THE MAN WHO MARRIED HIS DAUGHTER

Eleven Meskwaki Winter Stories and Tales of Olden Times

Written by Alfred Kiyana

Edited by Ives Goddard and Lucy Thomason

Translated by Ives Goddard, Lucy Thomason, Horace Poweshiek, and Harry Lincoln

Petoskey, Michigan

Mundart Press

2023

Copyright © 2023 by Joshua Jacob Snider
Mundart Press, Petoskey MI 49770

 All rights reserved. No part of this book may be reproduced or transmitted in any form or by any means, electronic or mechanical, including photocopying, recording, or by any information storage and retrieval system, without permission in writing from the publisher.

The publisher hereby grants such permission to the Sac and Fox Tribe of the Mississippi in Iowa, for any tribal educational or cultural purpose.

The original manuscripts edited and translated here and translations of some of them are in the National Anthropological Archives (Department of Anthropology, National Museum of Natural History, Smithsonian Institution), housed at the Museum Support Center in Suitland, Maryland (NAA mss. 1875.16, 1879.15, 2432.1, 2655.1, 2664.1, 2664.3, 2664.7, 2788, 2794.80, 2794.86, and 2794.91).

A publication of the Recovering Voices Program of the Smithsonian Institution, supported in part by a gift from the Shoniya Fund.

Publisher's Cataloguing-in-Publication Data

Names: Kiyana, Alfred, 1877-1918, author. | Goddard, Ives, 1941- editor, translator. | Thomason, Lucy, editor, translator. | Poweshiek, Horace, 1891-1982, translator. | Lincoln, Harry (Tä wa ko ha ka), 1890- translator.
Title: The man who married his daughter : eleven Meskwaki winter stories and tales of olden times / written by Alfred Kiyana ; edited by Ives Goddard and Lucy Thomason ; translated by Ives Goddard, Lucy Thomason, Horace Poweshiek, and Harry Lincoln.
Description: Petoskey, Michigan : Mundart Press, 2023. | "A publication of the Recovering Voices Program of the Smithsonian Institution, supported in part by a gift from the Shoniya Fund."--Title page verso. | Includes glossary and bibliography. | Texts in Meskwaki with English translations.
Identifiers: ISBN: 979-8986545042 (paperback) | LCCN: 2023906155
Subjects: LCSH: Fox language--Texts. | Fox Indians--Folklore. | Fox Indians--Social life and customs--Fiction. | Sac & Fox Tribe of the Mississippi in Iowa--Folklore.
Classification: LCC: PM1195.Z77 K59 2023 | DDC: 497/.314--dc23

Contents

Abbreviations and References

acc.	accepted by		NB	note (this)
AI	animate intransitive		no.	number
AK	Alfred Kiyana (Keahna)		obv.	obviative
AW	Adeline Wanatee		p.	page
cf.	compare		SP-BSAB	Sam Peters, [The Boy who
C-Giants	Charley H. Chuck, "Giants"			was Set Adrift in a Bucket]
	(NAA 2794.12)			(NAA 2794.85(e))
C-WH	Charley H. Chuck,		TA	transitive animate
	"Wampumhead: A Winter		TM	Truman Michelson
	Story" (NAA 2794.46(b))		<	changed from

acc.   accepted by

AI   animate intransitive

AK   Alfred Kiyana (Keahna)

AW   Adeline Wanatee

cf.   compare

C-Giants   Charley H. Chuck, "Giants" (NAA 2794.12)

C-WH   Charley H. Chuck, "Wampumhead: A Winter Story" (NAA 2794.46(b))

EK   Everett Kapayou

ex., exx.   example, examples

FM   Frances Mitchell

Goddard 1994   Ives Goddard, *Leonard Bloomfield's Fox Lexicon; Critical Edition.* Algonquian and Iroquoian Linguistics Memoir 12.

HL   Harry Lincoln

HP   Horace Poweshiek

HWB   Horace White Breast

IG   Ives Goddard

IP   Ida Poweshiek

JAG   James A. Geary (Meskwaki vocabulary slip file in NAA 4860)

JM texts   Jim Mamasaw texts (NAA 2794.65(a,c,d,e))

Kiyana 2022   Alfred Kiyana, *Masahkamikohkwêwa (Grandmother Earth): a Synchretistic Meskwaki Cosmology.* Petoskey MI: Mundart Press, 2022.

K-FC   Alfred Kiyana, "How the Fox Clan was Blessed" (NAA 2957.1)

K-FW   Alfred Kiyana, "Fox and Wolf" (NAA 2490:1-15)

K-Kin   Alfred Kiyana, "Kinship Terminology and Archaic Vocabulary" (NAA 2232)

K-M   Alfred Kiyana, "Masahkamikohkwêwa" (Kiyana 2022)

K-MMD   Alfred Kiyana, "The Man who Married his Daughter" (see pp. 13-37)

K-MMGW   Alfred Kiyana, "The Man who Married a Giant Woman" (see pp. 223-241)

K-MOR   Alfred Kiyana, "The Man Who Had Pet Raccoons" (see pp. 39-73)

K-RP   Alfred Kiyana, "Redstone Pipe" (NAA 2720-1).

K-S   Alfred Kiyana, "Spider" (see pp. 123-147)

K-SSP   Alfred Kiyana, "Sky Sacred Pack" (NAA 2273)

K-TO   Alfred Kiyana, "Turkey Owner" (NAA 3065)

K-W   Alfred Kiyana, "Wisahkeha" (NAA 2958-a)

K-Wâpasaya   Alfred Kiyana, "Wâpasaya" (NAA 2122)

K-Words   Alfred Kiyana, [Words, Phrases, Sentences on Various Topics] (NAA 2841, 2778)

l.   line

lit.   literally

LT   Lucy Thomason

LYB   Leonard Young Bear

NAA   National Anthropological Archives

Introduction.

This book has editions and translations of eleven texts written in the Algonquian language Meskwaki by Alfred Kiyana over a century ago. The manuscripts of these are among the thousands of pages written by Kiyana in his native language for Truman Michelson of the Bureau of American Ethnology, which was a component of the Smithsonian Institution until 1965. An even greater number of pages was written by other Meskwaki speakers. The manuscripts are kept in the National Anthropological Archives in the Museum Support Center of the Smithsonian in Suitland, Maryland.

The editors are responsible for the translations given, but they benefited from translations by Horace Poweshiek and Harry Lincoln found with two of the manuscripts, as indicated. They are indebted to the Meskwaki speakers who helped with the interpretation of selected words and sentences: Adeline Wanatee, Everett Kapayou, Frances Mitchell, Leonard Young Bear, and Horace White Breast.

The first ten of the texts have what are called winter stories. They are set in ancient times when human beings and their world are not yet like they are today. There are powerful spirits (manitous), giants and monsters, talking birds and animals, and magical transformations. Even the ostensible human beings may have supernatural powers. Winter stories are to be told in winter, when the spirits who might not want to hear themselves being talked about are asleep. The final text brings together three brief thematically linked stories about people who lived in the world as we know it today.

As indicated by the choice of the title selection, these stories have sexual themes and some strong sexual content. They have been brought together not only because the treatment of these topics might be of interest, but equally also to make it easier for those who may wish to avoid having them crop up unexpectedly in future collections of Kiyana's stories, given their often inexplicit titles.

It is evident that Kiyana's writing of these stories for Michelson owed much to the personal relationship between to two men. (There is a photograph of them together in *Handbook of North American Indians* 17, *Languages*, p. 250.) Kiyana (1877-1918), who belonged to the War Chief lineage of the Fox Clan, was a widower raising three boys. Michelson (1879-1938) was the son of a prominent physicist, Albert A. Michelson (1852-1931), a secular Jew born in Prussia (in what is now Poland), and his mother was born Margaret McLean Heminway (1857-1939). He had married Katherine Trowbridge Harrison (1864-1953) in 1903. For a time during his fieldwork Michelson had a love affair with a Meskwaki woman, Mary Payoki (*pa yo ·hki ·ha*), and the men he worked with kidded him about this.[1] On the back of the last page of one of Kiyana's texts someone else wrote, amidst a series of vocables: *pa yo ·hki ·ha oši ·kani we ·wenetwi.* 'Mary

---

[1]Her son John Rein (b. 2/20/1913, d. 7/26/1930) was also called John Michelson and Mike Rein, but Michelson was not in Iowa from mid-August 1911 to mid-July 1912.

Payoki has pretty hips.'[2] In the manuscript of Kiyana's "Âmanôneniwa" ('The Story of Lady-Killer'), after a sentence that says, 'Then the women all saw him, the story goes,' a second hand wrote "mishilson."[3]

In two of the stories in the present collection the men who are the title characters are described as having hooked noses, in fact sharply or strongly hooked noses.[4] The verb for this is *waˑkikomeˑwa* 'he or she has a hooked nose', and this regularly makes the homophonous agent noun, *waˑkikomeˑwa* 'Jew', which appears in no text but Michelson told Leonard Bloomfield about (Goddard 1994:172). In "The Man who Married his Daughter" the man's wife is described as having a mildly hooked nose (1.ef). Now, Meskwaki stories do not have descriptions of irrelevant physical features, and it is pretty obvious that Kiyana's descriptions are a way of teasing Michelson, including even a reference to his non-Jewish wife. At the very end of Kiyana's longest text he addresses Michelson as *šato*, a word used between close male friends (Kiyana 2022:836, "Masahkamikohkwêwa" line 1200*s*).

The two stories with the apparent teasing allusions to Michelson are put first, but the other stories are in no particular order, except that the longest of the winter stories is placed last followed by the set of three short tales that are not winter stories.

---

[2]This is evidently a song of four-syllable lines (divided here with slashes): ⟨wi yo e e / wi yo e e . / wi| yo e e / wi yo e e / pa yo ki| a / o ši ka ni . / we we| ne twi / wi yo e e / wi yo e| e .|⟩ (in Alfred Kiyana, "The Wooden Manitou Buffalo," NAA 2221, p. 57, verso).
[3]In Alfred Kiyana, "Âmanôneniwa," NAA 2432.1, p. 2A, l. j.
[4]Alfred Kiyana, "The Man who Married his Daughter," 1*cd*, and "The Man who Had Pet Raccoons," 1*j*.

Synopses.

The Man who Married his Daughter. While a man with a hooked nose is away hunting, his daughter has her first period and goes into the prescribed menstrual isolation. When he returns, she breaks the taboo and rubs down the aching backs of both her parents. The man and his daughter become sexually attracted to each other, and after his wife (who had less of a hooked nose) dies, they eventually live together as a married couple and have a child.

People come to live where they are that include Âyahkôha and his sister, who are living as man and wife. Âyahkôha, a notorious sex fiend with a gigantic penis, takes up with the man's daughter-wife, and for a time the men trade wives back and forth. Eventually Âyahkôha's sister becomes angry, and the three of them plot to kill him. While he is engaged in a marathon copulation with her, she slides back, and the other man cuts off his penis with a knife that has been smeared with his daughter-wife's menstrual blood. Âyahkôha bolts away, and his penis goes flying and wraps around a tree.

The three of them go to live underground, and they arrange for a woman Âyahkôha and his sister had lived with and called grandmother to come and live with them as a co-wife. She is a virgin and reluctant at first, but after a long night of copulation she becomes young again and very pretty.

But the man's desire for sex is deemed to have gone too far. The culture hero Wîsahkêha, as an enforcer of cultural norms, sends his friend Turtle to seduce the three women, and they give birth to baby turtles. And two berdaches (transgender women) capture the man's son and turn him into a berdache. He threatens to kill his wives and chases them with a knife, but Wîsahkêha grabs him and turns him into a terrier. Wîsahkêha takes the women to a village and admonishes them not to be so generous with sexual favors.

The Man Who Had Pet Raccoons. A man with a hooked nose called Wêtêsepanemêha 'Raccoon-Owner' lives in one half of a longhouse with some raccoons in the other half. One raccoon goes missing, making him angry at whoever killed it. Then one day there is a pleasant smell on the breeze. In time the smell becomes more intense, and he has an erection that he can't fight off. He goes after the scent, followed by his raccoons.

After many days he comes to a house. Living there are an older woman, a man who is her husband, and her teen-age daughter, a young girl whose scent it was that he had followed. He is instantly smitten and follows her outside to see where she urinates. By urinating on the same spot he makes her pregnant, though she is still a virgin. He stays with them, as if courting the girl, forgetting about his raccoons, but she won't even speak to him.

When the girl eventually realizes she is pregnant and feels herself, she has lascivious thoughts. She begins to concern herself with the man, but now he stops paying attention to her. Her mother scolds her and gets after them for not getting married. After the man explains things, the woman tells her daughter how to arrange it so that the man will have sex with her. And she tells her husband how he can impersonate the younger man and have sex with the girl, and he does so.

The younger man knows about the girl and goes back home, but he has forgotten his raccoons. He goes back and finds them dead, but when he walks away they revive and come after him.

The woman persuades her daughter to be her co-wife for four years, but in time the old man is sleeping only with the younger woman. After four years he dies, and the older woman complains bitterly, blaming her daughter.

The man's raccoons go away for four years and then come back in greater numbers. Their report about the two women encourages him to go back to marry them. He takes them as wives, but always sleeps with the mother. Eventually he starts beating her, being jealous of Turtle. But the beatings have no effect, and the daughter urges him to kill her mother.

One of the raccoons warns him not to kill the older woman, as she would become a rolling-skull, and says she is a serpent-lady. He can escape the danger only by becoming an eagle and taking the younger woman to the sky. For a while he hunts, and the woman becomes fat. One time when she is bathing he sees that she has a tail, and she is flicking out her tongue. He fears her and hates her, and she becomes more and more jealous. When the man caches meat in scattered places and the older woman goes around to collect it, he becomes an eagle and takes the younger woman to the sky.

After gathering and butchering the meat, the older woman follows each of the others to where their tracks suddenly end. She cannot learn where they went and vows to kill them.

The raccoons shape their dung into dolls that look exactly like the couple then in the sky and have them come to where the older woman is. After four days the dolls turn back into dung, and she continues her search. Âyahkôha (see above) tells her where they have gone, in exchange for sex, and then kills her by copulation. Her head eventually detaches from her discarded body and becomes a rolling-skull. When it gets close to where they are, the man shoots it into the sea, and it is swallowed by a whale.

The couple later come back from the sky and go to the man's house. He tells the raccoons they may go wherever they like, and they are delighted and scatter. The raccoon that had earlier warned him explains what had happened.

People of Long Ago who Were Blessed. A young man joins a warparty to go against the Siouxs. He was made to fast as a boy and is not yet courting girls. (The writer feigns to have forgotten to mention that he had a sister. She is, in fact, an unmarried older sister.)

The warparty camps at places along the shore of a large lake. When they see a black wolf, the warparty-leader says it is a sign that he has arrived where he is going. And when they offer it tobacco, he warns them not to ask for anything or pray for life. They attack the Siouxs in the morning fog and run back to the canoes, but the young man loses his way. The others assume he has been killed and leave in the canoes.

After running off blindly, he eventually comes to a lake he cannot see across, and he lies on the shore eating small meals. (Although it is not stated explicitly, it appears from what happens later that he must have asked for and received the help of the black wolf seen earlier.) One day, when the sky is completely cloudless, a little old man comes out of the water and gives him some meat and some medicine. He drinks water from the lake and is completely recovered. The old man has him choose which way he will get across, and he walks across on the surface, taking several days and nights. At one point he hears a drum and singers and the voice of his grandfather.

The man's sister is fasting. While they are in different places sleeping, the man is told that his sister will be the first to see him, and he must put his arms around her neck and kiss her four times. The woman is told the same thing and is much relieved. In the morning she sets out. Meanwhile, the warparty-leader is fasting all the time, but the man's parents are not.
The man crosses a large river, walking across on it. As he continues on, he finds moccasins and firewood waiting for him along the way. After some time he is told that he will see his sister the next evening. His sister is told the same thing her brother was told, and also that a wolf will be watching them, and that they must travel together only at night.

The next evening they come out of two ravines where they head up opposite each other. They kiss repeatedly and are overjoyed. They travel at night with a wolf walking a little to one side. They sleep a little ways from each other during the day and set out at night.

When they get back, the woman goes to get their father. The father comes and embraces them together, and he is told they must have a clan feast that night. As they are sleeping during the day, the woman is told in a dream that if her brother doesn't know her intimately, he'll die before celebrating the clan feast. And he is told the same thing, but with the crude verb. When she wakes up, she goes to where he is, and they tell each other that they have had bad dreams about his fate. She then tells him the specific details, using the crude verb that, as his sister, she would never let him hear her say. She says she's worried that he will die and that they must do it, but he says it's out of the question. The old man that had blessed him comes and explains that a wolf wants to ruin them, by having them do what wolves do. He assures them that they will not die. The wolf is ashamed and stops appearing.

The unexpected return of the man is celebrated, and the warparty-leader who abandoned him gives him his two daughters to marry. His wives both give birth to boys at the same time. His sister remains umarried, and he asks her why.

Sometime later his sons both die at the same time, and he and his sister are broken-hearted. The wolf comes to them separately and tells them that the old man has taken the children and will continue to do so. It would not have happened if they had done what the wolf told them to do. But if they have sex, the old man will stop doing that. The woman finds her brother in a remote place and persuades him to do it. And as they are well into it, the old man comes carrying the boys on his back. The old man is furious and leaves.

After the man's wives are both pregnant, he joins in an attack on a Sioux village and is the only one slain. The warparty-leader fasts for many winters and turns to stone. People come and pray to him for life. The children of the one who was slain. a boy and a girl, are taken care of by their aunt. Some years later, when the three of them are hiding from attacks by Siouxs and Comanches, they turn to stone in the place where they are hiding and become eternal people. Later they disappear, but when people dance there the boy can be heard whooping under the ground.

The mothers fast for years and are told that their children are spirits. They are told to stop fasting, and that they will live to old age.

Kashawîha. A couple is living someplace off by themselves with their only child, a son named Kashawîha. He's a bad actor who talks back to his father and won't take advice. His father never makes him fast. But he has a knack for getting game.

One time his father sees him sneak up on a gigantic snapping turtle, having an arrow-shaped tail and tongue, and hurl fire at it, killing it. He gives a cry like a Thunderer, and when rain comes it disappears. Back home the father tells his young wife what he has seen and that he thinks their son is a manitou. The son brings home a load of game, and they roast meat on a rack and on spits, and afterwards the woman makes pemmican. The old man eats all day every day and smokes his pipes.

Eventually the young man has a desire to get married. His mother tells him there are no other people around. She and his father were survivors of a town eaten by the Golden Dragon, and she thinks it goes around doing that. He searches for other people without success and eventually tells his mother that she is the only woman there is.

One time he comes back from shooting and butchering softshell turtles and sees his parents in the water. He swims underwater from upstream and pushes up his mother's skirt. After some erotic play, she explains to her husband that she is being tickled by minnows. She will go to see her brother [who must live beneath the waters] and come up when it gets dark. Underwater again, she sees that it is her son, and they continue on making love all evening long and make plans. Back home she explains to her husband that she should go back to her brother's for four days to placate her niece.

Her son is already waiting for her and grabs her under the water. For four days they remain there having sex. He gets her to agree to be his wife and tells her how to kill her husband by putting one of his lice in his food. She does this, and he dies from it.

The couple live together and have children, who are nothing but girls, and there are many of them. After his wife dies in childbirth, he marries his oldest daughter. In time he marries all of his daughters, and their children are both boys and girls. He remains the same age.

After his wives are no longer bearing children, he seeks to find out how he might deal with his daughters. He has a dream of a medicine and digs it up. He starts having sex with his eldest daughter, and in time she gets pregnant. And then he does this with them all in turn, and the babies come quickly. His sons realize what he is doing, and one-by-one they move away and build houses, each taking with them several of their nieces, also their sisters, who agree to be their wives.

The man doesn't know where they are and loses all his children. After he is an old man, he has a vision of them, and he goes with his wives to the four large villages where his grandchildren are. After his wives die, he lives on until he is bent with age, hated by his children but on good terms with his grandchildren. Then one day he announces that a chief should be installed and falls over dead. And his sons are glad.

Spider. A handsome young man, who wears only a breechcloth, is a skillful climber. He sets out snares that he makes with Indian-hemp ropes and traps all manner and sizes of animals. At some point he sets a large snare near a village, mistaking a water-path for a bear trail, and eventually snares all the women. They are jerked upwards and unable to cry out.

The young man comes and finds the women tied in various ways, all with their private parts visible, including teenagers. He calmly unties them and takes the snare away, and the women agree among themselves not to tell the men.

The young man thinks that what he has seen was interesting, but it is only much later that he begins to have lascivious thoughts. And the next fall he makes a large snare for catching people and puts it on what he thinks is a water-path. But what he traps is a mountain lion, and after killing it he flees back home. He finds that his house has been wrecked, and he kills all the mice there.   (NOTE: It is always foxes that trash people's houses.)

The next fall, still angry, he makes several snares and sets them around in a circle before leaving. And when the foxes go to trash the house again, they are all caught in the snares. The young man has headed out and finds a village. Again he misinterprets the things he sees and sets a snare, and this time he catches a bear and kills it. He is furious.

When he gets home he finds foxes in his snares who say they were chasing a deer, and he believes them. As he releases them, they run off and befoul his house. And having made a pile of snares, he decides to move away from everyone. and the foxes warn each other.

After eight days he finds a village and puts a snare in place, with no results. An owl explains that it was the foxes and gives him advice. After scaring them away, he sets out and sees a young woman. He sets a snare and catches her. She keeps straining, unable to scream. Her skirts ride up exposing her, and he has sex with her as she grimaces. He does the same thing to the same girl several times and then goes away. And now he goes around doing that to young girls, having sex with every one of them.

One time an old woman is caught in his snare, and she is exposed with her head covered. With great effort he finally succeeds in having sex with her and discovers that she is not a young girl. She talks about her experiences and goes home. She tells her grandson Wîsahkêha what happened to her, and he misunderstands her words.

Wîsahkêha goes to where people are and sees a young girl being violated by the man after being caught in his snare. The man runs away, and after Wîsahkêha unties her she explains what happened.

Wîsahkêha constructs intimate female parts from buffalo organs, borrows skirts, and pretends to be a girl going for water. When he is snared, the man copulates with what he thinks is a girl and then falls asleep. Wîsahkêha squeezes him to death.

The next year there are many spiders there.   (This is the origin of spiders.)

The Story of Lady-Killer. When he fasts a boy dreams of women and is told that he will be good at marrying them. The first time he goes to a dance the women ignore him, but afterwards he invokes his dream and women who see him like him.

The next time he goes and dances, all the women admire him. And later when he goes back to get the dish he forgot, after taking his dance outfit off, the women smile at him and follow him home. When he goes out to take care of business, he is followed by a woman, and when he starts running many women come after him. They eventually catch up with him at a lake, and everyone goes back. But he has run through thorns, and his feet become too sore for him to go on. Two of the women, relying on the blessing that one of them has received, go to the shore and kill a man lying in a canoe (a Sioux hunter, it later turns out). They take turns carrying him while bringing the others back there. and everyone gets in the canoe and comes back home. He marries all nine of those maidens. He becomes a warrior and has a knack for getting game. He always kills exactly nine deer.

At some point they are attacked, and all of his wives are killed. He is devastated and moves away. Some young women follow after him, and he is told in a dream that his wives will be coming. He wakes up in the night and thinks that the ghosts of his dead wives are after him. He runs away but eventually gives up, and after daybreak he sees that they are sixteen young virgins. He marries them all, and they all get pregnant at the same time and have baby boys. Sometime later people get sick. Only *his* wives all die, and only *his* children all survive. After his release from strict mourning, when he is out hunting, his penis grows to an enormous length.

The second time this happens, a pretty young teenager sees it and makes use of it, and they decide to get married. This happens again, and he marries a second teenage virgin. Sometime later he has a premonition that he will marry many wives.

While he is hunting alone, the same thing happens yet again. One of his wives, bringing him some arrows, sees something flashing as it moves away all spotted. Some young maidens climbing around to pick cherries put their arms around it and lose consciousness, in fact hanging from his huge penis. After they come to, the man's wife urges him to accept their suggestion that he marry them. He does so and continues hunting. After they all have lots of meat, he takes all of his wives back to where they came from.

He grows old with his wives and never has any more children. He was a person of long ago, from the time before when all the tribes ganged up on them. He was the last one to have many wives, having married thirty-four virgins.   (Kiyana writes 'twenty-four', which cannot be right.)

An Indian of Long Ago who Was Blessed by an Owl. A young man who is a good hunter is given three young girls to marry, one after another, and each of them immediately goes back home and refuses to stay with him, the third one even starving to death rather than doing so.

He goes away to hunt and fast, seeking to get a penis, as the one he has is too small, and women always leave him. An owl comes to him and says he knows what the man's problem is and that he will come back with some penises. When he returns, he is wearing many small penises on his body. The owl makes a large penis of the size the man asks for and puts it on him, taking the small penis and hanging it with the others. But the owl tells the man that he will not be able to have sex with anyone, and this turns out to be true, as the penis is too large.

He goes back to the same place, and the owl comes and puts a different penis on him. When he returns, he has sex once with each of the women he had been briefly married to, with great success, and they are furious when he then marries a different young girl.

He tells his friend, who is similarly small, what he has done, and the friend goes to fast. An owl comes to him and agrees to help him, but warns him not to smile. If he does, they both will die. When the owl comes back, he laughs, and they both fall over dead.

The friend's younger brother finds him dead and reports back. The young man goes there and explains what must have happened, but he is not believed. He revives the owl, and the owl confirms his explanation.

Another friend of the one who laughed kills a deer quite far away. As he is carrying it home on his back, an owl comes and asks for a smoke, and he refuses. They get angry at each other and curse each other: if he puts his load down he will die, and if the owl lands, the owl will die. After they are exhausted, they both relent. They talk about how they were not serious, and about how both respect each other's power. The man massages the owl's wings, and the owl goes and finds a roasting stick of meat for them to eat.

When he gets home, he tells his parents what happened. His father scolds him severely, making him frightened and angry. So, he goes to fight the Siouxs ill-equipped and is killed. Now the old man weeps loudly instead.

The Older Woman who Had Manitou Power. An older woman with manitou power has a beautiful daughter who, when she comes of age, politely rejects all the young men who approach her. She tells her mother that she intends to remain a virgin, and her mother talks to her about men, and women, and sex.

Later on, in the summer, the daughter does not come home for four days. The woman goes to ask Wîsahkêha and finds her daughter (lifeless, as it turns out) lying on the floor under a blanket. Wîsahkêha drums, and the woman dances, for four days. After he tires first and admits defeat, he raises the daughter to her feet and she shows no effects. He explains that he intended for her to be a sister for his brother (who lives where the souls of the dead go), as she was so well-behaved. He lets her go home, telling her that she will be a midwife.

The woman tries again to instruct her daughter. She talks about how sex is a lot of fun, and about how men furnish meat to eat, and that it's the only way there will be children. Her daughter explains that her grandmother told her about the things about sex and marriage that could be bad, and the woman is angry and concerned.

One morning the woman finds her daughter enticing as she sleeps. She arranges her to be exposed and waits outside. When a man comes in and touches her, the mother comes in and tells her she must marry him, as he has seen her privates. When the man comes back that night, the daughter rejects him, and hits him, and tells him to leave. He leaves but tells people he is married.

Sometime later the daughter declares that she is going to get married and names an older man who is a good hunter as the one she has in mind. The man takes her away as a bride, but he is extremely jealous and often beats her. She follows her mother's advice and leaves him, and she takes as a husband a man who is well-behaved. The rejected man pleads with his one-time mother-in-law for a second chance, and they eventually become intimate.

The daughter begins coming over to where her former husband is living with her mother, now thinking better of him and less of her current husband. She resumes an intimate relationship with him, with the acquiescence of her mother, and eventually moves in to live with her and her former husband. He treats them both well, always hunting, and the three of them get along very well, having great fun.

At some point when they are away on a hunt, they are killed by Siouxs.

The Man who Married a Giant Woman. There is a large young man who is reluctant to get married or to have sex because his penis is so big and women reject him. At some point he sets out to go just anywhere.

After four years he reaches the ocean. He climbs onto a large log and commmands the wind to blow him across. When he reaches land, he feels hunger and eats a whole, small deer.
He meets a man, who invites him to come to the large grass-lodge where he is staying with his wife and sister, who are large women. At the urging of his host he marries the man's sister, and they are physically compatible and like each other a lot.

When they all get back to the town where they live, the people there are fascinated because they can see his heart beating. His wife explains that they all put *their* hearts up high someplace for safe-keeping. (This is what giants do.) He shows her his heart. It is flint, and he heats it in the fire and puts it back in place. The other people assemble and formally declare that his heart should be put up high. He says that is not possible and shows everyone what his heart is like.

A man who has spiritual power challenges him. He agrees to a contest, and the other man is burned up by his heart. The people see that he has manitou powers, and the men come and are served a feast and given pipes to smoke.

The woman's parents think the man should take her back home to where *his* parents are.
When he says it is too far, he is given the power to go either through the air or on the water. That

fall they head out across the water. His wife becomes smaller to be the size of the women on the other side, and she makes him a smaller penis. When they arrive, he asks her what kind of person she is, and she tells him that she and all the people he has been living among are giants. She has brought seeds, which they plant, and they give seeds to the other people.

When he wonders why they have not had a child, she gets pregnant and gives birth to a boy. After he grows up, they return with him to her people. He is admired and marries the daughter of the chief, and she grows smaller. Later, *he* becomes the chief there, and his parents go back. Eventually, he brings his parents to the giant country, and they stay there.

When the Spirit of Fire Was Made by the Manitous. There is a young man and a young woman who each are raised by a grandparent of the opposite sex, having no other close relatives. They are quiet and well-behaved and do not engage in courting activities. (This is at a time when people do not use fire for cooking or to keep warm, and they do not fast for spiritual power.)

The young woman is urged by her grandfather to go to where the young man lives with his grandmother and become his wife. She does so, and she shares his bed, but all they do is sleep. After several days, when it becomes clear that he is still completely innocent about what married couples do, his grandmother invokes her dream power and entices him into having sex with her outside. She tells him that that is what he should do with his wife, and it will be great fun. Back inside, though puzzled at first when he initiates things, the young woman soon enjoys it immensely and asks for more. But the grandmother soon falls ill, ages quickly, and dies.

The couple go to live with the young woman's grandfather, and he tells them about his medicine. The young man starts going hunting, and the grandfather is delighted. One day when he is away, the old man catches sight of his granddaughter's private parts. She sleeps soundly, having an erotic dream, as he gets her into position and has sex with her. When she wakes up, he pretends that another man had been there, but she tricks him into giving himself away. She beats him with a beaming tool and chases him out.

When the young man comes back from watching the manitous play the moccasin game, his wife tells him what happened, but he does not believe it would have been her grandfather and thinks it must have been Turtle. The young woman has doubts and weeps all the time. Manitous find the grandfather dead and bury him.

The couple lives by themselves. After twenty years, and ten years of pregnancy, the woman gives birth to a boy. An old woman tells the man how to make a cradleboard. The boy was cruel to small animals, and ate anything, and spoke any language.

After a discussion with his friend Wîsahkêha, God sends Jesus to call together the manitous to decide on a task to assign to the boy. They agree to make him be the Spirit of Fire (Ashkotênêsiwa), and they establish the kin relationships that Wîsahkêha, God, and the other manitous will have to the People-to-Come (the future human race), who the manitous will bless. The boy and his parents are then invited to a second council, where he is transformed. The charcoal becomes flint, which Wîsahkêha scatters for people to find later on, and the use of charcoal to paint the face when fasting is also established.

The parents provide fire to other people and explain that they should fast to know about their lives. People learn about the dangers of fire and to use it properly. After living long the parents die and turn to stone, and later they disappear.

Two manitous report that fire is treating people badly, and when nothing is done about it they start blessing even people who have not fasted. Wîsahkêha has bees sting them inside and out and convinces the two to stop doing this.

Wîsahkêha goes around to see how the manitous are treating fire. Mesôswa and Sâkimâwa have their fire in fine beds of coals. Two who are not treating fire well are turned into a mouse and a pocket gopher. A young man and an old woman whose fire has not been kept up are turned into a woodchuck and a possum. South Wind and Wind are taking good care of their fire. Others who are neglectful of their fires are turned into a bat, a badger, and a porcupine.

Wîsahkêha returns home to find his grandmother having chills. She is cured by medicine Old Lady Toad comes and makes. She burns herself while cooking but is cured the next day and is now proud of her fire. Wîsahkêha wonders what it was like to be sick, and his grandmother has him put on a ghost-shirt. After he has been screaming in agony and dies, she takes the shirt off him and he recovers.

Wîsahkêha gets God to put on the shirt, and he become extremely sick. Many come and try to doctor him, including the Thunderers, angels, and Jesus, but it is no use and he dies. Wîsahkêha then takes off the shirt, and God is soon cured.

Wîsahkêha is arrested by the Devil and imprisoned. He convinces the Devil to put on the shirt, and the Devil soon starts screaming, his looks are transformed, and he dies. After the shirt is taken off, he is cured and is given instructions. He is not to arrest living people, but only bad-actors that are dead.

Wîsahkêha had calmed the rage of the Spirit of Fire and controlled how hot he would be.

What Some Jealous Men Did Long Ago.

(1) A man comes to realize that his wife is being serviced by another man through the wall of their lodge at night. His friend even reports that he accompanied the other man once. He braids a sinew into some basswood-bark cordage and sharpens his knife. He manages to persuade his wife to let him sleep next to the wall, and he cuts off the penis that comes through and pokes him. The other man runs off, collapses, and dies, while the husband ties the penis to his sleeping wife's belt.

In the morning the woman's father-in-law jokes about her knife-case. A shout is heard when the dead man is discovered, and the woman is told to take the penis back and does so. When what the man had done is told, nothing is held against the man who killed him.

The man marries another young girl. At some point he begins to feel jealous, but her relatives can discover nothing to support his suspicion, He fashions a barbed stick and shoves it into her, and she eventually dies. The man falls sick, and his eyes burst open and his tongue rots before he dies.

(2) Another man who is jealous at first ignores the fact that his wife really *is* fooling around. He eventually loses his patience and informs her brothers, but when their mother does not object, the matter is dropped.

The next spring he sees that his wife is carrying on openly. One night he announces that he's leaving, shoves a sunfish he has caught into her, and walks out. After she is in a bad way, he is summoned but refuses to come. Her brothers explain to their mother that she must have been summarily divorced.

After the woman dies, a manitou appears to her mother. She is admonished not to blame her former son-in-law, as it was her daughter that was bad. The two of them are reconciled.

(3) At the urging of her older brothers, a pretty young girl marries a man who is ugly but an excellent hunter, despite the fact that she and another young man like each other. The woman dislikes her husband and is always thinking about the other one. One day they meet by accident and begin an affair.

Seeking to make her husband angry, she makes a giant cradle-board and entices him into a game of tying each other on it. She has him tie *her* on first, and then she ties *him* on. She leaves his penis exposed (in the normal way) and briefly has sex with him, leaving him filthy and immobile. She props him up on the water path with flies swarming on him, and he is seen by many women. One who is like his sister-in-law unties him. She urges him to take revenge, but he goes back to his wife after being told that her brother has threatened to kill her if he doesn't.

That fall he proposes a game and coaxes her into pretending to be a deer. He pretends to shoot her and skin her, taking off her clothes, and ties her bent double, with her privates exposed between her legs. He carries her to a moccasin game, where all the men can see her, and then to her family's house. Her father and her brothers are embarrassed, and it has to be her mother who unties her. Her parents tell her that it was her own fault and she should have behaved. Her brothers are told not to blame her husband but only her lover.

Not long after, she dies of shame, having been seen by so many men.

ota·nesani we·wi·wita, a·teso·hka·kana

The Winter Story of the Man who Married his Daughter

otânesani wêwîwita, âtesôhkâkana

Alfred Kiyana[*]

1 a   ota·nesani we·wi·wita, a·teso·hka·kana.[†]

b   meše=wi·na=’pi e·h=owi·ke·hiwa·či nekotayaki_neno·te·waki.

c   neniwa_e·h=wa·kikome·či,

d   po·si=meko| e·h=wa·kikome·či.

e   owi·wani meše=meko| e·h=ahpi·hči_wa·kikome·niči,_

f   a·kwi po·si.

g   o·ni_ota·neswa·wani,|

h   e·h=ki·ša·koči·=meko -nawe·nihkwe·he·hiniči| ota·neswa·wani.

i   e·h=menwi·hkwe·winiči=ke·hi,[‡]

j   e·h=menwi·_’nekino·hiniči.

k   ča·kenwi=meko e·h=iši-we·wenesiniči.

l   o·ni=ye·toke| nekotenwi e·h=ši·ša·či i·na neniwa,|

m   e·h=pešekesiwešihaki.

n   ki·ši_na·kwa·či, e·h=mya·no·te·nitehe ota·nesani,

o   e·h=aškihkwe·winiči.

p   e·h=mi·ša·te·nemoči mečemo·ka. ‖

2 a   pye·ya·niči=meko ona·pe·mani,

b   e·h=a·čimoha·či.

c   “keta·nesena·na=koči aškihkwe·wiwa,” e·h=ina·či.

d   (e·h=pwa·wi·=ke·hi ke·ko·h=_nehto·či.)

e   o·ni=ye·toke, e·h=a·hkwaha·hkwamataki=’yo=ke·hi opehkwani,

f   e·h=ši·ši·hkenekoči ota·nesani.

g   o·ni_mečemo·ka oškawaneki e·h=ši·ši·hkenekoči.|

h   e·h=ne·se·nekowa·či=meko ota·neswa·wani.

i   aškači e·h=pi·tike·niči| ota·neswa·wani.

j   e·h=mi·ša·te·nemoči e·h=še·škesi·hiwe·hiči še·škesi·he·ha.

k   e·h=we·pi-ašihašihto·či maškimote·hani, pe·škitye·ni.

l   meše=we·=meko·=’nahi ke·ko·hi| e·h=ašihašihto·či.

m   e·h=nahi·hta·či=meko ke·ko·hi,

n   ča·ki=meko_iši| e·h=nahi_mi·hkeče·wi·či. ‖

3 a   e·h=pemena·či=meko omeso·ta·nahi.

b   e·h=wača·ha·či,

c   e·h=manese·či.|

d   mehto·či=meko neniwa_e·h=išawiči.

e   o·ni=ye·toke e·h=a·mi·wa·či.

f   meše=meko·=’nahi inote·wa·či,[§]

---

[*]The manuscript is NAA 2664.3; it has 29 pages.

[†]Written as a title at the top of the page.

[‡]/menwi·hkwe·wi-/: HWB (1999).

[§]A narrative aorist with /e·h=/ omitted.

The Winter Story of the Man who Married his Daughter
Translated by Ives Goddard

1 a   The Winter Story of the Man Who Married His Daughter.

b   An Indian couple were living wherever it was, the story goes.
c   The man had a hooked nose,
d   a sharply hooked nose.
e   And his wife had a nose that was hooked mildly,
f   but not a lot.
g   And as for their daughter,
h   she was extremely beautiful, their daughter was.
i   And what's more she had a nice womanly figure,
j   and she was a nice size.
k   She was pretty in every way.
l   And then it seems one time the man went hunting,
m   going on a deer hunt.
n   After he had left, his daughter menstruated,
o   having her first period.
p   The older woman was delighted.
2 a   When her husband came back,
b   she told him about it.
c   "You know, our daughter has had her first period," she said to him.
d   (And here, he had not killed anything.)
e   And then it seems,—as, by the way, he had back aches—
f   his daughter rubbed him down.
g   And then she rubbed down the older woman below her ribs.
h   Their daughter's massages made them both get better.
i   And after a while their daughter returned to living in the main house.
j   The young maiden was delighted that she was now a young maiden.
k   She began making bags and baskets.
l   In fact, she would make just anything.
m   She knew how to do things,
n   and she did all kinds of work.
3 a   She really took care of her parents.
b   She cooked for them,
c   and she got firewood.
d   She was like a man.
e   And then, it seems, they moved.
f   They were moving to just anywhere,

g eʿh=pemahowaʿči.

h tepehki=keʿhi eʿh=aʿmiʿwaʿči.

i oʿni otaʿneswaʿwani niʿkaʿnimekyaʿneki eʿh=anemi-sasaʿkamišiniči.

j (eʿh=penaʿwiniki=ʾyo=keʿhi.)

k katawi=meko nehkanitepehkwe eʿh=pwaʿwi|-nepaʿči šeʿškesiʿheha.

l mečemoʿka=keʿhi eʿh=kehči-nepaʿči.

m neniwa| eʿh=pemi-nanaʿhehkweʿhaki oči·maʿnwaʿwi.|*

n kapoʿtwe eʿh=nekwaʿnahkwitepehkiʿniki,

o eʿh=wawaʿsetoniči nenemehkiwahi.

p meše nekotenwi mani eʿši-paʿhpaʿhketoniči,‖

4 a eʿh=meškekwaʿmeniči| otaʿnesani,

b eʿh=šowišiniči.

c waʿwiʿtawi=meko eʿh=oči-seʿsikaʿhiniči pemitoʿnaki| čiʿmaʿni.

d eʿh=naʿsaʿwaʿpamaʿči,

e eʿh=pwaʿwi|-menwi-waʿpamaʿči.

f kapoʿtwe=naʿhka eʿh=kiʿšaʿkoči-waʿsetepehkiʿniki.

g (iʿninaʿh=čaʿhi=ʾpi pašitoʿha eʿnemi|-očiʿkwanapiči.)

h eʿh=mesawinawaʿči otaʿnesani.

i kapoʿtwe eʿh=koči-soʿnepyeʿhwaʿči nepi.

j waʿnatohka=meko eʿh=kehči-nepaʿniči.

k keʿkeyaʿh=meko eʿh=anemi-nemasoči.

l keʿkeyaʿh=meko| iʿtepi eʿh=aʿči,

m kehčineʿhe=meko eʿh=anemi-waʿpamaʿči.

n keʿkeyaʿh=meko eʿh=meʿšenaʿči takaʿwi=meko eʿh=owiʿsayiweʿhiniči.†

5 a keʿkeyaʿh=meko šeʿški eʿh=sahkikweʿsetawaʿči.

b mani=meko eʿši-meʿšeškawaʿči,

c eʿh=nasahteʿči.

d kiʿšeʿwiʿči, neʿyaʿpi wiʿh=aʿtehe, eʿh=koʿhkaʿškaki oči·maʿnwaʿwi.

e waninawe| eʿh=oči-moʿhkiʿwaʿči.|

f pašitoʿha=keʿhi anemyaʿkaʿha eʿh=oči-moʿhkiʿči.

g šepawiʿhta=ʾpi čahkwiʿtemyaʿhinikweʿni.|

h aʿneta=ʾpi=meko otaʿhwiʿnemwaʿwani eʿh=akihtoʿwaʿči.

i aʿneta eʿh=mehkamowaʿči,

j aʿneta=keʿhi eʿh=akihtoʿwaʿči.

k "ohohwaʿ´," eʿh=išiteʿheʿči=ʾpi pašitoʿha waʿpamaʿčini otaʿnesani.

l oʿni=meše·=ʾnah=kapoʿtwe eʿh=nepeneči owiʿweʿhani.|

m eʿh=aʿmiʿwaʿči otaʿnesani nešihka.‖

6 a meše=meko·=ʾnahi eʿh=inoteʿwaʿči.

b eʿh=mahkateʿwiʿwaʿči, nešihka=meko.

c oʿni=yeʿtoke aškači=meko maʿnwaʿhiʿmakateniki eʿh=šiʿšaʿči pašitoʿha.

d eʿh=kiʿšaʿkoči-=meko -ayiʿhkwiči peʿhkoteʿhiniki| eʿh=pyaʿči.

---

*/nanaʿhehkweʿhaki/: AK syllable ⟨e⟩ changed from ⟨a⟩.

†/eʿh=owiʿsayiweʿhiniči/: AK ⟨.eowisa‖yeweiniči.⟩.

g   going by canoe.

h   Now, they were moving at night.

i   And their daughter rode lolling back comfortably as she lay in the prow of the canoe.

j   (Well, it was summertime.)

k   For almost the whole night the young maiden did not sleep.

l   And here now, the older woman was sleeping soundly.

m   The man was guiding their canoe along with his paddle.

n   Suddenly, the night sky clouded over,

o   and the Thunderers flashed lightning from their mouths.

p   One time, when the lightning was flashing,

4 a   there was his daughter, sleeping exposed,

b   lying with her legs apart.

c   She had her feet up on the rails on either side of the canoe.

d   He could see her only fleetingly

e   and did not get a good look at her.

f   Suddenly again, the night sky became extremely bright.

g   (Now, it was when the man was riding in a kneeling position.)

h   And when he saw his daughter he desired her.

i   Soon, he tried flicking some water on her with the paddle.

j   And she slept soundly as if nothing had happened.

k   Before long he began to ride standing up.

l   And before long he went up to where she was

m   and rode on watching her from up close.

n   And before long he touched her where she had a little hair.

5 a   And before long he put his prick up to her, nothing more.

b   And as soon as he touched against her,

c   he came.

d   Trying to move back after he was done, he overset their canoe.

e   They came to the surface in different places,

f   with the man coming up a little downstream.

g   And luckily, they say the water was shallow.

h   Some of their possessions they're said to have lost.

i   They found some,

j   and they lost some.

k   "Man!" the man thought whenever he looked at his daughter, to hear the tale.

l   And then the time came when his wife died.

m   He and his daughter moved away by themselves.

6 a   They moved to just anywhere.

b   And they were fasting, by themselves.

c   And then it seems, much later on, after many years, the man went hunting.

d   And he was extremely tired when he came back that evening.

e · h=ki·ša·koči-=ča·h=meko -kehči_nepa·či.

f a·šitami e·h=meša·pamekoči.

g to·hki·či| wi·na ihkwe·wa,

h e·h=meškekwa·mo·hiniči o·sani.

i pena=ta·taki e·h=pasipasi_wa·pama·či.*

j ke·keya·h=meko e·h=wa·pama·či pe·hki o·sani.

k e·h=mayakite·he·či, e·h=ma·čikanwe·kwa·meniči.

l (ma·maya·='yo=ke·hi.)

m ke·keya·hi e·h=pemi_pasekwi·či,|

n e·h=mawi_sa·kiči·či.

o e·h=wi·ša·ška·či=meko ihkwe·wa ke·keya·hi.

p ke·keya·hi·='pi e·h=so·kenamawa·či kena·či. ‖

7 a ke·keya·h=meko e·h=pemi_nasawape·piči ihkwe·wa.|

b kena·či=meko e·h=to·hki·či pašito·ha.

c e·h=wi·ke·tenaki neniwa.

d e·h=pwa·wi-=ke·hi -kano·na·či.

e wi·na=na·hka e·h=pwa·wi_kano·nekoči.

f ke·keya·h=meko,| "wi·ke·čišineta·we=pena´," e·h=ina·či o·sani.|

g e·h=meškwi·kite·či ihkwe·wa| e·h=pwa·wi-kaški-pi·tenamawoči.

h i·ni=ča·hi·='pi kete·='nahi e·h=taši_ša·šo·škika·hokoči| o·sani.

i e·h=mi·ša·te·nemoči neniwa.

j i·ni·='pi_i·nini wi·na=meko e·h=owi·wiči| ota·nesani.

k (e·h=neši-='yo=ke·h=meko -mehtose·neniwe·hiwa·či.)|

l meše·='nah=meko e·h=te·pahkwi-oni·ča·nesiha·či| ota·nesani.

m e·h=a·čimoha·či našawaye e·h=meša·pama·či.‖

8 a "kemeša·pamene=koči·='yo·we," e·h=ina·či,

b ki·ši-=pe·hki -owi·wiči.|

c e·h=ki·ša·koči-=meko| -menwi_pemenekoči,

d wi·na=na·hka e·h=menwi|-to·tawa·či ota·nesani.

e meše nekotenwi| e·h=po·ni_nota·kowa·či mehtose·neniwahi,_

f ma·ne=meko.

g wa·natohka_e·h=ki·wi_čako·še·hiwa·či,

h e·h=pwa·wi_kehke·nemeči.

i "ke·htena=meko owi·wani," e·h=ine·nemeči.

j e·h=nahi_nawihekoči| neniwahi če_w_ahpi·hčikičihi.

k o·ni=nekotenwi=tepehki e·h=ki·ke·noweči,

l e·h=natomeči,

m e·h=mawi_atama·či.

n e·h=ne·wokoči neniwani=nekoti me·sawinama·kočini.

o opye·ni=meko ‖ e·h=mawi_kakano·neti·heči,

9 a wa·natohka=meko| e·h=taši_kakano·neti·či.|

---

*/pena=ta·taki/: also in K-MOR 2*c*, written with a divider.

e So, he slept extremely soundly.

f And this time it was *his* privates that were seen by *her*.

g   When the *woman* woke up,

h there was her father, sleeping somewhat exposed.

i She couldn't help taking glances at him.

j And before long she looked at her father outright.

k She had a funny feeling as he slept with a hard on.

l (Now, it was still early.)

m   Before long she got up

n and went out to pee.

o The woman finally could not stand it any longer.

p And before long then, they say, slowly and carefully, she took hold of him.

7 a And before long the woman moved to sit with her thighs astraddle.

b   Slowly, the older man woke up.

c   The man used his hand to line things up.

d Now, he did not speak to her.

e And she also did not speak to *him*.

f   Before long she said to her father, "Why don't we lie the right way."

g   The woman became impatient at the manual efforts to stick it into her.

h And then they say, a change of mood, as her father's thrusts were making her legs
straighten out.

i   The man was delighted.

j He was then married to his very own daughter, the tale goes.

k (By the way, they were living just by themselves.)

l And in the course of time he fathered his daughter's child.

m   And he told her that he had seen her privates long ago.

8 a "You know, I saw your snatch once," he told her,

b after she was fully his wife.

c   She took extremely good care of him.

d And he treated his daughter well, also.

e   One time some people camped in with them,

f a lot of them.

g They showed no embarrassment at having a little baby,

h and they were not found out.

i It was thought that the woman was truly his wife.

j And men of her age used to visit her.

k   And then one night there was a clan feast,

l and he was invited

m and went to be a smoker.

n And a certain man saw him who had seen his wife and desired her.

o Without obvious haste, a conversation was struck up with him,

9 a and he continued the conversation without suspicion.

^b   aškačitepehki=meko,| "nahi´, ni·h=mawi‑sa·kiči," e·h=ina·či,

^c   e·h=nowi·či.

^d   i·ni=ke·h=wi·na=meko| i·tepi e·h=a·či,

^e   i·ya·hi e·h=pye·notawa·či ihkwe·wani.

^f   ihkwe·wa o·sani=meko e·h=išite·he·či.

^g   "e·h=pya·yani, ano·se," e·h=ina·či.

^h   "ehe·he," e·h=ina·či.|

ⁱ   ki·šišiki=meko e·h=pemi|‑či·kako·te·nike·či.

^j   ki·ši‑=meko ‑nehkeškamawoči ihkwe·wa,

^k   e·h=kehke·nema·či e·h=pehkiniči.|

^l   e·h=ki·ša·koči‑=či·h=meko ‑me·meta·ča·hiči.|

^m   mani wi·h=iši‑mi·winawi·nitehe,

ⁿ   e·h=kehtena·či.

^o   aškači·me·h=ča·hi, "ki·h=mi·wišine,"| e·h=išiwe·či ihkwe·wa.|

^p   ke·keya·h=meko na·hka| neniwa e·h=we·pisahoči.[*]

10 ^a   i·ni=ča·hi=ʼpi pe·hki| e·h=mešowe·či.

^b   (i·na=ke·h=wi·na=ʼpi ma·wači‑=meko ‑neškina·kaniwiwa.)

^c   nehkanitepehkwe=meko e·h=a·maneki ihkwe·wa.

^d   pye·ta·paniki=meko e·h=na·kwa·či| neniwa.

^e   "ohohya´," e·h=iči.

^f   i·ya·h=pye·ya·hiči,| e·h=kehči‑nepa·či.|

^g   o·ni e·h=pwa·wi‑=meko| ‑po·nite·he·či ihkwe·wa.|

^h   i·niye·ne=meko neniwani e·h=a·hpeči‑natawe·nema·či.

ⁱ   aškači e·h=meme·satesiči neniwa.

^j   e·h=ki·ša·koči‑=meko ‑pehki·nwe·nema·či owi·wani.

^k   e·h=ki·ša·koči‑=meko ‑ke·šawičiki.

^l   "ši·´," e·h=išite·he·či,

^m   "me·kwe·h=ni·hka| owiye·hani ke·ko·hi| išahišawi·toke,"| e·h=ine·nema·či. ‖

11 ^a   e·h=pwa·wi‑=ke·h=wi·na=meko ke·ko·hi ‑ina·či.

^b   nano·nemi=meko e·h=taši‑ i·ni ‑išite·he·či.

^c   o·ni=meše·=ʼnahi| nekotenwi_pe·hkote·niki,|

^d   "i·ya·ma·h=ča·h=ni·h=mawi|‑nepe·wowe, ano·se," e·h=ikoči.

^e   "metemo·he·ha ni·h=mawi‑natawiha·wa_ke·ko·hi_wi·h=iši‑wi·tawi·tamawiči," e·h=ina·či
ona·pe·mani.

^f   "hawo·?," e·h=iči_neniwa.|

^g   ke·htena=ke·h=wi·na=ʼpi_i·nahi awi·hiniwani metemo·he·hani.

^h   i·tepi e·h=a·či.

ⁱ   (nekoti·=ʼnahi ihkwe·wani, i·na_neniwa| otehkwe·mani.)[†]

^j   pe·hkote·niki e·h=wa·wa·tehkwe·hiwa·či| i·nini neniwani.

^k   mani=meko e·ši‑pehkote·seniki, ihkwe·wa| e·h=mawi‑wi·hpe·či.

---

[*] /e·h=we·pisahoči/: AK ⟨.ewepisa‖oči.⟩.

[†] /i·na/: AK ⟨i⟩ changed from ⟨ina⟩.

b   Late in the night (the other man) said to him, "Alright, I'm going to take a leak,"
c   and he went out.
d   But in fact he immediately went over there
e   and came to where the woman lived.
f   The woman thought it was her father.
g   "You're back, Father," she said to him.
h   "Yes," he said to her.
i   And after lying down, he pushed the skirt right up.
j   After she had had a man bury himself in her,
k   the woman knew he was someone else.
l   And she found that she was having a terrific amount of fun.
m   When he was about to slide away,
n   she held him.
o   And then, after a little while the woman said, "You can lie beside."
p   Before long the man jumped in again.
10 a Well, then he won his partner over completely, the story goes.
b   (But in fact, they say that man was the most hated of all.)
c   The woman had sex all night long.
d   And when dawn came the man left.
e   "Man!" he said.
f   When he got home, he slept soundly.
g   And then the woman couldn't stop thinking about it.
h   She wanted that other man all the time.
i   Sometime later the man wanted sex.
j   And he thought his wife was extraordinarily different.
k   He was extraordinarily loose in her.
l   "Gee!" he thought.
m   "I'll bet she's been getting it on with someone else," he thought.
11 a But he didn't actually say anything to her.
b   He was thinking that without letting on.

c   And then one evening
d   she said to him, "Well, I'm going to go spend the night over yonder, Father.
e   "I'm going to try to get the old lady to tell me about things," she said to her husband.
f   "O.K.," said the man.
g   Now, they say it was true that there was a little old lady in that place.
h   And she went there.
i   (And there was also another woman, the sister of that other man.)
j   At night she and that man lay head-to-head.
k   Just as soon as it was dark inside, the woman went and got into the other bed.

1   na·hka nehkanitepehkwe e·h=a·maneki. ‖
12 a   nehkanitepehkwe=meko e·h=a·manohkatawoči.|
b   ki·h=meči=ʼpi -mami·noči neniwa,*
c   oko·te·hani e·h=kehtenamawa·či.

d   i·na·ka=wi·na neniwa e·h=neši=nepa·či.|
e   wa·paniki e·h=pya·niči owi·wani.
f   "nehkanitepehkwe=ʼškwe=meko neta·čiha·čimohekwa," e·h=išiwe·či.†
g   " ʼno·make·we| ki·h=a·čimohene,ʼ netekwa.
h   ʼme·kwe·he nye·wokoni,ʼ netekwa," e·h=ina·či| ona·pe·mani.
i   "o·´, ki·h=nepa nehkaniki·šekwe," e·h=ineči,
j   e·h=nepa·či ihkwe·wa nehkaniki·šekwe.| ‡
k   neniwa e·h=pemeno·še·či.

l   e·na·kwi·hiniki=meko ihkwe·wa e·h=wača·hoči to·hki·či.
m   ki·ši·seniniči, e·h=na·kwa·či,|
n   e·h=mawi-a·maneki.
o   i·ya·h=e·h=pya·či,
p   na·hka=meko e·h=wa·wa·tehkwe·hiči. ‖
13 a   mani=meko e·ši-pehkote·seniki, e·h=we·pi=wi·hpe·ti·wa·či.
b   ka·hkami=meko e·h=a·manowa·či.
c   kapo·twe ihkwe·wa,| "anwa·či·yane=koči| owi·weti·hkakoha," e·h=išiwe·či.
d   "no·sa=koči=ʼna e taši-ona·pe·miya·na,|
e   pe·hki=ma·h=meko| no·sa," e·h=iči.
f   "o·´, ki·na=meko," e·h=ineči.
g   "o·´, ni·h=a·čimoha·wa=ča·hi," e·h=iči.
h   wa·pano·hiniki e·h=we·pi=wača·hoči.|
i   ki·ši·seniwa·či, e·h=na·kwa·či.
j   "we·nah=ketowi·wi,"| e·h=ikoči otehkwe·mani.
k   "ehe·he," e·h=ina·či.

l   o·ni i·ya·h=pye·ya·či,|
m   ke·waki=meko e·h=šekišiniči ona·pe·mani.
n   "e·h=pya·yani," e·h=ikoči.
o   "ehe·he," e·h=ina·či.
p   "nawači=pya·no," e·h=ikoči.
q   i·tepi e·h=a·či.
r   pa·pekwa=na·hka e·h=taši-‖awiwoči ihkwe·wa.§
14 a   e·h=ki·ša·kočikiniči=či·h=meko owi·wani.
b   "šihihwi·´," e·h=ina·či.

---

*Follows HWB (1998).
†/neta·čiha·čimohekwa/: AK ⟨.netačia|čimoeakwa.⟩.
‡The divider after ⟨ikwewa⟩ was added later.
§/pa·pekwa=na·hka/: AK ⟨papekwa|naka.⟩.

^l And again she had sex all night.
^{12 a} All night long she was serviced.
^b   Having overdone it completely, to hear the tale,
^c the man clung tightly to her skirts.

^d   Meanwhile the other man was sleeping alone.
^e And the next day his wife came back.
^f "She went on all night telling me things," she declared.
^g "She told me she'd instruct me for a little while.
^h For four days, she thinks," she told her husband.
ⁱ   "Oh, you must sleep all day," she was told.
^j And the woman slept all day.
^k   The man took care of the child.

^l   That evening the woman cooked after she awoke.
^m After he had eaten, she left,
ⁿ going to have sex.
^o She got there,
^p and once again she was head-to-head.
^{13 a} As soon as it was dark inside, they got to sleeping together.
^b They had sex right from the start.
^c   At some point the woman said, "You know, we could get married if you like.
^d   "The man I'm married to is my father, you know.
^e My real father, you understand," she said.
^f   "Oh, it's up to you," she was told.
^g   "Ah, so I'll tell him," she said.
^h   Early the next morning she set about cooking.
ⁱ And after they had eaten, she left.
^j   "I see you're married," his sister said to him.
^k   "Yes," he told her.

^l   And then, when she got home,
^m her husband was still in bed.
ⁿ   "You're back," he said to her.
^o   "Yes," she answered him.
^p   "Come here first," he said to her.
^q   She went to him.
^r And in no time the woman was being taken again.
^{14 a}   And he discovered how extraordinary his wife's anatomy was.
^b   "Jeepers!" he said to her.

c   "a·kwi=ni·hka='yo·we| i·ni išikiyanini," e·h=ina·či.
d   "ehe·he," e·h=ineči.|
e   "ano·se, we·nahi, pe·hki=meko keki·ša·koči_owi·wite·he ni·yawi?" e·h=ina·či.
f   "neto·si='yo=wi·na_ki·yawi," e·h=ina·či.
g   "ehe·he, e·h=owi·wemena·ni,"| e·h=ina·či.
h   "o·´,_i·ni e·ne·nemiwane·ni,
i   ki·h=nakanene," e·h=ina·či.
j   "ona·pe·miya·ne=ke·hi,
k   e·šenočini| wi·h=ona·pe·miwa·ne·na,|
l   meše·='nah=meko i·ni ki·h=to·tawi,"_e·h=ineči.
m   e·h=nakapehkwe·sa·či.
n   "o·´, ona·pe·mino=ni·hka," e·h=ina·či.
o   "ano·se, ayo·h=ni·h=awipena," e·h=ineči| neniwa.
p   e·na·kwi·hiniki e·h=na·kwa·niči.

q   kapo·twe_e·h=ka·škiha·či| metemo·he·ha ‖ e·h=wi·hpe·niči o·šisemani.
15 a   "ya·´,_we·nah=ketowi·weti·pwa?"_e·h=ina·či| i·nini o·šisemani.*
b   "ehe·he,"| e·h=iniči.
c   "ona·pe·miwa=ke·hi·='na.
d   wi·h=menwe·netaminiwani='h=we·na·='na!? ona·pe·mani!?" e·h=išiwe·či| metemo·he·ha.
e   a·kwi='yo=ke·hi·='pi·='na neniwa_i·nahi taši_ihkwe·wahi pešeke·nemekočini.

f   o·ni pe·hkote·niki| i·ni·='tepi e·h=išiweneči| neniwa.
g   meše·='nah=nekotenwi_to·hki·či,
h   e·h=ka·škiha·či pašito·ha nekotayahi aka·mete·ki,†
i   e·h=wa·se·šawe·či_kena·či.|
j   i·ya·ma·haki=ke·hi e·h=ma·tako·hkwe·šinowa·či.
k   kwi·yena=meko e·h=a·manowa·či.
l   ki·ši-aniweše·niki,
m   kena·či e·h=pa·hkitiye·na·či.
n   nanešiwi=či·hi e·h=inekihkwa·hkwateniki e·nemi_nehka·hkwiseniki. ‖
16 a   e·h=ne·ya·pi-ma·takona·či.
b   wa·natohka wa·paniki e·h=ki·wi_'šawiči.
c   e·h=na·kwa·či neniwa.
d   "ki·ši-anehkake ma·hiya| kena·pe·ma,_
e   ki·h=a·mi·pena,"| e·h=ina·či.
f   "hawo·?," e·h=iniči owi·wa·wani.
g   "a·kwi=we·=meko,? e·ye·h_nesapiya·ni?" e·h=ikoči.
h   "a·kwi," e·h=ina·či.
i   "nepe·we·nemo," e·h=ina·či.
j   "kaši=ča·h=e·h=teki," e·h=ikoči.
k   "ši·´,_pe·hki=ma·hi·='na| nešiwinakaye·wa kena·pe·ma," e·h=ina·či.

____

*/we·nah=ketowi·weti·pwa?/: also in K-M 523n, without elision.
†AK ⟨.nekota|yai.⟩: also JM-texts 2c, SP-BSAB 33q; accepted as /nekotayahi/ by EK.

c   "You weren't like that before," he said to her.

d   "You're right," he was answered.

e   And she said to him, "Listen, Father, do you consider me to be fully as much your wife
as could be?

f   "Given that I'm your daughter," she said to him.

g   "Yes, I've taken you as my wife," he said to her.

h   "Well, if that's what you consider me to be,

i   I'm going to leave you," she said to him.

j   "Oh, and when I'm married,

k   anytime whoever I marry is away,

l   you can do that to me, if you like," he was told.

m   And his head dropped.

n   "Well, get married, then," he said to her.

o   "Father, we'll come and live here," the man was told.

p   And early that evening she left.

q   At some point the old lady became aware that her grandson had a bedmate.

15 a   "Oh my, now are you two married?" she said to her grandson.

b   "Yes," he said.

c   "The thing is, she has a husband.

d   I doubt that her husband will like that!" the old lady declared.

e   Now, they say the women there were not fond of that man.

f   And then that night the man was taken to the other place.

g   One time when he woke up,

h   the older man became aware of the couple on the other side of the lodge.

i   Slowly and carefully he made some light.

j   And here, the others were lying with their heads under the blanket.

k   And just at that moment they were having sex.

l   After the flame was burning bright,

m   he carefully lifted the blanket from the other's bottom.

n   He was astonished to see the enormous size of the shaft that was extending out of sight.

16 a   He covered him up again.

b   And the next day he acted unconcerned.

c   And the other man left.

d   "After your husband has settled in,

e   we'll all move," he said to her.

f   "O.K.," said their wife.

g   "Aren't we going to, then, while I'm left here by myself?" she asked him.

h   "No, " he told her.

i   "I'm giving up," he told her.

j   "How come?" she asked him.

k   "Gee, don't you see, your husband has a truly gigantic prick," he said to her.

l e·h=apahapane·niniči,
m "nahi´,| a·peči, ano·se," e·h=ikoči.|
n ke·keya·hi·='nahi e·h=mana·či.|

o e·na·kwi·hiniki=meko e·h=ki·ši-pya·niči i·nini| neniwani.
p "kaši='yo| ketešiso," e·h=ina·či.
q "a·yahko·he·ha," e·h=iniči.
r "o·ho·´," e·h=ina·či.

s ki·ši-anehkaminiči,
t e·h=a·mi·wa·či.
u otehkwe·mani e·h=awana·či. ‖
17 a i·na=ke·h=e·yi·ki i·ni=meko| e·h=išisoči.
b 'a·yahko·hihkwe·wa' e·h=išisoči.

c o·ni| meše=nekotenwi i·na| pašito·ha e·h=pana·čiha·či_i·nini a·yahko·hihkwe·wani,
d wi·h=kehči-nepa·niči e·h=ine·nema·či.|
e e·h=kehči-nepa·či i·na| še·škesi·ha.
f kena·či e·h=či·kako·te·na·či.*
g e·h=pwa·wi-=meko -ame·niči.|
h pašito·ha e·h=tanatahwa·či,
i e·h=pwa·wi-še·škesi·hiniči.
j kapo·twe e·h=to·hkahwa·či i·nini ihkwe·wani.
k "keme·meta·ča·hi?,| nesese," e·h=ikoči.
l "ehe·he," e·h=ina·či.
m nehkanitepehkwe=meko e·h=a·manohkatawa·či pašito·ha,|

n kapo·twe_e·h=kehke·nemekoči we·tehkwe·miničini.
o e·h=owi·wiči=ke·h=meko i·nini pašito·ha,
p i·nini še·škesi·hi·hka·soničini. ‖
18 a "netona·pe·mi=ke·h=mana| ki·mo·či," e·h=iniči.|
b "i·noki='yo_a·yahpi·hčina·h=meko_i·ni_e·h=to·tawiči," e·h=ikoči.
c a·ya·šo·hka=meko e·h=ki·mo·či|-matama·ti·wa·či owi·wa·wahi.
d pašito·ha=ke·hi ota·nesani a·yahpi·hčina·h=meko e·h=mana·či.
e wi·na=na·hka a·yahko·ha otehkwe·mani a·yahpi·hčina·h=meko e·h=mana·či.

f o·ni kapo·twe e·h=a·hkwe·či a·yahko·hihkwe·wa.
g "nesakwe=wi·na| mana a·yahko·ha," e·h=ikoči we·tawe·ma·winičini.
h "meškwa·wa·hkwi-ma·tesi ki·h=ašihto.
i atehči=ča·h=meko ki·h=tana·hkasa," e·h=ineči pašito·ha.
j "hawo·?," e·h=iči.|
k "o·ni_keta·nesa_mya·no·te·te, wi·h=ki·menači.
l ki·ši-ki·menate, i·ni·='ni ma·tesi‖ wi·h=pešepa·pite·namani," e·h=ineči._

____

*AK ⟨ka⟩ changed from ⟨ke⟩.

l   And she laughed.
m   "Let's, Father, come on!" she said to him.
n   Finally, with that, he fucked her.

o   By the early evening the other man had come back.
p   "Well, what's your name?" he asked him.
q   "Little Âyahkôha," he said.
r   "Oh, I see," he said to him.

s   After he had settled in,
t   they moved.
u   And he brought along his sister.
17 a   Now, she had the same name, as well.
b   Her name was Âyahkôhihkwêwa ('Âyahkôh-Woman').

c   And then one day the older man bewitched Âyahkôhihkwêwa,
d   willing her to sleep soundly.
e   And the maiden fell into a deep sleep.
f   Slowly and carefully he pushed up her skirt.
g   And she did not react.
h   And when the older man was shafting her,
i   he knew she was not a virgin.
j   Before long his shafting woke the woman up.
k   "Are you having fun, elder brother?" she asked him.
l   "Yes," he said to her.
m   And all night long the older man serviced her.

n   Before long, the girl's brother found out about her.
o   And indeed, the older man took her as his wife,
p   the one that had pretended to be a virgin.
18 a   "I'm secretly married to him," she said.
b   "As these days he does that to me once in a while," she told him.
c   They took turns secretly fucking each other's wives.
d   What's more, the older man fucked his daughter once in a while.
e   And once in a while Âyahkôha also fucked his sister.

f   And then at some point Âyahkôhihkwêwa became angry.
g   "How about if we kill Âyahkôha," the man's sister said about him.
h   "You must make a cedarwood knife.
i   And you must cure it someplace not nearby," the older man was told.
j   "O.K.," he said.
k   "And when your daughter has her period, you must feel her up.
l   And after you have felt her up, you must smear the blade of that knife," he was told.

19 a "meše=we·=meko·='nahi menehta=meko mya·no·te·kwe·na| i·na_i·ni wi·h=to·tawata,"|
e·h=ineči.

b o·ni ota·nesani menehta e·h=mya·no·te·niči,|

c kwi·yena=meko ki·šihto·či.

d o·ni·='na| a·yahko·ha otehkwe·mani atehči e·h=mawi_taši-manamana·či.

e e·h=mayo·ha·či i·ya·h=taši.

f e·h=mya·ne·netaki e·h=ona·pe·miniči.

g o·ni| pašito·ha ota·nesani| e·h=awiniči e·h=a·či.

h e·ši_pya·či=meko e·h=a·htawa·na·či.

i e·h=meškowa·hkosiniči.

j e·h=šešo·ya·pite·nike·či.

k ki·ši·=meko -meškowiniki_i·ni ma·tesi,

l e·h=na·kwa·či.

m "ano·se," e·h=ikoči.

n "wa·y," e·h=ina·či.*

o "pya·no=pena´," e·h=iniči. ‖

20 a i·tepi_e·h=a·či.

b "pe·hki=kohi| neta·neha·nemahokwa,"| e·h=iniči.†

c "wa·pamino| e·nekihkwa·nakesiya·ni,"| e·h=iniči.

d mani e·ši|-to·kenoniči, e·h=pi·tanwa·pama·či.

e e·h=se·kinotawa·či.

f " 'ki·h=nesenepwa,'_iwahiwa=ke·hi," e·h=ina·či o·sani.

g "o·ho·´," e·h=iči pašito·ha.

h o·ni| pe·hkote·niki, "i·ya·ma·hi ni·h=a·pena," e·h=ina·či| i·na a·yahko·hihkwe·wa.

i "mašite=ča·hi, ni·h=sakikwe·na·wa.

j o·ni wi·h=ki·škinakaye·šwači.

k ki·h=či·pinowe·tiye·ni wi·h=aše·nawi·ya·ni.‡/§

l aše·nawi·ya·ne, i·ni wi·h=ki·škinakaye·šwači," e·h=ineči.|

m wa·paniki, "ni·h=ki·yoki·yose=ča·hi," e·h=iči| pašito·ha.

n o·ni e·h=awahkye·či a·yahko·ha.

o kwi·yena=meko ‖ i·tepi e·h=iši_kehkahike·či.

21 a i·ya·hi e·h=taši-ma·hkwima·hkwiči.

b kaka·nwe·ši='yo e·h=ma·hkwiči.

c ki·hpene ma·hkwičini,| e·h=anawičike·či pašito·ha.

d e·h=či·pinowe·tiye·na·či owi·wani.

e e·h=aše·nawi·či| ihkwe·wa.

f e·h=ki·škinakaye·šike·či neniwa.|

g peno·či·me·h=meko e·h=ahkwi-ka·teče·ška·koči,

h e·h=ka·tanahami·niči i·nini a·yahko·hani.

---

*/wa·y/ is conjectural for AK ⟨.waye.⟩ (his consistent spelling); now always [wa·h].

†/=kohi/: ⟨i⟩ is flat and undotted.

‡/ki·h=či·/: AK ⟨.kiči.⟩.

§/wi·h=aše·nawi·ya·ni/: AK ⟨.wiašena.wiyani.⟩: the medial divider was added later.

19 a   "Or actually, whoever has their period first is the one you should do that to," he was told.

b   And then his daughter was the first to have her period,

c   exactly when he had finished making it.

d   And Âyahkôha went someplace else to fuck his sister for a while.

e   And he made her cry there.

f   He disliked the fact that she was married.

g   And the older man went to where his daughter was staying.

h   As soon as he got there, he put her on her back.

i   He could see that she was all bloody.

j   And he smeared the blade.

k   After the knife was bloody,

l   he started back.

m   "Father," she said to him.

n   "What?" he said to her.

o   "Wait, come here," she said.

20 a   And he went back to her.

b   "I have to tell you, his constant shafting is really too much for me," she said.

c   "Look at how big the hole in me is," she said.

d   When she took her fingers and spread herself open, he looked inside her.

e   And he was afraid for her.

f   "What's more, he's always saying he's going to kill us," she told her father.

g   "Oh, I see," said the older man.

h   And then that night Âyahkôhihkwêwa said to him, "We'll be going over yonder" (naming the place).

i   "So, when he fucks me, I'll hold his prick with my hand.

j   And then you must cut his prick off.

k   You must give me a poke in the rear end for me to slide back.

l   And when I slide back, you must cut off his prick," he was told.

m   The next day the older man said, "Well, I'm going to go walk around."

n   And then Âyahkôha took the woman with him,

o   precisely to where he had indicated.

21 a   And over there he fucked and fucked.

b   For he would fuck for a long time each time.

c   As soon as he would start fucking, the older man would sneak up.

d   And he gave his wife a poke in the rear end.

e   The woman slid back.

f   The man did the penis-severing.

g   And Âyahkôha knocked him quite a distance

h   as he bolted.

ⁱ   i·ni=ke·hi_mi·nakayi mehtekoki| e·h=tetepa·hkwisa·niki.
^j   e·h=ki·ši_nesa·wa·či.

^k   o·ni_ota·nesani_ki·ši_anenwi·niči,
^l   e·h=mawi_aneškaki wi·h=owi·ke·hiwa·či.
^m   e·h=po·si·=meko ·makinehpi_ki·ška·pehkateniki e·h=mawi|·owi·kiwa·či na·mahkamiki. ‖
22 a   e·h=ni·šo·hkwe·we·či neniwa,
^b   nekoti_ota·nesani e·h=owi·wiči.
^c   na·mahkamiki e·h=owi·kiwa·či,|
^d   pešekesiwahi e·h=otayiwa·či.
^e   e·h=ma·ne·ha·wa·či·=meko.

^f   i·niye=ke·hi e·h=akisowa·či we·či·wa·či.
^g   metemo·he·ha e·h=we·pi-ma·mahkate·wi·či.

^h   kapo·twe_wi·ša·či·=meko i·nahi tepina·hi e·h=pye·či_tanwe·kesiniči.
ⁱ   "nahi´,_ni·h=mawi|·wanima·wa," e·h=iči| we·yo·hkomesita.

^j   nepisi='yo=ke·hi i·nahi e·h=ahte·niki,
^k   e·h=mo·hki·či meše=meko na·hina·hi na·waka·me.
^l   "ano·hko," e·h=ina·či.
^m   man=e·na·piči| metemo·he·ha,
ⁿ   ke·htena=či·h=meko o·šisemani e·h=ne·wa·či._
^o   "kaši=ča·h=ketešawi e·h=taši-mayomayo·yani," e·h=ina·či ‖ o·hkomese·hani.[*]
23 a   "e·h=wanihenako·we=ča·hi we·či|-mayomayo·ya·ni," e·h=ineči ihkwe·wa.
^b   o·ni, "ni·na=kohi_mehteno·h=nene·se.
^c   netawe·ma·wa=ke·hi našawaye=meko nesekwa maneto·wani," e·h=iči.
^d   "ihkwe·wani='pi e·h=matama·ke·či e·h=ne·woči.
^e   we·wi·winičini=ča·hi='pi ne·wokočini,
^f   i·nini=ča·h=ne·sekočini," e·h=ina·či.|
^g   "neneškima·wa=ke·hi ka·hkami," e·h=iči.
^h   "ni·na=ke·h=wi·na netona·pe·mi,"| e·h=iči.
ⁱ   "ne·tawe·nemiyanini=ča·hi ayo·hi_ki·h=pya," e·h=ina·či.
^j   e·h=mi·ša·te·nemoči metemo·he·ha,
^k   o·šisemani e·h=maneto·wi-ošinetaminiči, e·h=išite·he·či.
^l   o·ni_metemo·he·ha e·h=anohka·hkye·či i·ya·hi| wi·h=mawi-ašikawoči. ‖

24 a   e·h=na·kwa·či_ihkwe·wa,_ki·ši_kakano·neti·či o·hkomese·hani.[†]
^b   i·ya·h=e·h=pya·či.
^c   "i·ni e·h=ki·ši|-kakano·neti·ya·ni neše·škesi·hi-no·hkomesa,"| e·h=ina·či ona·pe·mani.
^d   "we·nahi, še·škesi·hiwa?"| e·h=ikoči.
^e   "ehe·he, še·škesi·hiwa=kohi='pi," e·h=ina·či.|

---

[*]/e·h=ina·či/: AK ⟨eineči⟩.
[†]/o·hkomese·hani/: AK ⟨ko⟩ changed from ⟨š⟩.

ⁱ On top of that, the penis went flying and wrapped itself around a tree.
^j They had killed him.

^k   And then after his daughter had bathed (her period being over),
^l she went to arrange a nice place for them all to live.
^m They went and dwelt underground in some tall cliffs.
22 a The man had two wives,
^b one of his wives being his daughter.
^c They dwelt underground
^d and kept deer as stock.
^e They had a lot of them.

^f   Meanwhile, back where they had come from their whereabouts was unknown.
^g   And the old lady began fasting.

^h   Soon, to their great annoyance, the sound of her wailing came directly to that place.
ⁱ   "Alright, I'll go and tell her a tale," said the old lady's granddaughter.

^j   Now, there was a lake there.
^k And she came to the surface a little ways out in the middle.
^l   "Grandmother," she said to her.
^m   When the old lady looked,
ⁿ why, sure enough, here she saw her granddaughter.
^o   "What's the matter, that you keep weeping?" she said to her grandmother.
23 a   "Well, I'm weeping because I lost you," the woman was told.
^b   And then she said, "I have to tell you, I'm the only one still alive.
^c My brother was killed by a manitou long ago.
^d   "They say he was seen fucking someone else's wife.
^e Well, they say her husband was the one who saw him,
^f and he was the one that killed him," she told her.
^g   "Now, I warned him at the outset," she said.
^h   "And as for me, I'm married," she said.
ⁱ   "So, you can come here whenever you're wondering about me," she told her.
^j   The old lady was delighted,
^k thinking that her granddaughter had married into a manitou family.
^l   And the old lady asked to have a house built for her over in that place.

24 a   The woman left after talking with her grandmother.
^b And she got back.
^c   "I've had a talk with my maiden grandmother," she told her husband.
^d   "Wait, she's a virgin?" he asked her.
^e   "Yes, she says she's definitely a virgin," she told him.

^f   "o·ho·´," e·h=iči pašito·ha.

^g   mani=wi·na:
^h   maneto·wahi̲ e·h=taši-a·nwe·nemekoči e·šawiči,
ⁱ   e·h=asahasa·mi̲-wapašiha·či owi·wahi.

^j   o·ni=na·hka·='nini metemo·he·hani e·h=sa·kiči·niči.
^k   e·h=kekye·pi·kwe·na·či,
^l   e·h=šekiniči e·h=wa·pama·či.
^m   ke·htena=či·h=meko e·h=še·škesi·hiniči.
ⁿ   o·ni='pi owi·wani i·tepi e·h=išinehkawa·či.
^o   "mani wi·h=inači," e·h=ina·či.

^p   "ano·hko, wi·tapi·miyane='pi, na·mahkamiki‖ ki·h=awi," e·h=ina·či o·hkomese·hani.[*]
^{25 a}   "meči=ye·toke wi·h=pešeke·nemiči¡? wi·čawiwa·wate·na!?" e·h=ina·či o·šisemani.
^b   "kekye·htena·mowe·yane=koči=wi·na, i·ni=meko išawihka·ha," e·h=išiwe·či
      metemo·he·ha.
^c   "kaši´, nekekye·htena·mowe=kohi," e·h=ikoči o·šiseme·hani.
^d   "o·´, nahi´, i·ni̲ ni·h=išawi," e·h=iniči.
^e   "a·peči=we·na,̲ pya·no," e·h=ina·či,[†]
^f   e·h=awana·či o·hkomesani.
^g   i·ya·h=e·h=pye·na·či e·h=awiwa·či o·hkomese·hani.
^h   metemo·ka pe·hkote·niki e·h=wi·hpe·meči.|
ⁱ   kenwe·ši=meko e·h=taši·hkawoči mečemo·ka.
^j   saka·ki=meko| e·h=ki·ši-to·tawoči.
^k   mečemo·ka e·h=aka·wa·taki wi·h=a·či-aškiki·hiči.
^l   e·ye·ši-=meko -aka·wa·taki, e·h=aškikiči,|
^m   ki·ša·koči e·h=we·wenesiči.‖

^{26 a}   o·ni·='na neniwa,
^b   ke·htena=wi·na=meko e·h=maneto·wiči i·na o·šisemeti·hahi we·wi·wita.|
^c   šewe·na e·h=kwe·hkwe·wi-=meko -meme·satesiči.|
^d   e·h=pwa·wi-=ke·h=meko -ke·ko·hi -kaški-ine·neti·niči owi·wahi.
^e   e·h=tepa·neti·niči=meko.

^f   o·ni mešihke·ha, owi·hka·nani wi·sahke·hani, e·h=anohka·nekoči| wi·h=mi·hketama·ke·či
      i·nihi ihkwe·wahi.[‡]
^g   o·ni či·kwe·haki e·h=anohka·neči wi·h=pehtatahamo·hka·nowa·či.
^h   i·ni='pi e·h=pakatamowa·či i·ni nenemehkiwaki.
ⁱ   e·h=mehtapiwa·či i·niye·ka.
^j   o·ni metemo·he·ha e·h=owi·ke·hitehe e·h=a·wa·či,

———————————————

[*]/wi·tapi·miyane/: *lit.*, 'if you sit with me'.
[†]/=we·na/: AK ⟨wene⟩.
[‡]/mi·/: AK ⟨ni⟩.

f   "Oh, I see," said the older man.

g   But here's the thing:
h   The manitous had been disapproving of what he did,
i   as he demeaned his wives too much.

j   And then also, when the old lady went to pee,
k   he masked her eyes.
l   And he watched her take a piss.
m   And sure enough he could see she was a virgin.
n   And then he had his wife go to her.
o   "Here's what you must say to her," he told her.

p   She said to her grandmother, "Grandmother, if you're a co-wife with me, I'm told you
     can live underground.
25 a   And she said to her granddaughter, "I hardly think whoever you're married to would
     fancy me!
b   "But if you're serious, I would do that, of course," the old lady declared.
c   "Why, I'm definitely serious," her granddaughter said to her.
d   "Oh let's, I'll do that," she said.
e   "Well come on then, come," she said to her,
f   and she took her grandmother home.
g   She brought her grandmother to the place where they lived.
h   The old lady that night had a bed-mate.
i   Long was the old dear worked on,
j   and barely was the doing accomplished.
k   The old dear wanted to be young again,
l   and while desiring it, young she became,
m   and she was extremely pretty.

26 a   And as for that man,
b   he truly did have manitou powers, the one that married a grandmother and granddaughter.
c   But his desire for sex went too far.
d   At the same time, his wives never had any bad thoughts about each other.
e   They loved each other, indeed.

f   And then Turtle, the friend of Wîsahkêha, was given the task by him of paying court to
     those married women.
g   And the Thunder Beings were given the task of feigning an accidental lightning strike.
h   Then, the story goes, the Thunderers struck that place.
i   Those people were sitting out in the open,
j   And then they all went to where the old lady had lived,

k e·h=apahkwayike·wa·či.

l o·ni mešihke·ha e·h=we·pi-mi·hketama·ke·či ‖ i·nini ihkwe·wahi.

27 a e·h=mešoška·či=meko mešihke·ha.

b o·ni·=’nini kwi·yese·hani e·h=kemo·towa·či e·ye·hkwe·waki,

c e·h=e·ye·hkwe·wiha·wa·či i·nini_kwi·yese·hani=’yo·we.|

d e·h=we·pi_-ki·yose·či we·kwisita,

e e·h=natone·hwa·či| okwisani, ota·nesani| ki·šihtawa·čini.

f e·h=pwa·wi-=meko nana·ši| -mehkawa·či.

g ča·ki=meko na·mahkamiki e·h=ki·yose·či,

h ča·ki ahpemeki.

i nye·wenwi na·kwa·či, e·h=pe·we·nemoči.

j owi·wahi=ke·hi mešihke·hani| e·h=matamatama·koči.|

k kekimesi=meko e·h=ačihkwiniči owi·wahi.

l “netačihkwiha·waki=meko,” e·h=išite·he·či.

m kapo·twe_e·h=no·še·niči.

n če·wina·h=meko ‖ mešihke·he·hahi e·h=no·ša·na·niči owi·wahi.

28 a e·h=kehč_-a·hkwe·či.

b “ni·na=we·na, ‘ni·na=ye·toke neni·ča·nesaki,’_netešite·he.

c we·nahi mešihke·ha ona·pe·miwe·kwe·ni,” e·h=ina·či.

d “ni·na=ke·h=a·kwi,” e·h=iniči nekoti._

e “še·ški| nemanamanekwa,” e·h=iniči.

f ma·tesi e·h=we·pi-ki·nihto·či,

g e·h=ča·ka·mowa·či ihkwe·waki.|

h “o·´,_we·pa·moko=meko.

i kenepepwa=koh=meko,” e·h=ina·či owi·wahi.*

j o·ni_wi·sahke·ha e·h=wi·čipahwe·ma·či ihkwe·wahi.†

k o·ni| e·h=peminehkawoči, ma·wač_-ahkowi e·h=anemipahoči wi·sahke·ha.

l e·ye·hpahoči wi·sahke·ha e·h=sakihta·hpe·neči.|

m “hawo·ʔ,” e·h=iči,

n e·h=mawinaneti·či.

o no·make=meko mehči e·h=aseči ‖ ne·so·hkwe·wa·ta._

29 a nye·wenwi| ki·škatahoči, e·h=oči-pemi_-kehta·moči.

b wi·sakiti·he·ha e·h=kehta·moči.

c “i·ni wi·h=išawiyani,” e·h=ineči.

d “wi·sakiti·ha,” ki·h=iko·ki neki·haki, nešise·haki=ke·hi.

e a·kwi=wi·na·=’nahi amohkini,”| e·h=ina·či._‡

f e·h=awana·či| i·nihi ihkwe·wahi,

g e·h=ma·wa·seniki e·h=išiwena·či.

---

*/kenepepwa/: *lit.*, ‘you died!’, said without the diminutive element usual for this verb.

†/wi·sahke·ha/: the ⟨i⟩ is only partly present on the edge.

‡/=wi·na·=’nahi/: AK ⟨wi|nai.⟩.

^k and they made a winter lodge of cattail-mats.
^l   And then Turtle began paying court to the wives.
27 a And Turtle was smitten.

^b   And then berdaches kidnapped the boy.
^c They made the boy that had been into a berdache.
^d   And the boy's father began walking about,
^e searching for his son, the one he had fathered on his daughter.
^f He could never find him.
^g He walked around everywhere under the earth.
^h and everywhere in the heavens.
ⁱ After heading out four times, he gave up.

^j   At the same time, his wives were being serially fucked by Turtle.
^k And every one of his wives became pregnant.
^l   He thought that *he* must have gotten them pregnant.
^m And the time came when they gave birth.
ⁿ And at exactly the same time his wives all gave birth to baby turtles.
28 a   He was furious.
^b   "I had rather supposed that they were my own children.
^c But I see now you must have taken Turtle as your husband," he said to them.
^d   "Not me," said one.
^e "It was just that he kept fucking me," she said.
^f   He began sharpening a knife,
^g and the women all ran away.
^h   "Oh, go run away.
ⁱ Make no mistake, I'm killing you," he said to his wives.

^j   And then Wîsahkêha ran with the women.
^k As they were being pursued, Wîsahkêha ran in the rear.
^l And as Wîsahkêha was running along, he was grabbed by the back of the neck.
^m   "Hello!" he said
ⁿ and went on the attack.
^o   In short order, the man with three wives was thrown to the ground.
29 a And after being whipped four times, he bolted away at top speed.
^b A little terrier fled at top speed.
^c   "That's how you will be," he was told.
^d   "My aunts and uncles will call you a terrier, a 'bitter-tail.'
^e But for all that, they won't eat you," he said to him.
^f   He took the women away
^g and brought them to where there was a village.

^h   "ka·ta=na·hka i·ni=ʼši-anwa·či·hke·ko wi·h=asahasa·mi‿wapašihena·kwe neniwaki,"
e·h=ineči ihkwe·waki.
ⁱ   "ahpene·či=meko ayo·čiwe·pi ka·ta| i·ni iši-še·še·hkosihke·ko," e·h=ineči‿ihkwe·waki.
^j   e·h=po·ta·nekowa·či wi·sahke·hani,|
^k e·h=se·kinawe·ška·wa·či i·niki ihkwe·waki.

^l   i·ni=ča·h e·hkwiči. ‖

h   "Don't be willing again like that to have men degrade you so much," the women were told.

i   "From now on and always, don't be generous like that," the women were told.

j   Wisahkeha blew on the women,

k   and a scary feeling came over them.

l   So, that's the end.

wêtayita êsepâhahi

The Man Who Had Pet Raccoons.

wêtayita êsepâhahi
Alfred Kiyana[*]

1 a   we·tayita_e·sepa·hahi.[†]

b   neniwa=ʼpi ke·no·te·hi e·h=owi·kiči,|

c e·h=ma·ne·ha·či e·sepa·hahi,

d e·h=wi·čihekoči.

e e·sepa·hahi=meko e·h=otayiči.

f mahkate·wa·kete·wi e·h=nemate·niki e·h=otaškwa·te·miči,[‡]

g otaškwa·te·mi ahkiki oči| e·h=ča·keškaminiči.

h   e·h=pwa·wi-=ke·hi -nahi_ši·ša·či.

i mi·škota=ke·hi e·h=meši_neniwiči,

j e·h=mi·škawi_wa·kikome·či.

k   nekotah=e·ya·čini, meše·=ʼnah=meko kekimesi_e·h=wi·te·mekoči otaye·hi e·sepa·hahi.

l e·h=anehka·koči.

m po·hkote=ʼpi e·sepa·hahi=meko ne·htawi, o·ni=wi·na po·hkote.

n   wa·panikini ma·maya e·h=kehči-či·kakohike·či pe·pye·to·niči, aša·hki·wahi,

o meše=we·=meko·=ʼnahi_ša·ši·kwataminiči.

p e·hkwaškaha·te·ki·=ʼni wi·kiya·pi e·h=mesiwe·ya·kwate·ki aša·hki·wi_ohka·tani.

q   kapo·twe=ʼpi aškači e·h=akiha·či nekoti.‖

2 a "we·ne·h=ča·h=ye·toke ne·htamawita," e·h=išite·he·či.

b wi·h=kehke·nema·či=meko e·h=išite·he·či e·šawinikwe·ni otaye·ni.

c pena=ta·taki, še·ški=meko e·h=šekišekišiki| e·h=taši-natawe·nema·či| e·šawinikwe·ni.[§]

d nekoti=ke·hi·=ʼnini e·sepa·hani.

e   meše·=ʼnah=nekotenwi pye·ta·nemateniki,

f e·h=ki·ša·koči-=meko -menwiya·kwateniki,

g e·ye·ši-=ke·h=meko -a·hkwe·či e·h=akiha·či ote·sepa·hemani.

h e·h=a·nawihto·či=meko wi·h=pwa·wi-apane·niči.

i i·ni=meko e·h=išawiči e·taswi-=meko -pye·ta·nematenikini.

j ke·keya·h=meko e·h=po·siya·kwateniki e·šiya·kwatenikwe·ni.

k e·h=menwiya·kwateniki=meko.

l apina=meko kapo·twe e·h=ma·čikanwe·či.

m e·h=a·nawihto·či=meko wi·h=pwa·wi- i·ni_ineška·niki owi·nakayi.|

n ke·keya·h=meko e·h=pemi|-nowi·či, ‖

3 a e·h=na·čiye·či.

b   meše·=ʼnah=či·h=meko nano·pehka·čina·hi e·h=pya·či,

c mehto·či=ke·h=wi·na=meko e·h=katawi_pye·notaki we·čiya·kwateniki e·h=išite·he·či.

---

[*]The manuscript is NAA 2794.91; it has 38 pages.

[†]Written as a title at the top of the page. The man's name is /we·te·sepaneme·ha/ (20k).

[‡]/mahkate·wa·kete·wi/: also K-TO 8e; the transcription of /-a·k-/ is uncertain.

[§]/pena=ta·taki/ (EK; K-MMD 6i): AK ⟨pena.tataki⟩.

The Man who Had Pet Raccoons
Translated by Ives Goddard

1 a   The Man Who Had Pet Raccoons.

b   There was a man, they say, who lived in a longhouse,
c and he had lots of raccoons.
d They lived with him.
e The raccoons were his pets.
f There was a fire-blackened bole standing by his door,
g and they had worn down his door at the bottom.
h   Moreover, he never went hunting.
i And on top of that, he was a large man,
j and he had a strongly hooked nose.
k   Whenever he went anywhere, pretty nearly all of his pet raccoons went with him.
l They were at ease with him.
m Half the house is said to have been just for the raccoons, and the other half was his.
n   Early every morning he swept out what they had brought in, the crawfish,
o and in fact any of the refuse from their eating.
p At the edge of the yard around that house crawfish feet were strewn all over.

q   After a long time, the story goes, he noticed that one was missing.
2 a "Well, I wonder who killed it on me," he thought.
b He was intent on knowing what had happened to his pet.
c He couldn't help just lying there trying to think what could have happened to it.
d And here it was a single raccoon.
e   One time when a breeze came
f it brought an extremely pleasant smell,
g and this while he was still angry over losing his raccoon.
h He couldn't help smiling.
i It was the same for him every time the breeze came.
j In time the mysterious smell became even more intense.
k It was a pleasant smell, indeed.
l Suddenly he even had an erection.
m He couldn't get his penis not to do that.
n At length he got up and went out,
3 a going after the scent.
b   He was surprised to find that he had gone a very great distance
c when it seemed to him as if he had almost arrived at the source of the scent.

^d me·čimo·wi=meko e·h=na·kwa·či, otaye·hi·=’nahi e·sepanahi.
^e meše·=’nah=meko meta·sokoni e·h=anemehka·či.
^f i·ni=ke·h=meko=nehki e·h=pwa·wi-wi·seniči,
^g na·hka i·ni=meko nehki e·h=pwa·wi-nepa·či.
^h na·hka i·ni=meko nehki| pwa·wi-a·kwapiči.
ⁱ   kapo·twe e·h=pe·pye·ta·moniči ote·sepa·hemahi,
^j e·h=ma·wačipahoniči.
^k na·htaswi e·h=pwa·wi-pya·niči.
^l e·h=a·nawihto·či=meko wi·h=a·hkwe·wite·he·či.

^m   man=e·ši-keči·či,
ⁿ i·nah=či·h=wi·na wi·kiya·pi| e·h=ahte·niki.
^o [waninawe e·h=ki·wa·kwasoniči otaye·hi·=’yo·we.
^p a·kwi=’pi=meko ke·ko·hi| išite·he·čini,
^q e·h=ne·wa·či e·h=ša·ša·kwitepe·šiniči. —ne·pehe ..][*]
^r meše=na·hina·hi| e·h=ča·ki-aškwi·niči ‖ ote·sepa·hemahi.
^{4 a}   e·h=pi·tike·či=meko.
^b ke·hkya·hiničihi=či·hi,
^c nekoti metemo·he·hani, nekoti pašito·he·hani,
^d o·ni| nekoti e·škiki·he·hani.
^e e·h=ki·ša·koči·=meko -me·nawa·čike·či i·nini ihkwe·he·hani.
^f   “wahahwa·´,” e·h=išite·he·či.
^g e·h=wača·heči takwaha·ni,
^h e·h=wača·hekoči i·nini ihkwe·he·hani.
ⁱ mani e·ši-šahkamoči| takwaha·ni,
^j apina=meko e·h=saya·winawe·ška·či.
^k e·h=wi·kaniki i·ni takwaha·ni.
^l   i·nini=ke·hi·=’pi keye·hapa na·čiya·ma·čini.
^m še·kiničini=ke·hi·=’pi keye·hapa apina=meko e·h=ma·čikanwe·či.
ⁿ   ki·ši-wi·seniči, e·h=nowi·či,
^o e·h=mawa·pama·či| ote·sepa·hemahi.
^p ke·waki=či·hi e·h=apwi·hekoči.
^q (mehto·či| e·h=mama·kanahkahki mehtekwi| e·h=ina·pata·niki.)[†]
^r waninawe e·h=nepa·niči ahpemeki,[‡]
^s i·ya·h=e·h=apihapiniči.^{§/¶}
^t wi·na=ke·hi aya·pami ‖ wi·kiya·peki e·h=a·či.
^{5 a}   wa·natohka=meko e·h=taši-ašihto·niči maškimote·hi,
^b wi·na=ke·hi e·h=me·nawa·čike·či.

---

[*]In 3*o*-3*q* the writer wrongly skips to 16*j* before catching himself and then continuing with 3r.
[†]The explanatory aside is set off by the use of proximate inanimate intransitive verbs.
[‡]/waninawe/: following divider added later.
[§]/i·ya·h=/: following divider added later.
[¶]/e·h=apihapiniči/: AK ⟨niči⟩ changed from ⟨či⟩.

d   He pressed on, he and his pet raccoons.
e   He walked for about ten days.
f   And for that same length of time he didn't eat.
g   And also for that same length of time he didn't sleep.
h   And that same length of time was how long he didn't rest.
i   Suddenly his raccoons came fleeing back to him,
j   running all together.
k   Several didn't come back.
l   And he was quite unable to be angry.

m   As soon as he came out into the open,
n   he could see a house there.
o   [On all sides his slain pets lay scattered about.   (See note * to 3q.)
p   He thought nothing of it, they say,
q   when he saw them lying there with their heads smashed in. —Oh, I should have said ..]
r   His raccoons all stayed back a little ways off.
4 a   He walked right in.
b   And there he found two people who were up in years,
c   an older woman and an older man,
d   and one young person.
e   And he was greatly smitten by that young woman.
f   "Gee, I *like* her!" he thought.   (Translation from AW.)
g   Corn mush was cooked for him,
h   with that young woman cooking it for him.
i   As soon as he put the mush in his mouth,
j   there was even a tingling sensation that came over him.
k   The mush was delicious.
l   And they say she turned out to be the one whose scent he had gone after.
m   And they say it turned out that every time she had peed he had even gotten a hard on.
n   After eating, he went out,
o   going to see his raccoons.
p   And here, he found they were still waiting for him.
q   (Actually, there was a tree that looked like it had thick branches.)
r   They were sleeping all over up there.
s   And they *stayed* up there,
t   while *he* went back to the house.
5 a   She was making a bag, showing no concern,
b   but he was smitten with her.

^c e·h=še·škesi·hiniči=ʼyo=ke·hi i·nini.

^d aškači e·h=pemi_nowi·niči.

^e aškači meki·h=wi·na e·h=pemi|-nowi·či,*

^f e·h=ki·ma·ha·či e·h=taši-šekiniči.

^g ki·ši|-nehki·niči, e·h=mawi-na·piša·ma·či i·nini ihkwe·wani.

^h i·ni=ke·hi=ʼpi=meko·=ʼna| ihkwe·wa e·h=ačihkwiči,

ⁱ e·h=na·piša·meči.

^j kenwe·ši=meko e·h=taši-wa·wi·čihiwe·či i·nahi.

^k ote·sepa·hemahi=ke·hi| ke·keya·hi e·h=ke·hte·ke·škaminiči i·ni mehtekwi e·h=kahkisoniči.

^l e·h=pwa·wi- owiye·hani -ne·wokoniči,|

^m wi·na=meko mehteno·hi.

ⁿ ke·keya·h=meko e·h=kehke·nemeči.

^o e·h=kehke·nemekoči| i·nihi_we·ta·nesiničihi| e·h=mi·hkemehkwe·we·či,

^p e·h=tašite·he·či i·nini ‖ še·škesi·he·hani.

^{6 a} e·h=neškina·koči=ke·hi.

^b kwe·či_kakano·neti·ha·čini=ke·hi_atehči·me·h=taši,

^c e·h=pwa·wi-kano·nekoči.

^d ke·keya·h=meko ote·sepanemahi e·h=ahkahahkani·hiniči, e·h=menimeniški·kwe·niči,

^e e·hpi·hči-mi·hkemehkwe·we·či.

^f o·ni meše·=ʼnah=nekotenwi atehči·me·hi e·h=ne·wa·či,

^g e·h=mešena·či=meko.

^h "mahkwa·či," e·h=ikoči.

ⁱ "pe·hki=ma·h=ni·na keki·ša·koči-neškino·ne," e·h=ikoči.

^j "o·ho·´, neškinawino=ni·hka," e·h=ina·či.†

^k "keki·ši-=koh=mo·hči -ačihkwihene," e·h=ina·či.

^l e·h=pwa·wi-kehke·netaki ihkwe·wa ke·ko·h=wi·h=to·ta·koči.

^m "ke·nema·pi=ʼh=we·na e·h=nepa·ya·ni ke·ko·hi_to·tawite," e·h=išite·he·či,

ⁿ e·h=ki·menetisoči.

^o ke·waki=či·hi_e·h=še·škesi·hiči.

^p "a·kwi=ča·h=ye·hapa ke·ko·hi_to·tawičini," e·h=išite·he·či.

^q i·na=ke·h=neniwa, ‖

^{7 a} apina=meko ote·sepa·hemahi e·h=po·ni-nenehke·nema·či,

^b e·h=maki-wani·hke·či.

^c e·sepa·haki=ʼpi,

^d kapo·twe=meko ne·nekoti e·h=iši-pema·ška·wa·či.

^e e·sepa·haki e·h=pahkipahkihte·pene·wa·či.

^f i·na·ka=wi·na neniwa,‡

^g wa·natohka=meko e·h=taši|-mi·hkemehkwe·we·wite·he·či.

---

*/=wi·na/: AK ⟨.wina.⟩.

†/ški/: the ⟨s⟩ was added later.

‡The divider before /neniwa/ was added later.

^c   Now, she was a teenager.
^d   After a while she got up and went out.
^e A short time later he got up and went out himself,
^f and he spied on her while she peed.
^g After she was out of sight, he went and peed on the same spot where she had.
^h   In that very instant, the story goes, the younger woman became pregnant,
ⁱ when her urine was urinated on.

^j   For a long time he stayed there, living with the other people.
^k And the tree where his raccoons were hiding eventually came to look old and withered
     from their being there.
^l No one saw them,
^m except for him.
ⁿ   And eventually he was found out.
^o The girl's parents came to know that what he was doing was courting,
^p that his heart was set on that young girl.
^{6 a}   What's more, she disliked him.
^b Whenever he tried to talk with her away someplace,
^c she wouldn't speak to him.
^d And eventually his raccoons became skinny and bleary-eyed,
^e so long did his courting go on.

^f   And then one time he saw her a little way from the house,
^g and he grabbed ahold of her.
^h   "Calm down!" she said to him.
ⁱ "You know I really hate you a lot," she told him.
^j   "Oh, really, so hate me," he said to her.
^k "I've actually even already made you pregnant," he told her.
^l   She didn't know how he would have had sex with her.
^m "I wonder if maybe he had sex with me while I slept," she thought,
ⁿ and she felt herself.
^o And she discovered she was still a virgin.
^p "So, it turns out he didn't have sex with me," she thought.
^q   And as for that man,
^{7 a} he didn't even think about his raccoons anymore.
^b He forgot all about them.
^c   And as for the raccoons,
^d they say at some point they began tumbling down, one by one.
^e The raccoons were starving to death.
^f   Meanwhile, as for the man,
^g his mind was on courtship, as if nothing else mattered.

h   aškači šeˑškesiˑheˑha eˑh=kehkeˑnetaki eˑh=ačihkwiči.
i   "wihihwiˑ´, keˑhtena=weˑ=meko ačihkwihikweˑni," eˑh=išiteˑheˑči.
j   meše=nekotenwi| peˑhkoteˑniki naˑhka eˑh=kiˑmenetisoči.
k   meˑmeˑčiki=meko eˑh=šeˑškesiˑhiči.
l   eˑh=taši|-mamiˑnaˑwihetisoči.
m   meˑmeˑčiki=meko eˑh=šeˑškesiˑhiči.
n   eˑyeˑši-=meko -taši|-mamimamiˑnaˑwihetisoči,|
o   kapoˑtwe eˑh=memeˑsačiteˑheˑči.*
p   "oˑhwaˑ´," eˑh=išiteˑheˑči.
q   eˑh=weˑpiˑhkawaˑči iˑnini neniwani.
r   ahpeneˑči=meko| eˑh=memeˑsačiteˑheˑči.
s   eˑh=poˑni-=meko ‖ -wiˑkwaˑnekoči.
8 a   eˑškami=meko eˑh=ahpiˑhčiteˑheˑči,
b   eˑh=kaˑhkaˑhki-akaˑwaˑnaˑči| iˑnini neniwani.†
c   iˑna=keˑh=neniwa,
d   eˑh=kwayaˑši-=meko -aˑhkweˑhtawaˑči.
e   keˑkeyaˑh=meko ihkweˑwa eˑh=meškwiˑkiteˑči,
f   eˑh=kaˑhkaˑhki-akaˑwaˑnaˑči iˑnini.
g   mešeˑ-='nah=nekotenwi eˑh=mawi-saˑkičiˑči| neniwa.
h   iˑyaˑh=eˑh=pyeˑnotaˑkoči iˑnini ihkweˑheˑhani.
i   eˑh=kiˑši-=keˑh=meko -paˑsaˑhkočeˑhiniči.
j   eˑh=aˑhtawaˑsaheči| neniwa.
k   eˑh=šekinekoči ohkiwaneki iˑnini ihkweˑwani,
l   eˑh=apahapaneˑnemekoči waˑnatohka.

m   kapoˑtwe_okyeˑni eˑh=kehči-neškimekoči.
n   "kaši=weˑ=ketešawi eˑh=pwaˑwi-kwayahkwi-onaˑpeˑmiyani," eˑh=ineči_iˑna ihkweˑwa.|
o   "šeˑški=mani eˑh=ačihkwiheneki.
p   keˑkisaki=čaˑh=meko onaˑpeˑmeˑhiyane kiˑh=menwawi,"_eˑh=ineči. ‖
9 a   "aˑkwi=maˑhi keˑkoˑhi niˑnaˑ='na| toˑtawičini," eˑh=inaˑči okyeˑni.
b   iˑnini=ʼyo=keˑhi=ʼpi nehpenekwa pašitoˑhani.
c   aˑkwi=ʼpi| oˑsičini.
d   "kaši=weˑ=čaˑhi| eˑh=teki mani eˑh=ačihkwiyani," eˑh=ineči.
e   "šeˑna.
f   keˑwaki_nešeˑškesiˑhi," eˑh=iči,
g   eˑh=iči=meko.
h   keˑkeyaˑh=meko okyeˑni eˑh=aˑhkweˑniči,
i   wiˑna| naˑhka.
j   eˑyeˑnweˑweˑtiˑwaˑči,|
k   iˑniyeˑne eˑh=pyaˑniči_wiˑčihaˑwaˑčini,
l   miˑhkemehkweˑwaˑničini.

---

*/kapoˑtwe/: the following divider was added later.
†/kaˑhkaˑhki/ (AW); also heard as /kaˑkaˑhki/ (AW).

^h After a while the girl knew that she was pregnant.
ⁱ "Oh my! He really did get me pregnant after all," she thought.
^j Sometime that night she again felt herself.
^k And she was certain she was a virgin.
^l She was examining herself very thoroughly.
^m And she was certain she was a virgin.
ⁿ While she was examining herself repeatedly and thoroughly,
^o she suddenly had lascivious thoughts.
^p "Oh! Oh!" she thought.
^q And she began to concern herself with that man.
^r She had lascivious thoughts all the time.
^s And he completely stopped paying attention to her.
8a She felt it more and more
^b and had an intense longing for the man.
^c But as for the man,
^d his anger against her was already set.
^e Eventually the girl became frustrated
^f as she longed for him intensely.
^g One time the man went out to take a leak.
^h And the girl came to where he was.
ⁱ (Her belly was already swelling out a little.)
^j The man was thrown on his back.
^k And the girl peed on his nose
^l and nonchalantly laughed at him.

^m The time came when her mother got after her.
ⁿ "What's the matter with you that you don't marry him and be done with it?" the younger
woman was told.
^o "As it is, all you've done is to be made pregnant.
^p So, you'll do well to waste no time to marry him," she was told.
9a "But you see, he didn't have sex with me," she told her mother.
^b (Now, the older man is said to have been her step-father.
^c He was not her father.)
^d "Well, how come you're pregnant now?" she was asked.
^e "Whatever.
^f I'm still a virgin." she said,
^g and she insisted.
^h Eventually her mother got angry,
ⁱ and she as well.
^j While they were arguing,
^k that one they were living with came back,
^l the suitor.

^m   ahpene·či·=ʼnahi!
ⁿ   aškači·meki·h=mečemo·ka e·h=wi·ša·ška·či,
^o   e·h=pemi-we·petone·moči.
^p   "e·šiwe·pesiwe·kwe·ni=mani
^q   e·h=taši|-pwa·wi-mehč̲owi·weti·ye·kwe," e·h=išiwe·či mečemo·ka,_
^r   e·h=ina·či.
^s   če·wi·šwi=meko e·h=neškima·či.
^t   e·h=nakapehkwe·sa·či i·na neniwa.
^u   "a·kwi menwikekini mana neta·nese·ha še·ški e·h=ačihkwihači.*
^v   mya·netwi i·ni| e·h=išawiyani," ‖ e·h=ineči neniwa.†
10 a   "nahí, ke·htena| kete·pwe e·na·čimoyani," e·h=ina·či i·nini metemo·he·hani.
^b   "a·kwi=koči mana keta·neswa·wa ke·ko·hi me·h̲to·tawakini,
^c   i·noki=ke·h=mani e·h=ačihkwiči.
^d   mani=we·či-ačihkwiči:
^e   e·h=meškwi·kite·ya·ni,
^f   wi·h=owi·wiya·nehe=mekoho, e·h=išite·he·ya·ni.
^g   i·ni=ča·h=we·či-ačihkwiči," e·h=ineči mečemo·ka.‡
^h   "mani=ke·h=e·šawiya·ke:
ⁱ   še·ški nena·piša·ma·wa.
^j   i·ni=ča·h we·či-ačihkwiči," e·h=ineči.
^k   "a·kwi=ke·h=ke·ko·hi to·tawakini," e·h=ineči.§
^l   "aše=ma·hi mani e·h=išiči:
^m   ʻpe·hki=ma·h=ni·na keki·ša·koči-neškino·ne,' e·h=išiči,
ⁿ   i·ni=ča·hi·=ʼni we·či-to·tawaki," e·h=ineči metemo·ka.
^o   "a·kwi=kohi ke·ko·hi to·tawakini mana keta·nese·ha," e·h=ineči.
^p   "i·ni=ča·hi e·h=ki·ši-mehta·čimohena·ni," e·h=ineči.
^q   e·h=po·nite·he·či mečemo·ka,
^r   e·h=ki·ši-mehta·čimoheči ‖ e·šawiniči mi·hkemehkwe·wa·ničini,
11 a   ota·nesani mi·hkema·ničini.
^b   wi·na=ke·hi metemo·ka kete·=ʼnahi e·h=me·nešite·he·či.
^c   kapo·twe ota·nesani, "neta·ha, wi·kopihke·yakwe=wi·na," e·h=ina·či.
^d   e·h=anwa·či·či še·škesi·ha.
^e   e·h=opiškwe·če·wa·tesiči=meko po·si.
^f   i·ya·h=nekotahi ahkwič̲asenye| e·h=apihapiwa·či ota·nesani.
^g   aškači=meko, "nahí, neta·ha," e·h=ina·či,
^h   "ona·pe·mino| i·niya wi·čihenakwa neniwa," e·h=ina·či.
ⁱ   "nepo·ni·hka·kwa=ma·hi," e·h=iniči.
^j   "neta·nawiha·wa=meko wi·h=kakano·neti·hiči," e·h=iči i·na| ihkwe·wa.
^k   "a·kwi, we·činowesiwaki=kohi neniwaki," e·h=iči ihkwe·wa,

---

*/mana/: the preceding divider was added later.
†Starting on page 10 the word dividers are doubled.
‡/i·ni=ča·h=we·či-/: AK ⟨.iniča.|weči.⟩; /mečemo·ka/: AK ⟨.|meče.moka.⟩.
§/a·kwi=ke·h=ke·ko·hi/: AK ⟨.akwi.kekeko|i.⟩.

^m No one knew what to say.

ⁿ After a little while the older woman got agitated

^o and started holding forth.

^p "I wonder what's the matter with the two of you now,

^q that you're not openly married," the older woman declared,

^r speaking to them.

^s She scolded them both together.

^t The man hung his head.

^u "It's not a good thing that all you did was make my daughter here pregnant.

^v It was bad for you to do that," the man was told.

10 a "Alright, it's true, you're correct in what you say," he said to the older woman.

^b "Understand that I did not have sex with your daughter,

^c even though she is pregnant now.

^d This is the reason why she became pregnant:

^e Because I was frustrated,

^f having in mind that I was going to marry her.

^g So, that's why she became pregnant," the older woman was told.

^h "And here's how it happened with us:

ⁱ All I did was urinate on the same spot where she had.

^j So that's why she became pregnant," she was told.

^k "But I didn't have sex with her," she was told.

^l "Mind you, she just said *this* to me:

^m She told me, 'You know I really hate you a lot.'

ⁿ So, that's the reason why I did that to her," the older woman was told.

^o "I assure you that I did not have sex with your daughter here," she was told.

^p "So, now I've explained to you everything that happened," she was told.

^q The older woman ceased her concern,

^r now that everything had been explained to her that the suitor had done,

11 a the one courting her daughter.

^b The older woman was now embarrassed instead.

^c At some point she said to her daughter, "Daughter, why don't we go gather basswood bark?"

^d The girl agreed.

^e She had the swollen belly of someone in an advanced condition.

^f Over someplace she and her daughter sat on top of a stone.

^g After some time she said to her, "Alright, daughter.

^h Marry that man that lives with us."

ⁱ "He doesn't bother with me anymore, you know," she said.

^j "I can't get him to talk with me," the younger woman said.

^k "No, I assure you that men are easy to get," the woman said,

l   eˑh=inaˑči otaˑnesani.

m   "peˑhki=čaˑh=meko netaˑnawihaˑwa.

n   aˑkwi=meko kanaˑkwa," eˑh=iniči.

o   "'šinaˑkwa, mani=čaˑh wiˑh=toˑtawači: ‖ *

12 a   kiˑh=naˑkatawexnemaˑwa eˑšihiši-saˑkičiˑkweˑni maˑmaya," eˑh=inaˑči otaˑnesani.†

b   eˑh=wiˑkeˑčiˑpeseˑčiˑ=meko ihkweˑwa.

c   "oˑni maˑmaya=meko kaškiški_wiˑh=aˑyani wiˑh=anemihaˑči.

d   mani=meko iši-kaškaˑpamate, iˑtepi wiˑh=inaˑsamapiyani wiˑh=pyeˑčihaˑči,

e   wiˑh=saˑkičiˑhkaˑnoyani.

f   mešeˑ='nah=meko kiˑh=meškapi,

g   kiˑh=maˑtakoˑhkweˑpi=keˑhi.

h   taˑni=čaˑhiˑ='nahi wiˑh=išawiči.

i   mešeˑ='nah=meko iˑnahi kiˑh=taši- keˑkoˑhi_-toˑtaˑkwa," eˑh=ineči ihkweˑwa.

j   "kiˑšiˑ-='ni_-toˑtoˑhke,

k   iˑni wiˑh=onaˑpeˑmiyani," eˑh=inaˑči otaˑnesani.

l   eˑh=anwaˑčiˑči ihkweˑwa.

m   "naˑpi=weˑna, iˑni niˑh=išawi," eˑh=inaˑči okyeˑni.

n   eˑh=naˑkwaˑwaˑči.

o   eˑnaˑkwiniki iˑyaˑh=eˑh=pyaˑwaˑči.

p   oˑni| mečemoˑka, "pašito, anwaˑčiˑyane=wiˑna,

q   netaˑnesa keˑkoˑh=toˑtawiyeˑkapa," eˑh=inaˑči.

r   pašitoˑha eˑh=niˑmeˑškaˑči.

s   "mani=keˑhi wiˑh=išawiči:

t   wiˑh=pyeˑtaˑsamapiwa ‖ wiˑh=pyeˑčihaˑyani.

13 a   wiˑh=čiˑkakonamwa okoˑteˑhani.

b   kiˑh=naˑsehkawaˑwa=čaˑh=meko.

c   kiˑh=maˑtakoˑhkweˑho," eˑh=inaˑči onaˑpeˑmani.

d   "oˑ´, iˑni ni_-h=išawi," eˑh=iči pašitoˑha.

e   oˑni=na waˑpaniki, "niˑh=šiˑša=čaˑhi," eˑh=iči.‡

f   paˑpekwa=='nah=metemoˑheˑha, "taˑtepi=čaˑhi| otaˑhkwe," eˑh=inaˑči iˑnini neniwani.

g   "weˑči_-kesiˑyaˑki," eˑh=iniči.

h   "taˑni=čaˑh=kwiˑyena wiˑh=anemihaˑyani," eˑh=inaˑči.

i   "ayoˑh=meko oči_-nowiˑyaˑne, tepinaˑh=meko weˑči_-kesiˑyaˑki wiˑh=aˑyaˑni," eˑh=iniči.

j   "nahi´," eˑh=išiˑkweˑhtawaˑči otaˑnesani.

k   oˑni ihkweˑwa eˑh=naˑkwaˑči.

l   eˑh=anemi-=meko -memeˑsačiteˑheˑči.§

m   iˑyaˑh=meše=naˑhinaˑhi, penoˑčiˑmeˑh=meko, eˑh=mawi-apihapiči.

n   "naˑpi=wiˑna manahka mawi-nesate peneˑwaki weˑči_-naˑwahkweˑhiki.

o   ayoˑh=meše=naˑhinaˑhi pehkwaˑhkwaˑwiwi.

---

*The ⟨ta⟩ is uncrossed.

†AK ⟨.ma[[ma]]|maya.⟩.

‡/iˑna/ 'that one' (with a proximate shift) is translated as 'the other man'.

§/-memeˑsačiteˑheˑči/: AK ⟨.memesači.te|eči⟩.

l she said to her daughter.

m "Nevertheless, I really couldn't succeed with him.

n It was impossible," she said.

o "Well, here is what you must do to him:

12 a You must pay attention to where he goes when he goes out first thing in the morning," she said to her daughter.

b The younger woman listened intently.

c "Then very early you must go to a place on the path that he's going to take.

d Just as soon as you can see him, sit facing the way he will come

e and pretend to be urinating.

f You can spread you legs apart as you squat.

g And you must have your head covered.

h So, with all that, what's he going to do?

i Just let him have sex with you there," the younger woman was told.

j "After he does that to you,

k then you'll be married to him," she told her daughter.

l The younger woman agreed to it.

m "Alright, I'll do that," she told her mother.

n And they went back.

o They got home in the evening.

p And then the older woman said, "Husband, if you are agreeable,

q you could have sex with my daughter," she said to him.

r The older man raised up.

s "This is what she will do:

t She'll sit facing the way you'll be coming.

13 a She'll raise up her skirts.

b So you must go straight to her.

c You must cover your head," she told her husband.

d "Oh, I'll do that," said the older man.

e And the next morning the other man said, "I guess I'll go hunting."

f Right away the older woman asked the man, "In what direction?"

g "North," he replied.

h "So, what way will you go, exactly?" she asked him.

i "When I go out the door here, I'll go straight north," he replied.

j With her expression she signaled to her daughter to go.

k Then the younger woman left.

l On the way she thought lascivious thoughts.

m She went to someplace nearby, but at a good distance, and was sitting there.

n "Maybe it would be better if you went off to the south to kill turkeys.

o There's a grove of trees near here.

p i·ni=ča·h=a·pehe mana_pašito·ha wa·woto·ma·či=’yo·we anašawaye,” e·h=iči ‖ metemo·ka.

14 a “o·´,_ni·h=kočawi,”| e·h=ina·či.*

b “i·tepi_ni·h=a ota·hkwe,” e·h=iniči,

c e·h=na·kwa·niči.

d i·na·ka=ke·hi=’hkwe·wa e·h=mehči-pehkwapiči.

e “nahi´,_pašito, kekeni=na·kwa·no·=’nahi.

f na·hka=we·na e·škiki·heki i·ni ki·h=to·tawe·hi,” e·h=ina·či.†

g “ki·h=anemi-=meko -ma·tako·hkwe·wose,” e·h=ina·či.‡

h e·kwihakwiniči e·h=anemi-akwiči.

i kapo·twe=wi·na ihkwe·wa:§

j e·h=pye·či-sa·sa·kitepe·wose·niči,¶

k e·h=nana·hapiči,

l e·h=meškapiči, e·h=ma·tako·hkwe·piči.*

m metemo·ka=ke·hi ahkowi·me·hi e·h=anem_osa·pama·či ona·pe·mani.

n e·h=te·pahkwa·pama·či=meko ota·nesani.

o pašito·he·ha e·h=šo·ški·=meko -a·htawa·nike·či.

p metemo·ka e·h=wa·wana·tesiči,

q na·hka=ke·hi=’pi nekotahi e·h=ihpahoči.

r ke·keya·h=meko mehtekwi e·h=mawinataki,

s e·h=taši-ma·ma·hkwitiya·taki metemo·he·ha.

t i·na·ka=ke·hi še·škesi·ha i·niye·ne=meko e·h=a·we·nema·či.

u aškači=meko e·h=kehke·nema·či, ‖

15 a ki·ši-=meko -kehči-to·ta·koči.

b e·h=me·nešite·he·či ihkwe·wa.

c e·h=pwa·wi-=ke·h=meko ke·ko·hi -ina·či.

d wa·natohka pašito·he·ha, “wi·h=na·kwa·ya·ni,” e·h=iči,

e e·h=na·kwa·či.

f i·ya·h=pye·ya·či i·na_pašito·ha,

g “e·h=a·pi_a·maha·mano·hiya·ni,” e·h=ina·či metemo·he·hani.†

h pe·hkote·niki metemo·ha e·h=nana·toše·či,

i “še·škesi·hikwe·ni?” e·h=išiwe·či.

j “meše=we·na e·h=še·škesi·hiči,” e·h=iči| pašito·ha.

k i·na=ke·hi=’pi ihkwe·wa atehči=meko nepe·wa,

l e·h=me·nešite·he·či.

m e·h=me·nešihekoči ne·hpenekočini e·to·ta·koči.

n e·h=ačihkwitehe=ke·hi=’pi·=’niye e·h=akeniki,

---

*/e·h=ina·či/: a one-line proximate shift; perhaps emend to /e·h=iniči/.

†/e·škiki·heki/: AK ⟨.eški|kiaki.⟩.

‡/wo/: AK ⟨o⟩.

§The extra-syntactic noun is a point-of-view adjunct.

¶/wo/: AK ⟨o⟩.

*/ta/: AK ⟨te⟩.

†/metemo·he·hani/: emending AK ⟨.metemoeA.⟩.

^p This old man used to come back from that place loaded down with them in times past,"
the older woman said.

14 a   "Oh, I'll try that," he said to her.

b   "I'll go in that direction," he said,

c   and he left.

d   Meanwhile the younger woman sat out in the open, exposed.

e   "Alright, husband, now go quickly.   (*Lit.*, 'old man'.)

f   Like a lad again, after all, are you to do that to the young thing," she told him.

g   "Make sure you walk with your head covered on the way," she told him.

h   He left wearing the other one's clothing.

i   All of a sudden the younger woman [could see]:

j   there was someone's head bobbing in and out if view as he walked toward her,

k   and she sat in position,

l   with her legs spread apart and her head covered.

m   Now, the older woman went along watching her husband from a little behind.

n   And she could just see her daughter in the distance.

o   The older man moved swiftly to place his quarry on her back.

p   The older woman was beside herself.

q   She's said to have run from one place to another.

r   Eventually she made straight for a tree

s   and stayed there thrusting her pelvis against it, did the older woman.

t   Meanwhile, that girl thought it was the one who was elsewhere.

u   It was some time before she knew who it was,

15 a   after he had already had great copulation with her.

b   The younger woman was ashamed.

c   And she didn't even say anything to him.

d   Nonchalantly the older man said, "I'll be going,"

e   and he left.

f   When the older man got home,

g   he said to the older woman, "I've been having a nice bit of nooky."

h   That night the older woman inquired,

i   asking, "I take it she was a virgin?"

j   "It was basically *because* she was a virgin, after all," said the older man.

k   The younger woman, meanwhile, is said to have been sleeping somewhere else,

l   being ashamed.

m   Her step-father made her ashamed by what he did to her.

n   And what's more, her erstwhile pregnancy is said to have disappeared.

o eʹh=poʹni-opiškweʹčeʹči.

p eʹh=kehkeʹnemekoči=meko miʹhkemekočini.[*]

q aše=keʹh=meko=ʼyoʹwe eʹh=toʹtaʹkoči.

r eʹh=nawači-kekyeʹškačihekoči mehtoʹči, eʹh=aʹšitawaʹhekoči,

s weʹči-=ʼpi=ʼyoʹwe_-toʹtaʹkotehe.

t wiʹna=keʹhiʹ=ʼniya ihkweʹwa,

16 a meše=mekoʹ=ʼnahi_nekotahi taʹtwaʹhkiʹki eʹh=nepaʹči ‖ peʹhkoteʹniki.[†]

b mešeʹ=ʼnah=meko_nyeʹwokoni iʹnahi_eʹh=awihawiči.

c nyeʹwokonakateniki eʹnaʹkwiʹhiniki eʹh=naʹkwaʹči neʹyaʹpi.

d iʹniya=keʹhi eʹh=naʹkwaʹči| neniwa.

e iʹyaʹh=pyeʹyaʹči eʹh=owiʹkiči, eʹh=mehkweʹnemaʹči oteʹsepaʹhemahi.

f "ehehyeʹʹ," eʹh=iči,

g eʹh=naʹkwaʹči.

h meʹh-=meko -wiʹsenikwe, ayaʹpami eʹh=ihpahoči.

i aškači iʹyaʹhi eʹh=pakamipahoči eʹh=awinitehe.

j waninawe=meko eʹh=kiʹwaʹkwasoniči otayeʹhi=ʼyoʹwe.

k našawaye=meko eʹh=išinaʹkosiniči.

l kenaʹči eʹh=pemi-kohkikaʹpaʹči,

m eʹh=pemi|-weʹposeʹči.

n meše=naʹhinaʹhi| eʹnemehkaʹči,

o eʹh=čaʹki-matanekoči,

p eʹh=miʹšaʹteʹnemoči.

q eʹh=aʹčimohekoči.

r "niʹh=nawači-kiʹyoseʹpena| nyeʹwawahiʹme," eʹh=iniči.

s "meše=mekoʹ=ʼnahi niʹh=kiʹkiʹwipahopena," eʹh=ikoči.

t eʹh=nahkomaʹči,

u eʹh=kwaʹpipahoniči. ‖

17 a oʹniʹ=ʼniya ihkweʹwa, okyeʹni, "taʹtepi=čaʹh aʹpihaʹyani," eʹh=ikoči.

b "meše=čaʹh=mekoʹ=ʼnahi taʹtwaʹhkiʹki netaʹpi-nepanepa," eʹh=inaʹči.

c "iʹni=yaʹpi=ʼyoʹwe eʹnaʹčimohenaʹni?"

d "eheʹhe," eʹh=iči._

e naʹhka okyeʹni, "šeweʹna mani_eʹšawiyaʹni:

f maʹhiya kenaʹpeʹma—iʹni_eʹtoʹtawiči wiʹna.[‡]

g nekiʹši-=keʹh=meko iʹni_-toʹtaʹkwa.

h ʼnekya aʹčimoheʹtoke,ʼ netešiteʹhe=čaʹhi,

i weʹči-pwaʹwi- keʹkoʹhi -inaki," eʹh=iči.

j " ʼmeʹmešihka=meko nekya iʹni išiteʹheʹtoke wiʹh=toʹtawiniči,ʼ netešiteʹhe=čaʹhi," eʹh=ineči metemoʹka.

____

[*]⟨.|meko.⟩.

[†]/peʹhkoteʹniki/: AK ⟨ekoteniki⟩.

[‡]⟨ta⟩ is uncrossed.

o　　Her belly was no longer swollen.

p　　　　And her suitor knew about her.

q　　He hadn't done that to her seriously.

r　　He was at first as if begrudging her by getting back at her.

s　　That was the reason, as the story has it, that he had done that to her.

t　　　　As for the younger woman,

16 a　she slept that night just anywhere out in some ravine.

b　　She even remained there for four days.

c　　In the early evening of the fourth day she left to come back.

d　　　　Meanwhile the younger man departed.

e　　When he got all the way back to his house, he remembered his raccoons.

f　　　　"Uh-oh!" he exclaimed,

g　　and he set out.

h　　Before even eating a meal he went running back again.

i　　　　After a long run, he arrived at the place where they had been.

j　　On all sides the animals that had been his pets lay dead.

k　　They looked like they had been there for some time.

l　　Slowly he turned on his heel

m　　and started walking.

n　　　　After he had gone a little ways,

o　　they all caught him up from behind,

p　　and he was delighted.

q　　They explained to him.

r　　　　"First we want to wander around for four years," they said.

s　　"We want to run around just anyplace," the said to him.

t　　He gave his consent,

u　　and they ran off in all directions.

17 a　　And meanwhile the younger woman was asked by her mother, "Where have you been?"

b　　　　"Well, I've been sleeping out in some ravine," she told her.

c　　　　"Now tell me, was it the way I told you?"

d　　　　"Yes," she said.

e　　And continued on to her mother, "But here's what happened to me:

f　　it was your husband—that's what *he* did to me.

g　　And to be clear, he *has* done that to me.

h　　Well, I thought to myself, 'My mother must have told him,'

i　　which is why I didn't say anything to him," she said.

j　　　　"So, I thought, 'My mother must certainly have wanted him to do that to me," the older
woman was told.

k “mani=kohi we·či-_i·ni -ine·nemena·ni:
l e·h=menwi-pemenakwe.
m še·škesi·hani=ča·h=a·pehe aka·wa·ne·wa_i·ni wi·h=to·tawa·či.
n i·ni=ča·h=we·či- i·ni_-inaki,
o i·ni_wi·h=to·to·hki.
p ke·htena e·h=še·škesi·hiyani,
q ‘meči=’hi=’yo anwa·či·sa, mehči i·ni_inake,’ e·h=ine·nemena·ni=ke·hi, ‖
18 a we·či- i·ni_-inena·ni e·na·čimohena·ni.”
b “wa·wosa·h=ye·toke[!?] a·mi_a·nomiyani[!?] i·ni išiyane!?” e·h=ineči mečemo·ka.
c “ya·´,_neta·ha, nye·wawahi·me a·kwi_wi·h=ona·pe·miyanini.
d nye·wawahi·makahke=ča·hi i·n=a·mihtahi i·ni_i·h=išawiyani.
e me·nwe·nema·wate·na=meko.
f ata·hpesamo·nesa neniwani ma·hiya_pašito·ha,” e·h=iči ihkwe·wa.
g “nye·wawahi·me nešihka ayo·hi ki·h=taši-ona·pe·mipena ma·hiya| pašito·ka,” e·h=ina·či ota·nesani.
h “na·piwe·na.
i awita=koči nana·ši wi·h=a·hkwe·hkapa?” e·h=ina·či okye·ni.
j “ohoho·´, wa·wosa·h=ye·toke,[!?]| neta·ha, wi·h=oč_a·hkwe·ki!?” e·h=ina·či ota·nesani.
k o·ni| metemo·ka kapo·twe_e·h=po·ni_wi·hpe·mekoči ona·pe·mani.
l e·h=anemi-=meko| -mya·ne·netaki e·škami, ‖
19 a ota·nesani e·h=mi·wihekoči| metemo·ka.[*]
b ke·keya·h=meko e·h=we·pi-ki·weki·we·kesiči.

c pašito·ka_ne·nehkaniki·šekwe=meko e·h=wi·hpe·či.
d kwi·yena=meko nye·wawahi·makateniki, e·h=nepo·hiči pašito·he·ha ni·šo·hkwe·wa·ta.
e i·ni=ča·hi=’pi pe·hki e·h=kehči-mayo·či metemo·he·ha we·na·pe·me·hita._
f pe·hki ota·nesani e·h=kehči-neškima·či.
g “e·h=pi·ke·nana·či mana wi·čawiwomečini,” e·h=ina·či ota·nesani.[†/‡]
h “’šina·kwa=’škwe, e·h=še·škesi·hiya·ni=ma·hi,|
i mehto·či ki·na nanawi=meko we·či-ina·hpenašiki,
j e·h=a·čimohatehe_i·niya kena·pe·mena·na,” e·h=ina·či okye·ni.
k o·ni_metemo·ka e·h=kehč_a·hkwe·či.
l e·škami=meko e·h=anihaniwa·naki·kwe·či,
m e·h=mečimečima·pama·či ‖ ota·nesani,
20 a e·h=kehči|-tanwe·we·ma·či.
b o·ni, “ane·he,” e·h=ina·či we·kita,|
c “keta·čimohene=koči=’yo·we,
d ‘awita_wi·h=a·hkwe·hkapa?’| ketene=koči=’yo·we,
e ‘wa·wosa·h=ye·toke,’ keteši=ča·hi=’yo·we.
f kwi·yena=ča·h=meko e·šimena·ni ketešawi.

---

[*]NB: the antecedent of the pronominal possessor follows the possessed noun.
[†]A third person insult.
[‡]AK ⟨ča⟩ changed from ⟨če⟩.

^k "Let me tell you the reason why I wanted that to be done to you.
^l It's because he takes good care of us.
^m Well, he's always wanted to do that to a virgin.
ⁿ So, that's why I told him that,
^o to do that to you.
^p Because you really were a virgin,
^q and because I thought to myself besides, 'There's no way she'd assent if I tell her to do that in plain words,'
18 a that's why I gave you the instructions I did."
^b "It hardly seems likely that I'd have refused you if you'd asked me to do that!" the older woman was told.
^c "Say listen, Daughter, you're not to marry anyone for four years.
^d So, after four years, then you could do that.
^e Whoever you want.
^f The old man could use his medicine to draw a man to you," the woman said.
^g "For four years we'll be married here to just this old man," she said to her daughter.
^h "Alright, why don't we.
ⁱ And of course, you wouldn't ever get angry?" she asked her mother.
^j "Oh, don't worry, Daughter, it hardly seems likely there'd be a reason to be angry!" she told her daughter.
^k Then at some point the older woman's husband stopped sleeping with her.
^l She became increasingly bitter as time went on,
19 a did the older woman, being cut out by her daughter.
^b In time she began going about wailing.

^c The old man spent all his days in bed with company.
^d And after exactly four years the old man with two wives died.
^e So then the older woman that had been his wife really wept bitterly, the story goes.
^f And she really scolded her daughter severely.
^g "Look at what you did! You wore my husband down till he died," she told her daughter.
^h "Well, come on, when I was a virgin, as you know,
ⁱ you were basically the cause of my ruination,
^j when you gave your plan to that late husband of ours," she told her mother.
^k And then the older woman got extremely angry.
^l Her eyes got bigger and bigger,
^m and she stared fixedly at her daughter,
20 a and railed at her.
^b And then her daughter said to her, "Mother,
^c I asked you back then, remember,
^d 'You wouldn't get angry?'
^e And you told me, 'There'd be no reason to.'
^f So, you're doing just exactly what I talked about you doing.

g a·kwi=’še·=’nahi_wi·h=nešiyani wi·h=išite·he·yanini,” e·h=ina·či okye·ni.*
h “a·kwi.
i aše=koh=meko ma·mahka·či e·h=pi·ke·nane·hiyani ma·hiya pašito·ha,” e·h=inekoči.
j “a·kwi=ke·hi| nekotahi wi·h=otenakwini ‘neniwa’ e·neta,”| e·h=ikoči okye·ni.

k o·ni we·te·sepaneme·ha kapo·twe_e·h=kwi·noma·či| otaye·hi nye·wawahi·makateniki.
l aškači=meko e·h=ma·wači·niči ote·sepa·hemahi.
m kekimesi=meko e·h=anahanakwiniči. ‖
21 a a·wasi=ke·h=meko e·h=tašiniči e·tašinitehe.
b a·wasi=meko e·h=mi·ša·te·nemoči.
c aškači nekoti ote·sepa·hemani e·h=a·čimohekoči.†
d “ni·šwi=ma·hi ihkwe·waki ki·ša·koči-aka·wa·tamo·ki wi·h=ona·pe·miwa·či,
e če·wi·šwi=ke·h=meko wi·h=ona·pe·miwa·či aka·wa·tamo·ki.‡
f nekoti| metemo·hiwa,
g nekoti aškiki·hiwa.
h šewe·na nekoti=meko wi·h=ona·pe·miwa·či išite·he·waki, me·kwe·he,”_e·h=iči e·sepana.
i “e·škikita we·wenesiwa,| menwina·kosiwa.”
j “ta·nahi=ča·hi ota·hkwe_e·h=awiwa·či,” e·h=ineči e·sepa·ha.
k “i·nah=ni·hka=’yo·we ketaši-na·piša·ma·wa še·škesi·ha.
l i·na·ča·hi·=’na·=’na.
m o·ni_metemo·he·ha, we·ta·nesita.
n i·ni=meko wi·h=iši-ni·šo·hkwe·wa·sowa·či ‖ išite·he·waki.”
22 a “ni·h=mawi-=ča·h=_ni·šo·hkwe·we,” e·h=ina·či otaye·hi e·sepanahi.
b “ka·ta,” e·h=ikoči a·neta,
c a·neta=ke·hi, “ke·htena,”_e·h=ikoči.
d ke·keya·h=meko e·h=na·kwa·či i·tepi.
e kapo·twe, “o·ho·´, meše·=’nah=ta·ni mawi-ni·šo·hkwe·we·no,” e·h=ikoči otaye·hi.
f e·h=na·kwa·či, e·h=pwa·wi-wi·te·mekoči.
g e·h=nešike·wa·či e·sepanaki.

h aškači i·ya·hi e·h=pya·či,
i e·h=šo·ški-=meko -pemi_pi·tike·či.
j “hawo·ʔ,”| e·h=iči.
k “hawo·ʔ,”_e·h=iči metemo·ka.
l o·ni_metemo·ka e·h=we·pi-ašama·či i·nini neniwani,
m ki·ši·seniniči:
n “nekotahi·=’niya iha·kwe·ni pašito·ha,” e·h=ina·či.§
o “nepo·hiwa=ča·hi·=’yo·we,” e·h=iniči.
p “o·ho·´,” e·h=ina·či,

---

*/=iše·=’nahi/ ‘it’s hard to believe; I doubt it’ (also K-W 664, K-SSP 80h).
†The ⟨te⟩ is uncrossed.
‡/če·/: AK ⟨še⟩.
§22*l-n*: punctuated to correspond to the proximate shift between 21*l-m* and 21*n*.

g   It's hard to believe you won't have it in mind to kill me," she said to her mother.
h   "No.
i   It's just that there was certainly no call to wear the poor old man down till he died," she said to her.
j   "And what's more we won't be getting what's called a man from anywhere else," she said to her daughter.

k   And as for Raccoon-Owner, the time came after four years that he missed his pets.
l   It was some time before his raccoons all came back together.
m   Every one of them was fat.
21 a   And what's more there were even more of them than there had been before.
b   He was even more delighted.
c   After a time one of his raccoons told him something.
d   "You know, there are two women who very much want to get married.
e   What's more, the two of them want to get married together.
f   One is an older woman,
g   and one is young.
h   But they have in mind to marry just one man, I believe," the raccoon said.
i   "The young one is pretty and easy to look at."
j   "So, in which direction do they live?" the raccoon was asked.
k   "Where you peed where the girl had peed some time back.
l   So, she's the one.
m   And the older woman is her mother.
n   They have in mind to be the joint wives of someone, just the two of them."
22 a   "So, I'm going off to marry two wives," he told his pet raccoons.
b   "Don't do it," some told him,
c   while at the same time some told him, "Go ahead."
d   Eventually he left to go there.
e   And with that his pets said to him, "Oh, I see. Well, go ahead. Go marry two wives."
f   When he left they didn't go with him.
g   The raccoons had the house to themselves.

h   After some time he arrived there.
i   And he walked right straight in the door.
j   "Hello," he said.
k   "Hello," said the older woman.
l   And then the older woman set to getting that man something to eat,
m   and after he had finished eating:
n   He said to her, "I guess the old man went somewhere."
o   "He died some time ago," she said.
p   "Oh, I see," he said to her.

^q "meči=keˑhi nekehkeˑnemaˑwa^{!?} eˑh=nepoˑhitehe!?" eˑh=inaˑči.

^r "eheˑhe," eˑh=iči metemoˑheˑha.

^s "iˑni=čaˑh=ninaˑna weˑči- iˑnoki -ketemaˑkesiˑhiyaˑke mana ‖ netaˑneseˑha," eˑh=iniči.

23 a "eˑh=nepoˑhiči peˑmeniyameta,"| eˑh=iniči.

^b "oˑhoˑ´, kete=ʼnah=niˑhka," eˑh=inaˑči

^c peˑhkoteˑniki neniwa metemoˑkani eˑh=waˑwaˑtehkweˑhiči.

^d metemoˑka| eˑh=taši-kosetawaˑči wiˑh=čiˑpenaˑči iˑnini neniwani.

^e keˑkeyaˑhi=ʼnahi=ʼpi eˑh=ataˑhpahoˑnaˑči.

^f eˑh=wayeˑneškaˑči neniwa, metemoˑheˑhani eˑh=ataˑhpahoˑnekoči.

^g mečemoˑka eˑh=miˑšaˑteˑnemoči eˑh=wiˑhpeˑmeči.

^h eˑh=ahpihoweˑči opwaˑmi mečemoˑka,

ⁱ eˑh=pwaˑwi-=meko -ameˑniči.

^j šeˑški=meko eˑh=taši-wiˑhpewiˑhpeˑmekoči.

^k niˑšokonakateniki čeˑwiˑšwi=meko eˑh=owiˑwiči otaˑneseˑtiˑhahi.

^l eˑh=owiˑtoˑšetiˑwaˑči otaˑneseˑtiˑhaki.

^m eˑh=miˑšaˑteˑnemoči mečemoˑka,

ⁿ eˑh=aˑhpečiˑwiˑhpeˑmeči.

^o eˑh=miˑwihaˑči=meko otaˑnesani,

^p eˑh=kehči-ʼšiteˑheˑči. ‖

24 a "eˑšiweˑpeˑnemikweˑni=ʼškwe eˑh=aˑhpečiˑwiˑhpeˑmiči," eˑh=inaˑči=ʼp=aˑpehe otaˑnesani.

^b iˑna=keˑh=wiˑna=ʼpi weˑkita aˑšotamwa iˑni wiˑh=toˑtawomeči okyeˑni.

^c "mešeˑ=ʼnah=kapoˑtwe kiˑh=kyaˑwe," eˑh=inaˑči.

^d "mešeˑ=ʼnah=meko wiˑh=iši-nesači kiˑh=toˑtawaˑwa," eˑh=išiweˑči weˑkita.

^e oˑni=ʼna neniwa| kapoˑtwe eˑh=kyaˑweˑči,

^f eˑh=neˑnesaˑči iˑnini metemoˑheˑhani.

^g mešihkeˑhani=ʼpi| kyaˑwamaˑčini.

^h eˑh=neˑnesaˑči=meko iˑnini metemoˑheˑhani.

ⁱ eˑh=miˑšaˑteˑnemoči metemoˑheˑha waˑnatohka eˑh=neˑneseči.

^j kapoˑtwe atehči eˑh=išiwenaˑči,

^k iˑyaˑhi eˑh=taši-kehči-nesaˑči.

^l aˑyaškači=meko eˑh=neˑmoči metemoˑheˑha.

^m eˑh=poˑniˑhkawaˑči neniwa,

ⁿ eˑh=naˑkwaˑči.

^o "kašinaˑkwa, kenesaˑwa?" eˑh=inaˑči onaˑpeˑmani ‖ [weˑkita].

25 a "saˑsakaˑki=koh=meko=ʼyoˑwe| neˑmowa," eˑh=inaˑči weˑkiničini.[*]

^b "oˑhoˑ´," eˑh=iči ihkweˑwa.

^c "iˑyaˑhi apihapino," eˑh=ikoči owiˑwani.

^d iˑyaˑhi eˑh=apihapiči,

^e eˑh=šekišekišiki=ʼh=weˑna.

^f aškači keˑhtena eˑh=pyeˑči-piˑtikeˑniči.

^g wiˑnа=keˑhi eˑh=maˑtamaˑtakwišiki.

---

[*]/neˑmowa/: AK ⟨|nemowa.nemowa.⟩.

q   "I obviously had no idea that he had died!" he said to her.

r   "Yes," said the older woman.

s   "So, that's why my poor daughter here and I are now in such bad straits," she said.

23 a   "Because the one who took care of us died," she said.

b   "Oh, I see. Bad luck," he said to her.

c   That night the man lay head-to-head with the older woman.

d   The older woman was holding back from giving the man a poke.

e   Finally, the story goes, she went ahead and dragged him over.

f   The man seemed ready to be moved when the woman dragged him over.

g   The older woman was delighted to have a man in her bed.

h   The older woman put her weight on his thigh,

i   and he didn't react.

j   All he did was to keep sleeping with her.

k   After two days he was married to both the mother and the daughter.

l   The mother and daughter were co-wives.

m   The older woman was delighted,

n   as she always had a man in her bed.

o   She cut out her daughter,

p   and she felt great.

24 a   "I wonder what he thinks of me that he always sleeps with me," she would say to her daughter.

b   But the daughter herself, to hear the tale, was urging that that be done to her mother.

c   "Maybe the time will come when you get jealous," she said to him.

d   "Maybe you'll do things to her like you're going to kill her," said the daughter.

e   And then the time came when that man did get jealous.

f   And he would give the older woman beatings.

g   The story goes that Turtle was the one he was jealous of.

h   He would give the older woman serious beatings.

i   And the older woman was glad to get beatings, as if they were nothing.

j   At some point he took her away someplace

k   and gave her a great beating there.

l   The older woman was breathing at long intervals.

m   The man left off dealing with her,

n   and went back.

o   "Well, did you kill her?" [the daughter] asked her husband.

25 a   "Actually, she was just barely breathing," he said to the daughter.

b   "Oh, I see," said the woman.

c   "Sit over in the other place," his wife told him.

d   He sat over there,

e   or rather lay there.

f   After a while she came back in, sure enough.

g   And he was lying there covered up.

^h mahkwa·či=meko e·h=we·pi-kakano·neti·ha·či ota·nesani.

ⁱ e·h=mi·ša·te·nemoči=meko i·nahi e·h=šekišekišiniči ona·pe·mani we·tapiči.

^j aškači e·h=natota·sa·či ota·nesani.

^k "a·kwi=ye·toke=meko aškwisenye·hiyanehe," e·h=ina·či.

^l "netaškwisenye=ča·hi," e·h=ina·či.

^m "mana=ča·h=ki·ši·seniwa?" e·h=iči.

ⁿ "a·kwi,"| e·neči metemo·ka,

^o e·h=menwite·he·či.

^p "i·ni=ča·h=meko e·h=nana·hisahoči pye·ya·či," e·h=iniči ota·nesani.

^q "o·ho·´," e·h=ina·či.

^r mahkwa·či=meko, ‖ "wi·senino=wi·na," e·h=ina·či ona·pe·mani.

26 ^a e·h=wana·ki·či neniwa.

^b e·h=wa·pama·či wa·wotatahwa·tehe,

^c e·h=pwa·wi·=meko ke·ko·hi -išikiniči.

^d wa·natohka=meko e·h=ki·wi-'šawiniči.

^e e·h=keša·čihkwe·wiči metene·ka.*

^f aškači=na·hka, "nahi´, koči-=meko -neši," e·h=ikoči [we·kiničini].†

^g o·ni=meše=nekotenwi e·h=pye·nota·koči nekoti ote·sepa·hemani,

^h i·niye·ne ne·škimekočini e·sepa·hani.

ⁱ "nahi´, a·kwi=kohi| wi·h=kaško·hpenanačini," e·h=ikoči.

^j "mo·hči=ke·hi nesate, wi·h=we·wi·še·hiwa.

^k e·hkwi-nesa·wate·ni i·ni=meko i·h=išawiči.

^l i·ni=ke·hi='yo·we we·či-neškimena·ni wi·h=owi·wiyani.

^m maneto·wi-metemo·hiwa.

ⁿ i·na=ke·hi we·kita·kwi kehke·nema·čini i·nini okye·ni e·h=maneto·winiči," ‖ e·h=ineči.

27 ^a "mehteno·h=mani| išawiyane: ketiwiyane.

^b i·ni=me·kwe·h=mehteno·hi," e·h=inekoči ote·sepa·hemani.

^c "o·n=a·mihtahi·-'na ahpemeki išiwenači ihkwe·wa,

^d 'ni·h=owi·wi,' išite·he·yane.

^e i·ni| a·mi-'ši-konakwiwenači,

^f a·mi-'ši-konakwi·ye·kwe.

^g ayo·h=wi·na, a·kwikana·kwa=meko wi·h=konakwi·ye·kwe, ayo·h=mehči·ki," e·h=ineči.

^h "i·ni wi·h=iši-konakwiweneti·ye·kwe išawiye·kwe," e·h=ikoči e·sepa·hani,

ⁱ e·h=na·kwa·či.

^j wa·natohka=meko e·h=ki·wi-'šawiči, e·h=pya·či.

^k e·h=keša·či·neniwiči.

^l e·h=nawači-ša·ši·ša·či.

^m e·h=anakwiči metemo·he·ha,

ⁿ e·h=makihkwe·wiči.

---

*/metene·ka/ (phonetics conjectured): also C-WH 25*q*; cf. /mečene·ka/ (EK 2003).
†/we·kiničini/: as in 24*o*; compare 25*a*.

h   She began conversing quietly with her daughter.
i   She was so glad that her husband was lying there in her spot.
j   After a while she made a request of her daughter.
k   "You wouldn't by chance have had any leftovers," she said to her.
l   "I do have leftovers," she replied to her.
m   "And has he eaten?" she said.
n   When the older woman was told, "No,"
o   she was glad.
p   "He flopped down right away when he came back," her daughter said.
q   "Oh, I see," she said to her.
r   Softly she said to her husband, "Have something to eat."
26 a   The man sat up.
b   He looked at the places where he had beaten her,
c   and she had no marks on her at all.
d   He saw that she was acting as if nothing had happened.
e   The old girl was a nice lady.
f   And then at a later time [the daughter] said to him, "Alright, try to kill her."

g   And one time one of his raccoons came to where he was,
h   the raccoon that had warned him before.
i   "Listen, you must know that you won't be able to succeed with her," it told him.
j   "What's more, even if you kill her, she'll become a rolling-skull.
k   If you should end up killing her, that's just what will happen to her.
l   Frankly, that's why I warned you against marrying her before.
m   She's a serpent lady.   (/maneto·wi-/ 'serpent': not 'god, spirit, monster'; see 28bc.)
n   And what's more, the daughter doesn't know that her mother is a serpent," he was told.
27 a   "Only if you do this: if you become an eagle.
b   That would be the only way, I believe," his raccoon told him.
c   "Then you could take that younger woman up to the sky,
d   if your thought is to marry her.   (*Lit.*, 'if you think, "I want to marry her." ')
e   That's how you could get her through the danger,
f   how you could both get through.
g   But here, it would not be possible for the two of you to get through safely, here below," he
    was told.
h   "If you do that you will get each other through the danger," the raccoon told him,
i   and he went back.
j   He was acting as if nothing had happened when he got back.
k   He was a nice man.
l   And, before anything else, for a while he hunted.
m   The older woman got fat.
n   She became a large woman.

^o e·h=anakwiniči.[*]

^p "nemi·wihto=meko," e·h=išite·he·či metemo·he·ha.|

^q meše=nekotenwi e·h=mawi‿anenwi·wa·či.

^r "meše·='nah=meko ča·ki-ketenano ‖ keko·te·hani," e·h=ina·či.

28 a metemo·ka e·h=we·pi|-ketenaki oko·te·hani.

^b maneto·wani=či·hi.

^c e·h=osowa·nakwiniči,

^d wa·natohka=meko e·h=ki·wi|-sa·sa·kinaniwe·niči.[†]

^e "šihihwi·´," e·h=ina·či.

^f "kemayakiki=meko, metemo·ke," e·h=ineči.

^g "hwi·´," e·h=išiwe·či metemo·he·ha,

^h e·h=kosa·či ača·hmeko,

ⁱ "ke·htena·we·=meko," e·h=išite·he·či.

^j "nesowa·nakwi=ma·hi·='ni e·taši‿mayake·netamawiyani," e·h=išiwe·či metemo·he·ha.

^k "a·kwi=ča·h=ke·ko·hi iši‿mayake·nemena·nini," e·h=ina·či kakišaši·pye.

^l e·h=na·kwa·wa·či e·h=owi·kiwa·či.

^m e·h=anemi‿kosa·či.

ⁿ e·h=aya·wi‿'šimekoči=meko i·nini owi·wani.

^o "tani·hka=mana," e·h=išite·he·či‿na·mite·he,

^p e·h=neškinawa·či. ‖

29 a e·škami=ke·h=meko e·h=kya·kwiniči i·nini metemo·he·hani.

^b kapo·twe, "i·ya·ma·h=ki·h=a," e·h=ina·či i·nini ote·škiki·h‿owi·wani.

^c " 'ni·h=wi·kopihke,' ki·h=ina·wa kekya," e·h=ina·či.

^d e·h=a·čimoha·či okye·ni.

^e "ni·h=wi·kopihke=ča·hi," e·h=ina·či okye·ni.

^f "hawo·ʔ," e·h=ikoči.

^g o·ni·='na neniwa e·h=kehči‿wi·hpe·či.

^h aškači, "ši·ša·yane=wi·na," e·h=ineči.

ⁱ saka·ki=meko e·h=anwa·či·či,

^j e·h=na·kwa·či,

^k e·h=ši·ša·či.

^l e·h=nesa·či ma·ne=meko pešekesiwahi,

^m e·h=sa·sanakišima·či.

ⁿ a·neta=ke·hi='pi e·h=we·pa·hke·či,

^o "peno·či=meko," e·h=iči.

^p peno·či='pi=meko e·h=mawi-apiniči, waninawe=meko.

^q e·h=na·kwa·či.

^r e·h=mawinana·či metemo·he·hani.

^s metemo·he·ha e·h menwinawe·heči.

---

[*]Proximate shift to a virtual point-of-view adjunct; cf. the overt adjunct in 14i.

[†]/sa·sa·kinaniwe·niči/: AK ⟨|sasakineniweniči.⟩.

o	He saw that she was fat.
p	"Now I've cut out my rival," the older woman thought.
q	One time they went to bathe.
r	"Feel free to take off all your skirts," he told her.
28 a	The older woman set to taking off her skirts.
b	And he saw that she was a serpent.
c	She had a tail,
d	and she was nonchalantly flicking out her tongue.
e	"Jeepers!" he said to her.
f	"You have quite an unusual body, wife," she was told.
g	"Oh, my!" replied the older woman.
h	He was afraid of her for the first time.
i	"So it's true," he thought.
j	"My tail is obviously what you're thinking is unusual on me," said the woman.
k	"Well, I don't think you're unusual at all," he said to her, measuring his words.
l	They went back to where they lived.
m	He continued to fear her.
n	And that wife of his really ordered him around.
o	"What have I gotten myself into with her!" he thought, deep in his heart,
p	and he hated her.
29 a	And what's more he could see that the older woman was getting more and more jealous.
b	Then at some point he told his young wife to go to a certain place some ways off.
c	He said to her, "Tell your mother you're going to gather basswood bark."
d	And she told her mother.
e	She said to her mother, "Well, I'm going to gather basswood bark."
f	"O.K.," she said to her.
g	And then the man had a great time in bed.
h	After a while he was asked, "What if you go hunting."
i	Only barely willing,
j	he left
k	and went hunting.
l	He killed many deer indeed
m	and cached them in hard-to-get places.
n	Some he even threw,
o	saying, "Far away!"
p	And it's said they *did* come to rest far away, in all directions.
q	And he went back.
r	He rushed back to the older woman.
s	The older woman's heart was gladdened.

t e·h=a·ya·čimoha·či e·h=pemi|-taši-se·sahwa·či.*

u metemo·ka,| "ki·h=pako·ši-nasikanehke," e·h=ina·či ‖ ona·pe·mani.

30 a "e·h=pwa·wi·-='niya_-natomači kete·škiki·hi|-ki·wa," e·h=išiwe·či metemo·he·ha.

b "nawači-=ke·h=mo·hči -awihkapa," e·h=ina·či ona·pe·mani.

c "nahi´,_ni·na='h=we·na·='na!? ni·h=mehkawa·wa!? e·ya·kwe·ni!?" e·h=ina·či a·šitami.|

d mečemo·ka e·h=a·šotaki ota·nesani wi·h=nesemeči.

e "meše·='nahi," e·h=ikoči ona·pe·mani.

f "ši·´,_pena´, ni·h=natawi-na·čiko·hi," e·h=iči metemo·he·ha,

g e·h=na·kwa·či.

h neniwa_ma·tesi e·h=anemi|-keki·či.

i mani e·ši_-nehki·či, e·h=anisa·či,

j e·h=ketiwiči.

k e·h=apihapiniči e·h=pakišiki.

l "nahi´, nasawape·pino nehkwe·kaneki," e·h=ina·či.

m e·h=nasawape·piči ihkwe·wa.

n e·h=ka·tanahami·či neniwa.

o meše=meko e·h=anema·ška·wa·či,

p ahpemeki e·h=a·wa·či.

q e·h=po·hkya·niki ki·šekwi e·h=pya·wa·či. ‖

31 a wa·natohka=meko e·h=menwina·kwateniki.

b o·ni_metemo·ka wa·natohka=meko e·h=tana·wata·soči.

c meše·='nah=meko e·h=ča·ka·wana·či i·nihi pešekesiwahi.

d meše·='nah=meko na·hka e·h=ča·ki-wi·naniha·či.

e meše·='nah=meko=na·hka e·h=neši_-nepa·či.

f e·h=pwa·wi·=meko ke·ko·hi -išite·he·či.

g nye·wokonakateniki=ča·hi·='pi i·ni e·h=a·hkwe·či, e·h=neškite·he·či.

h e·h=na·wanone·hwa·či e·nemi_-'šihkawe·niči.

i ayo·h=či·hi e·h=ahkwihkawe·niči,

j e·h=pwa·wi·=meko -kehke·nema·či e·nemiha·nikwe·ni.

k e·h=kehč_-a·hkwe·či.

l o·ni ota·nesani e·h=na·kana·či.

m ayo·h=či·h e·h=anemihkawe·niči,

n ayo·h=či·h e·h=ahkwihkawe·niči,

o e·h=pwa·wi·=meko -kehke·nema·či e·nemiha·nikwe·ni.

p e·h=we·patone·hwa·či.

q menehta=meko ahkwitahkamiki meše·='nah=meko e·h=ča·katone·hwa·či,†

r o·ni na·mahkamiki. ‖

32 a meše·='nah=meko e·h=ča·katone·hwa·či na·mahkamiki ona·pe·mani, ota·nesani·='nahi.

---

*An inanimate singular participle is here used with a plural oblique reference.

†/e·h=ča·katone·hwa·či/: AK ⟨.eča|ketonewači.⟩.

^t He recounted to her all the places where he had stashed his game.
^u "Make some roasting spits, to be ready," the older woman told her husband.
30 a "Not asking your young wife," the older woman said.
^b "Anyway, you should have them first," she said to her husband.
^c And this time she said to him, "Listen, why don't *I* find where she went?"
^d The older woman's suggestion was so that her daughter would be killed.
^e "Never mind," her husband said to her.
^f "Say, I'd better go get the meat now," said the older woman,
^g and she left.

^h And the man went off with a knife.
ⁱ As soon as he was out of sight, he flew up,
^j becoming an eagle.
^k He landed where she was sitting.
^l "Alright, sit astride my neck," he said to her.
^m The woman sat astride him.
ⁿ And the man shoved off.
^o They flew on their way unimpeded,
^p going up.
^q And they came to where there was a hole in the sky.
31 a It looked fine, like it would not be a problem.

^b And the older woman was having no problem hauling her loads.
^c In the course of time she hauled in all the deer.
^d And in time she also butchered them.
^e And in time she also went to bed alone.
^f She had no inkling that anything was amiss.
^g Well, after four days they say she got mad, and her thoughts then turned dark.
^h She went in pursuit of him, following his tracks.
ⁱ And suddenly, here his tracks ended.
^j She had no idea which way he had gone.
^k And she got very angry.
^l And then she tracked her daughter.
^m Suddenly, here were her tracks going off,
ⁿ and suddenly, here her tracks ended.
^o She had no idea which way she had gone.
^p And she began looking for them.
^q First on top of the earth she in time searched for them all over,
^r and then under the earth.
32 a In time she searched all over under the earth for her husband, and her daughter.

^b "a·kwi=ča·h=meko kehke·nemakini,"_e·h=ikoči=meko na·mahkamiki we·wi·kiničih maneto·wahi.

^c ki·ši-ča·ki-nana·toše·či,

^d aya·pami_e·h=pya·či e·h=owi·kiči.

^e "ki·hpene=ʼškwe=meko kehke·nemake e·h=awikwe·hiki,

^f ni·h=nesa·waki=meko," e·h=išite·he·či,

^g e·h=iči=ʼh=we·=meko.

^h wi·h=nesa·či=meko e·h=ki·šowe·či.

ⁱ o·ni e·sepanaki e·h=ašiha·wa·či ni·ča·pahi.

^j omo·weči·wa·wi e·h=anawa·hkonamowa·či ni·šwi,|*

^k nekoti ihkwe·wani, nekoti neniwani.

^l e·šina·kosiniči=meko ahpemeki e·šiweneti·ničihi e·h=išina·kwihto·wa·či.

^m o·ni na·meki e·h=ahto·wa·či mehtekominani,

ⁿ e·h=ne·nye·wo·seto·wa·či.

^o "ki·h=anemi-kakano·neti·pwa,"_e·h=itamowa·či.

^p tepehki=ke·hi e·h=we·pose·mikihto·wa·či. ‖

^q e·h=ma·ne·wa·či.

33 a kekimesi=meko i·tepi e·h=a·wa·či.

^b meše=meko na·hina·hi e·h=oči-anemi-kakano·neti·mikahki i·ni e·sepani-mo·weči.

^c ihkwe·wani=ʼpi e·h=anemi-apahapane·niniči.

^d kapo·twe metemo·ka e·h=ka·škiha·či e·h=pya·niči.

^e apina=meko e·h=pemi-pasekwi·či.

^f e·h=a·hkwe·či=meko.

^g "ki·h=nesenepwa=kohi," e·h=iči.

^h kehčine·he=meko pye·či|-ka·škiha·či,

ⁱ e·h=pemi-pasekwi·či metemo·ka.

^j aseni-papakye·he·hi·=ʼnahi če·ka·heno·hiniki e·h=keki-wana·ki·či.

^k ke·htena=meko ota·nesani e·h=pye·ta·ye·niniči.

^l ona·pe·mwa·wani·=ʼnahi e·h=pye·ta·ye·niniči.

^m ke·htena=meko e·h=pye·či-pi·tike·niči.

ⁿ apina=meko e·h=pemi-kohkapiči.

^o "ohoho·´, metemo·ke," e·h=ikoči.†

^p e·h=pwa·wi-ke·hi·=ʼnahi -pye·či-nana·hapiniči.

^q e·h=ni·šo·piniči=meko. ‖

34 a še·ški e·h=ki·wi-kekapiči aseni-papakye·he·hi e·h=mawi-nana·hapiniči.

^b e·h=pwa·wi-ke·hi·=ʼnahi ke·ko·hi-išawiči.

^c e·h=wi·hpe·mekwiči e·sepani-mo·weči.

^d nehkanitepehkwe=meko e·h=taši-ana·swihto·či.‡

---

*/anawa·hkon-/ ʻmold into shapeʼ (phonetics conjectured); also /ana·waken-/ (C, AW, EK).

†/metemo·ke/: AK ⟨.metemoka.⟩.

‡/=meko/: AK ⟨neko.⟩.

b   "Well, I don't know anything about them," she was told by the spirits that dwelt under the earth.

c   After asking everywhere,

d she came back to where she lived.

e   "Once I do learn where they are,

f I'll certainly kill them," she thought,

g or rather, she said out loud.

h She vowed to kill them.

i   And then the raccoons made dolls.

j They molded two of them out of their dung,

k one woman and one man.

l They made them look exactly the way the ones that had gone together to the sky looked.

m   And then they put acorns inside,

n putting four in each.

o   "You must keep talking," they told them.

p And then at night they had them start walking.

q There were a lot of *them*.

33 a Every one of them went there.

b   From a little ways away that raccoon dung was having a conversation as it went.

c The woman (so to say) went along laughing.

d   All of a sudden the older woman heard them coming.

e She even got to her feet.

f She was angry indeed.

g   "I'll kill you for sure," she said.

h   When she heard them come closer,

i the older woman got to her feet.

j And in doing so, she got up holding a little stone hatchet in her hand.

k Sure enough, her daughter was laughing as she came.

l And their husband was laughing as he came.

m Sure enough, they came in.

n She even sat with her back turned.

o   "Oh, the idea of it, wife," he said to her.

p What's more, he didn't come and sit by her.

q Those other two sat right together.

34 a All she did was sit there with the stone hatchet in her hand as they went to sit down.

b But with all that she didn't do anything.

c   The raccoon dung slept with her.

d All night long she was making out with it.

e   e·h=taši-=ke·hi -kakano·neti·hto·či,
f   e·šawiči e·h=tana·čimoči.
g   "e·h=nesapiya·ni," e·h=iči.

h   nye·wokonakateniki e·h=ahkwa·ška·niči.
i   kapo·twe̲ma·maya to·hkisa·či,
j   e·h=nešiwiya·kwateniki.
k   e·h=pa·hki·kwe·sahoči.
l   "to·hki·no.
m   pe·hki=ma·hi mya·šiya·kwatwi," e·h=ina·či ona·pe·mani.
n   e·h=memekwisaha·či, e·h=ši·keče·nike·či,
o   e·h=wi·nineče·či.
p   e·h=wa·pataki onehki.
q   meči=meko ke·ko·hi e·h=ine·netaki.
r   keye·hapa=ke·h=wi·na·ʼpi·=ʼni e·sepani-mo·weči.
s   a·šowi=na·hka aka·mete·ki e·h=taši̲o·če·winiki.
t   pa·hkisahto·či=či·hi e·yi·ki=meko mo·weči.
u   e·h=če·če·keki metemo·he·ha.
v   a·wi·te·ni=meko, "o·hwa·´, ‖ nena·pe·me·ha," e·h=iči,
35 a   a·wasi=meko e·h=iši̲ka·htosiči ona·pe·mani.
b   o·ni=ča·hi=ʼpi e·h=a·če·wi·či.
c   me·mečine·h=meko a·yahko·hani e·h=pi·tikawa·či.
d   "we·kone·hi=ʼyo=ča·hi," e·h=ineči ihkwe·wa.
e   "o·´,̲nena·pe·me·ha=ča·hi nenatone·hwa·wa," e·h=ineči a·yahko·ha.
f   "o·ho·´," e·h=išiwe·či.
g   "na·kwe·waki=ma·h=wi·na·=ʼniki," e·h=ineči ihkwe·wa.
h   "keta·nesa̲ketawata·kwa," e·h=ineči.
i   "nahi´,̲a·yahko, wi·tamawino," e·h=išiwe·či metemo·he·ha.
j   "o·´, we·kone·h=we·=ča·h wi·h=tepahwiyani," e·h=ineči metemo·he·ha.
k   "ʼšina·kwa, ni·yawi.
l   meči=ča·hi!ʔ netota·hwi·hemi=ke·ko·hi!?" e·h=ina·či a·yahko·hani.
m   "o·´, ki·h=a·čimohene," e·h=išiwe·či‖ a·yahko·ha.
n   "awana·pi=ča·hi·=ʼna keta·nesa ki·šekoki," e·h=ineči metemo·he·ha.
o   "i·ni‖ e·h=ki·ši-=meko=ye·toke -tepe·nemena·ni," e·h=ina·či metemo·he·hani.
p   "meše=meko," e·h=ineči a·yahko·ha. ‖
36 a   " ʼki·h=tepahone ni·yawi,ʼ ketene=koči.
b   ki·na=ča·h=meko wi·h=išawiwane·ni ki·h=išawi,"̲e·h=ineči a·yahko·ha.
c   i·ni=ʼpi=meko a·yahko·ha e·h=pemi-a·htawa·nike·či.
d   metemo·ka, kapo·twe=meko e·h=če·če·keki.
e   kana·kwa=meko.
f   kapo·twe=meko e·h=pahkihte·hoči metemo·ka.
g   sa·kiči‖ e·h=mawi-pakineči.
h   aškači=meko e·h=mahkeška·niki owi·ši,
i   e·h=we·pipaho·te·niki.

e   What's more, she was having a conversation with it,

f   telling about what she had done,

g   saying, "I've been home alone."

h   After four days their time ran out.

i   Suddenly, when she awoke in the morning,

j   there was a terrible smell.

k   She threw the covers off her face.

l   "Wake up.

m   There's a really bad smell, as must be obvious," she said to her husband.

n   She shook him hard and made the crust come off,

o   and she got her fingers filthy.

p   She looked at her hand.

q   She suspected something was wrong.

r   And after all, the story goes, it turned out to be raccoon dung.

s   And over on the other side of the lodge it was swarming with flies.

t   When she threw off the covers, here she found dung there as well.

u   The older woman let out a scream.

v   The first thing out of her mouth was, "Oh no! My poor husband."

35 a   She grieved for her husband more.

b   So then it's said that she started over again.

c   The very last person whose house she entered was Âyahkôha.

d   "So, what is it?" the woman was asked.

e   "Ah, I'm searching for my husband," Âyahkôha was told.

f   "I see," he said.

g   "You realize that they have left," the woman was told.

h   "He took your daughter," she was told.

i   "Come on, Âyahkôha, tell me what happened," the older woman said.

j   "Well, so what will you give me as payment, after all?" the older woman was asked.

k   "Why, my body.

l   I obviously don't have anything else!" she said to Âyahkôha.

m   "Well, I'll tell you," said Âyahkôha.

n   "So, your daughter was taken to the sky," the older woman was told.

o   "And now it seems I have you in my power," he said to the older woman.

p   "If you like," Âyahkôha was told.

36 a   "I did tell you, after all, that I would pay you with my body.

b   So, you may do with me as you will," Âyahkôha was told.

c   Right away, to hear the tale, Âyahkôha placed his mount on her back.

d   And as for the older woman, she soon let out a scream.

e   It was to no avail.

f   Soon the older woman was rogered to death.

g   And she was taken outside and discarded.

h   Much later, her head came off,

i   and it started running.

ᴶ   e·h=we·pi-na·ni·me·ya·ška·ki.
ᴷ   i·ya·h=meko ašiči e·h=a·yahkwa·ška·ki.
ᴸ   meše·=ʼnah=mani e·ši-pye·či-we·pa·ška·niki,
ᴹ   kehčikami·ki e·h=ineče·pemotaki.
ᴺ   na·waka·me=meko e·h=pakiseki.
ᴼ   meši·name·wi-mečemo·ka| e·h=mesisahto·či i·ni we·wi·še·h-owi·še·hi.

ᴾ   aškači=meko e·h=na·kwa·wa·či i·niye·ka| mehči·ki.
ᵟ   na·hka=meko e·h=ketiwiči i·na neniwa.
ᴿ   e·h=ni·sa·ška·wa·či.
ˢ   i·ya·hi e·h=pya·wa·či ‖ e·h=owi·kiwa·tehe.
37 a   e·h=aye·ši|-ki·ki·wihkawe·niči ihkwe·wa okye·ni.
ᵇ   e·h=pwa·wi-=meko| -nenehke·nema·či.
ᶜ   e·h=pwa·wi-=ke·hi| -nahi-nepa·wa·či,
ᵈ   e·h=na·kwa·wa·či neniwa e·h=owi·kiči.
ᵉ   "me·me·čiki=meko ča·kiha·petoke nete·sepa·heme·haki," e·h=iči neniwa.
ᶠ   "we·nah=ketotayi e·sepa·haki," e·h=išiwe·či ihkwe·wa.
ᵍ   "ehe·he," e·h=ineči.
ʰ   i·ya·h=pye·ya·wa·či, š=anano·pehka·či e·h=tašiniči.
ⁱ   e·h=mi·ša·te·nemowa·či e·sepa·he·haki e·h=pya·niči oto·te·meko·hwa·wani,
ʲ   e·h=ašinawe·wa·či.
ᵏ   "nahi´, nete·sepa·hemetike, meše=meko·=ʼnahi ayahaya·ko.
ˡ   e·ši-menwe·netame·kwini=meko iha·ko," e·h=ina·či.
ᵐ   e·h=kwa·pi·wa·či e·sepa·haki.
ⁿ   e·h=mi·ša·te·nemowa·či,
ᵒ   e·h=ča·ki·wa·či.

ᴾ   aškači·=ʼniya e·h=pya·či ne·škima·ta wi·h=mawi-ni·šo·hkwe·we·niči,
ᵟ   e·h=a·čimoha·či.
ᴿ   "nemo·weči·hena·ni·=ʼyo·we netašihčike·we·pena ‖ ni·ča·pa,
38 a   e·h=ašihakeči ni·ča·paki.
ᵇ   ni·šwi netašiha·pena,
ᶜ   nekoti ihkwe·wa, nekoti neniwa, owi·weti·haki.
ᵈ   ki·nwa·wa=ta·taki e·h=a·we·hčike·ya·ke ki·ya·wa·wi," e·h=ina·či.
ᵉ   "nye·wokoni=ča·hi·=ʼnini neniwi-ni·ča·pani taši-ona·pe·miwa," e·h=ina·či.*
ᶠ   "nye·wokonakateniki e·h=kehke·nema·či," e·h=ikoči ote·sepa·hemahi. ‖ †

---

*/wo/: AK ⟨o⟩.
†Followed by a blank half page.

^j And now it began jumping up in the air.
^k It was getting close to the place up there.
^l As soon as he saw it beginning to succeed in coming up,
^m he shot it into the great sea.
ⁿ It went and landed right out in the middle of the water.
^o And an old lady whale swallowed that puny rolling-skull head in a single gulp.

^p Much later, those two left to come down to earth.
^q Once again the man turned into an eagle.
^r And they flew down.
^s They got to where they had lived before.
37 a The tracks of the woman's mother were still visible in many places.
^b She summoned no thoughts of her.
^c What's more, they didn't stop to sleep.
^d They left to go to the man's house.
^e "I'm sure my raccoons have all been killed," said the man.
^f "I gather you have raccoons as pets," said the woman.
^g "Yes," she was told.
^h When they got there, say, there were so many they couldn't count them.
ⁱ The raccoons were delighted with the arrival of their master,
^j and they greeted his return.
^k "Alright, my faithful raccoons, go where you please.
^l Go to wherever you like," he told them.
^m The raccoons scattered.
ⁿ They were delighted,
^o and they all left.

^p Later on, the one that had warned him before not to go to marry two wives came back,
^q and it explained things to him.
^r "We used some of our dung to make a doll before,
38 a in making some dolls.
^b We made two of them,
^c one woman and one man, a married couple.
^d We made them pretty much like the two of you," it told him.
^e "So, for four days she was married to that male doll," it told him.
^f "After four days she found out about it," he was told by his raccoons.

kêteminawesichiki nashawaye-mehtosêneniwaki

People of Long Ago Who Were Blessed.

kêteminawesichiki nashawaye-mehtosêneniwaki
Alfred Kiyana[*]

1 a   ke·teminawesičiki našawaye-mehtose·neniwaki.[†]

b   nekoti=ʼpi našawaye kwi·yese·ha e·h=ma·mahkate·wi·nekoči o·sani.

c   "nahi´, nekwi·hi, mahkate·wi·no," e·h=ikoči=meko| ahpene·či.

d   pa·ši=meko e·h=ki·šikiči e·h=mahkate·wi·či.

e   kapo·twe| pe·hki e·h=ki·šikiči,

f   e·h=po·nahkate·wi·neči.|

g   o·ni e·h=mo·šoči,

h   omo·šo·ni e·h=ašihtawoči.

i   e·h=wa·wa·pimatete·či.[‡]

j   e·h=oškinawe·hiči=ta·taki,

k   e·h=ki·ki·wita·či.

l   e·h=pwa·wi-=ke·hi -ma·mi·hkemehkwe·we·či.|

m   še·ški=meko e·h=ki·wita·či.

n   o·ni=ye·toke kapo·twe e·h=natopaniwenahkiwiniki,

o   e·h=wi·če·we·či=ke·hi.

p   (ne·pehe, e·h=otehkwe·miči.)

q   "o·´,_peno·či=meko neta," e·h=ikowa·či me·ya·wosa·ničini.

r   e·h=pemahowa·či=ke·hi, ‖

2 a   meše=meko e·h=anemi-_tanahowa·či.[§]

b   o·ni meše·=ʼnah=kapo·twe e·h=mo·hkise·howa·či kehčikami·wi.

c   či·kepye·ki=meko e·h=anemi-pa·po·ni·wa·či.

d   o·ni=ye·toke kapo·twe,_"e·h=pya·ya·ni e·ya·ya·ni," e·h=iniči.

e   "kekye·hkinawa·či ki·h=ne·wa·pena mahwe·wa me·hkate·wesita.

f   i·nina·h=ča·h=meko wi·h=po·ni·yakwe,

g   na·hina·h=meko e·h=ne·wa·wakwe·ni," e·h=ineči ne·topa·haki.

h   "hawo·ʔ," e·h=iyowa·či.

i   kwi·yena=meko na·wahkwe·niki| e·h=ne·wa·wa·či i·ni e·šikiničini,

j   mahwe·wani me·hkate·wesiničini.

k   "ayo·h=ča·h=ye·toke wi·h=po·ni·heti·yakwe,"| e·h=iniči me·ya·wosa·ničini.

l   e·h=po·ni·heti·wa·či.

m   i·nini=ke·hi e·h=sahkahamawa·wa·či ‖ mahwe·wani,

3 a   e·h=neškimeči ke·ko·hi wi·h=ina·wa·či,

b   wi·h=natota·sa·wa·či pema·tesiweni.

c   še·ški=meko, "kesahkahamo·ne mana ase·ma·wa," e·h=ina·wa·či.|

---

[*]The manuscript is NAA 2794.86; it has 30 pages.

[†]Written as a title at the top of the page.

[‡]/e·h=wa·wa·pimatete·či/: AK ⟨.ewawapi.ma|teteči.⟩.

[§]/e·h=anemi-_tanahowa·či/ (AW): AK ⟨.eanemi|tanatowači.⟩.

People of Long Ago who were Blessed
Translated by Ives Goddard

1 a   People of Long Ago Who Were Blessed.

b   There was a certain boy long ago, the story goes, whose father made him fast.
c   "Alright, son, fast," his father would always insist.
d   He fasted until he was grown up.
e   The time came when he was fully grown up,
f   and he no longer fasted.
g   And then his hair was cut,
h   and his scalplock was made for him.
i   And he had white leggins.
j   He was basically just a young man,
k   staying around.
l   He didn't go courting girls, either.
m   He just stayed around unmarried.
n   And then it seems that at some point a warparty was organized,
o   and he went along as well.
p   (Oh, I should have said, he had a sister.)
q   "Well, I'm going far away," the warparty-leader said to him and the others.
r   Now, they went in canoes,
2 a   and went paddling along without incident.
b   And then eventually at some point they emerged onto a large lake.
c   They followed the shore, camping as they went.
d   And then it seems at some point they heard him say, "I've come to where I'm going.
e   "It will be a sign when we see a wolf that is black.
f   So, then we'll camp right away,
g   at whatever time we see it," the warriors were told.
h   "O.K.," they said.
i   Exactly at noon they saw a creature of that description,
j   a wolf that was black.
k   "So, it seems here's where we're to make our camp," the warparty-leader said.
l   And they made camp.
m   And another thing, when they offered tobacco to the wolf,
3 a   they were warned against saying for it to do anything,
b   or praying to it for life.
c   The only thing they said to it was, "I offer you this tobacco."

d   "nye·wi‗wa·se·ya·we ayo·hi ki·h‗owi·kipena," e·h‗iyoweči.*

e   e·h‗po·si‗=meko ‑ša·kwe·nemowa·či| a·neta kenwe·ši e·h‗naki·wa·či.

f   o·ni nye·wokonakateniki e·h‗na·kwa·wa·či,

g   e·h‗we·pahowa·či.

h   i·ni=ke·h‗mani nano·pehka·čina·h=meko e·h‗pya·wa·či.

i   nye·wokonakateniki e·h‗pye·notawa·wa·či e·h‗ma·wa·seto·niči aša·hahi,

j   kohpiči e·h‗po·ni·heti·wa·či.

k   e·h‗ana·hpawa·niči.|†

l   "wa·pake ma·maya| wi·h‗awanwi.

m   a·kwi=meko wi·h‗nenwa·pata·nikini," e·h‗iniči. ‖

4 a   "ki·h‗sese·satahwa·pwa=ča·hi," e·h‗ineči.

b   "sese·si=meko ayo·h=ki·h‗ma·wači·pwa," e·h‗ineči,

c   či·ma·nani e·h‗ahte·niki.

d   "ki·h‗kahkami·pena=ke·hi," e·h‗ineči.

e   "wi·h‗to·hkamepye·senwi mani nepi," e·h‗iniči me·ya·wosa·ničini.

f   wa·pano·hiniki e·h‗mo·hki·htamowa·či.

g   o·ni| i·niya oškinawe·ha e·h‗ki·wa·ni·či.

h   e·h‗apwi·heči=ke·hi kenwe·ši·me·hi.

i   "nahi´, nesa·petoke=kohi´," e·h‗iyowa·či we·wi·hka·ničiki,‡

j   e·h‗we·pahowa·či.

k   wi·na=ke·hi·‗'na po·si·ni·me·ška·niki pe·keše·niki e·h‗ne·taki e·h‗akwa·howa·tehe.

l   nano·škwe e·nemi‗'ši‑nehkya·niki e·h‗anemi‗'šisa·či.

m   meše·=‑'nah=meko| nehkaniki·šekwe e·h‗pemipahoči. ‖

5 a   kapo·twe e·h‗mi·na·wite·he·či.

b   "ši·´, meše=ni·hka, e·h‗wa·se·ya·ki nepapa·mehka," e·h‗išite·he·či.

c   o·ni kekye·hči‑ke·nwa·sowe·wahi e·h‗a·naha·nemihekoči tepehki e·h‗pemehka·či.

d   na·hka e·h‗kohtaki.

e   ahpene·či‗wi·na=meko e·h‗wi·sewi·seniči ne·no·či‑ki·šikeno·hiniki.

f   o·ni kapo·twe e·h‗wa·sikami·niki,§

g   e·h‗pwa·wi‗=meko ‑te·pa·pata·niniki e·nekihkwaka·maki·nikwe·ni.

h   i·ni=ča·hi·‗'pi e·h‗mayo·či,

i   ne·kawahki·ki=meko e·h‗tanwe·kesiči nye·wokoni.

j   nye·wokonakateniki e·h‗mi·na·wite·he·či.

k   "ši·´, meše=ni·hka,| netaši·wi·škwe·we·kesi,"| e·h‗išite·he·či.

l   "mani=ke·h‗wi·na‗ye·toke e·h‗ahte·ki wi·h‗tahpene·ya·ni," e·h‗išite·he·či, ‖

6 a   e·h‗po·nwe·we·kesiči.

b   o·ni‗še·ški=meko e·h‗šekišekišiki.‗

____

*/e·h‗iyoweči/: AK ⟨we⟩ changed from ⟨wa⟩.

†Explained in K-Kin 38*a-g*.

‡/=kohi´/: AK ⟨i⟩ changed from ⟨.⟩.

§/wa·/ (emended; word not attested, but /‑ikami·/ is 'be a lake, sea'): AK ⟨na⟩.

d   "We must camp here for four days," were the orders.

e Some were very much against the extended halt.

f   And then after four days they headed out

g and went paddling on.

h Now to be clear, there was then a huge number of them that came along.

i   After four days they came to where the Siouxs had a village,

j and they camped up away from the water.

k They heard him recite his dream.

l   "Early tomorrow morning there will be fog.

m It won't be possible to make things out," he said.

4 a   "So, you must hurry to club them," they had him say.

b   "You must hurry, indeed, to come together here," they were told,

c meaning where the canoes were.

d   "To be clear, you must cut cross-country," they were told.

e   "This water will lie calm and flat," the warparty-leader said.

f   Early in the morning they attacked the place.

g   And then that young man lost his way.

h And here, he was waited for for quite a long time.

i   "Alright, he must have been killed, for sure!" his companions said.

j And they paddled off.

k   And as for him, after the fog had lifted sufficiently, he saw the place where they had earlier beached their canoes.

l He ran off into the murk without knowing where he was going.

m He ran pretty much all day long.

5 a   At some point he had a thought.

b "Gee, what am I doing traveling in the daytime!" he thought.

c   And then he was beset by huge mountain lions as he traveled at night.

d And again he was fearful.

e He always had meals of wild plants, however.

f   And then at some point there was the gleam of a lake.   (See note.)

g And it was not possible to see how wide it was across.

h So then they say he wept.

i He wept right there on the beach for four days.

j   After four days he reflected.

k "Gee, what the heck am I doing just bawling away!" he thought.

l "After all, this is probably the place where I'll die," he thought.

6 a And he ceased his weeping.

b   And then all he did was lie there.

^c wi·ša·pene·čini, wi·škeno·he·hahi e·h=pemwa·či,

^d e·h=apo·so·hiči.

^e ke·keya·hi=ʼpi_nekoti e·h=te·pama·či=meko wi·škeno·he·hani.

^f e·h=po·ni- ma·ne·he -ča·kisenye·či.|

^g kapo·twe meše=nekotenwi wa·paniki e·h=nekotwa·nahkwateniki,

^h e·h=ne·htawi-=meko -mešahkwateniki.

ⁱ či·kepye·ki| e·h=šekišekišino·hiči.

^j kapo·twe_e·h=pye·či|-akwa·pye·ki·niči pašito·he·hani,

^k e·h=ašamekoči owi·ya·se·hi.

^l ohkone·he·heki=meko e·h=pye·či-wi·hkwe·naminiči.

^m e·h=šekišiki=meko e·h=taši-mi·či·hiči.

ⁿ "ča·katano=meko," e·h=ikoči,*

^o e·h=ča·kataki=meko.

^p ki·ši-ča·kataki, mehktekwina·ka·heki e·h=ahte·niki ‖ na·tawino·na·powi.

^{7 a} "nahi´,_noši·hi, mani=na·hka meno·hino," e·h=ikoči,

^b e·h=ča·kataki=meko.

^c ki·ši_ča·kataki, e·h=pasekwi·tenekoči,

^d e·h=we·pa·ška·či=meko.

^e e·h=ana·po·hke·niči na·tawino·ni,_

^f e·h=seswamekoči.

^g ki·ši_seswamekoči, e·h=pasekwi·tenekoči,

^h e·h=ne·se·či.

ⁱ e·h=pwa·wi-=meko ke·ko·hi -iši-mya·ši_pema·tesiči.

^j "nahi´, nepi·=ʼnahi mawi-menono," e·h=ikoči,

^k e·h=mawi_menoči,

^l e·h=menoška·kwiči.

^m ki·ši_menoči, e·h=ki·ša·koči-pi·no·sowiči.

ⁿ ne·ya·pi=meko e·hpi·hčina·kositehe e·h=ahpi·hčina·kosiči,

^o e·h=na·pye·we·sa·či.

^p aya·pami e·h=a·či omešo·hani e·h=apihapiniči.

^q i·ya·hi e·h=mawi|-nana·hapiči. ‖

^{8 a} "nekotahi ketoči?" e·h=ikoči.

^b e·h=a·čimoha·či.

^c "nemešo, na·hkataho·ši·ke·ni e·h=mo·hki·htama·ke," e·h=ina·či.

^d e·h=pešikwi-=meko -wi·tamawa·či omešo·mesani.

^e "o·´,_we·nahi·=ʼni," e·h=ikoči.

^f "we·nahi keta·tesehkwe·šine| ayo·hi," e·h=ikoči.†

^g "o·´,_mani ki·h=a·šo·hka," e·h=ineči.

^h "ki·na=meko ki·h=we·we·ne·neta wi·h=anemiha·wane·ni,"_e·h=ineči.

ⁱ "na·mepye·ki=ke·hi, ahkwitepye·ki=ke·hi," e·h=ineči.‡

---

*In 6n-8.l 'the man' translates the obviative inflection, which marks a secondary third person.

†/keta·tesehkwe·šine/ EK: AK ⟨.ketatesakwešine|⟩.

‡/ahkwitepye·ki/ AK and others, many exx.; AW: AK ⟨akwitapyeki⟩.

c Whenever he got hungry, he shot little birds with his bow
d and roasted a small meal for himself.
e In time, it's said that one small bird filled him right up.
f He no longer needed several to make a complete meal.
g   And at some point when day dawned one time the sky was a uniform hue.
h It was clear from horizon to horizon.
i And he was just lying there on the shore.
j And at some point a little old man came out of the water
k and gave him a piece of meat to eat.
l He came carrying it wrapped in his little blanket.
m And he ate it right where he lay.
n   "Eat all of it," the man told him.
o And he all of it.
p After he had eaten all of it, there was some medicine to drink in a little wooden bowl.
7 a   "Alright, my grandchild, just drink this also," the man told him.
b And he drank all of it.
c After he had drunk it all, the man lifted him to his feet,
d and he fell right down.
e The man boiled some medicine
f and sprayed it on him with his mouth.
g After spraying it on him, he lifted him to his feet,
h and he was cured.
i He didn't feel bad in any way at all.
j   "Alright, now go and drink some water," the man told him.
k He went and drank some,
l and it had a good effect on him.
m After drinking it, he was completely recovered.
n He looked just the same as he had looked before,
o and he had his strength back.
p   He went back to where his grandfather was sitting.
q He went and sat over there.
8 a   "Are you coming from someplace?" the man asked him.
b And he explained to him.
c   "Grandfather, it seems I was left behind by the canoes on our raid," he told him.
d He told his grandfather the straight story.
e   "Oh, so that's it," the man said to him.
f "So, here you are, stranded on the wrong side," he said to him.
g   "Well, you'll get across this," he was told.
h "It will be up to you to decide which way you want to go," he was told.
i "Whether under the water, or on top of the water," he was told.

j	e·h=kohtaki na·mepye·ki,
k	"ahkwitepye·ki," e·h=ina·či omešo·mesani.
l	"hawo·?," e·h=inekoči.
m	"nahi´, mehčika·nono," e·h=ikoči.
n	nepi e·h=kwa·pane·htaminiči,
o	e·h=seswatama·koči ohka·tani.
p	"i·ni.
q	i·ni=meko wi·h=anemi-'ši-a·šoha·šo·hkamani.
r	se·nakahkini, ‖ ki·h=konakwi=meko," e·h=ikoči omešo·mesani.
9 a	e·h=na·kwa·či,
b	ahkwitepye·ki‖ e·h=anemiha·či,
c	nehkaniki·šekwe, meše·='nah=meko nehkanitepehkwe.
d	na·waka·me·pye·ya·či, e·h=ka·škehtawa·či ahkohko·ni, ne·kamoničihi·='nahi.
e	e·h=nenohtawa·či=meko omešo·mesani e·h=taši-kanakanawiniči.‖
f	ši·ši·kwanani=ke·hi e·h=ka·škehtaki.
g	ni·šwitepehkwe='pi anemehke·wa.
h	e·na·kwi·hiniki_i·ya·h=e·h=pya·či e·hkwi-ahkiwiniki.
i	(e·h=pwa·wi-=ke·h=meko·='nahi nana·ši -wi·ša·pene·či.
j	meše=meko e·h=anahanemehka·či,
k	ahpene·či=meko‖ či·kepye·ki e·h=anemiha·či.)
l	na·pi='pi=meko·='nahi e·h=išite·he·či.
m	i·na·ka=na·hka ihkwe·wa we·tawe·ma·wita e·h=ki·ša·koči-=meko ‖ -mami·kwa·soči e·h=mahkate·wi·či.
10 a	e·h=ki·ša·kotwe·we·kesiči,
b	e·h=mawima·či otawe·ma·wani.
c	i·na·ka neniwa e·h=nepa·či.
d	"ketehkwe·ma‖ wi·h=aški-=meko -ne·wata,"‖ e·h=ineči.
e	"i·na=meko‖ wi·h=aški_-ne·wata," e·h=ineči.
f	"nye·wenwi=ča·hi ki·h=po·tetone·hpwa·wa," e·h=ineči.
g	"ki·h=kehkitehkwe·na·wa," e·h=ineči.
h	o·ni ihkwe·wa‖ e·h=mo·šiha·či otawe·ma·wani.
i	"wi·h=pye·wa ketawe·ma·wa," e·h=ineči.
j	"ki·na=meko ki·h=menehta·mi-ne·wa·wa," e·h=ineči.
k	"nye·wenwi=ča·hi‖ ki·h=po·tetone·hpwa·wa," e·h=ineči.
l	na·pi=meko·='nahi_e·h=išite·he·či.
m	o·ni ma·maya=meko e·h=to·hki·či,
n	e·h=na·kwa·hiči.
o	na·hka a·pi_-maya·wosa·ta e·h=mahkate·wi·či,
p	e·h=natokwawa·či ‖ e·šawinikwe·ni.
11 a	i·nini=ke·h=meko mehteno·hi e·h=nakana·či.

^j He was afraid of being under the water,
^k and he told his grandfather, "On top of the water."
^l   "O.K.," the man said to him.
^m   "Alright, uncover your feet," he told him.
ⁿ And he took a big mouthful of water
^o and sprayed it on his feet.
^p   "That's it.
^q *That* is how you'll keep going right on across it.
^r Whenever it gets difficult, you'll come through fine," his grandfather told him.
9 a   He set out,
^b going on top of the water,
^c all day and eventually all night.
^d   When he got to the middle of the lake, he could hear a drum and singers.
^e And he recognized the voice of his grandfather giving a speech.
^f He heard rattles as well.
^g   He walked on for two nights, they say.
^h And in the early evening he got to the edge of the dry land.
ⁱ (Now, he was never at all hungry in all that.
^j He just kept on walking right along,
^k all the time going on top of the water.)
^l And with that he's said to have felt much relieved.

^m   Meanwhile, the young man's sister was making extreme efforts fasting.
10 a She wailed terribly,
^b weeping over her brother.

^c   Elsewhere the man was asleep.
^d And he was told, "Your sister will be the very first one you see."
^e   He was told, "*She'll* be the one that you see first."
^f   He was told, "So, you must kiss her four times."
^g   He was told, "You must put your arms around her neck."

^h   And the woman then had a vision of her brother.
ⁱ And she was told, "Your brother will come back."
^j   She was told, "*You'll* be the first to see him."
^k   She was told, "And you must kiss him four times."
^l   And at that, she felt much relieved.
^m   And then early in the morning she woke up,
ⁿ and she set out.

^o   And the man who had been the warparty-leader fasted also,
^p seeking to learn in a dream what had happened to him.
11 a Now, he was the only one he had left behind.

b   ahpene·či=meko e·h=mahkate·wi·či.
c   o·ni kakata·ni we·ni·ča·nesičiki e·h=pwa·wi|-mahkate·wi·wa·či.

d   o·ni| aškači i·na neniwa| e·h=pye·notaki=na·hka kehči-si·po·wi e·h=mo·hkise·ya·niki.
e   ke·htena=meko e·h=a·šo·hkaki šo·ški, ahkwitepye·ki e·h=anemiha·či.
f   wa·natohka=meko e·h=anemehka·či.
g   ke·keya·hi·'pi=meko e·h=anemi-kesikesi·ya·hiniki.
h   omahkese·hani=ke·hi wi·h=po·ni·čini=meko e·h=anemi-ahte·niki.
i   ahpene·či=meko e·h=ki·šiseniki wi·h=po·ni·čini.
j   o·ni_po·si-=meko -kesi·ya·hiniki, ahpene·či=meko e·h=ki·šiseniki mese·he·hani,
k   i·ni=meko e·h=išikeniki. ‖
12 a   aškači_i·ni e·h=a·čimoheči.
b   "nahi´, wa·pake ana·kwi·hike wi·h=ne·wači ketehkwe·ma," e·h=ineči.
c   "i·ni=ča·h=meko wi·h=išawiyani na·hina·h=meko e·h=ne·wa·wate·ni ketehkwe·ma.
d   ki·h=mawinana·wa,
e   wi·h=kehkitehkwe·ne·hiyani,
f   wi·h=po·tetone·hpwači," e·h=ineči.

g   i·na·ka=na·hka ihkwe·wa i·ni=meko e·h=ineči.
h   "mahwe·wa=ke·hi ki·h=wa·pamekowa·wa," e·h=ineči ihkwe·wa.|
i   "mani=ča·hi wi·h=išawiye·kwe:
j   a·kwi wi·h=anemi-mehči-wi·te·mačini," e·h=ineči.
k   "tepehki=meko ki·h=anemehka·hipwa," e·h=ineči.

l   ma·maya=meko| e·h=na·kwa·či,
m   nehkaniki·šekwe e·h=anemipahoči.|
n   e·h=pwa·wi-=ke·hi_-nah-ahkwima·či·či.
o   aye·niwe=meko e·h=ahpi·hčipahoči.|
p   e·na·kwi·hiniki e·h=ne·wa·či.
q   ta·twa·hkiwani ‖ e·h=wa·wa·tanahkiseniki wa·wi·tawa·hkiwe_e·h=oči-keči·wa·či.
13 a   ayo·nina·h=či·hi otawe·ma·wani e·h=oči-pye·či_-keči·niči,
b   e·h=mawinana·či.
c   e·h=wa·wa·či-=meko| -mawinaneti·wa·či,|
d   e·h=po·tepo·tetone·hpoti·wa·či.
e   e·h=na·kwa·wa·či.
f   e·h=ki·ša·koči-=meko -mi·ša·te·nemowa·či e·h=ne·woti·wa·či.
g   tepehki='pi e·h=na·kwa·wa·či.
h   ahpene·či=meko mahwe·wani pemičinawe·me·hi e·h=pemehka·niči.

i   wa·pano·hiniki e·h=kesi·ya·niki,
j   e·h=nana·hišinowa·či me·meše na·na·hina·hi,
k   e·h=nepa·hiwa·či wa·paniki.|
l   o·ni pe·hkote·niki e·h=na·kwa·wa·či,

^b   He fasted all the time.
^c   And his parents, despite being that, were not fasting.

^d   And then after a while the man came to where another large river flowed out.
^e   Sure enough, he crossed it with ease, going on top of the water.
^f   He walked on without giving it a further thought.
^g   Eventually, we're told, the days were getting colder and colder.
^h   And there were moccasins for him along the way right in the places where he would camp.
ⁱ   Wherever he was going to camp there were always some ready for him.
^j   And when it got even colder, there was always some firewood ready,
^k   in the same way.
12 a   After some time then he was instructed.
^b   "Alright, tomorrow in the early evening you will see your sister," he was told.
^c   "So, that is, indeed, what you must do the moment you see your sister.
^d   You must run to her,
^e   and you must put your arms around her neck,
^f   and must kiss her," he was told.

^g   And elsewhere the woman was also told the same thing.
^h   "And what's more, a wolf will be watching the two of you," the woman was told.
ⁱ   "So, here's what the two of you are to do:
^j   you're not to go along in plain sight with him," she was told.
^k   "The two of you must only travel at night," she was told.

^l   Early in the morning she set out,
^m   and she went running along all day.
ⁿ   What's more, she never became exhausted from running.
^o   She ran steadily at the same pace.
^p   In the early evening she saw him.
^q   Where two ravines headed up opposite each other, the two of them came out into the open
     on either side of the ridge.
13 a   All of a sudden here was her brother coming out of there,
^b   and she ran to him.
^c   They ran right to each other
^d   and kissed each other repeatedly.
^e   And they set out.
^f   They were overjoyed to see each other.
^g   They set out at night, we're told.
^h   And there was always a wolf walking along a little to one side.

ⁱ   At dawn it was very cold.
^j   They lay down a little ways from each other
^k   and slept a bit the next day.
^l   And then at night they set out,

^m wa·pano·hiniki i·ya·hi e·h=pya·wa·či.

ⁿ o·ni otawe·ma·wani, "nahi´, ko·sena·na natomi.

^o "wi·h=pye·wa," ‖ e·h=ina·či.

14 a "meše·='nah=meko| ki·h=pye·či_wi·te·ma·wa," e·h=ineči ihkwe·he·ha.

^b "ka·ta=wi·na,| 'pye·wa,' išiye·kani," e·h=ineči.

^c "še·ški=meko, 'wi·te·mino,' ki·h=ina·wa_ko·sena·na," e·h=ineči ihkwe·wa.

^d e·h=na·kwa·či e·h=owi·kiwa·či.

^e "ano·se," e·h=ina·či o·sani,

^f "pena´,| wi·te·mino," e·h=ina·či.

^g "no·make·we=meko ki·h=wi·te·mi," e·h=ina·či.

^h "hawo·?," e·h=iči pašito·ka.

ⁱ e·h=wi·te·ma·či ota·nesani,

^j e·h=anemi-ahko·wa·či.|

^k ayo·h=či·hi okwisani e·h=apihapiniči.

^l e·h=aka·wi|-mayo·či.

^m ki·ši-mayo·či, e·h=so·kena·či oni·ča·nesahi,

ⁿ e·h=ni·šo·če·na·či.

^o ki·ši-so·kena·či, e·h=a·čimoheči.

^p "ki·h=ki·ke·nopena," e·h=ineči.

^q "i·noki=meko| i·ya·h=pya·yane, ki·h=anohka·na·waki ‖ kemami·ši·hemena·naki," e·h=ineči.

15 a "i·noki=ča·h=meko pehkote·ke i·ni wi·h=ki·ke·noyakwe,"| e·h=ina·či o·sani.*

^b "ka·ta=ke·h=wi·na a·čimihke·ko e·h=pya·ya·ni," e·h=ineči pašito·ha.

^c e·h=na·kwa·či.

^d i·ya·h=meko pye·ya·či e·h=a·čimoha·či me·mi·šama·kowa·čini.

^e i·na=ke·hi neniwa e·h=wa·se·ya·niki e·h=nepa·či.

^f ihkwe·wa=na·hkači.

^g "nahi´, mana_ketawe·ma·wa pwa·wi-kehke·nemehke, wi·h=nepo·hiwa.

^h a·kwi_wi·h=te·pahkwi-ki·ke·nočini," e·h=ineči.

ⁱ (e·h=še·škesi·he·hiči='yo=ke·hi.)

^j o·ni=na·hka neniwa,

^k "nahi´, mana ketehkwe·ma pwa·wi-manate,

^l a·kwi wi·h=te·pahkwi-ki·ke·noyanini," e·h=ineči.

^m e·h=to·hkisa·či ihkwe·wa,|

ⁿ e·h=na·kwa·či=meko.

^o i·ya·h=pye·ya·či ‖ e·h=apihapi·hiniči otawe·ma·wani,

16 a e·h=či·tapiniči=meko e·h=mawi|-nana·hapiči._

^b "nahi´, nesi·hi, kemya·na·hpawa·nene=kohi," e·h=ina·či osi·me·hani.

____

*/e·h=ina·či/: AK ⟨|eineči.⟩.

^m and at dawn they got there.
ⁿ   And then her brother (said), "Alright, go get our father.
^o   He said to her, "Tell him to come."
14 a   "You may come with him," the young woman was told.
^b   "But don't tell him I've come back," she was told.
^c   "You must only tell our father to come with you," the woman was told.
^d And she set out for their house.

^e   "Father," she said to her father,
^f "Now, come with me," she said to him.
^g   "I'd like you to come with me for a short while," she said to him.
^h   "O.K.," said the older man.
ⁱ He went with his daughter,
^j going behind her as they went.

^k   All of a sudden he saw his son sitting there.
^l And he briefly wept.
^m And having wept, he held his children,
ⁿ embracing both of them together.
^o   After holding them, he was told what he should do.
^p "We must have a clan feast," he was told.
^q   "Right now when you get back, you must give orders to our ceremonial attendants," he
was told.
15 a   "So, right now tonight is when we must give the clan feast," he told his father.
^b   "But don't either of you tell that I've come back," the older man was told.
^c And he left.
^d When he got back there, he informed the one that served them as ceremonial attendant.

^e   Now, the man slept during the day.
^f   And the woman also.
^g And she was told, "Now listen, if your brother here doesn't know you intimately, he'll die.
^h He won't live to celebrate the clan feast."
ⁱ (Now, bear in mind, she was a virgin.)
^j   And the man also was told,
^k "Now listen, if you don't fuck your sister here,
^l you won't live to celebrate the clan feast."

^m   The woman awoke with a start
ⁿ and set out directly.
^o   When she got to the place where her brother was, by himself,
16 a she went and sat down right where he was sitting.
^b   "Listen, little brother, you must know that I had a bad dream about you," she said to her
younger brother.

c   "e·´," e·h=iniči,

d   "ni·na=ča·h=ne·hi nemya·na·hpawa·to=ni·yawi," e·h=iniči=meko.

e   "ke·htena.

f   a·kwi=ʼpi| wi·h=te·pahkwi-ki·ke·no·hiya·nini.

g   no·ta=meko=ʼpi ni·h=nepo·hi," e·h=iniči.

h   apina=meko ihkwe·wa e·h=mayo·či.

i   o·ni=wi·na e·h=a·čimoči ihkwe·wa.

j   "ni·na=ke·hi e·na·hpawa·ya·ni:

k   ʽpwa·wi-manehke, wi·h=nepo·hiwa.

l   a·kwi wi·h=te·pahkwi-ki·ke·nočini,ʼ neteko·pi,| netena·hpawa," e·h=ina·či.|

m   "a·kwi=ča·hi tepa·tamo·na·nini ni·yawi.

n   meše·=ʼnah=meko i·ni ki·h=to·tawi._

o   i·ni=we·=meko ki·h=išawipena.

p   ketahkwiya·te·nemene wi·h=nepo·hiyani," ‖ e·h=ina·či osi·me·hani.

17 a   "a·kwi=ča·h=kana·kwa," e·h=iniči.*

b   "na·piwe·na.

c   neki·ši_-pya," e·h=iniči.†

d   "neme·nešite·he i·ni wi·h=to·to·na·ni.

e   i·ni=koči=ye·toke| e·ne·nemiči maneto·wa,"| e·h=iči.

f   kapo·twe=meko e·h=pya·niči omešo·mesani.

g   "ni·na=ma·hi keketemino·ne," e·h=ikoči.

h   "mahwe·wa=ke·hi·=ʼna wi·h=nešiwana·čihena·kwe e·šite·ha·ta.|

i   wi·nwa·wa i·ni e·šawiwa·či.

j   meše=meko·=ʼnahi anemi_-maneti·waki," e·h=ineči.

k   "i·ni=ča·hi wi·h=išawiye·kwe e·šite·he·či.|

l   pwa·wi-=ʼh=we·na!ᵀ_ka·hkami| -ketemino·nwa·sa!?"_e·h=ineči.

m   "a·kwi=ča·hi wi·h=nepo·hiyani ayo·nina·hi ine·nemena·nini," e·h=ineči.

n   e·h=me·nešimeči mahwe·wa.

o   i·ni=meko e·h=iši-po·ni-na·kwiho·noči i·nahi. ‖

18 a   aškiča·h=ke·h=wi·na i·nah=meko_e·h=a·hpeči-ki·wita·či.

b   o·ni pe·hkote·hiniki, e·h=na·kwa·či.

c   ki·ši-po·ta·hkwawoči wi·h=ki·ke·nowa·či,

d   e·h=omači·kwe·wa·či| mehtose·neniwaki,‡

e   i·niye·ne †ne·kehkamiki| e·tašihemečini e·h=ne·wa·wa·či.§

f   "šihihwi·´," e·h=iyowa·či.

g   nehkanitepehkwe=meko e·h=ki·ke·noniči.

---

*/e·h=iniči/ ʽ(obviative) saidʼ: translated ʽhe said, sitting thereʼ.

†/e·h=iniči/ ʽ(obviative) saidʼ: translated ʽshe said, sitting thereʼ.

‡/e·h=omači·kwe·wa·či/: AK ⟨|eomačikwawači|⟩.

§/ne·kehkamiki/: shape and meaning conjectured by AW; /neke·hkamiki/ HWB.

c   "Ah," she heard him say,
d   "Well, I, too, had a bad dream about myself," he said.
e   "It's true.
f   I'm told I won't live to celebrate the clan feast.
g   And I'll die beforehand," he said.
h   The woman even wept.
i   And then the woman told about her *own* experience.
j   "To be precise about what *I* dreamt:
k   'If he doesn't fuck you he'll die,' I was told in my dream.
l   He won't live to celebrate the clan feast,' " she told him.
m   "So, I don't hold back my body from you.
n   You can go ahead and do that to me.
o   In fact, that's just what we must do.
p   I'm really worried about you, that you'll die," she said to her younger brother.
17 a   "Well, it's out of the question," he said, sitting there.
b   "We'd better do it.
c   I'm already here," she said, sitting there.
d   "I'm ashamed to do that to you.
e   That must be what a manitou wants me to do, of course," he said.
f   At some point his grandfather came,
g   telling him, "*I'm* the one that blessed you, you understand."
h   "But there's a wolf besides that wants to ruin the two of you.
i   That's what *they* do.
j   Anyone fucks anyone," they were told.
k   "So, that's what he wants you to do.
l   I should have blessed the two of you right from the start," they were told.
m   "So, it is my will that you shall not die at the present time," he was told.

n   The wolf was shamed hearing this.
o   He immediately stopped appearing there.
18 a   Although at first he had stayed around there all the time.

b   And then early in the night he set out.
c   After the food for their clan feast had been put in the pots to boil,
d   the people stared in surprise
e   when they saw the one that had been killed in the place far away.
f   "Oh my!" they exclaimed.
g   He celebrated the clan feast all night long.

^h		oˑni waˑpaniki meˑyaˑwosaˑta_aˑpi-pakinaˑta| iˑnini neniwani=ʼyoˑwe| eˑh=wačaˑhaˑči,
ⁱ		eˑh=natomaˑči.
^j	otaˑnesahi=keˑhi_eˑh=kiˑšaˑkoči-=meko -naˑnaweˑnihkweˑheˑhiniči.|
^k	eˑh=miˑnaˑči kiˑšiˑ-wiˑseniniči.
^l	čeˑwiˑšwi=meko eˑh=miˑnaˑči.
^m		eˑh=niˑšoˑhkweˑweˑči neniwa.
ⁿ	keˑhtena=meko šeˑškesiˑheˑhahi.
^o	nekoti atenaˑwiˑmeˑhi eˑh=ahpiˑhtesiˑhiniči,
^p	nekoti ‖ aˑwasiˑmeˑhi eˑh=ahpiˑhtesiˑhiniči.
19 a	eˑh=kiˑšaˑkoči-=meko -kehtweˑwesiniči,|
^b	wiˑna,_iˑna neniwa.*
^c		oˑni iˑnihi owiˑwahi eˑh=ačihkwiniči čeˑwiˑšwi.|
^d	oˑni noˑšeˑniči, eˑh=čeˑwi-_ʼšinaˑkosiˑhiniči=meko oniˑčaˑneseˑhahi.
^e	čeˑwiˑšwi=keˑh=meko=ʼpi kwiˑyeseˑheˑhahi.
^f	čeˑwinaˑh=keˑh=meko eˑh=noˑšeˑniči| owiˑwahi.
^g		oˑni=wiˑna,
^h	ačaˑhmeko=meko=ʼpi eˑh=weˑpi-aˑčihaˑčimoči| eˑšahišawiči naˑhinaˑhi_eˑh=aˑpi-pakineči.
ⁱ	kiˑkeˑnowečini eˑh=aˑčihaˑčimoči eˑši-sanasanakihtoˑči iˑna_neniwa,
^j	eˑh=meˑmetaˑtehtawoči aˑtotakini owiˑyawi.

^k		oˑni kapoˑtwe=meko eˑh=anemi|-kehtesiči.
^l	omiseˑhani=keˑhi awiyaˑtoke=meko eˑh=šeˑškesiˑhiniči. ‖
20 a	kapoˑtwe,_"kaši=ʼyo=kiˑna| ketešawi eˑh=pwaˑwi- owiyeˑha -wiˑčawiwači," eˑh=inaˑči
		omiseˑhani.

^b		oˑni oniˑčaˑnesahi naˑhka=meko čeˑwinaˑhi eˑh=nepoˑhiniči.
^c	eˑh=kweˑhtaˑniteˑheˑči,
^d	eˑh=mayomayoˑči.
^e		weˑnekwaˑhita=keˑhi eˑyiˑki=meko eˑh=kweˑhtaˑniteˑheˑči.
^f	eˑh=mayomayoˑwaˑči.
^g	aˑšitami eˑh=pyeˑnotaˑkowaˑči mahweˑwani.
^h		"eheheˑ´, teˑpweˑhtawiyeˑkoha, awita| maˑhaki nepoˑhiwaˑsa,"| eˑh=ineči_neniwa.
ⁱ		"iˑniya=čaˑhi pašitoˑheˑha kiˑh=anemi-=meko -ataˑhpenamaˑkwa," eˑh=ineči.|
^j		"aˑkwi nanaˑši wiˑh=menwi-_kiˑšikiwaˑčini keniˑčaˑnesaki," eˑh=ineči_neniwa.
^k		"mana=mata ketehkweˑma manate,
^l	iˑni=mata ‖ wiˑh=poˑneˑnemehki_iˑniya| keˑteminoˑhka," eˑh=ikoči| mahweˑwani.
21 a		oˑni naˑhka| ihkweˑwa iˑni=meko eˑh=ineči.†
^b	(eˑh=šeˑškesiˑhiči=ʼyo=keˑhi.)
^c	eˑh=anwaˑčiˑči=meko iˑni wiˑh=išawiči.
^d		otaweˑmaˑwani eˑh=neˑwotiˑwaˑči,

---

*The line repairs the obviative in 19*a*.
†/oˑni/: follows a divider added later.

^h And then the next day the warparty leader that had earlier abandoned that man prepared a meal for him

ⁱ and invited him to come.

^j Now, his daughters were extremely beautiful.

^k And he gave them to him after he had finished eating.

^l He gave them both to him.

^m The man had two wives.

ⁿ They were true virgins.

^o One was a little younger than he was,

^p and one was a little older.

19 a And he was extremely good at getting game,

^b the man was.

^c And then his wives both got pregnant.

^d And when they then gave birth, his children both looked just alike.

^e And what's more, they say both were little boys.

^f And what's more, his wives both gave birth at the same time.

^g And as for him,

^h it's said to be only then that he began telling about the things that happened to him at the time when he'd been abandoned.

ⁱ Every time there was a clan feast, that man told about the difficulties he had had.

^j People enjoyed listening to him when he talked about himself.

^k In time he was getting older.

^l His elder sister, meanwhile, remained unmarried as before.

20 a In time he asked his elder sister, "Tell me, what gives with you that *you* aren't married to anyone?"

^b And then his children, again at the same time, both died.

^c He was broken-hearted,

^d and he wept and wept.

^e And their aunt was broken-hearted as well.

^f They wept and wept.

^g And this time it was the wolf that came to them.

^h The man was told, "Now now, if you two had done what I said, these two wouldn't have died."

ⁱ "So, that old man will continue to take them from you," he was told.

^j "Your children will never have the good fortune of growing up," the man was told.

^k "If, on the other hand, you fuck your sister,

^l then, in that case, that one that blessed you will stop scheming against you," the wolf said to him.

21 a And the woman also was told the same thing.

^b (Remember, she was a virgin.)

^c And she was completely willing to do that.

^d Encountering her brother someplace,

e e·h=a·čimoha·či ihkwe·wa otawe·ma·wani e·ši-kehke·nema·či,

f e·h=a·čimoči.

g e·h=a·čimoha·či,

h "i·ni='pi wi·h=po·ne·nemehki ke·temino·hka," e·h=ina·či.

i "a·kwi=ča·h=ni·na ni·yawi tepa·tamo·na·nini," e·h=ina·či.

j "ni·na=ča·hi neme·nešite·he," e·h=ina·či omise·hani.*

k e·h=ki·hki·hkimekoči=meko omise·hani.

l (nanawi='yo=ke·hi.)

m ke·keya·hi·='nahi, "o·´,_nahi=we·na´," e·h=ina·či.

n e·h=pemi-nana·heškawa·či.

o kapo·twe=meko ‖ i·ni e·h=to·tawa·či.

22 a me·kwe·tanekowa·či=meko, e·h=pya·niči i·niye·ne pašito·he·hani._

b kete·='nah=či·hi e·h=ki·yo·ma·niči i·niye·he oni·ča·nesahi.†

c (e·h=ki·ši-nepo·hiniči='yo=ke·hi.)

d e·h=kehč_a·hkwe·niči omešo·mesani.

e e·h=anemetone·moniči=meko.

f e·h=a·čimoči ihkwe·wa,

g e·h=a·čimoha·či okye·ni.

h "ane·he," e·h=ina·či okye·ni,|

i e·h=we·pi-a·ya·čimoha·či.

j ke·keya·h=meko e·h=a·čimoha·či e·šawiwa·či osi·me·hani.

k e·h=me·nešite·he·či=wi·na neniwa.|‡

l peno·či=meko e·h=iši-me·neši·htawa·či omise·hani.

m o·ni kapo·twe| e·h=na·kwa·niči ne·topa·hahi,

n e·h=wi·če·we·či.

o še·ški e·h=ačihkwiniči owi·wahi če·wi·šwi,

p wi·na=ké·hi e·h=natopaniči.‖ §

23 a aškači e·h=pye·notamowa·či aša·hi-ma·wa·ka·hi,

b meše=meko e·h=inekihkwa·hiniki.

c a·kwi=ke·hi='pi wi·h=po·si|-ma·nwikamikesiniči,¶

d anehki·h=meko.

e wi·nwa·wa=na·hka a·kwi='pi ma·ne·wa·čini.

f e·h=a·čimoči.|

g "nahi´, ni·hka·netike, i·noki a·kwi=ni·na wi·h=pya·ya·nini.

h i·ni=meko e·h=a·hpeči·ya·ni," e·h=ina·či owi·hka·nahi.

i mo·hki·htamowa·či, i·ya·hi e·h=tašiheči.

---

*/omise·hani/: AK ⟨.oniseAni.⟩

†/oni·ča·nesahi/: AK ⟨.oničanesani.|⟩.

‡/wi·na/: a preceding divider was added later.

§/=ké·hi/: to bear emphatic stress (IG).

¶/kamike/: AK ⟨kemike⟩.

e   the woman reported what she had learned about her brother,

f   and she told about herself.

g   Telling him about it,

h   she said to him, "Then, I was told, the one that blessed you will stop scheming against you."

i   "So, I do not hold back my body from you," she told him.

j   "Well, *I'm* ashamed," he told his sister.

k   His sister pressed him hard.

l   (Now, it was in a remote place.)

m   Finally, with all that, he said to her, "Oh, alright, let's get to it!"

n   He nudged her legs into position with his body.

o   And right soon he did it to her.

22 a   When they were well into their coupling, that old man came there.

b   And here he was, with a change of heart, carrying on his back those children he had had.

c   (Remember, they had died.)

d   His grandfather was furious

e   and went away muttering.

f   The woman told what had happened to her.

g   She told her mother about it.

h   "Mother," she said to her mother,

i   and she started in telling her about it.

j   And eventually she told her what she and her younger brother had done.

k   The man was ashamed, however.

l   For a long time he was ashamed around his older sister.

m   Then some time later a warparty set out,

n   and he went along.

o   Only when both his wives were pregnant

p   did *he* go to war.

23 a   After a while they came to a small Sioux village,

b   one of modest size.

c   Now, they were said not to be going to have a whole lot of tepees,

d   only a few.

e   And there were also said not to be many of *them*.

f   And he made a statement about himself.

g   "Listen, my friends, as for me, this time I shall not come back.

h   Now I have gone for good," he said to his companions.

i   When they attacked, he was killed over there.

j   i·ni=meko iši|-nekoti e·h=neseči.

k   i·nihi=wi·na=’pi_mo·hki·htawa·wa·čihi e·h=ča·katahwa·wa·či=meko.

l   o·ni me·ya·wosa·ta i·ya·h=meko meše=na·hina·hi e·h=aškwi·či.

m   i·ya·h=meko e·h=tanahkate·wi·či.

n   e·h=natomeči=ke·hi,

o   wi·h=na·ni·miniči e·h=išimeči a·pi-awana·čihi,

p   e·h=ša·kwe·nemoči=meko— ‖ *

24 a   wi·h=na·ni·miniči e·h=išimemeči.†

b   e·h=pwa·wi-ma·mata·nahkiwihto·wa·či.

c   o·ni e·h=kehči-mahkate·wi·či i·niya a·pi|-mečimi·ta.

d   “nemečimi=koči,” e·h=iči.

e   ma·nwipepo·nwe=meko i·nahi e·h=taši-ma·mahkate·wi·či.

f   o·ni kapo·twe e·h=nekwačihike·weniwiniki na·hina·hi,

g   e·h=po·ni-=meko -ka·škiheči.

h   o·ni nekoti i·tepi e·h=a·či oškinawe·ha.

i   aseni=či·hi e·h=či·tapihte·niki.‡

j   e·h=wa·pataki,

k   e·h=na·kwa·či,

l   we·to·škinawe·miničihi e·h=a·čimoha·či.§

m   “me·kwe·he·=’niya me·hkate·wi·ta aseniwi·toke,” e·h=ina·či.

n   “a·kwi·=’nahi ne·wakini.

o   ke·keya·h=meko i·tepi neta e·h=owi·ke·hiči.

p   i·ya·h=pye·ya·ya·ni, aseni=či·hi| i·nahi ‖ či·tapihte·wi,” e·h=iči.

25 a   e·h=natomeči a·ya·či·hpana·ha,¶

b   e·h=kwa·koho·taki.

c   “aseniwikwe·ni·=’pi me·hkate·wi·ta,” e·h=iči.

d   e·ški=meko mehtose·neniwaki| e·h=se·kesiwa·či.

e   i·tepi| e·h=ina·waneti·wa·či,

f   e·h=ma·ne·wa·či.

g   o·ni nese·ma·wani e·h=sahkahamawa·wa·či.

h   asayani=’pi wa·peškye·ki·hiničini e·h=neneškišima·wa·či,

i   wa·peškye·ki·hiničini e·na·samapiniči e·h=neneškisetawa·wa·či.

j   i·na=’pi=meko·=’na nese·ma·wa se·hkahama·ke·ka.

k   e·h=kehči-natota·sowa·či mehtose·neniwiweni neno·te·waki.

l   nehkaniki·šekwe=meko e·h=ma·ne·wa·či.

m   e·h=owi·kinitehe e·h=wi·ke·čina·kwihto·wa·či,

---

*/mo/: has an extra stroke.

†/e·h=išimemeči/: the shift to the obviative is translated by supplying ‘the men’.

‡/či·tapihte·-/ ‘sit (inanimate)’ (a guess by AW; the word is otherwise unknown).

§‘the warparty-leader’s men’; *lit.*, ‘his young men’.

¶/a·ya·či·hpana·ha/ (FM, HWB, LYB): also heard as /a·ya·hči·pana·ha/ (HWB 2x) and
 /a·ya·hči·hpana·ha/ (LYB).

^j He was the only one killed.

^k But it is said that they clubbed to death all of the ones that they attacked.

^l   And back home the leader of the warparty stayed behind a little ways off.

^m And over there he fasted.

ⁿ What's more, when he was asked to come

^o and told that the ones he had taken with him should have a war dance,

^p he was quite unwilling—

24 a when the men were told they should have a war dance.

^b And they had no celebration.

^c   And then that leader who had lost a man fasted intensely.

^d "Remember, I did lose a man," he said.

^e For many winters he fasted there.

^f   And then one year at the time when the corn was being hilled,

^g all at once he could no longer be heard.

^h   And then a certain young man went there.

ⁱ And what he saw was a stone in a sitting position.

^j He looked at it

^k and came back,

^l and he informed the warparty-leader's men.

^m   "I think the one who was fasting must have turned to stone," he told them.

ⁿ   "I didn't see him now.

^o Ultimately, I went to his camp.

^p And when I got there, I found a stone in a sitting position there," he said.

25 a   The town-crier was called for,

^b and he shouted,

^c saying, "The one who's fasting is reported to have turned to stone."

^d   The people were scared as the dickens.

^e They went there in a group,

^f a lot of them.

^g And then they offered tobacco to him.

^h They're said to have spread out a small white (deer) hide,

ⁱ spreading out a small white one in front of where he sat.

^j   That was said to be (for) the tobacco that was offered.

^k   The Indians prayed a great deal for life.

^l All day long there were a lot of them.

^m They fixed up the house he had lived in to look neat and tidy,

n   e·h=menwapahkwawa·wa·či. ‖ *
26 a   meše=we·=meko e·h=wi·ke·či·hkamowa·či i·ni| wi·kiya·pi.
b   ki·ši-menwi·hkamowa·či i·ni wi·kiya·pi, e·h=na·na·kwa·wa·či.

c   o·ni oni·ča·nesahi=ʼpi i·niya aša·hi-ma·wa·ka·neki e·tašiheta,|
d   nekoti ki·yese·hani, nekoti iškwe·se·hani.
e   a·kwi=ke·hi·=ʼnahi=ʼpi na·hka| ke·ko·hi išawiničini,
f   e·h=mehtose·neniwiniči=meko.
g   e·h=tepa·na·sowa·či,
h   wa·wi·tawi=meko oči e·h=tepa·neči.
i   o·ni osekwiswa·wani e·h=pemenekowa·či.
j   e·h=nešikaheči,
k   nešihka=meko osekwiswa·wani e·h=wi·čiha·wa·či.
l   mahkwa·či=meko e·h=pemena·či i·nihi apeno·hahi.
m   o·ni| aškači=meko meše ki·h-a·ya·nekineniči,
n   e·h=mi·ka·ti·wa·či, ‖
27 a   aša·hahi, kome·či·hahi e·h=iši-ni·šo·hka·kowa·či,†
b   e·h=kehteneti·wa·či| meškwahki·haki.
c   o·ni·=ʼniki=ye·toke·=ʼpi e·h=pema·mowa·tehe ošemi·hani na·hka onekwa·hani.
d   e·h=kahkisowa·či=meko| e·h=taši-aseniwiwa·tehe.
e   e·h=ašwahte·či kwi·yese·ha.
f   po·neneti·hkiwiki, e·h=kwi·nomeči i·niki.
g   "mešena·petoke," e·h=iyowa·či.
h   o·ni e·h=natomeči ne·ha·pi·ha, wi·h=te·pa·pama·či.
i   "o·´, ayo·h=meko anemya·ka·ha e·h=a·tesa·pehkateniki e·h=awiwa·či," e·h=iči.
j   "šewe·na aseniwiwaki," e·h=iči.
k   i·tepi e·h=a·wa·či e·h=tana·čimoweči.
l   ayo·h=či·hi e·h=či·tapiniči ihkwe·wani,
m   iškwe·se·hani e·h=so·kenemeči. ‖
28 a   o·ni kwi·yese·ha e·h=nemasoči, e·h=ašwahte·či.
b   e·h=se·kina·kwahki.
c   e·h=mayo·wa·či we·ni·ča·nesičiki,
d   e·h=neškimeči.|
e   "a·kwi=ma·h=ma·haki nepo·hiwa·čini," e·h=ineči.
f   "ka·kike·neniwaki=ma·h=ma·haki,"| e·h=ineči.
g   "wi·h=ka·kike·neniwiwaki," e·h=ineči.
h   nye·wokoni e·h=pemi|-ma·ne·wa·či mehtose·neniwaki i·nahi.
i   o·ni nye·wokonakateniki e·h=sahkahamawa·wa·či.
j   ča·ča·tepi=meko asayahi neswi wa·wa·peškye·kiničihi i·nahi e·h=neneškisetawa·wa·či.
k   nenešiwi=taswi nese·ma·wa i·nahi e·h=apiči.
l   na·kwa·wa·či,

---

*AK ⟨kwawa⟩ was changed from ⟨kwewe⟩.
†The preverb /iši/ is rendered 'in it', as if literally 'to do so'.

n putting nice cattail mats on it for him.

26 a In fact, they fixed up that whole house with care.

b And after they had put the house in good shape, they left.

c And as for what's said of the children of the one who had been killed in the Sioux village,

d one was a boy and one was a little girl.

e And another thing, in this case it's said that nothing happened to them.

f They lived.

g And they were cherished.

h They were loved by both families.

i And their aunt took care of them.

j A house was built just for them,

k and they lived alone with their aunt.

l She gave those children a quiet upbringing.

m And then much later, after they had gotten to be a pretty good size,

n the Meskwakis fought,

27 a being ganged up against in it by the Siouxs and the Comanches together,

b and having a big war.

c And apparently they then fled, the story goes, she and her niece and nephew.

d And they turned to stone in the place where they were hiding.

e The boy was holding his bow ready to shoot.

f After the fighting stopped, those people were missed.

g People said, "They must have been captured."

h And a seer was called for, to use his power to see them.

i "Oh, they're a little downstream from here where the rock stands separate," he said.

j "But they've turned to stone," he said.

k They went to the place referred to.

l And here was the woman sitting,

m and the girl being held.

28 a And the boy was standing, holding his bow ready to shoot.

b It was a scary scene.

c The mothers wept,

d and they were admonished.

e "They aren't dead, you understand," they were told.

f "These are eternal people, you understand," they were told.

g "They will be eternal people," they were told.

h For four days there were many people there.

i And then after four days they offered tobacco to them.

j They spread out three white deerskins there, one for each of them.

k There was a tremendous amount of tobacco there.

l When they left,

m eˑh=aˑčimohaˑwaˑči wiˑh=poˑni-wiˑčeˑnomaˑwaˑči.

n oˑni weˑyoˑšisemita iˑtepi_eˑh=aˑči. ‖ *

29 a eˑh=ašenoniči=čiˑhi iˑniyeˑhe.

b eˑh=aˑčimoči.|

c "ašenowaki iˑniyeˑke," eˑh=iči.†

d mesoˑteˑwe=meko eˑh=wiˑtamaˑtiˑwaˑči eˑh=ašenoniči.|

e "ašenowaki=koči| iˑniyeˑka eˑseniwičiki," eˑh=itiˑwaˑči.

f oˑni| naˑhka=meko iˑyaˑhi eˑh=mawi_taši-opahkiwihtoˑwaˑči eˑh=apinitehe.

g eˑh=naˑniˑmiwaˑči,

h eˑh=kaˑškehtawaˑwaˑči naˑmahkamiki waˑwaˑkahaminičini kwiˑyeseˑhani.

i iˑnah=čaˑhi=ʼpi taneˑnemeˑwaki naˑmahkamiki iˑnihi.|

j oˑni weˑniˑčaˑnesičiki eˑh=kehči-mahkateˑwiˑwaˑči,

k eˑh=nataweˑnemaˑwaˑči eˑšawinikweˑni oniˑčaˑneswaˑwahi.

l mešeˑ=ʼnah=meko meˑmetaˑswawahiˑme eˑh=pemi-‖ mahkateˑwiˑwaˑči.

30 a eˑh=aˑčimoheči eˑh=awiniči.

b keˑhtena=meko| iˑnahi eˑh=kehkahamoweči eˑh=awiniči.

c "aˑkwi_nanaˑši wiˑh=neˑweˑkwini," eˑh=ineči.

d "manetoˑwiwaki.

e aˑkwi-kanaˑkwa mešeˑ=mekoˑ=ʼnahi wiˑh=kiˑwi-_noseˑwaˑči," eˑh=ineči.

f "kekehkeˑnemekowaˑwaki eˑši_natawenemeˑkwe.

g ašeweˑna| aˑkwi-kanaˑkwa wiˑh=mehtoˑči-neˑweˑkwe," eˑh=ineči.

h "mešeˑ=ʼnah=meko kiˑh=nanoˑči-kehkyaˑpwa.

i iˑni šeˑški eˑneˑnemenaˑkwe," eˑh=ineči.

j "kiˑh=poˑni-=čaˑhi_mahkateˑwiˑpwa,"| eˑh=ineči iˑniki| ihkweˑwaki.

k eˑh=poˑni|-maˑmahkateˑwiˑwaˑči.

l iˑni eˑnaˑčimekosiwaˑči. ‖

---

*Lit., ʻone who had him, her, or them as grandchild(ren)ʼ, but presumably the mothersʼ father.

†/iˑniyeˑke/: an unusual variant of /iˑniyeˑka/ for AK, but used by others.

^m they told them that they would not be joining them in activities anymore.

ⁿ And then the children's grandfather went there.

^{29 a} And he found that they were gone.

^b He reported it,

^c saying, "They are gone."

^d Everyone told everyone else that they were gone,

^e saying, "You know, the ones that turned to stone are gone."

^f And then they went over to the place where they had been again and had a jolly time.

^g And when they danced,

^h they could hear the boy whooping under the ground.

ⁱ So it's said they concluded that they were under the ground there.

^j And the mothers fasted hard.

^k seeking to learn what had happened to their children.

^l They kept on until they had both fasted for a good ten years.

^{30 a} And they were told where they were.

^b Sure enough, they were where it had been said they were.

^c "You will never see them," they were told.

^d "They are spirits.

^e It's not possible for them to roam about at will," they were told.

^f "They know that you sought to find out about them.

^g But it's impossible for you to see them openly," they were told.

^h "You will keep on living until old age.

ⁱ That is your only blessing," they were told.

^j "So, you must stop fasting," those women were told.

^k And they stopped fasting.

^l That's the story that's told about them.

Kashawîha

Kashawiha

kashawîha

Alfred Kiyana[*]

1 a   kašawi·ha.[†]

b   o=meše=wi·na=ʼpi=ma·haki| nekotayaki e·h=owi·kiwa·či owi·weti·he·haki.

c   e·h=nekotiha·wa·či=ʼpi oni·ča·nese·hwa·wani.

d   kašawi·ha=ʼpi, išisoniwani,

e   e·h=wa·waneška·hiniči.

f   "nahi´, nekwi·hi,"| e·h=ina·či meše·=ʼnah=nekotenwi,

g   "mahkwa·či_wi·h=awihawiya·ni ketene·nemene," e·h=ina·či.

h   meše=mekoho e·h=inekineniči.[‡]

i   aškači=meko, "a·kwi=ča·h=meko kana·kwa," e·h=ikoči okwisani.

j   "a·kwi=ča·h wi·h=pešeke·neta·kaniwiyanini i·ni=meko išawiyane," e·h=ina·či=meko.

k   ke·keya·h=meko, "ano·se, a·kwi=ma·h=natawe·nemena·nini ke·ko·hi wi·h=išihišimiyani.

l   na·hka=ke·ko·hi e·šiwane·ni, kwayahkwi=mekoho ‖ na·kwa·hka·ha," e·h=ina·či o·sani.

2 a   e·h=po·ni·=meko -kanawiči neniwa.

b   "a·kwi=koči mahkwa·tesiye·kwini ayo·h=mani e·h=ki·wita·ye·kwe,

       e·h=mehtose·neniwiye·kwe," e·h=ineči neniwa.

c   "ne·škinawiwane·ni=ke·hi, kwayahkwi=meko na·kwa·hka·ha.

d   meše=meko iha·hka·ha,"_e·h=ineči pašito·he·ha.

e   "a·kwi=koči e·h=neškino·na·ni oči·=mani -išihišimena·nini.[§]

f   e·h=tepa·nena·ni| we·či-a·yaha·ya·čimohena·ni.

g   neškino·na·ne·=ke·hi, awita=meko nana·ši kano·nenaka·ha.

h   ʼmeše=meko e·šawikwe·ni išawiče,' ine·nemenaka·ha," e·h=ineči kwi·yese·ha.

i   "a·kwi=ča·h| wi·h=kaški·=ne·h=ni·na -te·pwe·hto·na·nini,"

       e·h=iši·=meko| -ki·hki·hkowe·či.

j   "o·ho´, kete·=ʼnah,=nekwi·hi," e·h=ineči,‖

3 a   e·h=ina·či okwisani.

b   e·h=po·ni·=meko ke·ko·hi -ina·či.

c   "meše=meko e·šawikwe·ni kwi·yese·ha," e·h=ine·nemekoči.[¶]

d   e·h=pwa·wi·=ke·hi -nahi-mahkate·wi·na·či_okwise·hani.

e   (i·ni·=ʼyo=ke·h=meko e·h=iši_nekotiha·wa·či.)

f   e·h=kehtwe·wesiniči=ke·hi ki·h_ki·šikiniči.

g   ča·ki=meko ke·ko·hi e·h=no·hkihto·niči.

h   šewe·n=e·yi·ki e·h=ki·ša·koči·=meko| wa·waneška·hiniči,

i   e·h=pwa·wi·=meko -nenohta·koči.

---

[*]The manuscript is NAA 2664.7; it has 25 pages.

[†]Written as a title at the top of the page.

[‡]/meše=mekoho/: AK ⟨.me|še.mekoo.⟩.

[§]/ški/: AK ⟨ki⟩.

[¶]/e·h=ine·nemekoči/: AK ⟨.ei|nenekoči.⟩.

Kashawiha
Translated by Ives Goddard and Lucy Thomason

1 a   Kashawiha.

b   They say there was one married couple living someplace or other, just them.
c   And they had only one child.
d   His name was Kashawiha,
e   and he was a bad actor.
f   "Listen, son," [the man] told him one time,
g   "I want you to always stay around quietly."
h   The boy was fairly big.
i   After quite some time his son responded, "Well, that's really not possible."
j   And he insisted to him: "Well, no one will care to have you if you're that way."
k   Eventually he said to his father, "See, father, I don't want you to tell me to do things.
l   And, if you should tell me to do things, I'd have done with it and leave."
2 a   The man said nothing more.
b   "You know, you aren't exactly of a quiet nature staying here, you of the human race,"
   the man was told.
c   "And another thing, if you should dislike me, I'd have done with it and leave.
d   I'd go just anywhere," the older man was told.
e   "I don't keep telling you to do this because I dislike you, you know.
f   It's because I love you that I always keep giving you advice.
g   Also, if I disliked you, I would never speak to you.
h   My thought for you would be, 'Let him go ahead and do whatever he may do,' " the boy
   was told.
i   And he persisted, saying, "Well, *I* won't be able to do what *you* say."
j   "So *that's* it. Well, that's too bad, my son," was the reply,
3 a   what the man said to his son.
b   And he didn't say anything more to him,
c   thinking, "Let the boy go and do what he will."

d   And another thing: he never made his young son fast.
e   (By the way, he was the only child they had.)
f   And another thing: their son had a knack for getting game when he grew up.
g   He killed everything with ease.
h   But he was an extremely bad actor, as well,
i   and didn't mind him at all.

j   eˑh=nekotikamikesiˑhiwaˑči=keˑhi.

k   eˑh=pwaˑwi-wiˑčikeˑkeˑwaˑči.

l   eˑh=pwaˑwi-wiˑči-maˑwaˑsetoˑkeˑwaˑči.

m   mešeˑ=ʼnah=nekotenwi eˑh=šiˑšaˑči| pašitoˑha,

n   eˑh=kiˑmaˑhaˑči okwisani,

o   eˑh=anawičikeˑniči.

p   kehči-mešihkeˑhani eˑh=anawinaˑniči,

q   eˑh=kahkisoˑhtawaˑči okwisani. ‖

4 a   kapoˑtwe eˑh=weˑpinekweˑsaˑniči,

b   eˑh=sesekešeˑniki.|

c   aškoteˑwi=meko eˑh=neˑtaki,

d   okwisani naˑhinaˑhi peˑkačikeˑniči.

e   iˑna=keˑhi| apina=meko eˑh=aˑpoˑškečeˑhoči kehči-mešihkeˑha.

f   mešeˑ=ʼnah=meko niˑšenwi_eˑh=aˑči-pakamemeči| mešihkeˑhani.

g   niˑšoˑnameki peˑkamemeči,

h   iˑnini mešihkeˑhani=čiˑhi manetoˑwani=čiˑhi.

i   nanoˑpehka=meko eˑh=ahkwiniči,

j   eˑh=ašaˑtiˑhaˑnoweˑniči,

k   naˑhka| eˑh=ašaˑtiˑhinaniweˑniči.

l   eˑh=seˑkesiči.

m   kiˑši-=meko meˑmeˑčiwi -nesaˑniči,

n   eˑh=ketoniči,

o   eˑh=nenemehkiwimoniči.|

p   seseˑsi=meko eˑh=pyeˑtaˑnahkwateniki.

q   noˑmake=meko eˑh=kiˑši-pyeˑmikateniki,

r   eˑh=kehči-kemiyaˑniki.

s   kiˑši-kemiyaˑniki, eˑh=ašenoniči| iˑniyeˑne‖ eˑšaˑtiˑhaˑnowaˑničini.|

5 a   "šihihwiˑ´," eˑh=išiteˑheˑči.

b   nešihka_okwisani waˑnatohka eˑh=kiˑkiˑyoseˑniči.|

c   "šiˑ´,_weˑnah=nekwisa manetoˑwiwa," eˑh=išiteˑheˑči.|

d   iˑni=meko eˑh=iši-naˑkwaˑči.

e   iˑyaˑh=meko pyeˑyaˑči,| eˑh=aˑčimohaˑči owiˑweˑhani._

f   "metemoˑke, weˑnahiˑ=ʼniya_kekwiseˑhenaˑna manetoˑwiwa," eˑh=inaˑči.

g   "eˑh=aˑpi-šiˑšaˑyaˑni iˑnoki,

h   neneˑwaˑwa eˑh=nesaˑči| manetoˑwani,

i   aškičaˑh=keˑhi kehči-mešihkeˑhani.

j   keyeˑhapa-keˑh=wiˑnaˑ=ʼna meˑnetoˑwitehe mešihkeˑha._

k   niˑna=keˑhi, 'keˑhtena=meko mešihkeˑhiˑtoke,' netešiteˑhe," eˑh=iči.

l   "keyeˑhapa=keˑh=wiˑna| eˑšaˑtiˑhaˑnowaˑta,

m   naˑhka=meko eˑšaˑtiˑhinaniwaˑta," eˑh=iči.

n   "kiˑši-=čaˑh=_nesaˑči, eˑh=ketoči.

o   nenemehkiwa=meko mehtoˑči tanweˑtamwa," ‖ eˑh=iči pašitoˑheˑha.

6 a   "naˑhinaˑhiˑ=ʼyo=keˑhi_peˑkamaˑči,|

^j And one more thing: there was just that one family of them.

^k They didn't live where there were other people.

^l Their house wasn't with any other house.

^m One time the older man went hunting,

ⁿ and he spied on his son

^o as he was sneaking up on his prey.

^p His son was sneaking up on a gigantic snapping turtle,

^q and he hid from him.

4 a Suddenly he saw him swing his arm,

^b and there were sparks.

^c He actually saw fire

^d at the moment his son struck his prey.

^e What's more, that gigantic snapping turtle was even flipped over by the strike.

^f Even a second time he saw the snapping turtle struck again.

^g And the second time it was struck,

^h what he saw as a snapping turtle he could see was a manitou.

ⁱ It was massively long

^j and had an arrow-shaped tail

^k and also an arrow-shaped tongue.

^l He was frightened.

^m After the one being watched had killed it utterly,

ⁿ he gave a cry,

^o making the sound of a Thunderer.

^p Clouds quickly came flying.

^q And in a very short time they had arrived,

^r and it rained hard.

^s After the rain, that one that had had a tail like an arrow had disappeared.

5 a "Criminy!" he thought.

^b His son was walking about by himself as if nothing had happened.

^c "Gee, so my son is a manitou!" he thought.

^d And right away he set out for home.

^e When he got back there, he told his young wife.

^f "So, my wife, it turns out, that that young son of ours is a manitou!" he told her.

^g "Coming back from hunting now,

^h I saw him kill a manitou.

ⁱ What's more, at first it was just a gigantic snapping turtle.

^j But in fact, as it turns out, that snapping turtle was a manitou.

^k Understand, I thought it must really be a snapping turtle," he said.

^l "But as it turns out, it was one not only with a tail like an arrow,

^m but with a tongue like an arrow, as well," he said.

ⁿ "So, after he killed it, he gave a cry.

^o It was as if a Thunderer was making the sound," the older man said.

6 a "And by the way, when he struck it,

^b mani=meko e·ši-we·pinekwe·sa·čini, se·sesekeše·niwi," e·h=iči.

^c "i·ni=ča·hi,_'we·nahi maneto·wiwa,"| we·či-išite·he·ya·ni," e·h=iči pašito·ha.

^d kwi·yena e·hkwa·čimoči, e·h=po·našiniči sa·kiči,

^e e·h=pye·či-pi·tike·niči.|

^f e·h=we·pi-ašama·či okwiswa·wani.

^g o·ni·='na pašito·he·ha nasikanani e·h=ki·wi-ki·škahaki.

^h na·hka=meko apwa·čikanek=oči e·h=apwa·čike·wa·či.[*]

ⁱ ahpeme=ke·hi e·h=nasa·hkohesowa·či.

^j ki·ši-ča·ki-ki·šesamowa·či,

^k e·h=kehči-ašihto·či| metemo·he·ha no·hkaha·ni,|

^l na·hka opiškwa·ki e·h=ahto·či,

^m keneki=meko ašihkanwi, e·h=kenekiseto·či.

ⁿ ma·ne=meko e·h=ki·ši-anaho·to·či ‖ opiškwayani,

^{7 a} na·hkači| no·hkaha·ni e·h=ki·šihto·či,|

^b ma·ne·he=meko, ma·ne=we·=mekoho.

^c še·ški=meko ne·nehkaniki·šekwe e·h=wa·wi·seniči pašito·ha.

^d ki·ši|-wi·seničini, e·h=kehč_atama·či.

^e ki·ši-atahatama·čini, e·h=kehči_nepa·či.

^f pa·pekwa=meko to·hki·čini,| e·h=we·pisenye·či pašito·ha.

^g kapo·twe_e·h=aka·wa·taki wi·h=owi·wiči oškinawe·ha,

^h e·h=a·čimoha·či| okye·ni.

ⁱ "a·kwi=ča·h=meko kehke·nemena·nini a·m_otena·wate·ni ihkwe·waki," e·h=ikoči okye·ni.

^j "ni·na·na='yo=wi·na mana ko·sa| aye·=meko našawaye netowi·weti·pena.|

^k šewe·na ča·katamwa| o·te·weni asa·wišo·niya·hi-šo·kesi·ha," e·h=iniči.|

^l "o·ni=ni·na·na mana| ko·sa e·h=pi·tahwi·namekehe=ye·toke, ‖

^{8 a} a·kwi=ke·hi_tahtakwi.

^b a·yatehči·me·h=meko taši-pi·tahwi·nami·ke·ni.[†]

^c kapo·twe=ča·h=meko neka·ška·škehtawa·wa| me·yo·ta._

^d keye·hapa=ke·h=mana_ko·sa me·yo·tehe.

^e wi·na=menehta_keči·kwe·ni.

^f me·menwina·h=meko_neka·ška·škehtawa·wa.

^g kapo·twe e·h=keči·ya·ni,

^h keye·hapa=ke·hi pe·hkote·kehe.

ⁱ nekeči=meko.

^j 'aše=ye·toke=meko·='ni e·šikeki,'| netešite·he.

^k man=e·na·piya·ni,| nene·ta aškote·wi e·taneše·ki,

^l i·tepi e·h=a·ya·ni.|

^m keye·hapa=ke·h=mana=ko·sa e·h=mehči_pehtawasotehe.

ⁿ i·ya·h=pye·ya·ya·ni, neniwa·či·hi.

^o meše=we·=meko ahpi·htesi·hiwa,

---

[*]/kanek=o/ (LT): AK ⟨kanako⟩.

[†]/pi·tahwi·nami·ke·ni/: AK ⟨.pitawi|nemikeni.⟩.

just as he swung his arm each time, sparks flew," he said.

"So that's why I thought, 'Well, that's it: he's a manitou!' " the older man said.

Just as he finished his telling, they heard him drop his load of game outside,

and he came on in.

She set about giving their son something to eat.

At that, the older man went around to different spots and cut roasting spits.

And they roasted meat using a roasting rack besides.

They roasted their meat on spits set in the ground at the same time.

When they had finished cooking all of it,

the young old lady made a lot of pemmican,

and she put it in bladders,

mixed with suet, mixing it together.

She had filled a good many bladders

and made pemmican,

a good bit of it, quite a lot, in fact.

All the older man did all day every day was eat meal after meal.

Whenever he had finished his meals, he would smoke up a storm.

And whenever he had smoked his pipes, he would sleep a deep sleep.

And whenever he woke up, the older man would immediately start eating.

And there came a time when the young man had a longing to get married,

and he informed his mother.

"Well, I don't know where you might get women from," his mother told him.

"Your father here and I were actually married already long ago.

But the Golden Dragon ate up the whole town," she said.   ["lizard, salamander"]

"Your father and I were buried in the ground then, apparently,

though not together.

It seems we were buried a little ways from each other.

Well, at some point I kept hearing the sound of someone weeping.

And it turned out to be your father weeping.

He must have come out first.

And I kept hearing him every so often.

When at some point I came out,

I didn't realize it was night.

I came on out

and thought, 'I guess that's just how it is.'

As soon as I looked around, I saw a fire burning,

and I went to it.

And it turned out that your father had made a fire for himself out in the open.

When I got to it, I saw there was a man there.

But actually he was pretty young,

p   ki·šiki·hiwa=meko.

q   e·ši-=meko -ne·wiči, pye·či|-pasekwi·wa,_

r   e·h=pemi_nawateniči

s   (ki·šišinwa=’yo)|

t   e·h=wi·hpe·maki.

u   natawa·či=meko·=’ni e·h=ona·pe·miya·ni,” e·h=iči.

v   “ ‘ki·h=owi·weti·pena=meko,’ ‖ netekwa=’yo=ke·hi.

9 a   ni·na=ke·hi| neteškwe·se·h=meko,” e·h=iči.|

b   “natawa·či·=’nahi netona·pe·mi,” e·h=iči.

c   okwisani,| “me·kwe·h=ča·hi·=’na=meko=ye·toke ki·wi_ča·ča·kataka o·te·wenani,”
e·h=iniči.

d   okye·ni, “a·kwi=ča·h,=nekwi·hi,| kehke·nemakini a·mi|-otena·wate·ni ihkwe·waki,”
e·h=ineči neniwa.|

e   “a·kwi=me·kwe·h=meko ayo·hi awiwa·čini mehtose·neniwaki,

f   ayo·hi ahki·ki,” e·h=ina·či okwisani.

g   “o·´,_ni·h=kehke·nema·waki=meko e·h=awikwe·hiki,” e·h=iči i·na neniwa.

h   e·h=ši·ša·či.|

i   ahpene·či=meko e·h=natawe·nema·či mehtose·neniwahi.

j   ke·keya·h=meko e·h=ka·hka·hki-aka·wa·na·či ihkwe·wahi,*

k   meše=meko·=’nahi.|

l   a·kwi=ke·h=me·mye·hči we·wenesiničihi,

m   meše=meko·=’nahi.

n   “kaši=meko wi·h=towi kehtesi·hinite,” ‖ e·h=išite·he·či.

10 a   a·kwi ma·mahka·či wi·h=aškikiniči,

b   meše=meko·=’nahi.

c   e·h=wa·waneška·hiči=ke·h=meko ahpeme.|

d   meše=nekotenwi [e·h=mi·na·wite·he·či,] mehteno·h=meko okye·ni
e·h=neši_ihkwe·winiči.†

e   e·h=a·čimoha·či okye·ni.

f   “kete·pwe,” e·h=ina·či.|

g   “a·kwi ayo·h=nekotahi awiwa·čini mehtose·neniwaki.

h   ki·na=meko=ye·hapa keneši-ihkwe·wi,” e·h=ina·či.‡

i   “kašina·hi,” e·h=išite·he·či.|

j   meše·=’nah=nekotenwi e·h=pena·winiki,

k   “awahi·maki=ča·h=ni·h=ki·wi-pi·pemwa·waki papahki·haki,” e·h=iči.

l   “ke·htena. pe·hki=koh=wi·keno·ki,” e·h=iči pašito·he·ha.

m   e·h=na·kwa·či.

---

*/ka·hka·hki/ (AW); also heard as /ka·ka·hki/ (AW).

†Word omitted.

‡/=ye·hapa/: AK ⟨.yeapa.⟩.

^p   just barely grown up, in fact.
^q   As soon as he saw me, he stood up facing me,
^r   and he took me in hand directly
^s   (he having lain down again),
^t   and I slept with him.
^u   There was nothing for it then but for me to take him as my husband," she said.
^v   "I should say, he told me, 'We must get married.'
9 a   And consider that *I* was then still just a girl," she said.
^b   "With all that, there was nothing for it but for me to take him as my husband," she said.
^c   And her son said, "Well, I believe it was quite likely that creature that goes around eating up whole towns."
^d   And his mother: "So, my son, I don't know where you might get women from," so the man was told.
^e   "I don't believe there are any of the human race here,
^f   on this earth," she told her son.
^g   "Well, I shall discover where they might be," that man said.

^h   And he hunted.
ⁱ   Always he sought to find others of the human race.
^j   And in time he yearned with a deep longing for women,
^k   any at all.
^l   So it wasn't necessary for him that they be pretty ones—
^m   any at all.
ⁿ   And he thought, "What difference will it make if they're the older ones!"
10 a   For him it didn't have to be that they were young—
^b   any at all.
^c   And, remember, he was at the same time quite a bad actor.

^d   And a time came when he [realized] that there was just his mother as the only woman.
^e   And he said this to his mother.
^f   "What you say is true," she told him.
^g   "There aren't any human beings anywhere here.
^h   So, it turns out *you're* the only woman there is," he told her.
ⁱ   "Well now!" she thought.

^j   One time in the summer
^k   he said, "Well, I'm going to go different places and shoot soft-shell turtles."
^l   "You should do that. They certainly do taste good," the older man said.
^m   And he set out.

n   o·ni e·h=ki·wi-pi·pemwa·či papahki·hahi.

o   ma·ne=meko e·h=nesa·či.

p   ki·ši-wi·nawi·naniha·či,|

q   e·h=na·kwa·či aya·pami.

r   (wa·siki·nahte·hani=’yo| e·h=ki·wi-ayo·či e·h=papahki·hehke·či.) ‖

11 a   meše·=’nah=nekotenwi_i·ya·h=ašiči pye·ya·či_e·h=owi·ke·hiwa·či,

b   mani e·h=ši_keči·či, e·h=taši-anenwi·niči omeso·ta·nahi,

c   aya·pami e·h=oči·kwe·sahoči.

d   a·sami e·h=oči|-mawi-kotawi·či,

e   e·h=kotawi·htawa·či._

f   meše·=’nah=meko e·h=pye·tana·moči e·h=taši-anenwi·niči okye·ni,

g   e·h=nemasoniči,

h   e·h=wa·pama·či.

i   e·h=ki·ša·koči-mama·kipwa·me·niči.

j   ke·keya·h=meko e·h=pemi_či·kako·te·na·či.

k   mečemo·ka=ke·hi,

l   “aše=meko či·kakwipoko·te·wani,” e·h=išite·he·či| mečemo·ka._*

m   kapo·twe mečemo·ka po·si=na·waka·me=meko e·h=ina·šowi·či.

n   i·ya·hi ohkwe·kaneki ki·š_ahkomi·či, e·h=ketenaki oko·te·hi,

o   e·h=ko·kepye·naki.

p   o·ni·=’na_i·nah=meko e·h=ki·wi_tašikwe·šiki ‖ neniwa._

12 a   o·ni_pemičinawe e·h=ta·keškawa·či,

b   “mehtekwi=meko,” e·h=išite·he·či metemo·ka,

c   e·h=nasawape·piči,

d   e·h=we·pi-na·no·misahoči.

e   kapo·twe=meko e·h=meme·sačite·he·či| mečemo·ka._

f   “ta·ni·=’nah=mani_makwikeno·hike,” e·h=išite·he·či,

g   e·h=nana·toče·naki.|

h   ayo·h=či·hi e·h=mehkoče·naki ne·tawe·netaki.

i   okwisani owi·naka·hi e·h=nana·henaki.

j   ki·ša·koči=meko e·h=iši-menwamataki.

k   ke·keya·h=ke·h=meko=’pi e·h=we·pi- pe·hki -ma·ma·hkwitiye·či mečemo·ka,|

l   e·h=apahapane·niči.

m   “kaši=ča·h=ketešawi,” e·h=iči_pašito·ka._

n   “neme·si·haki=ča·hi nekenikeni·kika·hpoko·ki,” e·h=iči mečemo·ka.|

o   o·ni ahkiki e·h=išinawi·či mečemo·ka,

p   e·h=kotawi·či.

q   “ ‘na·hina·hi_wi·h=mo·hki·wa·ne·ni,’ ki·h=ina·wa| kena·pe·ma,” e·h=ina·či‖ okye·ni.

13 a   “kenwe·ši·me·h=ča·h=meko ki·h=kotawi.

b   meše=ke·hi,| ‘aški-=meko -pehkote·hike_ni·h=mo·hki,’ ki·h=ina·wa_kena·pe·ma,”_e·h=ina·či.

c   e·h=mo·hki·či,| e·h=a·čimoha·či.

d   “nahi´,_pašito,| ka·ta_na·kwa·hkani.

---

*She refers to her skirt (see 11*n*) as if she were wearing the usual multiple skirts.

n   He went from place to place then, shooting soft-shell turtles.

o   He killed a good many of them.

p   And after butchering all of them,

q   he headed back.

r   (Actually, it was sharp wooden arrows he used to hunt soft-shell turtles.)

11 a   When, at some point, he got back near the place where the three of them lived,

b   as soon as he came out into the open, and there were his parents in the water,

c   he ducked back.

d   He slipped under the water upstream,

e   and went underwater towards them.

f   He came swimming underwater to about where his mother was in the water,

g   standing,

h   and looked at her.

i   She had extremely big thighs.

j   And before long he pushed up her skirt.

k   And as for the woman,

l   her thought was, "They're just being pushed up by the current."   (See note *.)

m   At some point the woman waded out further, into the middle of the stream.

n   After she was out in water up to her neck, she took off her skirt

o   and washed it in the water.

p   And then that man had his cock floating about right there.

12 a   And then he touched her with it on one side.

b   "It's a stick," the woman thought,

c   and she straddled it with her thighs

d   and began to rock herself back and forth.

e   And the woman was soon having erotic thoughts.

f   "How I wish this had a little knob!" she thought,

g   and she felt along for it.

h   And here her fingers found what she was seeking.

i   And she took her son's young cock and put it in place.

j   She felt incredibly good.

k   And here before long the woman began to really thrust her hips erotically,

l   laughing away.

m   "What's the matter with you?" said the older man.

n   "Well, minnows keep nibbling at my feet and tickling me," said the woman.

o   And then the woman slipped down,

p   going under the water.

q   "You should tell your husband, 'I'll come up when I come up,' " he told his mother.

13 a   "So, you'll be under water for a pretty long time.

b   Or maybe you should tell your husband, 'I'll come up when it's just getting dark,' " he told her.

c   She came up and explained to him.

d   "Listen, my husband, don't go home.

e aški-=meko_-pehkote·hike, ni·h=mo·hki.

f netawe·ma·wa_ni·h=mawi-wa·pama·wa," e·h=iči mečemo·ka.

g wa·natohka_e·h=awata·hiwe·či neno·te·wi·hani| pašito·he·ha.

h "o·´,_ni·h=awatawa·wa=ča·hi," e·h=išiwe·či metemo·he·ha,

i e·h=kotawi·či.

j mani=meko e·ši_-kotawi·či, e·h=ki·ši-mešenekoči okwisani.[*]

k wi·na=ke·hi e·h=mešena·či.

l "nahi´,| wa·pamino·='nahi," e·h=ineči metemo·ka.

m okwisani=či·hi.

n e·h=mehčikiči='yo=ke·hi.

o natawa·či,| "keki·ši-=koči -kwaya·ši|- i·ni_-to·tawi," e·h=iči.

p o·ni=ča·hi='pi pe·hki nehkanana·kwe e·h=taši-ona·pe·miči‖ okwisani.

14 a "wa·pake=meko-na·hka i·noki.

b ma·maya=meko, 'nye·wokoni ni·h=ašeno,'| ki·h=ina·wa.

c ki·h=ča·ki-=meko_-nakatamawa·wa_keta·hi·hemani," e·h=ina·či okye·ni.

d "ši·´,_na·piwe·na,"| e·h=iči ihkwe·wa.

e e·h=na·kwa·wa·či.

f kapo·twe=meko| e·h=če·če·keki metemo·ka,

g e·h=mayo·či,

h e·h=kehči|-mayo·či.

i aškači po·nwe·kesiči, e·h=a·čimoha·či ona·pemani.|

j "mani=kohi we·či_-kehči|-mayo·ya·ni:

k netawe·ma·wa oni·ča·nese·hani| wi·h=pwa·wi-=meko ašitahi_-pye·čipenoya·ni,_išite·he·wa.

l anwa·či·yane=ča·hi,_nye·wokoni i·ya·hi mawi|-awihka·ha," e·h=ina·či| ona·pemani.

m "kaši=ya·pi=ki·na iši_-pye·čipenowane·ni," e·h=ina·či| owi·wani. ‖

15 a "wi·h=pwa·wi-=ča·hi_-aki·hiya·ni we·či-pye·čipenoya·ni," e·h=ina·či ona·pe·mani.

b i·niya=ke·hi oškinawe·ha aye=meko i·ya·hi| e·h=ki·ši-awihawiči.

c metemo·ka, e·h=me·neši·htawa·či=meko mya·ši| okwise·hani.[†]

d o·ni ma·maya=meko, "ni·h=anawi=ča·hi| anemya·ka," e·h=iči oškinawe·ha.

e ma·maya=meko e·ye·h-pehkote·hiniki e·h=ki·ši_-šekišekišiki i·ya·hi.

f ("kekye·hkinawa·či meše·='nah=meko kepwa·meki ki·h=mešenene.

g i·ni=meko wi·h=kotawi·yani," e·h=ineči='yo=ke·h=ne·pehe.)

h meše=meko e·nemi_-ahkomi·či, e·h=ata·hpipwa·me·neči,

i e·h=šekisahoči wa·natohka e·h=kenwi·temya·niki.[‡]

j na·waka·me| e·h=mawi_-taši-‖wi·hpewi·hpe·ti·wa·či.

16 a ki·h_-meči-mami·noči, e·h=ona·pe·mehka·soči okwisani.[§]

b nye·wokoni| na·mepye·ki e·h=tahitana·manowa·či.

---

[*]/e·h=ki·ši/: AK ⟨.ekeši.⟩

[†]/mya·/: AK ⟨nya⟩ with a line added.

[‡]/te/: AK ⟨ta⟩.

[§]/mami·no-/ 'overdo it': HWB.

^e When it's just getting dark, I'll come up.

^f I'm going to go see my brother," the woman said.   (So, he must live beneath the waters
like Panânwa in Kiyana's "Masahkamikohkwêwa.")

^g Unsuspecting, the older man wanted to send along some Indian tobacco.

^h "Ah, well, I'll take it to him," the woman declared,

ⁱ and she went under the water.

^j And the moment she was under, her son had already taken hold of her.

^k And *she* took hold of *him*.

^l "Alright, *now* look at me!" the woman was told.

^m And here it was her son!

ⁿ Remember, her body was completely bare.

^o And it took her no time to say, "Well, obviously what you've already done to me can't
be undone."

^p So she then had her son for her husband in every way all evening long.

14 a "Tomorrow again, now.

^b You must tell him early in the morning that you'll be gone for four days.

^c You must leave all your things with him," he told his mother.

^d "Say, alright, I will!" the woman said.

^e And they headed for home.

^f At some point the woman cried out

^g and wept,

^h weeping loudly.

ⁱ And later, when she had stopped crying, she explained to her husband.

^j "This is why I'm weeping so loudly, let me say:

^k my brother's little child thought I shouldn't come back here for a long time.

^l So, if it's alright with you, I'd go stay over there for four days," she told her husband.

^m "So tell me, how is it, then, that you came back here?" he said to his wife.

15 a "Well, I came back so I wouldn't just sort of disappear," she told her husband.

^b Now, that young man was elsewhere, already over there.

^c As an older woman, she was sort of embarrassed in front of her young son.

^d Then bright and early, the young man said, "Well, I'm going to hunt downstream."

^e And bright and early, while it was still a bit dark, he was already lying around over there.

^f (I forgot to say: she'd been told, "To signal you, I can grab you on your thighs.

^g Then you should right away go under the water.")

^h As she was getting in fairly deep, she was grabbed by the thighs

ⁱ and, with no concern, threw herself down into the deep water.

^j They went out to the middle of the stream and coupled repeatedly.

16 a Having overdone it completely, she was acting as if her son was her husband.

^b For four days they were having sex underwater.

c kwi·yena=ke·h=meko e·h=menwa·ko·ma·či okwisani.

d   (pašito·ha=wi·na e·h=taši|-ne·nesapiči.)

e   ne·sokonakateniki e·h=kano·na·či wi·h=owi·wiči okye·ni,
f wi·h=mehči-=meko| -owi·wiči.

g   e·h=anwa·či·či wi·h=ona·pe·miči| okwisani.

h   "mani=ča·hi| a·mi_to·tawači mana=kena·pe·ma,
i ke·htena_i·ni_e·šite·he·wane·ni.

j otehkomani owi·ya·seki sanakwi ki·h=ahtawa·wa," e·h=ina·či.

k   "wi·h=kehkahamani na·hina·hi_wi·h=nepokwe·ni i·nina·h=meko wi·h=nepeki,"| e·h=ina·či.

l   nye·wokonakateniki ‖ e·h=na·kwa·či a·pi-ona·pe·mita.

17 a i·na·ka=na·hka_a·pi-anawita e·h=po·ni·či,|

b e·h=pye·ta·wato·či owi·ya·se·hi.

c   o·ni·='na pašito·ha e·h=natonamawoči,

d e·h=kehči-ne·tamawoči otehkomahi.

e   "aye=meko| ki·ši_kehči-otehkome·hiwane·ni
f no·make·we e·h=a·pi-ašenoya·ni," e·h=ineči.

g   "ehe·he," e·h=išiwe·či.

h   o·ni e·h=ašihto·či čaki|-nasika·he·hi_metemo·ka.

i ki·šesaki, ki·ši-=meko -tahkiseniki, i·nahi e·h=ne·kona·či nekoti ahkwani.

j   "na·hina·h=meko ki·ši-komehke,| i·ni wi·h=nepeki," e·h=ina·či_i·nini ahkwani.

k   o·ni| e·h=we·pi-mi_či·či pašito·ha i·ni nasikani.|

l kapo·twe=meko e·h=me·me·menataki,

m no·make·he e·h=neseči.

n e·h=nepeki pašito·ha.|

o   o·ni meše=meko·='nahi‖ či·ka·hkwe e·h=mawi-apiha·wa·či,

18 a e·h=pwa·wi-=ke·hi| ma·mahka·či -mi·ša·čiha·wa·či.

b pe·hkote·niki e·h=aški-wi·hpe·ti·wa·či| we·wi·weti·čiki.

c e·h=owi·wiči okye·ni pe·hki.|

d   ki·ši-owi·wiči, e·h=ačihkwiha·či,

e e·h=oni·ča·nesiwa·či.

f okye·ni| e·h=oni·ča·nesiha·či.

g meše·='nah=meko na·htaswi e·h=ki·šihtawa·či| apeno·he·hahi.

h e·h=na·htaswiha·či=meko oni·ča·nese·hahi.

i mo·šaki=ke·h=meko iškwe·se·he·hahi.

j e·h=pwa·wi_okwisiči.

k   o·ni e·h=no·še·niči_owi·wani e·h=nepo·hiniči,

l e·h=wi·čiha·či ota·nese·hahi.

m ke·keya·h=meko e·h=mama·kekino·hiniči.

n   o·ni po·si-=meko -makekineničini e·h=ki·ma·ha·či| e·h=pesehkaminiči,

o e·h=meša·pama·či ‖ ota·nesani.

^c And what's more, her son's ways suited her exactly right.

^d (The older man, for his part, was staying home by himself every day.)

^e At the end of three days he spoke to his mother about wanting to marry her,

^f about wanting to have her openly as his wife.

^g And she consented to having her son be her husband.

^h "So, here's what you should do to this husband of yours,

ⁱ if you truly want that to be.

^j You must slip one of his lice into his meat," he told her.

^k "The time you shall name for him to die is the exact time that he shall die," he told her.

^l At the end of four days the one back from getting a husband headed home.

17 a And separately the one back from hunting had a camp

^b and brought home a load of meat.

^c And then the older man's lice were looked for on him,

^d and a great many lice of his were seen on him.

^e "You must already have had a good many lice,

^f as I was away for a bit," he was told.

^g "Yes," he declared.

^h And then the woman made a little roasting spit of meat.

ⁱ And after she had cooked it and it had cooled, she slipped a single louse into it.

^j "The moment he has swallowed you, he shall die," she told that louse.

^k And then the older man started eating that skewer of meat.

^l At some point he vomited repeatedly,

^m and in a short time he was killed.

ⁿ The older man was dead.

^o And then they took him and sat him up in no particular place next to a tree.

18 a And they also didn't feel the need to dress him in finery.

^b That night the married couple slept together for the first time.

^c And his mother really was his wife.

^d Having married her, he got her pregnant,

^e and they had a child.

^f He had a child by his mother.

^g And in the course of time he fathered several babies on her.

^h He had several little children.

ⁱ And what's more, they were nothing but baby girls.

^j He didn't have a son.

^k And then his wife died while giving birth,

^l and he lived with his little daughters.

^m In time, they grew bigger.

ⁿ And then he spied on the biggest one as she was putting on her moccasins,

^o and he saw his daughter all the way up.

19 a   e·h=ki·ša·koči|-mama·kipwa·me·niči,

b   e·h=mesawinawa·či.

c   kapo·twe e·h=a·mi·wa·či,|

d   e·h=ni·ši·hiwa·či=meko| i·nini ota·nesani.

e   (e·h=nesapiwa·či atena·wi| e·ya·nekino·hičiki.)*

f   e·h=anawiwa·či.

g   peno·či ki·ši_pya·wa·či, e·h=ma·či·hkawa·či wi·h=owi·wiči,

h   e·h=anwa·či·niči ota·nesani.

i   e·h=owi·wiči.

j   e·ya·wi_-’ši-=meko -ki·šiki·hiničini e·h=anemi-owi·wiči.

k   meše·=’nah=meko e·h=ča·ki-owi·wiči ota·nesahi.|

l   e·h=keneko·še·či iškwe·se·hahi kwi·yese·hahi,_

m   meše=meko e·h=ino·še·či.|

n   e·h=ma·ne·ha·či oni·ča·nesahi.

o   wi·na=ke·hi_aye·niwe=meko| e·h=ahpi·htesiči._

p   a·kwi=ke·hi=’pi_kehtesičini. ‖

20 a   meše=meko e·h=menw-ahpi·htesiči,

b   e·h=ča·ko·hkwe·wa·na·či ota·nesahi=’yo·we.

c   o·ni ki·h-=meko -po·nopo·no·še·niči owi·wahi,

d   e·h=we·pi-=meko -natawe·nema·či wi·h=ina·hpenana·kwe·ni ota·nesahi.†

e   e·h=ma·ne·ha·či=’yo=ke·hi,

f   na·hka_e·h=we·wenesiniči| kekimesi.

g   meše·=’nah=nekotenwi e·h=nepa·či,|

h   e·h=mo·šihto·či na·tawino·ni,

i   we·weneteniki=ke·h=meko.

j   wa·paniki=meko apina_e·h=pwa·wi|-nawači-wi·seniči.|

k   ma·maya=meko e·h=mawi_ketahaki.

l   me·h-=meko| -keči·nikwe ki·šeso·ni,| e·h=ki·ši-ketahaki.

m   “me·h-=meko -keči·kwe, ki·h=ki·ši_-ketaha,” e·h=ineči,

n   i·ni=ča·h=meko=’pi e·šawiči,

o   e·h=na·kwa·či.

p   pe·hkote·niki e·h=kočawiči.|

q   ke·htena=meko ‖ e·h=pwa·wi_-ka·škihekoči| ota·nesani me·kekineničini.

21 a   meše·=’nah=meko ke·ko·hi_e·h=to·tawa·či nye·wenwi.

b   i·ni e·h=to·tawa·či, i·nini=meko e·h=ka·škihekoči kena·či.

c   ke·htena=či·h=meko e·h=to·hki·či ihkwe·wa.|

d   pe·hki=či·h=meko e·h=me·kwa·či-me·meta·ča·hiči,

e   e·h=pwa·wi-=meko| ke·ko·hi_-ina·či o·sani.

f   i·ni=’pi=meko i·ni e·h=we·pi_to·tato·ta·koči,

g   kapo·twe_e·h=ačihkwihekoči.

---

*/ya·/: AK ⟨ye⟩.

†/=meko/: AK ⟨.meko.⟩.

19 a　Her thighs were extremely large,

b　and he desired her.

c　　　Some time later they went out to camp,

d　just the two of them, he and that daughter.

e　(The smaller ones stayed at home.)

f　They were hunting.

g　And when they had gone far away, he got after her to be his wife,

h　and his daughter consented.

i　He married her.

j　　　He continued on marrying each one in turn as she grew to maturity.

k　And in the course of time, he married all of his daughters.

l　And his offspring were a mix of girls and boys,

m　as he had either kind.

n　And he had lots of children.

o　At the same time, he himself stayed just the same age.

p　That is, they say he didn't get old.

20 a　He stayed contentedly at a good age,

b　while marrying all of those that had been his daughters.

c　　　And after his wives were all no longer bearing children,

d　he then began seeking to find out how he might deal with his daughters.

e　Remember, he had lots of them,

f　and also every one was pretty.

g　　　One time as he was sleeping

h　he had a vision of a medicine,

i　and moreover a good one.

j　The next morning he didn't even stop to eat.

k　He went out bright and early and dug it up.

l　By the time the sun had risen he had already dug it up.

m　"By the time it has risen you must already have dug it up," he had been told.

n　So, that's exactly what he did

o　and headed home.

p　　　That night he tried his luck.

q　And sure enough his eldest daughter was not aware of him.

21 a　He was easily able to have sex with her, four times.

b　As he did that to her, she for her part became aware of him slowly.

c　　　And here, sure enough, the woman now woke up.

d　And here, she was really well into having a good time.

e　She didn't say a word to her father.

f　And starting then, he did that to her repeatedly.

g　And at some point he got her pregnant.

^h   o·ni=na·hka_kotakani e·h=we·pi-_i·ni_-to·tawa·či.
ⁱ   ki·ši·-='ni=_-'šawiči,| kotakani=meko na·hka.
^j   ke·keya·h=meko e·h=ča·ki·-='ni_-to·tawa·či| ota·nesahi.
^k   i·ni=ča·hi='pi pe·hki e·h=kekenesiwa·či apeno·he·hahi.
^l   na·na·htaswi=meko e·h=iši-||ni·kini·ki·hiniči apeno·he·hahi,
22 a   e·h=ma·ne·ha·či.|
^b   e·h=pwa·wi-=ke·h=meko ke·ko·hi=_-'koči owi·wahi metemo·kahi.
^c   kapo·twe e·h=a·čimoha·wa·či_ota·neswa·wahi metemo·he·haki.
^d   "kwayahkwi=meko mehči-ona·pe·miko," e·h=ina·wa·či ota·neswa·wahi._
^e   e·h=mehčimehči-ona·pe·miwa·či.
^f   e·h=ma·ne·wa·či=meko ihkwe·waki.
^g   e·h=katawi-=meko mo·šaki_-ihkwe·winiči.[*]

^h   meše·='nah=nekotenwi e·h=ši·ša·wa·či_okwisema·waki,
ⁱ   e·h=kakano·neti·wa·či.
^j   "meše·='nah=meko=wi·na mana=ko·sena·na owihowi·wiwa ota·nesahi," e·h=ina·či.
^k   awiya·toke=ke·h=meko e·h=na·no·še·niči.[†]

^l   o·ni=nekoti| e·h=a·mi·či neniwa,|
^m   e·h=mawi-_ašike·či.|
ⁿ   ki·šike·či, || e·h=nawasehkawa·či_neswi ošemi·hahi,
23 a   ki·šiki·hiničihi=meko.
^b   e·h=pwa·wi-=ke·h=meko -kehke·nečike·či pašito·ha.
^c   aškači=meko e·h=kehke·nečike·či, e·h=akiha·či neswi ota·nesahi.
^d   nekoti·='nahi okwisani e·h=natone·hwa·či,
^e   e·h=pwa·wi-=meko -mehkawa·či.
^f   aškači e·h=mehkoškawa·či nekoti we·sese·hita.
^g   ayo·h=či·hi e·h=owi·kiniči,|
^h   e·h=neso·hkwe·we·niči.
ⁱ   i·ni='pi-ne·h=wi·na_e·na·čimoweči_e·h=išawiči,
^j   e·h=mawi-_ašike·či atehči.
^k   ki·ši-=meko_me·me·čiwi -ki·šike·či, e·h=nawasehkawa·či otehkwe·mahi nye·wi.[‡]
^l   i·ya·h=meko pye·na·či, wi·h=owi·wiči e·h=išima·či.
^m   kekimesi=meko e·h=owi·wiči| i·nihi. ||
24 a   a·ya·nehke·wi=meko='pi·='ni e·h=išawiwa·či.
^b   e·h=pwa·wi-=ke·h=meko -mehkawa·či pašito·he·ha ne·tone·hwa·čini.
^c   ke·keya·h=meko e·h=ča·ki_akiha·či oni·ča·nesahi.
^d   kwi·yena=meko e·h=ča·ki-owi·wiwa·či otehkwe·mwa·wahi.

---

[*]The force of the obviative (/-ni-/) is translated 'those with him'.
[†]/awiya·toke/: AK ⟨awiyatoka⟩.
[‡]/me·me·čiwi/: JAG, who earlier also had /me·mečiwi/ from HL.

h And then he started doing that to another one, in turn.

i And after he did that, yet another one in turn.

j And in time he did that to all his daughters.

k So, then the babies really came quickly.

l The babies were being born several at a time,

22 a and he had lots of them.

b And what's more, his wives, the older women, didn't say a word to him.

c At some point the older women explained things to their daughters.

d "Make the best of it and marry him openly," they told their daughters.

e They each married him openly,

f and there were lots of women.

g Those with him were almost exclusively women.

h One time the sons were hunting

i and they had a conversation.

j "Our father here just goes right on marrying his own daughters," one said to the others.

k Moreover, they continued to give birth as before.

l And then one man moved away,

m going to build a house.

n After building it, he went and asked three of his nieces to come with him,

23 a ones who were grown up.

b And what's more, the older man was not at all aware of it.

c He became aware after a long time that he had lost three of his daughters.

d And with that realization, he went searching for one of his sons,

e and he couldn't find him.

f After a while one of his younger brothers came across him.

g He unexpectedly found where he was living,

h with three wives.

i Then they say he himself also did what the tale tells

j and went and built a house some distance away.

k After he had completely finished the house, he went and asked four of his sisters to come with him.

l And when he brought them over there, he asked them to be his wives.

m He married every one of them.

24 a And one after the other, they all did that (all the sons).

b What's more, the older man couldn't find the one he went searching for.

c And in the end, he lost all his children.

d Doing exactly the same, they married all their sisters, the sons did.

^e　aškači, ki·h-=meko -po·si-pašito·he·hiči, e·h=mo·šiha·či,

^f　e·h=pemi_awiniči e·h=kehke·nema·či.*

^g　e·h=na·kwa·wa·či,|

^h　owi·wahi e·h=wi·te·ma·či| kekimesi.

ⁱ　e·h=pye·notamowa·či kehči_ma·wa·ka·ni, o·šisemahi='yo·we.

^j　　o·ni_e·h=na·kwa·wa·či,|

^k　a·č_a·wasi·me·h=meko e·h=inekihkwa·niki ma·wa·ka·ni.

^l　ne·so·nameki a·wasi=meko e·h=inekihkwa·niki,

^m　nye·wo·nameki a·wasi=meko e·h=inekihkwa·niki,

ⁿ　e·h=ma·ne·niči.

^o　i·ni='pi iši_nye·wenwi ma·wa·seto·niči_o·šiseme·hwa·wahi.†

25 ^a　kekimesi=meko e·h=o·šisemiwa·či i·nihi.

^b　nye·wawahi·me_i·nahi e·h=awiwa·či.

^c　　menehta=meko owi·wahi e·h=ča·ki_nepo·hiniči.

^d　o·ni=wi·na e·h=nano·či-=meko -šekwi_pašito·he·hiči,

^e　e·h=neškina·koči| oni·ča·nesahi.

^f　mehteno·h=meko o·šiseme·hahi| e·h=menwi_wi·čiha·či.

^g　i·nihi=wi·na='pi pe·hki_oni·ča·nesahi, e·h=neškina·koči=meko.

^h　　kapo·twe='pi e·h=maneto·wa·čimoči,

ⁱ　wi·h=ašihemeči wi·h=okima·winičini e·h=iči.|

^j　ki·ši-=meko -kwayahkwa·čimoči, e·h=a·htawa·sa·či.

^k　e·h=nepo·hiči| pašito·he·ha ma·ne| ki·šiha·ta apeno·hahi,

^l　e·h=te·pesiniči okwisahi.

^m　　i·ni.‡

ⁿ　　e·hkwiči kašawi·h. ‖ §

---

*This idiom is also in K-S 19*k*.

†/ma·wa·seto·niči/: AK ⟨.mawasetoni‖či⟩.

‡Followed by space for four syllables.

§On the last line, preceded by one syllable space; /kašawi·h/: AK ⟨.kašawi.‖⟩.

e   Later, having now become a very old man, he had a vision of them,
f   and he knew where the different ones were.
g   They set out,
h   he taking with him every one of his wives.
i   And they came to a large village, and in it ones that had been his grandchildren.
j   And they went on,
k   and there was an even larger village.
l   The third one was still larger,
m   and the fourth one was still larger,
n   with many in it.
o   Those were the only four villages their grandchildren had.
25 a   Every one of them was a grandchild of theirs.
b   And they stayed in them for four years.
c   His wives all died first.
d   And then *he* lived on until he was bent with age.
e   He was hated by his children.
f   It was only with his young grandchildren that he lived on good terms.
g   But as for his original children, they indeed hated him.

h   And there came a day when he spoke from his spiritual power,
i   saying that one who would be chief should be installed.
j   And after he had said what he had to say, he fell over backwards.
k   The old man who had fathered many children died,
l   and his sons were glad.

m   That's it.
n   The end of the story of Kashawiha.

êsapîhkêha

Spider

êsapîhkêha

Alfred Kiyana[*]

1 a   e·sapi·hke·ha.[†]

b   nekoti=ʼpi oškinawe·he·ha| e·h=ki·ša·koči-=meko -nawe·nineni·he·hiči,_

c   e·h=a·hpeči|-mehčinameške·či.

d   e·h=naha·si·či=ke·hi,

e   e·h=a·hpeči-ma·ne·ha·či asapye·hi.|

f   i·nihi=meko_še·ški e·h=tašitaši·hkawa·či.

g   e·nemi-takwa·kinikini e·h=awahawana·či.

h   pe·po·nikini e·h=we·pi|-ašihto·či a·čipanakiči=meko iši-nekwa·pičikanani.

i   ki·ši-ča·ki- waninawe_-ahto·čini, še·ški=meko e·h=ki·yoki·yose·či.

j   na·nano·pehka=meko wi·yaki|-mi·čipe·he·hahi e·h=nekwanekwa·pina·či,

k   pešekesiwahi=ke·hi, mahkwahi=ke·hi, kohpiči·hahi—[‡]

l   meše=meko·=ʼnahi,

m   a·čipanakiči| iši-mi·čipe·he·hahi,

n   ki·wisa·ničihi=ke·hi—‖

2 a   meše=meko·=ʼnahi.

b   e·h=owi·ke·hiči=ke·hi e·h=meso·te·wa·pye·niki=meko.

c   nepi·ki=ke·hi ki·wita·hiničihi,

d   e·yi·ki=meko amehkwahi,_ašaškwahi, neme·sahi,|

e   meše=meko·=ʼnahi owiye·he·hahi:

f   i·ni=meko e·to·tawa·či.

g   še·ški e·h=nekwanekwa·pina·či.

h   e·h=pwa·wi_-omehte·hiči.

i   ki·hpene=ʼpi ča·ki-ki·šiseto·čini, še·ški=meko e·h=awahawatašiči| mi·čipe·hi.

j   ča·ki=meko| iši-mi·čipe·he·hi=ké·hi.| [§]

k   e·h=pwa·wi-=ke·h=meko -paši_-natawe·netaki| wi·h=owi·wiči.

l   e·h=menwe·netaki=meko e·h=mo·šaki·hiči.

m   ke·keya·h=meko=ʼpi mehtose·neniwahi e·h=we·pi-nekwa·pina·či,

n   e·h=pehtapehtapina·či.

o   a·kwi=ke·h=wi·na=ʼpi aše=meko nekwa·pina·čini,

p   e·h=pehtapina·či. ‖

3 a   meše·=ʼnah=kapo·twe_keye·hapa ašiči=meko| e·h=ma·wa·seniki e·hto·tehe_me·ša·niki nekwa·pičikani.

b   "mahkwi_-mye·wi,"| e·h=išite·he·či.[¶]

---

[*]The manuscript is NAA 2794.80; it has 31 pages; edited by Lucy Thomason.

[†]At the top as a title.

[‡]/mahkwahi=ke·hi/: written twice, perhaps displacing /meše·we·wahi=ke·hi/ 'and elk'.

[§]/=ké·hi/: AK ⟨.kei|⟩.

[¶]/mahkwi_-mye·wi/: AK ⟨.makwimewi|⟩.

Spider
Translated by Ives Goddard and Lucy Thomason

1 a   Spider.

b   The tale is told of a certain very young man who was extremely handsome,
c   and he always wore only a breechcloth.
d   What's more, he was a skillful climber,
e   and he always had lots of Indian-hemp ropes.
f   He would be occupied only with those.
g   During the fall he would always take home lots of them.
h   And in the winter he would set about making all different kinds of snares.
i   After he had set all of them all over, he would always simply walk around.
j   He would always snare considerable numbers of small game animals,
k   as well as deer, and bears, and buffalos—
l   just anything;
m   all kinds of small game,
n   and fowl, as well—
2 a   just anything.
b   Another thing: his little house had ropes strung all over it.
c   And what's more, the smaller creatures that live in the water,
d   the beavers, muskrats, and fish, too,
e   and any kind of small animals:
f   that same way is how he dealt with them.
g   He would only snare them.
h   He had no bow.
i   Once he'd set them all out, he did nothing but take home load after load of game.
j   *All* different kinds of small game.
k   And another thing, he didn't at all want to have a wife.
l   He liked being a bachelor.

m   And the time came, the story goes, when he began to snare *people,*
n   snaring them by accident.
o   They say he didn't snare them just to be doing it, though.
p   He snared them by accident.
3 a   At some point it turned out he had set a large snare right near where there was a village.
b   "It's a bear path," he thought.

c   keye·hapa=ke·h=wi·na=’pi·=’ni nepina·to·hkanawi.

d   ma·maya e·h=a·hpeha·hpeči·wa·či ihkwe·waki ne·pina·tekiki,

e   mo·šaki=ke·h=meko ihkwe·waki.

f   a·kwi=’yo=ke·hi·’pi, owiye·ha ne·kwa·pisočini,

g   a·kwi=’pi kaški‗wi·škwe·we·kesičini.*

h   nano·nemi=meko e·h=ma·kwima·kwinawi·či.†

i   i·ni=ča·hi·’pi·=’niki e·šahišawiwa·či, i·niki ihkwe·waki.

j   meše=ke·h=meko na·hina·hi_e·h=oči-ata·hpisa·wa·či,

k   i·tepi e·h=ina·ška·wa·či.

l   i·ni=ča·hi·’pi e·šawiwa·či i·niki‗ihkwe·waki.

m   kapo·twe_e·h=ča·ki·niči ihkwe·wahi. ‖

4 a   we·to·hkwe·yo·mičiki wa·natohka=meko_e·h=pwa·wi‗kehke·nema·wa·či| e·šawinikwe·ni.

b   e·h=pwa·wi·=ke·h=mo·hči=meko -mi·na·we·nema·wa·či.

c   o·ni·=’na i·ni e·h=mawa·pataki.

d   i·ya·h=pye·ya·či, e·h=mayaka·piči.

e   a·neta e·h=mehta·nakitiye·pisoniči,

f   a·neta| e·h=meškapisoniči.

g   a·čipanakiči=meko e·h=ihpisoniči.

h   še·škesi·he·haki=ke·hi·=’niye·ka.|

i   apina_a·neta e·h=pepye·tekwapisowa·či,

j   a·neta| e·h=šowapisowa·či.

k   kekimesi=meko e·h=meša·pama·či ihkwe·wahi,‡

l   še·škesi·hahi=ke·hi.

m   e·h=ča·ki·=meko -meša·pama·či.

n   i·nahi·=’ni ma·wa·ka·neki taši|-ihkwe·wahi e·h=ča·ki-a·pihwa·či.

o   opye·ni=ke·h=meko e·h=a·pihwa·či. ‖

5 a   e·h=pwa·wi·=ke·h=meko ke·ko·hi iši‗meme·sačite·he·či,| ma·ne e·h=ne·wa·či ihkwe·wahi.

b   mahkwa·či=meko e·h=taši‗a·piha·pihwa·či.

c   e·h=me·nešite·he·wa·či ihkwe·waki wi·h=a·čimowa·či.

d   e·h=tepowe·wa·či ihkwe·waki.

e   “ ‘aše=koh=meko i·ya·h=netaši-ka·kakano·neti·pena,’ ki·h=ipena=ma·h=ki·na,” e·h=iči=nekoti.‗

f   “a·kwi, mani=kohi wi·h=iyakwe.

g   ‘netaši-=meko -mačina·ti·pena| wi·h=ko·nano·hiya·ke,’ ki·h=ipena=ma·h=ki·na.”§

h   “o·´, ke·htena,” e·h=iyowa·či.

i   i·nini=ke·h=wi·na wa·natohka e·h=we·po·taminiči,

j   e·h=anemi‗nehki·niči.

---

*/a·kwi=’pi /: written twice.

†/nano·nemi/: AK ⟨.nano|memi⟩.

‡/=meko/: AK ⟨me.⟩.

§/netaši-=meko/: AK: uncrossed ⟨t⟩, ⟨.meko.⟩.

^c They say, though, that it turned out to be a water-path.
^d   Before long women who went for water were not coming back,
^e and no one but women, to be precise.
^f And by the way, when anyone was snared,
^g they say she was unable to scream.
^h They kept straining hard with their bodies, silently.
ⁱ So, that's what they say they would do, those women.
^j And furthermore they were jerked up a short distance
^k and went flying there.
^l So, that's what they say happened to those women.
^m   At some point all the women had gone.
4 a   And their menfolk were unconcerned and unaware of what had happened to them.
^b And they didn't even notice anything about them.

^c   And then he went to look at the thing.
^d And when he arrived over there, he saw a strange sight.
^e Some were tied with their butt-holes showing,
^f and some were tied with their privates exposed.
^g They were tied in all different ways.
^h   Young teenage girls, for example, were the ones over there,
ⁱ Some of them were even tied doubled-over,
^j and some were tied with their legs spread.
^k   He saw the private parts of every one of the women,
^l including the teenagers.
^m He saw the private parts of all of them.
ⁿ   In those circumstances he untied all the women of that village.
^o What's more, he took his time untying them.
5 a What's more, he didn't have any lascivious thoughts, seeing lots of women.
^b He was occupied with calmly untying them, one after another.

^c   The women were ashamed to relate what had happened to them.
^d And the women held a discussion.
^e   "Look, we should say we've obviously been having conversations over there," said one.
^f   "No, here's obviously what we should say.
^g Look, we should say we've been challenging each other to play shinny."
^h   "Oh, we should do that!" they said.
ⁱ   He, though, carried the thing away on his back, unperturbed,   (The snare in 4c.)
^j and went out of sight.

^k   ayi·ne·hka=wi·nwa·wa e·h=pepye·hkwika·pa·wa·či.
^l   "šihihwi´," e·h=iyowa·či a·neta ihkwe·waki,
^m   e·h=me·nešihekowa·či ‖ i·nini neniwani.|

^{6 a}   o·ni='pi i·ni e·h=iyowa·či,
^b   e·h=pašitowe·wa·či, e·h=wanima·wa·či_oteneni·mwa·wahi,
^c   e·h=me·neši·htamowa·či wi·h=a·totamowa·či e·na·pameči,
^d   kekitiye=meko e·h=ina·pameči.

^e   o·ni·='niya_neniwa, i·ya·h=pye·ya·či, e·h=we·pi-mami·na·wite·he·či.|
^f   "ši·hče´, we·nahi·='ni e·šikiwa·či ihkwe·waki," e·h=išite·he·či.|
^g   "i·ni=ye·toke wa·woči|- ke·ko·hi -to·tawoči," e·h=išite·he·či.
^h   e·h=pwa·wi-=ke·h=meko -meme·sačite·he·či.
ⁱ   e·h=pwa·wi-='pi=meko ke·ko·hi -iši_-wa·waneška·hite·he·či i·na_neniwa.

^j   aškači=ča·hi·='pi=meko e·h=meme·sačite·he·či i·na_neniwa. ‖
^{7 a}   o·ni_na·hka te·kwa·kiniki ača·hmeko e·h=ašihto·či mehtose·neniwi|-nekwa·pičikani.
^b   meše=meko e·h=inekihkwa·heniki i·ni nekwa·pičika·hi.
^c   ki·šihto·či_te·kwa·kiniki, e·h=na·kwa·či,
^d   e·h=natone·hwa·či mehtose·neniwahi e·h=awinikwe·ni.
^e   nye·wawahi·makateniki e·h=mehkawa·či_i·na_neniwa,
^f   e·h=nana·hiseto·či·='pi nepina·to·hkana·ki.
^g   o·ni| meše=na·hina·hi e·h=mawi_-šekišekišiki.|
^h   i·ni=ye·toke='pi e·h=nepa·tehe i·na neniwa.
ⁱ   aškači e·h=to·hkisa·či,
^j   a·wi·te·ni=meko e·h=wa·pataki i·ni onekwa·pičikani.
^k   ke·htena nekoti e·h=pepye·tekoče·pisoniči.
^l   e·h=pwa·wi-=meko -kehke·nema·či| e·wiye·hinikwe·hini, ‖
^{8 a}   i·tepi e·h=a·či.
^b   ašiči| pye·ya·či, e·h=ma·kwima·kwinawi·niči.
^c   e·h=pwa·wi-=ke·h=meko -nenawa·či.
^d   po·si_kehčine=meko_pye·ya·či, e·h=papahkeškaminiči,
^e   e·h=mawinanekoči.
^f   ka·pa·čiči=meko e·h=te·pi·hiwe·či si·po·wi.|
^g   e·ši-=meko -pakamipahoči, e·h=očisahoči.
^h   man=e·na·piči,|
ⁱ   ayo·nina·h=či·h=meko| e·h=pye·či-me·meškineče·ya·ška·niči.
^j   ke·kya·ta=meko e·h=te·pi_-a·wahkitepe·sahekoči.
^k   i·ni=meko e·h=iši|-pemi_-kotawi·či, e·h=se·kihekoči.*
^l   na·waka·me e·h=mawi_-mo·hki·či, e·h=se·kesiči.
^m   "šihihwi´," e·h=išite·he·či,| e·h=anemičime·niči.| †

____

*/i·ni=meko/: AK ⟨.enimeko.⟩.

†AK ⟨.|šiiwi.⟩: syllable ⟨i⟩ over start of ⟨w⟩.

k   And *they* still lingered together, standing close in knots.
l   "Oh my!" said some of the women,
m   as that man had made them ashamed.

6 a   And then they said that, the story goes,
b   telling a lie and deceiving their men,
c   as they were ashamed to tell how they'd been seen,
d   having been seen bottoms and all.

e   Meanwhile, that man, when he got back home, began thinking everything over.
f   "What a thing to see! So that's how women's bodies are!" he thought.
g   "That must be the hole where they have the business done to them," he thought.
h   Now, his thoughts were not at all lascivious.
i   That man didn't think wicked thoughts of any kind, to hear the tale.

j   Well, a long time later, that man did have lascivious thoughts, the story goes.
7 a   And then the next fall he, for the first time, made a snare for catching people..
b   The snare was pretty big.
c   And after he made it, that fall he set out,
d   searching for where people might be.
e   After four years the man found them,
f   and they say he set it on the water-path.
g   Then he went some ways off and was lying there.
h   And that's where, it seems, the man then slept, to hear the tale.
i   After a while he started awake,
j   and before anything else, he looked at that snare of his.
k   Sure enough, something was tied up with its body bent over double.
l   He didn't know what kind of creature it might be,
8 a   and he went to it.
b   When he got near, it kept straining hard with its body.
c   And he did *not* recognize it at all.
d   When he got right up close, it snapped the ropes
e   and attacked him.
f   He just barely reached the safety of the river.
g   And just as he got to it on the run, he jumped in.
h   And as soon as he looked,
i   here it was, coming at him with paws flexed wide.
j   And it very nearly succeeded in clawing up his head with a swipe.
k   Right away, he proceeded to dive under the water in fear of it.
l   And he went out into the middle of the stream to come up, frightened as he was.
m   "Jeepers!" he thought, as it swam off.

n nano·pehka=meko e·h=ahkwa·nowe·niči. ‖

9 a e·h=mawinana·či ki·ši-nenawa·či.

b keye·hapa=ke·hi=ʼpi·=ʼnini kehči-ke·nwa·sowe·wani.|

c e·h=kehtena·či=meko.

d e·h=nano·či-=meko i·nahi_-taši-aškepyana·či.*

e ki·ši-aškepyana·či, e·h=akwa·pye·ki·či,

f e·h=na·kwa·či.

g keye·hapa=ke·hi=ʼpi-wi·na·=ʼni e·h=ma·mawi-menoniči nepi pe·pa·miha·nitehe.

h o·ni=wi·na ʻnepina·to·hkanawiʼ e·h=išite·he·či.

i i·nini-ke·hi| ʻwi·kiya·pye·niʼ e·šite·he·čini, e·ye·ni·hi-wi·kiya·pye·ni.

j neniwa| we·ta·moči aya·pami e·h=ihpahoči,

k e·h=pema·moči.

l e·h=na·kwa·či=meko kwayahkwi.

m meše·=ʼnah=meko| aškači aya·pami_e·h=pya·či e·h=owi·ke·hiči,

n e·h=ni·škina·kwateniki owi·ki. ‖

10 a "šihihwi·´," e·h=išite·he·či.

b "we·ne·h=ča·h=ye·toke e·taši-wa·wapašihtawita e·h=owi·ke·hiya·ni," e·h=išite·he·či.

c omaškimote·hani=ke·hi e·h=kwa·pa·kwate·niki,

d oto·sapi·me·hahi=ke·hi.|

e e·h=neškinawe·hekoči=meko.

f wa·pikono·hahi=wi·na i·nah=meko e·h=taši-ča·kiha·či, e·tašiniči=meko.

g o·ni=ʼpi ošihoši=meko te·kwa·kiniki_na·hka e·h=ašihto·či nekwa·pičikani.

h e·h=a·hkwe·či=meko.

i ki·šihto·či, e·h=we·pi-ašihto·či| na·hka kotakani.

j meše=meko e·h=tetepa·kwato·či nekwa·pičikanani,

k e·h=na·kwa·či.

l o·ni| wa·koše·haki e·h=kehke·nema·wa·či e·h=na·kwa·niči.

m "nahi´, na·hkači,"| e·h=iyowa·či,

n wi·h=mawi_-tahitanenekowa·či. ‖

11 a i·tepi_e·h=a·wa·či._

b i·ya·h=ašiči pye·ya·wa·či, waninawe=meko e·h=taši-nekwa·pisowa·či.†

c wi·na=ke·hi_e·h=na·kwa·či atehči, meše=meko·=ʼnahi.

d kapo·twe| e·h=ne·taki ma·wa·ka·ni.

e e·na·kwi·hiniki=meko, me·me·čiki=meko mehtose·neniwahi| e·h=tanetone·moniči.|

f e·h=na·kataki nepina·to·hkanawi.

g ayo·h=či·hi| e·h=ahte·niki mehtekwina·ka·hi, kwa·pahikani.

h e·h=nana·hiseto·či onekwa·pičikani,| ke·tawi_-meko -wa·paniki.

i o·ni mahkwa_e·h=nekwa·pisotehe.‡

j wi·na=ke·hi i·niye=meko e·h=išawitehe.

k e·ye·ši_-meko -menokwa·meki,_e·h=to·hkisa·či,

---

*Divider added before ⟨meko.⟩.

†/waninawe/: AK ⟨.waninanawe⟩.

‡/e·h=ne/: AK ⟨ena⟩, with ⟨e⟩ over unlooped ⟨e⟩.

n   It had a terrifically long tail.
9 a   And he attacked it, after he'd recognized it.
b   Now, they say it turned out it was a large mountain lion.
c   He held it tightly.
d   And he kept it up until he drowned it there
e   After drowning it, he got out of the water
f   and set out.
g   But they say it turns out that was the route they always took when they went to drink water.
h   And *he* thought it was a water-path.
i   What's more, the things he thought were wickiups were possum lodges.
j   The man ran back to where he had fled from
k   and fled on by.
l   He thought he might as well go back home.
m   Some time later he got back to where he lived alone,
n   and his house looked a mess.
10 a   "Jeepers!" he thought.
b   "So, who was here wrecking my poor house, I wonder?" he thought.
c   His bags were even scattered about,
d   as well as his pieces of Indian hemp.
e   They *did* make him angry.   (It is always foxes that trash people's houses.)
f   But he killed all the *mice* there, as many as there were.
g   And taking his time then, they say, that fall he made another snare.
h   He was definitely angry.
i   And when he finished it, he set to making others as well.
j   And he simply placed the snares around in a circle
k   and set out.
l   And then the foxes knew that he had left.
m   "Alright now, one more time!" they said,
n   for them to go and mess around.
11 a   They went there,
b   and when they got near there, they were caught in snares on all sides.
c   He, meanwhile, headed out to go away somewhere, anywhere.
d   And at some point he saw a village.
e   Early in the evening people could definitely be heard talking.
f   He followed a water-path.
g   And suddenly here was a little wooden bowl and a dipper.
h   He set his snare in place, when it was nearly dawn.
i   And then a bear had been caught in the snare.
j   But *he* had done the same thing as before.
k   While he was sleeping soundly, he started awake,

l e·h=mawi‿wa·pataki.

m ke·htena=či·hi mahkwayi‿e·h=ohkone·hiniči. ‖

12 a keye·hapa=ke·hi=ʼpi mahkwani=meko.

b e·h=kehč‿a·hkwe·či.|

c keye·hapa=ke·hi=ʼpi mahkwani i·nahi wa·woči|‑menonitehe nepi.

d i·ni=ke·hi ana·ka·hi e·šite·he·či, mahkwa·hke·hi‑ohkena·hko·hani.

e ača·hmeko| e·h=mi·na·wa·pama·či.

f i·nini=ke·h=mahkwani i·nah=meko e·h=taši‿pa·pakama·či.

g i·niye·ne·=ke·hi‿wi·kiya·pye·ni kekye·hči‑wa·pikono·hi‑wi·kiya·pye·ni.

h   "šihihwi·ʹ," e·h=išite·he·či.

i "i·noki ni·h=nawači‑=meko ‑mami·na·wesi," e·h=išite·he·či.

j e·h=na·kwa·či nawači=meko e·h=owi·ke·hiči.

k   i·ya·h=pye·ya·či, e·h=nešiwi‿tašiniči wa·koše·hahi ne·kwanekwa·pisoničihi.

l a·neta=ke·hi našawaye=meko e·h=nekwa·pisonitehe.

m   o·ni, "kaši=ča·hi ‖ išawiwe·kwe·ni," e·h=ina·či.*

13 a   "o·ʹ,‿mani=ča·hi e·šawiya·ke:

b pešekesiwa nepeminehkawa·pena ayo·h=meše=na·hina·hi," e·h=iniči.†

c   "o·ni| kapo·twe=meko e·ya·wi‿ʼši‑=meko ‑pya·ya·ke e·h=iši‑nekwa·pisoya·ke," e·h=iniči.

d   "ma·haki=ke·hi=ʼyo·we ni·ka·ni·čiki,"| e·h=iyoweči ke·tawi‿nepo·hiničihi.

e   e·h=te·pwe·htawa·či.

f mahkwa·či=meko e·h=a·ya·pihwa·či i·nihi,

g e·h=na·kwa·niči.

h   "ke·htena=meko," e·h=išite·he·či.|

i menehta=meko e·h=keteškena·či ke·tawina·hiničihi.

j e·h=anemi‑=meko| ‑we·pipahoniči i·nihi,‿

k ma·wač‿ahkowi=meko keye·či·hi ki·ši‑nekwa·pisoničihi.

l   —ne·pehe=ʼpi, e·nemi‿ʼši‑=meko ‑ki·ši‿a·piškona·čini, e·h=nawači‑=meko ‖ ‑pi·tike·niči.

14 a keye·hapa=ke·hi=ʼpi‿ma·mawi‿mi·čitama·kotehe owi·ki| pi·tike,

b e·h=pekowa·hkwihto·niči pi·tike.

c   "pe·hki mena·nina·kwato·ni| wi·kiya·pye·ni,

d anemi|‑mehtose·neniwaki owi·kewa·wani," e·h=iti·niči.‿

e   wi·na=ke·hi, "ke·htena=meko," e·h=išite·he·či.—

f   ki·ši‑=meko‿ča·ki‑a·piškona·či,

g sese·si=meko e·h=mawi‑pi·čisa·niči nekoti.‿

h   i·ni=ʼpi‑=ʼna‿e·h=so·naso·nepye·škaki mo·weči.

i   wi·na=ke·hi opahopye·ni=meko e·h=nawači‑šekiči| neno·te·wa,

j e·h=na·kwa·či.|

k   mani=meko e·ši‿pi·tike·či,

l   "e·h, e·h," e·h=iči.‡

---

*AK ⟨we⟩: ⟨e⟩ over ⟨a⟩.

†/e·h=iniči/: AK ⟨einači⟩.

‡/e·h, e·h/: phonetics conjectured; AK ⟨‑ę‑ę‑⟩ (written so).

l   and he went to look at it.

m   And sure enough, here he saw someone wearing a bearskin robe.

12 a   But it turned out, they say, that it actually was a bear.

b   He was furious.

c   Now. it turns out, they say, that the bear had been drinking water from there.

d   And here, what he thought was a little bowl was in fact a little mud-turtle shell.

e   Only then did he look closely at the creature.

f   And the bear, as it was, he clubbed to death on the spot.

g   And what's more, those wickiups he had seen were rat lodges.

h   "Jeepers!" he thought.

i   "This time I'll first examine things closely," he thought.

j   And he set out first of all for his poor house.

k   When he arrived over there, there were a great many foxes that had been snared.

l   And some had been snared long before.

m   And then he said to them, "So, what happened to you, I wonder?"

13 a   "Well, so this is what happened to us:

b   we were chasing a deer some ways from here," they said.

c   "And then at some point, as each of us got here we were snared," they said.

d   And the ones that were nearly dead were described as having been the leaders.

e   He believed them.

f   And he calmly untied them, one by one,

g   and they left.

h   He thought it was true.

i   First of all, he freed the poor things that were all but dead,

j   and those set off at a run,

k   and last of all the ones that had been snared most recently.

l   —Oh, I forgot: as he had untied them, they would first go inside, the story goes.

14 a   And it turns out, they would each go and dung up the inside of his house

b   and cover the inside with ashes.

c   "Wickiups really look strange,

d   the houses of the People-to-Be," they said to each other.

e   And for his part he thought it was true.—

f   After he had untied them all,

g   one of them, in a great hurry, went rushing in.

h   And that one, the story goes, had then splattered watery dung about.

i   And the Indian, for his part, taking his time, stopped to take a leak

j   and went home.

k   As soon as he went inside,

l   "Ehh! Ehh!" he said.

m   e·h=mya·šiya·kwateniki.[*]

n   e·h=kehč‑a·hkwe·či.

o   aye=ke·h=meko e·h=ki·ši-anemi‑nehka·ška·niči| ma·wač‑ahkowi ‖ nwe·wa·ška·ničini.[†]

15 a   "šihihwi·´," e·h=išite·he·či.|

b   pepehči·me·hi e·h=iši-mawi‑ki·hkike·či kwayahkwi._

c   o·ni_wa·koše·haki e·h=meso·te·we‑=meko -a·čimoheti·wači,

d   wi·h=po·ni|‑ na·hka a·ye·niwe -pemiha·wa·či, e·h=iti·wa·či,

e   mo·hči peminehkawote,| wi·h=pwa·wi‑=meko a·ye·niwe_-pemi_-'hpahowa·či, e·h=iti·wa·či.[‡]

f   e·h=te·pwe·hta·ti·wa·či=meko.

g   i·ni='pi·='na e·h=ašihto·či ma·ne=meko nekwa·pičikanani.

h   ki·ša·kwato·či, e·h=nakataki=meko owi·ki.[§]

i   o·ni_šwa·šika| e·tasokonakateniki_e·h=mehkawa·či| mehtose·neniwahi e·h=ma·wa·seto·niči.

j   kete·='nah=meko mehtose·neniwahi e·h=mehkawa·či.

k   "i·ni=yá·pi," e·h=išite·he·či. ‖

16 a   e·h=nana·hiseto·či onekwa·pičikani, e·h=nana·hišiki,[¶]

b   meše=na·hina·hi| e·h=mawi‑šekišekišiki.

c   meše·='nah=meko e·h=nano·či-apete·niki.

d   e·h=pe·we·nemoči,_

e   i·tepi_e·h=a·či.

f   aye=či·h=meko e·h=ašehašenoniki wi·kiya·pye·ni.

g   "šihihwi·´,"_e·h=išite·he·či.

h   kapo·twe e·h=mi·na·wa·piči.

i   waninawe=či·hi e·h=ahte·niki owa·si·sanani še·ški.

j   keye·hapa=ke·hi='pi i·niye·he wa·koše·hahi.

k   wi·teko·wani e·h=a·čimohekoči,

l   "wa·koše·haki=ma·hi·='niki," e·h=ikoči._

m   e·h=a·čimohekoči wi·h=a·niči.

n   "mani=ča·h=wi·h=to·tawači, ma·ne·wa·te:

o   še·ški=meko če·winehki ki·h=nana·hišine," e·h=ikoči.

p   "ki·h=taši-mamamama·čišine," e·h=ineči.

q   "hawo·?," ‖ e·h=iči.

17 a   "kekimesi ki·ši_to·hki·wa·te, i·ni wi·h=pemi_pasekwi·yani," e·h=ineči.

b   "a·kwi=na·hka_wi·h=asipi_nepa·wa·čini.|

c   ki·h=meso·te·we‑=meko| -nenye·škwinehkawa·waki," e·h=ineči.

d   e·h=na·kwa·či.

---

[*]/mya·/: AK ⟨ma⟩.

[†]/nehka·/: AK ⟨k⟩ begun as ⟨s⟩.

[‡]AK ⟨pa⟩ changed from ⟨pe⟩.

[§]AK ⟨.meko.⟩.

[¶]/e·h=nana·hišiki/: AK ⟨nana⟩ < ⟨nena⟩.

^m It stank.

ⁿ And he was furious.

^o And here, the last one to rush out had already sped off out of sight.

^{15 a} "Criminy!" he thought.

^b He decided to go and move his house some ways away from everyone and be done with it.

^c And then the foxes went all over informing each other,

^d telling each other not to keep going that way,

^e telling each other that, even if they were chased, they should not run that way.

^f And they heeded each other.

^g And then, the story goes, he made a great many snares.

^h And after he had made a pile of them, he left his house behind.

ⁱ And eight days later he found where some people had a village.

^j His luck had changed and he had found some *people*!

^k "Here we go!" he thought.

^{16 a} He put his snare in place and lay down,

^b going to lie some distance away.

^c And as he waited and waited, it got warm.

^d He gave up

^e and went over there.

^f And here he saw that the wickiups had all been gone for some time.

^g "Jeepers!" he thought.

^h Finally he took a hard look.

ⁱ And he could see that on all sides there was nothing but nests.

^j What's more, it turns out that it had been those foxes from before, as he heard.

^k It was explained to him by an owl,

^l who told him, "It was those foxes, you understand."

^m And it told him where they would be going.

ⁿ "So, here's how you should deal with them if there are lots of them:

^o you should simply lie down in the middle of them," it told him.

^p "You should keep shifting about as you lie," he was told.

^q "Alright, I'll do that," he said.

^{17 a} "After they all wake up, then you should get up," he was told.

^b "Also, they won't sleep all in a bunch.

^c You should chase them all over in all directions," he was told.

^d And he set out.

e   no·make·tepehki·niki e·h=pye·notaki.[*]
f   i·niye=meko e·h=išina·kwateniki ma·wa·ka·ni.
g   "šihihwi·´," e·h=išite·he·či.
h   če·winehki e·h=nana·hišiki ma·wa·ka·neki.|
i   e·h=taši-sesosesotaki.
j   kapo·twe e·h=we·pi-to·hki·wa·či wa·koše·haki.|
k   ayo·h=či·hi_i·niye·ne| neniwani.
l   e·škami=meko e·h=to·hkito·hki·wa·či.|
m   ki·ši-=meko -ča·ki-to·hki·niči, e·h=kehke·nema·či,
n   e·h=pemi_pasekwi·či.
o   e·h=ča·ki-=meko -pasekwi·čisa·niči,
p   e·h=se·kiha·či.|
q   e·h=nenye·škwa·mowa·či‖ wa·koše·haki.
18 a   e·h=ki·ša·koči-=meko_-se·kiheči wa·koše·haki,
b   wanahkamiki=meko e·h=ina·mo·hiwa·či.

c   o·ni·='na| ki·ši-se·kiha·či, e·h=na·kwa·či._
d   e·h=ne·taki_pehkwika·hi,
e   e·h=ne·wa·či ihkwe·wani.|
f   "ši·='ni=ya·pi," e·h=išite·he·či.|
g   e·h=mi·ša·te·nemoči.|
h   ke·tawi-=meko_-wa·pano·hiniki, e·h=mawi_nana·hiseto·či i·ni onekwa·pičikani.
i   meše=na·hina·hi či·kasaki e·h=mawi-nana·hisahotehe,_[†]
j   ke·htena e·h=pye·tose·niči,_e·h=we·wenesi·hiniči ihkwe·wani,
k   mahkahko·hi e·h=pye·či-ni·pikwito·škwana·taminiči,|
l   e·h=nekwa·pina·či.
m   e·h=pwa·wi-=ke·hi -kaški_-wi·škwe·we·kesiči ihkwe·he·ha.
n   e·h=ma·kwima·kwinawi·či,|[‡]
o   nano·nemi=meko.
p   ahkiki=meko ‖ e·h=ineška·či e·škami.|
19 a   oko·te·hani=ke·hi_ahpemeki e·h=e·mikateniki.|
b   e·h=nano·či-=meko -meškapisoči.
c   (pe·hki='yo=ke·h=meko_še·škesi·he·ha.)
d   i·tepi e·h=e·notawa·či.
e   e·h=mawi-=ke·ko·hi -to·tawa·či._
f   še·škesi·he·ha še·ški=meko e·h=taši-wi·sawi·saki·kwe·ška·či ke·ko·hi e·h=to·tawoči.
g   ki·ši·-='ni_-to·tawoči, e·h=a·pihoči.
h   meše·='nah=meko na·htasenwi i·ni| e·h=to·tawoči.
i   i·nini=ke·h=meko nekoti ne·kwanekwa·pina·čini.| [§]

---

[*]/ma/: AK ⟨na⟩.

[†]/či·kasaki/: spelling and meaning conjectured, assuming /-asak-/ 'log'.

[‡]/nawi·či/: ⟨nawači|⟩.

[§]/-na·čini/: AK ⟨-nekočini⟩ (as if she kept snaring him). Emended to fit the context.

^e Part way through the night he got there.
^f It looked like the very same village as before.
^g "Jeepers!" he thought.
^h He lay down in the middle of the village
ⁱ and kept coughing repeatedly.
^j Finally the foxes began to wake up.
^k And here they saw that man from before.
^l They woke up gradually, one after the other.
^m After they were all awake, he knew that they were
ⁿ and stood up.
^o And they all sprang to their feet,
^p being frightened by him.
^q The foxes fled in all directions.
18 ^a The foxes were extremely frightened.
^b The poor things ran away in all directions.

^c And he, after he had scared them, then set out.
^d And he saw a small dome-shaped lodge,
^e and he saw a woman.
^f "Gee, here we go!" he thought.
^g And he was glad.
^h When it was very nearly first light, he went and set his snare in place.
ⁱ He had gone and flung himself down a little ways off alongside a log,
^j and sure enough, here she came walking along, a rather pretty woman,
^k coming with a bucket hooked on her elbow,
^l and he caught her in his snare.
^m Now, the young woman was unable to scream,
ⁿ and she kept straining hard with her whole body,
^o in utter silence.
^p She slid down gradually,
19 ^a and as she did her skirts went up.
^b Until in the end she was tied there completely exposed.
^c (Now, she was a true young virgin.)
^d And he went to where she was there.
^e He went and did the business to her.
^f The young girl merely kept grimacing as it was done to her.
^g And after it was done to her, she was untied.
^h And in the course of time, that was done to her several times.
ⁱ Now, it was only just that same one that he kept snaring.

j   aškači e·h=na·kwa·či.|

k   i·ni=ʼpi kete·=ʼnahi, e·h=kehke·nema·či=meko e·h=pem_awiniči mehtose·neniwahi,
l   e·h=we·pi- i·ni -to·tato·tawa·či,
m   še·škesi·he·hahi=meko,
n   a·kwi_meše=meko·=ʼnahi. ‖
20 a   meše=meko e·h=ki·wi_tahitananohkye·či.
b   še·škesi·haki, e·h=ča·ki-=meko -kehke·nemekowa·či i·nini.

c   meše=nekotenwi| na·hka e·h=we·patone·hwa·či mehtose·neniwahi,_
d   e·h=ne·taki pehkwika·hi, meše=meko e·h=inekihkwa·heniki,
e   e·h=menwi-=meko -inekihkwa·heniki.
f   e·nemihe·weniwiniki e·h=mawi_šowapito·či onekwa·pičikani.
g   o·ni metemo·he·ha e·h=nepina·to·hiči,|
h   e·h=nekwa·pineči._
i   (e·h=ki·ša·koči-=ʼyo=ke·h=meko i·na| -aka·wa·taki neniwa.)|
j   o·ni-=ʼna metemo·he·ha aškiča·hi e·h=ma·kwima·kwinawi·či.
k   ki·ši-=meko -ča·ki-meškapisoči,
l   e·h=po·ni_ma·kwima·kwinawi·či.
m   e·h=na·kwa·či.|
n   aye·či·h=meko e·h=ki·ši|-meškapisonitehe.
o   e·h=ki·ša·koči-‖me·menwipwa·me·niči,|
21 a   e·h=wa·wa·peškipwa·me·niči.
b   kapo·twe=wi·na| metemo·ka_e·h=ta·kenamawoči ota·hwi·hemani.
c   (e·h=ma·tako·hkwe·pisoči=ʼyo=ke·hi oko·te·hani metemo·ka.)
d   e·h=saya·weneči.
e   kete·=ʼnah=meko| e·h=kehke·nema·či ke·ko·hi| wi·h=to·ta·koči,
f   e·h=sahpwi·htawa·či.
g   (o·šisemani=ke·h=meko e·h=a·we·nema·či.)
h   neniwa e·h=taši-a·noha·nohwa·či.|
i   ke·keya·h=meko e·h=meškwi·kite·či e·h=taši-a·noha·nohesoči metemo·ka.
j   ke·keya·hi e·h=ka·šahoči.
k   ke·keya·h=meko=ʼpi e·h=awana·či| atehči,
l   e·h=anemi_so·kena·či.
m   meše=meko·=ʼnahi e·to·tawe·hi·ke·ni_metemo·he·ha.
n   o·ni=ʼpi e·h=pye·na·či na·wi_masa·nimišihkiwe,[*]
22 a   e·h=taši·hkawa·či| metemo·he·hani.
b   ke·keya·h| metemo·he·ha e·h=pakisa·hkwi·či.
c   ki·h-=meko -mečimatahoči, e·h=ča·kahamawoči oto·wi·sa·me·hani.
d   ki·h-=meko -meči_po·ni-owi·sayiwiči, e·h=pakisa·hkwi·či.
e   e·h=kaški- i·ni -to·tawa·či i·na| neniwa.
f   meše·=ʼnah=meko=na·hka nye·wokoni| e·h=pwa·wi-kaški_pahkwinawi·či.

____

[*]⟨.nawimasanimiši‖kiwe.⟩

^j   And later on he went away.

^k   Then, with a change of mind, the story goes, knowing (as he did) the places where people were,
^l   he began doing that to them,
^m   to young girls,
ⁿ   not just anyone.
20 a   He went around as he pleased doing what he did.
^b   And the girls he knew intimately, every one.

^c   One time, as he had again set out to search for people,
^d   he saw a dome-shaped lodge, and it was a nice size,
^e   a pretty good size.
^f   And he went and tied his snare spread open where the path went.
^g   And then an old woman was going for water,
^h   and she was caught in the snare.
ⁱ   (Now, that man really wanted it.)
^j   And the old woman at first kept straining hard with her whole body.
^k   And after she had become wholly exposed as she was tied,
^l   she stopped her straining.
^m   He headed out.
ⁿ   And here he found that one had already been snared with her privates exposed.
^o   And she had extremely nice thighs,
21 a   thighs that were white.
^b   The old lady soon felt her thing being touched by someone.
^c   (Remember, the old lady's head was covered by her skirts.)
^d   And the touch made her tingle.
^e   And then things changed, and she knew he was doing the business to her,
^f   and she clamped up on him.
^g   (Now, she thought he was her grandson.)
^h   The man kept failing to get it done with her.
ⁱ   And eventually the old lady became exasperated that she kept failing to have it done.
^j   Eventually, she got sore from it.
^k   And eventually, the story goes, he took her away,
^l   carrying her off with him.
^m   Any and every possible thing was tried with the old woman.
ⁿ   And then he brought the old woman to the middle of a nettle patch
22 a   and went at it with her.
^b   Eventually the old lady gave up.
^c   After she had been pounded repeatedly, her short hairs were all worn off.
^d   And after she had no more hairs left at all, she gave up.
^e   The man was able to do that to her.
^f   And for as many as four more days he was not able to pull out.

g wi·na=ke·hi·=’na| metemo·he·ha aše=meko e·h=to·tawa·či.

h nye·wokonakateniki, e·h=pahkwinawi·či.|

i aškači=meko e·h=kaški-mama·činawi·či.

j ki·ši-mama·činawi·či,

k i·ni=’pi=meko na·hka e·h=mawinana·či i·nini| metemo·he·hani,

l i·ni| e·h=to·tawa·či. ‖

23 a “ni·h=owi·wi=meko,” e·h=išite·he·či, i·nini metemo·he·hani.

b e·h=pwa·wi-=ke·h| -kehke·nema·či e·h=metemo·he·hiniči, wi·h=owi·wiči=meko
e·h=ine·nema·či.

c e·h=we·pi-a·pihwa·či.

d e·h=ne·wa·či e·šina·kosiniči.

e metemo·he·hani=či·hi.

f e·h=se·kesiči.

g “na·kwi·´, kwi·yese·ha,” e·h=ikoči.|

h “we·nah=no·šiseme·ha| e·taši-meškwimeškwi·kite·taneko·hita,” e·h=ikoči.

i “a·wasi=ma·h=ki·na| e·hpi·hči-sanakesiwa·či aškehkwe·he·haki,” e·h=ikoči.

j “aše=koh=meko, noši·hi, ketaši-wi·čewi·če·nomene,” e·h=ikoči.|

k “awita=ča·h=ye·hapa paši-=meko -kaškahwiye·kapa aškehkwe·haki,” e·h=ikoči.

l e·h=nakanakapehkwe·piči.

m “aše=kohi, noši·hi, kewi·tamo·ne,” ‖ e·h=ikoči.

24 a “a·kwi-ke·hi mya·ne·netama·nini,” e·h=ikoči.

b “ni·na=’yo, noši·hi, e·ye·hi-aškehkwe·hiya·ni, wi·čawiwaka nye·wawahi·me
nepemi·hka·kwa.

c nye·wawahi·makateniki ača·hmeko e·h=kaški-pi·tenamawiči,” e·h=iniči.*

d “i·ni e·hpi·hči|-sanakesiya·ni,

e e·h=wi·šiki·hkama·ni=ni·yawi wi·h=pwa·wi-=ke·ko·hi| owiye·ha -to·tawiči,” e·h=iniči.

f e·h=se·kesiči.|

g “šihihye·´, metemo·he·ha e·h=me·nešihiči,” e·h=išite·he·či.

h “mya·ne·netama·ne=ke·hi, mani:†

i nene·kwičine,” e·h=iniči.‡

j nano·pehka=meko e·h=ahkwa·pehkateniki ma·tesi, e·h=oči_pemi-ketenaminiči.

k “nahi=’škwe·´, noši·hi, ni·h=natawi-na·kwa·hi,” e·h=iniči,

l e·h=na·kwa·niči. ‖

25 a e·h=pwa·wi-=ke·hi·=’nahi -wa·wane·netaminiči we·čiwena·či i·na| neniwa.

b e·h=šo·ški-=meko_-na·kwa·niči.

c i·ya·h=pye·ya·či e·h=owi·ke·hiwa·či,

d “ta·tepi=ča·h=ki·na| a·piha·yani, ano·hko,” e·h=ikoči o·šisemani| wi·sahke·hani.

e “’šina·´, wa·waneška, menipopi=ma·h=ki·na ni·yawi,” e·h=iniči o·hkomese·hani.

f “ano·hko, šepawi·hta=ča·h=ye·toke pwa·wi|-ča·kamenekehe,” e·h=inekoči o·šisemani.

---

*/nye·/: AK ⟨ne⟩.

†/=ke·hi/: AK ⟨keii.⟩.

‡/nene·kwičine/ (a conjecture, assuming /ne·kw-/ ‘slide in, slip in’: AK ⟨nenekwačini⟩.

g   And for her part, the old lady did it to him just for fun.
h   And after four days he pulled out.
i After a long time he was able to move around.
j And after he was moving around,
k he again rushed over to the old woman, the story goes,
l and did that do her.
23 a   "I'm going to marry her," he thought, meaning the old woman.
b Now, he didn't know she was an old woman when he thought he would marry her.
c And he set about untying her
d and saw what she looked like.
e And here, she was an old woman.
f He was scared.
g   "Goodness me! It's a boy!" she said to him.
h   "So it was my young grandson being exasperated in the task," she said to him.
i   "Let me tell you, much more difficult is how young girls are," she said to him.
j   "I promise you, I was just playing with you for fun, grandson," she said to him.
k   "So, I suppose you wouldn't at all be able to get it done with girls," she said to him.
l   He was sitting there with his head down.
m   "Really, I'm just telling you, grandson," she said to him.
24 a   "I'm not out of sorts over it," she said to him.
b   "After all, grandson, when *I* was a young girl, my husband worked on me for four years.
c Only after four years was he able to shoot it into me," she said.
d   "That's how difficult I was to succeed with,
e working myself up to be tight, so no one would do the business to me," she said.
f   And he was scared.
g "How pitiful! The old woman has embarrassed me," he thought.
h   "And another thing, if I'm out of sorts, there's this.
i I slide right in," she said.   (A conjectural emendation; see note ‡.)
j Huge was the length of the knife he saw as she drew it out.
k   "*Alright*, grandson, it's time for me to toddle off," she said.
l And she left.
25 a And for all that, she was not at a loss about where the man had taken her from, either.
b She went straight back.

c   When she got to the house they shared,
d her grandson Wîsahkêha said to her, "So, where have you been, Grandmother?"
e   "Oh gosh, you naughty boy, see, I was gang-raped," his grandmother said.
f   And her grandson said to her, "So I guess it's lucky you weren't completely devoured,
Grandmother."

g "'šina·kwa='škwe=wi·na·='na.

h e·h=manamaneči=ma·h=ki·na owiye·ha, i·ni| 'menipopi,' " e·h=ina·či o·šisemani.

i "o·ho·´, mani=koh=e·šiwe·pehto·na·ni:[*]

j mehči=meko 'e·moti·kini'| ketešiwe·pehto·ne."

k e·h=apahapane·nema·či o·hkomese·hani. ‖

26 a "ano·hko, i·ni=ye·toke wi·h=oni·ča·nese·hiyani?"| e·h=ina·či o·hkomese·hani.

b metemo·he·ha e·h=kehč‿a·hkwe·či.

c "kete·ke·h=ni·hka keta·čimo," e·h=ina·či.

d "ki·na=koh=ne·hi.

e i·ni=meko e·h=nana·tohtawiyani wi·h=oni·ča·nese·hiya·ni,"| e·h=išiwe·či metemo·ka.|

f "ano·hko, wi·škeno·he·haki=ni·hk=a·pehe e·h=ašiha·wa·či apeno·he·hahi, keteši._

g i·ni=ča·h=we·či- i·ni -inena·ni,|

h 'i·ni=ye·toke‿no·hkomese·ha| wi·h=oni·ča·nese·hiči,'‿išite·he·yani," e·h=ina·či.

i "te·pi=ye·toke·='ni nekotenwi‿wi·h=oči-maki-oni·ča·nese·hiki," e·h=iči| metemo·he·ha.

j e·h=pemi‿kohkapiči, e·h=apahapane·niči wi·sahke·ha,

k o·hkomese·hani=meko e·h=apahapane·nema·či.| [†]

l "we·=tani·hka, no·hkomese·ha," e·čini=meko, ‖ e·h=apahapane·niči.

27 a "i·na‿wi·na‿wi·h=ka·htwe·neke·mowa=kana·hi?" e·h=inekoči.

b "o·ho·´. nahi´, ano·hko, ki·h=ka·htwe·nemene=ta·ni," e·h=ikoči metemo·ka.[‡]

c o·ni='pi, "no·hkomesa neka·htwe·nema·wa,"| e·h=iči wi·sahke·ha.

d aškači=meko='pi e·h=nana·tohtawa·či,

e "ano·hko, we·ne·ha='yo·='na we·pašihehka," e·h=ina·či.

f "'šina·kwa, ne·kwa·pičike·ha," e·h=inekoči.|

g aškači·me·h=meko‿na·hka,|

h "ano·hko, we·ne·h=ya·pi·='na| ne·kwa·pičike·ha," e·h=ina·či.

i "'šina·kwa='škwe, ihkwe·wahi ne·kwanekwa·pina·ta,

j še·škesi·he·hahi," e·h=iniči o·hkomese·hani.| [§]

k "we·ne·ha='yo," e·h=ina·či.

l "'šina·kwa, we·to·sapi·me·ha," e·h=iniči na·hka.

m "a·kwi=ča·h=ye·hapa‿kehke·nemakini we·to·sapi·me·hikwe·na," e·h=ina·či. ‖ [¶]

28 a "kana·kwa, ano·hko; ki·h=po·nimene.

b meči=‛h=we·na i·na i·ni išitehka·sosa,!?[*]

c i·na a·čipanakiči e·ši-memememe·sačitehka·nata,"‿e·h=ina·či o·hkomese·hani wi·sahke·ha.[*]

d aškači e·h=na·kwa·či e·h=ma·wa·seto·niči ošise·hahi,‿oki·hahi=ke·hi,

e i·ya·h=e·h=pya·či.

---

[*] /o·ho·´/: AK ⟨.o.o.⟩.

[†] Second ⟨pa⟩ changed from ⟨pe⟩.

[‡] /o·ho·´/: AK ⟨.o.o.⟩; AK ⟨mo⟩ changed from ⟨no⟩.

[§] /še·škesi·he·hahi/: AK ⟨.šeškesiea.i.⟩.

[¶] AK ⟨pi⟩ over the start of ⟨n⟩ or the like.

[*] /i·na/: AK ⟨na.⟩ changed from ⟨ni.⟩

g   "Oh, listen to this one!

h   See, when someone is fucked over and over, that's 'she's gang-raped'," she told her grandson.

i   "Oh I see, but here's what I certainly understood you to mean:

j   I understood you to mean plainly, 'when people are eaten'."

k   He was laughing at his grandmother.

26 a   And he said to his grandmother, "Grandmother, are you now maybe going to have a baby?"

b   The old woman was furious.

c   "Well, it was your fault for telling about it," he said to her.

d   "And yours, for sure.

e   Just now you asked me if I was having a baby," the old woman said.

f   "Grandmother, the little birds always make babies, you tell me.

g   So, that's why I said that to you

h   and thought, 'Now my grandmother will probably have a baby,' " he told her.

i   "Would one time seem to be enough to have a whole, big baby?" said the old woman.

j   Wîsahkêha turned around where he sat and laughed,

k   laughing at his grandmother.

l   "Oh, my poor grandmother," he would say, and every time he did, he laughed.

27 a   "But will he at least feel sorry for someone?" she said, directed at him.

b   "So that's it! Alright, Grandmother, I'll feel sorry for you, O.K.?" he said to the old lady.

c   And then, the story goes, Wîsahkêha said, "I feel sorry for my grandmother."

d   And after a while, the story goes, he asked her,

e   "Grandmother, by the way, who was it that violated you?"

f   "Why, it was the snare-maker," she told him.

g   And a little later, again,

h   he said to her, "Now tell me, Grandmother, who is the snare-maker?"

i   "Why, the one who snares women,

j   young teenagers," his grandmother said.

k   "So tell me who," he said to her.

l   "Why, it's The-One-with-the-Indian-Hemp-Rope," she said.

m   "Well, I guess I don't know who has the Indian-hemp rope," he said to her.

28 a   "It's no use, Grandmother; I'll stop asking you.

b   It's hardly likely that that's his name!—

c   the one you give all kinds of randy names to," said Wîsahkêha to his grandmother.

d   After a while he left to go to where his uncles and aunts had a village.

e   And he arrived there.

f meše·=’nah=nekotenwi ma·maya=meko e·h=to·hki·či wi·sahke·ha,|

g e·h=mawi‿sa·kiči·či.

h i·nah=či·h=wi·na nekoti| e·h=taši·hkawa·niči ihkwe·wani.

i “wihihwi·´,” e·h=ina·či,*

j nano·škwe=meko e·h=iši-pemipenoniči.|

k e·h=a·pihwa·či.

l “šihihwi·´, meše=ye·toke e·nwa·či·yanehe e·h=taši-sanasanakapineneki,” e·h=ina·či.

m e·h=a·čimoči.

n “nenekwa·pineko·pi=ma·hi,” e·h=iniči. ‖

29 a “’ši‿mani=ni·hka pemičinawe pemi-we·wenetwi,”| e·h=ina·či.

b “i·tepi·me·h=meko neteši-ata·hpisa.”

c o·ni=’pi i·nah=meko e·h=nekwa·mehkenoči.

d aškači=meko e·h=pye·či-na·teniči i·ni nekwa·pičikani.

e i·ni=meko e·h=ki·ši-kehke·nema·či na·hina·hi wi·h=pya·niči.

f o·ni=’pi tepehki wi·sahke·ha e·h=natone·haki nenos‿okota·kani,

g e·h=mehkaki,

h nenoswi‿=meko ‿oteški·hani.|

i “i·ni,” e·h=išite·he·či,

j e·h=ki·wi-apahapane·niči.|

k o·ni meko·te·wenani| e·h=awihiwe·či.

l e·h=pa·sikešwa·či i·nini‿nenos‿oteški·hani.

m ke·kya·ta=meko e·h=te·pahkwi-po·hkešwa·či.

n o·ni·=’ni nenos‿okota·kaneki| nepi e·h=anaho·to·či| e·pa·po·hte·niki,

o e·h=si·na·hkoškaki. ‖

30 a oteški·hani oneškoki| e·h=asa·či.

b mehto·či=meko=’pi ke·htena ihkwe·wa.|

c e·h=neškimeči ihkwe·waki‿wi·h=nepina·towa·či.|

d wi·sahke·ha ki·ši·hta·či, e·h=nepina·teki,

e e·h=anemi|-ma·tako·hkwe·hoči.

f ke·htena| e·h=šowe·kapite·niki nekwa·pičikani.

g e·ye·nose·či=meko, i·tepi e·h=išisahoči.

h e·h=ki·ši‿mehči·ka·hkwisahto·či oko·te·hani wi·sahke·ha,

i e·h=taši-ma·kwima·kwinawi·hka·noči.

j i·na·ka=ke·hi kena·či=meko i·tepi e·h=a·či.

k aye=či·h=meko e·h=ki·šapisonitehe.

l opahopye·ni=meko e·h=nawači-so·kena·či oteški·hani.|

m kapo·twe e·h=we·pitanekoči, e·h=awiwa·či.|

n wi·sahke·ha, na·hina·hi ke·tawi-po·hkahamawoči| oto·teški·hemani, ‖

31 a “nekatawi‿šeki, nekatawi‿šeki,” e·h=iči.

b i·ni=ke·h=meko=’pi e·h=po·hkahesoči| neniwa,‿

c e·h=šekiniči,| e·h=išite·he·či.

---

*AK ⟨wiiw⟩ has a long link above.

f   One time early in the morning Wîsahkêha woke up
g   and went to pee.
h   And there he was surprised to see someone busily engaged with a woman.
i   "Well now!" he said to him,
j   and he ran off in a random direction.
k   And he untied her.
l   "Jeepers! It looks like you just let yourself be completely tied up tight," he said to her.
m   And she told what had happened.
n   "I was caught in a snare, obviously," she said.
29 a   "Well, it's nice along this side," he said to her.
b   "And I was jerked up there a little ways."

c   And then, the story goes, he buried himself in the dirt right there.
d   And some time later the other one came for the snare.
e   And then he had learned the time when he would come.
f   And that night, the story goes, Wîsahkêha went looking for a buffalo throat,
g   and he found one,
h   and the spleen of a buffalo.
i   "That's it," he thought,
j   and he laughed as he went from place to place.
k   And then he borrowed some skirts.
l   And he split that buffalo spleen in half with a knife.
m   And he cut a hole nearly all the way through it.
n   And then, they say, he filled that buffalo throat with warm water
o   and clamped it between his legs.
30 a   And he placed the spleen on his groin.
b   He was just exactly like a woman, the story goes.
c   The women were told not to go after water.
d   And Wîsahkêha, after he was all set, went after water,
e   going with his head covered.
f   Sure enough, the snare was tied there spread open.
g   And as he was walking along, he shot into it.
h   Wîsahkêha had shoved down his skirts,
i   and was pretending to strain hard with his body.
j   Meanwhile, the other fellow went there, approaching with care.
k   And here he found "her" already snared.
l   Taking his time, he first held the spleen in his hand.
m   And at some point he started in and took "her."
n   And Wîsahkêha, at the moment his spleen was almost poked through,
31 a   said, "I have to pee! I have to pee!"
b   And just then, they say, the man drilled a hole through,
c   and "she" peed, as he thought.

^d wi·sahke·ha| ki·mo·či e·h=papahkenaki i·ni nekwa·pičikani.

^e e·ye·ši-=meko -me·kwe·wi-anwe·we·kome·niči, e·h=ata·hpehkwe·na·či.|

^f ke·keya·h=meko e·h=po·ni_-ne·moči=kaški.

^g e·h=ma·kwima·kwinawi·či.

^h ke·keya·h| e·h=opiškwe·ška·či, e·h=pwa·wi-kaški_-ne·moči.

ⁱ i·na·='na_we·nekwa·pičikanemita.

^j aškači=meko e·h=pahkihte·neči,| e·h=neseči.

^k i·nah=meko| e·h=taši-ča·kaneneki.|

^l no·hka·winiki e·h=ma·ne·wa·či i·nahi e·sapi·hke·haki.*

^m ma·ne=meko i·nahi e·h=oči_-keta·waneti·wa·či.

ⁿ "i·niki," e·h=ina·či| wi·sahke·ha.

^o i·ni_e·hkwiči. ‖

---

*AK ⟨niki⟩: a following divider was added later, below the dot of the ⟨ki⟩.

^d   Wîsahkêha secretly broke the ropes of the snare.

^e   And while the other fellow was well into snoring, he grabbed him by the head.

^f   Before long he was no longer able to breathe.

^g   He kept straining hard with his body.

^h   And soon he swelled up, not being able to breathe.

ⁱ   That was the one who had the snare.

^j   After a while he was squeezed to death and killed.

^k   He rotted all away right there.

^l   And the next year there were many spiders in that place.

^m   Many came swarming out of there.

ⁿ   "There they are," said Wîsahkêha about them.

^o   That's as much as there is about him.

âmanôneniwa

The Story of Lady-Killer

âmanôneniwa

Alfred Kiyana[*]

1 a   e·šawiči_nekoti a·mano·neniwa.

b   e·h=ma·mahkate·wi·či,
c   e·h=mehkokwawa·či ihkwe·wahi.
d   e·h=kwi·yese·hiči=ke·h=meko, e·h=mehkokwawa·či.
e   "ki·šikiyane,| ki·h=nah_owi·wi," e·h=ikoči| ke·temina·kočini.

f   kapo·twe_e·h=ki·šiki·hiči.
g   kapo·twe e·h=mi·ša·čiheči.
h   menehte·wi·me·h=ke·hi·='nahi e·h=katawi-nepo·hiči,
i   e·h=ahkani·hiči.
j   ki·h_ki·ši-=ča·hi='pi -ne·se·či, i·ni e·h=mi·ša·čiheči.
k   e·h=ni·mihete·niki='yo=ke·hi.
l   "ki·h=mawi-ni·mi," e·h=ineči.
m   "hao·ʔ," e·h=išiwe·či,
n   i·tepi e·h=a·či.
o   e·h=pwa·wi|-nenawoči._
p   "we·ne·h=ča·hi·='na," e·h=ineči.
q   ahpene·či=meko_wa·pamekočini,| e·h=apahapane·niniči. ‖
2 a   e·h=we·pi_mi·hkemehkwe·we·či,
b   ahpene·či=meko=na·hka e·h=a·neha·nawesiči.[†]
c   ki·ši-=meko| -ča·ki-kočawiči_ihkwe·wahi, e·h=pe·we·nemoči.
d   "ta·ni=ye·toke a·mi-'ši-kakano·neti·ya·ni,"| e·h=išite·he·či.
e   e·h=pwa·wi-=ke·h=meko_-nenehke·netaki e·na·hpawa·či.
f   wa·wosa·h=meko kapo·twe_e·h=mya·šite·he·či.

g   kapo·twe,_"ši·´,_ne·pehe,_man=e·na·hpawa·ya·ni," e·h=išite·he·či.
h   "ki·hpene=meko i·noki kemiya·ke," e·h=iči,
i   "e·ye·ši-=ma·h=meko mani| -mešahkwahki," iči.[‡]
j   kapo·twe=meko e·h=we·pi|-kemiya·niki. ‖
2A a   e·h=mi·ša·te·nemoči.|
b   kapo·twe_ki·ši-kemiya·niki, e·h=ki·yoki·yose·či.
c   meše=meko·='nahi e·nemi-=meko| -ne·wokočini ihkwe·wahi,
d   e·h=menwe·nemekoči.

e   kwi·yena=meko=na·hkači e·h=ni·mihete·niki,
f   i·tepi e·h=a·či.|

---

[*]The manuscript is NAA 2432.1; it has 32 pages. Michelson's title was "Homo Stuprator."
[†]/e·h=a·neha·nawesiči/: ⟨a⟩ in ⟨na⟩ is written over ⟨e⟩.
[‡]/iči/: AK ⟨iči⟩ with the syllable ⟨i⟩ changed from ⟨e⟩ by adding a dot; cf. 18d.

The Story of Lady-Killer
Translated by Ives Goddard

1 a   The story of one Lady-Killer.

b   When he fasted,
c   he had dreams of women.
d   Even as a boy he had dreams of them.
e   "When you grow up, you'll be good at marrying them," the one blessing him told him.

f   At some point he became grown up.
g   And at some point he was given fancy clothes to dress up in.
h   But a little before that he had almost died,
i   and he was just skin and bones.
j   So, it was after he had recovered, the story goes, that he was given the fancy clothes.
k   Now, there was a dance where he was.
l   "You must go and dance," he was told.
m   "Alright, I will," he declared,
n   and he went there.
o   And nobody recognized him
p   "So, who's that?" was the question asked.
q   And every time the others looked at him they were always laughing.
2 a   He began to try his luck with the women,
b   and time and again he failed.
c   After he had tried with all the women, he gave up.
d   "I wonder how I could get a girl into a conversation," he thought.
e   Now, he did not think of what he had dreamed.
f   And, not surprisingly, he eventually became depressed.

g   And at some point he thought, "Say, I forgot, this is what I dreamt about."
h   And he said, "If only it could rain now."
i   And he said, "Yes, with a clear sky as it now is."
j   Suddenly it started raining.
2A a   And he was glad.
b   Later, after the rain, he walked around.
c   And when any of the women saw him,
d   they liked him.

e   And there just happened to be another dance where he was,
f   and he went there.

g   wi·na=meko e·h=ki·wi|-na·katawe·nemekoči.*

h   me·mečine·h=ni·miwahamoweči, e·h=mawi‿ni·miči,

i   e·h=mi·ša·tesiči.

j   i·ni=’pi| ihkwe·waki e·h=ča·ki-=meko‿ne·wa·wa·či.†

k   wi·na=meko mehto·či| nešihka e·h=neniwiči.|

l   e·h=asipi-=meko -me·nawa·nekoči.‖

3 a   ki·ši-ki·ke·noweči,

b   wi·na=ke·hi e·h=na·kwa·či e·h=owi·ke·hiwa·či.

c   apina=meko e·h=wani·hke·či| oto·na·kani.‡

d   i·ya·h=meko| pye·ya·či, e·h=mehkwite·he·či, ki·ši-peninawi·či,

e   e·h=na·teki oto·na·kani.

f   e·h=mehčikahkwaki, e·h=mehtanasite·či.

g   i·ni=meko a·neta e·h=ki·ši-=meko -apane·nemekoči.

h   e·h=pwa·wi-=ke·h=meko| ke·ko·hi -iši‿mi·na·wite·he·či.

i   e·h=ki·ši-=’yo=ke·hi -ča·ki-neškina·koči ihkwe·wahi.

j   e·h=pwa·wi-=ča·h=meko -kehke·nema·či.

k   kapo·twe‿e·h=nowi·či,| e·h=ma·ne·niči ihkwe·wahi.

l   e·ški-=ke·h=meko -pehkote·hiniki. ‖

4 a   “kaši=ča·h=ma·haki-’šawi·toke·hiki,” e·h=išite·he·či, ihkwe·wahi.

b   e·h=mawi‿sa·kiči·či.

c   ki·ši‿peno·či·me·hi -anemehka·či,

d   nekoti peteki e·h=pye·či-ka·škiha·či.

e   man=e·na·piči, ihkwe·wani=či·hi.

f   pe·hki=ke·hi=’pi=meko-=’nini=’yo we wi·sakine·hokočini.

g   e·h=pemipenoči,

h   e·h=peminehka·koči.‿

i   wi·na=ke·hi-=’na oškinawe·ha e·h=kekye·htena·mi-=meko -se·kihekoči,

j   peno·či‿e·h=išihkana·či.

k   peteki| e·h=ina·piči,

l   e·h=pye·či-ma·ne·niči=či·hi.

m   i·ni=’pi| pe·hki=meko e·h=ki·ša·koči-=meko -kekye·htena·mi-=meko -se·kihekoči.

n   pe·hki=meko e·h=pema·moči.

o   kapo·twe=’pi‖ e·h=anemi-ayi·hkwiči.

5 a   i·ya·ma·haki=ke·hi‿ihkwe·waki, “netana·swihekona·na=meko,”| e·h=išiwe·pite·he·wa·či.§

b   e·h=ma·ma·neti·hiwa·či=meko.

c   “menehta‿me·tana·kwe·na i·na wi·h=owi·hka·nita,”‿e·h=iti·wa·či.

d   pe·hki=’yo=ke·h=meko e·h=ki·ša·koči-=meko -me·nawa·na·wa·či.

---

*/na·katawe·nemekoči/: AK ⟨nakatawepemekoči⟩.

†At the end of this sentence a second hand adds “mishilson,” a kidding reference to Michelson.

‡/apina=meko/: AK ⟨epi|nameko⟩, with ⟨pi⟩ changed from ⟨A⟩.

§/ihkwe·waki/: syllable ⟨i⟩ added later; /netana·swihekona·na/: AK ⟨netaneswiekonana⟩.

g It was *he* they were paying close attention to.

h And when the songs for the last dance were sung, he went to dance,

i decked out in his finery.

j   Then the women all saw him, the story goes.

k   It was as if he were the only man.

l All the women admired him.

3 a And after the clan feast,

b he left to go home by himself.

c Actually, he forgot his dish.

d And when he got back there, he remembered, after he had taken his outfit off,

e and he went to get his dish.

f His legs and feet were bare, without leggins or moccasins.

g   Some of them had immediately smiled at him.

h Now, he did *not* realize that anything was going on.

i Remember, he had been disliked by all the women.

j So, he did *not* understand about them.

k   At some point he went outside, and there were a lot of women.   (Back home.)

l Now, it was just beginning to get dark.

4 a "Well, what could be the matter with these people?" he thought, about the women.

b And he went off to take care of his business.

c After he had gone some ways away,

d he became aware of someone coming behind him.

e And as soon as he looked, why, here it was a woman.

f And it was precisely the one that had hit him and hurt him earlier.   (Not included above.)

g And he started running,

h with her in pursuit.

i Now for *his* part, the story goes, the young man was seriously frightened by her,

j and he left her far behind.

k   When he looked back,

l here were many of them coming towards him.

m And at that, they say, he was really, extremely seriously indeed frightened by them.

n And he fled for real.

o And at some point, the story goes, he was becoming tired.

5 a   Meanwhile, those women behind him imagined that he was playing with them,

b and they had a contest.

c "Whoever catches up to him first will have him as her friend," they told each other.

d Remember, they really admired him to an extreme degree, indeed.

e   wi·na=ke·hi·=’na| pe·hki=meko, “ši·´‚ kehke·nema·pi=’h=we·na
ki·šimiwa·te_wi·h=nešiwa·či,” e·h=išite·he·či.

f i·ni=’pi apina=meko e·h=po·ni-nenwišiki e·h=wa·wi·sakičiki a·hkwikoma·ničihi.

g e·h=kehta·moči.

h   ihkwe·waki=ke·hi‚ e·h=pwa·wi-=meko| owiye·ha -pe·we·nemoči.

i e·h=me·čimo·wi-=meko ‖-ki·wi_asipipahowa·či.

6 a   kapo·twe=meko=’pi_neniwa| e·h=we·pi-nahi-mehkawišiki.

b   ihkwe·waki=na·hka i·ni=meko e·h=išawiwa·či.

c peno·či=ke·hi=’pi·=’ni e·h=pye·nehkawa·wa·či.|

d   ke·tawi_wa·paniki=meko| neniwa e·h=pye·nehkawoči kehči_nepiseki.|

e waninawe e·h=sa·sa·kahaniki mehteko·ni, e·h=išite·he·či.

f nekoti_i·nah=meko e·h=oči_čapo·ka·hkwiseniki.

g “ni·h=nawači_meno| nepi,” e·h=išite·he·či.

h i·ni·=’nahi wi·h=anemi-’na·hkwišikehe| mehtekoki.

i mani=meko| e·ši-me·šenaki, e·h=čapo·ko·te·pahoniči=či·hi.

j mi·na·wa·piči, ko·hko·teni·hahi=či·hi. ‖

7 a   i·ni=ke·hi=’pi=meko e·h=we·pi-=meko -pakamipahoniči| ihkwe·wahi,

b e·h=ki·ši-matanekoči.

c   e·h=na·kwa·wa·či.

d   wi·na=ke·h=kapo·twe_e·h=anemi|-nenwamataki.

e e·h=mehčikahkwaki=’yo=ke·hi, e·h=mehtanasite·či,

f e·h=ohkone·hiči=wi·na.

g kapo·twe=meko| pe·hki e·h=mya·nawamataki ohka·tani.

h e·h=wa·pataki, pe·hki=či·h=meko e·h=makwimakwi·taki ohka·tani.

i ke·keya·h=meko e·h=nana·hapiči.

j i·ni=ke·hi=’pi=meko e·h=a·nawihto·či.|

k awiya·toke=ke·h=mani e·h=peno·ča·niki.

l meše=na·hina·hi e·h=pema·pye·niki si·po·wi we·wi·ki·notamowa·či.

m   i·ni=’pi ihkwe·waki ‖ ni·šwi e·h=kakano·neti·wa·či.

8 a “ki·na·na=ke·h=mana=wi·na we·či_ki·sa·čihakwe.

b a·kwi=ke·hi·=’nahi ki·na·na wi·h=kaški-awanakwini,” e·h=iti·wa·či.

c   o·ni=nekoti, “nahi·´, ayo·hi tepina·h=či·kepye·ki ki·h=a·pena.

d ke·htena ke·hke·nemikwe·ni| maneto·wa,

e ki·h=ne·ta·pena=meko=ke·ko·hi,” e·h=iči.

f   “hao·ʔ,” e·h=išiwe·či.

g e·h=na·kwa·wa·či.

h   i·nahi e·h=pya·wa·či,

i i·nah=či·h=wi·nwa·wa neniwani e·h=kehči|-nepa·niči.

j me·me·čiki=meko e·h=pehkiniči.

k e·h=mawi_keči·wa·či, i·nah=či·h či·ma·ni e·h=sakapite·niki,

l ke·ko·h=meko·=’nahi.|

e   And *he* wondered seriously whether they might have made plans to kill him.
f   Then he even stopped feeling the pain of the thorns he was running into, the story goes.
g   And he fled at top speed.
h   For their part, none of the women gave up.
i   They ran on persistently, keeping in a tight bunch.
6 a   At some point the man began to stumble, the story goes.
b   And the women also did the same.
c   Now, by then they had chased him a long way, the story goes.

d   When dawn was about to break, the man was chased up to a large lake.
e   There were logs lying all over partly exposed out of the water, as he thought.
f   And there was one that lay extending down into the water from there.
g   "I'll stop to get a drink of water," he thought.
h   And he was then going to stretch out on the log to reach it.
i   As soon as he touched it, he was startled to have it scamper into the water.
j   And taking a second look, he could see that they were alligators.
7 a   Now just then, the story goes, the women began running up,
b   having caught up to him.

c   They all went back.
d   And as for him, as he went along he soon was feeling where he was hurt.
e   Remember, he had bare legs and bare feet,
f   though he had a blanket.
g   Soon, he was completely overcome by the pain in his feet.
h   And when he looked at them, he could see that his feet were badly swollen.
i   Finally he sat down.
j   And he was immediately unable to stand and walk, the story goes.
k   What's more, there was now still far to go.
l   The river whose banks they all lived on was some ways off.

m   Then, the story goes, two of the women spoke with each other.
8 a   One of them said, "Now, *we're* responsible for putting *him* in this terrible fix.
b   And here, as it is, it's just that *we* won't be able to carry him back."
c   And then the other said, "Alright, let's go right to the shore here.
d   If a manitou truly knows me,
e   we shall see something."
f   "Alright," answered the other one.
g   And they set out.
h   When they got over there,
i   they saw a man right there sound asleep.
j   They were sure he was a stranger.
k   They went out into the open, and they saw a canoe tied up there,
l   with something in it.

^m i·ni=’pi e·h=sa·ka·hkwiseniki| aseni-papakye·hi. ‖

9 a   e·h=ata·hpenaki i·na=nekoti| ihkwe·wa, i·tepi.

^b (e·h=ni·šiwa·či=ke·h=meko.)

^c šewe·na=’pi nawači_či·hči·kwapisowaki.

^d e·ye·ši-=meko| -kehči_nepa·niči, e·h=pa·pakama·wa·či.

^e pe·hki=meko e·h=ša·ša·kwitepe·hwa·či.

^f   i·tepi| e·h=ihpahowa·či.

^g “ka·ta=meko a·čimohkani,” e·h=ina·či owi·či_ihkwe·wani.

^h (ma·haki=ke·hi še·ški=meko e·h=taši-ma·mi·wiheti·wa·či.)

ⁱ   i·ya·h=pye·ya·wa·či, e·h=a·čimoha·či_owi·či_ihkwe·wahi.

^j “ni·či_’hkwe·tike, pe·hki=meko| mana keki·sa·čiha·pena| oškinawe·ha.

^k ma·hani ohka·tani wa·patamawohko.|

^l pe·hki=meko=ma·hani·=’ni e·h=makwimakwi·taki.

^m ki·na·na=ke·hi| e·h=asa·mi-aka·wa·tamakwe‖ wi·h=a·maneyakwe.[*]

10 a   i·noki=ča·h=mana ni·na ni·h=awato·ma·wa.

^b ayi·hkwiya·ne, mana·=’ni ni·hka·na.

^c ni·na·na=meko a·ya·šo·hka ni·h=anemo·ma·pena,” e·h=iči.

^d   i·ni=ke·hi·=’pi=meko e·h=pemi|-wi·wahoči.

^e e·h=na·no·mipaho·hiči=meko.

^f   “če·winehki=meko, ni·hka·ne,” e·h=ina·či owi·či_še·škesi·he·hani.

^g i·ni=’pi=na·hka·=’na i·ni=meko e·h=išawiči.

^h e·h=na·no·mipaho·hiči=meko.

ⁱ i·ya·h=meko ašiči, “kana·kwa=yá·pi,=ni·hka·ne,”| e·h=išiwe·či.

^j   i·ni=’pi=meko=na·hka·=’na e·h=wi·wahoči,|

^k i·tepi e·h=ino·ma·či i·nini_ki·šatahwa·čini e·h=apiniči.

^l   “mana ki·na ki·h=nesa·wa.

^m kemi·nene,” e·h=ineči oškinawe·ha. ‖

11 a   ki·ši-mahkikwe·hwa·wa·či,_

^b e·h=we·po·ma·wa·či, či·kepye·ki.|

^c i·ni·=’ni_či·ma·ni e·h=ahte·niki.|

^d   (keye·hapa=ke·h=wi·na·=’pi·=’na aša·ha e·nawi·ha.)

^e   e·h=po·sa·waneti·wa·či,

^f e·h=we·pahowa·či.

^g ša·ka=ke·hi·=’niki še·škesi·haki,| o·ni·=’na oškinawe·ha.

^h ihkwe·waki e·h=pemahowa·či.

ⁱ   i·ni=’pi i·ya·hi e·h=pya·wa·či, e·h=akwa·sa·wa·či.

^j   e·h=se·kahkiwiki mehtose·neniwaki,

^k e·h=akiheči| i·niki.

^l e·h=mi·ša·te·nemowa·či e·h=pya·niči.|

^m   e·h=na·nekoči omeso·ta·nahi.

---

*/wi·h=a·maneyakwe/: ⟨e⟩ in ⟨ne⟩ has a small dot.

m   What lay in it partly sticking out was a stone axe, the story goes.

9 a   And one of the women picked it up, going there.

b   (Remember, there were two of them.)

c   But first they hiked up their skirts, the story goes.

d   And while he slept soundly, they clubbed him to death.

e   She really smashed his head to pieces with the axe.

f   And they ran there.

g   "Don't tell," she said to the other woman.

h   (Now, these were the only ones cutting each other out as rivals.)

i   When they got back there, they explained to the other women.

j   "Women, we have all really put this young man in a terrible fix.

k   Look at his feet here.

l   They're now badly swollen.

m   What's more, all of us were too eager for sex.

10 a   So, *I* will carry him home on my back now.

b   And when I get tired, then my friend here will.

c   The two of us will take turns carrying him on our backs," she said.

d   And here, right away she put him on her back to carry him, the story goes.

e   And she ran right along at an easy pace.

f   "Halfway, my friend," she said to the other young maiden.

g   The other one then did the same thing, the story goes.

h   And she ran along at an easy pace.

i   Near there she said, "O.K.! Can't go on, my friend!"

j   Right away the other one put him on her back again, the story goes,

k   and she carried him to where the one that was clubbed to death was.

l   "*You* must kill this one.

m   I give him to you," the young man was told.

11 a   After they had chopped off the head of the one,

b   they set about carrying the other one on their backs, to the shore.

c   That is where that canoe was.

d   (Now it turned out after all, that that one was a Sioux hunter, the story goes.)

e   The whole bunch of them got into the canoe,

f   and they paddled off.

g   That is, there were those nine maidens and that one young man.

h   The women did the paddling.

i   Then they got back home, the story goes, and ran the canoe up on the shore..

j   There was fear among the people there,

k   as those others had been lost.

l   And they were happy when the others came back.

m   His parents came to get him.

n   i·nihi=meko·='ni e·h=ča·ki-wi·te·mekoči še·škesi·hahi.

o   e·h=ča·k_owi·wiči.

p   e·h=we·pi-kekye·tahamawoči wa·wi·sakišikini ‖ a·hkwikoma·ničihi.[*]

12 a   ša·ka_e·h=owi·wiči, nekotenwi=meko e·h=pye·tehkwe·we·či.

b   apina=meko e·h=we·ta·se·wiči,

c   e·h=kehtwe·wesiči=ke·hi.

d   e·h=aniwa·šohwe·či| aša·ti·hani.

e   ši·ša·čini, ša·ka=meko pešekesiwahi| e·h=nesa·či.

f   kapo·twe_meše·='nah nekotenwi e·h=mo·hki·hta·kowa·či_ owi·či·škwe·hwa·wahi.

g   wi·na=meko owi·wahi e·h=ča·kihtawotehe| nanai·hta.[†]

h   e·h=ki·ša·kočite·he·či.

i   awiya·toke=ke·h=meko| e·h=menwe·nemekoči| ihkwe·wahi.

j   kapo·twe_e·h=ki·ši-pa·ni·či, e·h=nana·henoči.

k   pe·hki=meko=na·hka·='ni ihkwe·waki [e·h=menwe·nema·wa·či].[‡]

l   wi·na=ke·hi e·h=pwa·wi-=meko -kehke·nema·či e·h=menwe·nemekoči. ‖

13 a   e·h=a·mi·či.

b   e·h=pwa·wi-=ke·h -mi·hkemehkwe·we·či.

c   nešihka=meko| e·h=a·mi·či.

d   kapo·twe ki·ši|-nye·wokone·teki, e·h=na·wanone·hokoči iškwe·se·hahi,[§]

e   mo·šaki=meko=na·hka·='nihi še·škesi·he·hahi.

f   wi·na=ke·h=wa·natohka=meko e·h=owihowi·kiči.

g   e·h=a·hpawa·či._

h   "wi·h=pya·wa·či ki·waki," e·h=ineči, e·h=ina·hpawa·či.

i   e·h=mayakite·he·či, ke·htena to·hki·či, na·witepehki·niki.

j   mehči=meko e·h=kohta·čiči, e·šiwe·pesikwe·ni.

k   e·h=šekišekišiki, owiye·hani=meko e·h=tane·nema·či ke·htena.

l   me·h-=meko -po·ni-kohta·čikwe, e·h=pye·te·we·nema·či=meko owiye·hani.

m   ke·htena=meko e·h=to·hkenekoči._

n   "ayo·h=ye·toke e·h=po·ni·yanehe," e·h=ikoči._

o   wi·na=ke·hi·='na,_"či·paya=meko," e·h=išite·he·či. ‖

14 a   e·h=pemi_pasekwi·čisa·či.

b   man=e·ši_nowa·ška·či, i·nah=či·h| e·h=pehkwika·pa·niči,

c   "mawinanehko," e·h=iti·niči.

d   e·h=se·kesiči,

e   meškohpwa·ka·hani e·h=nenehke·nema·či,[¶]

f   e·h=kehta·moči.

---

[*] /we·pi/ 'began to be' is here translated 'one by one'.

[†] /nanaihta/ 'it just so hapened that', here 'and his alone' (following AW).

[‡] /e·h=menwe·nema·wa·či/ (IG); a word was omitted.

[§] /e·h=na·wanone·hokoči/: AK ⟨enawaneneokoči⟩.

[¶] /meškohpwa·ka·ha/ 'Redstone Pipe', a man pursued by the ghost of a woman in a story (K-RP).

n   And all those maidens then went along with him,

o   and he married them all.

p   And one by one the thorns were plucked from his wounds.

12 a   He married nine, while bringing home brides just once.

b   He even became a warrior,

c   and what's more he had a knack for getting game.

d   He was a good shot with arrows.

e   Whenever he went hunting, he killed exactly nine deer.

f   Suddenly at some point they were attacked by their enemies.

g   All his wives were killed, and his alone.

h   And he was devastated.

i   Now, women still liked him as before.

j   At some point, after he was released from strict mourning, he fixed himself up.

k   Women really [liked him] again, then.

l   But the thing is, he was unaware that they liked him.

13 a   He moved away to make camp.

b   That is to say, he did not court women.

c   He moved away and camped alone.

d   In time, after he had been away four days, girls went following after him.

e   Again they were nothing but young maidens.

f   Meanwhile, for his part he was living there without a care in the world.

g   And he had a dream.

h   "Your wives will be coming," he was told, in his dream.

i   And he had a funny feeling when he woke up for real, in the middle of the night.

j   He was plainly fearful, for whatever reason.

k   He lay there, thinking someone else was really there.

l   And before he was over being fearful, he was aware of someone coming.

m   Sure enough, they touched him to wake him.

n   "I guess this is where you camped," the voice said to him.

o   And here he was thinking, "It's a ghost."

14 a   And he leaped to his feet.

b   And as soon as he ran out, he found them standing there in a bunch,

c   saying to each other, "Get after him!'

d   And he was scared,

e   thinking about Redstone Pipe,

f   and he fled at top speed.

g   petek=e·na·piči,‿ke·htena=meko| e·h=pye·hpahoniči.

h   me·me·čiki=meko i·niye·he owi·wahi.

i   pe·hki='pi=meko·='ni e·h=se·kesiči.

j   kena·či=meko e·h=po·ni-kaškihto·či pe·hki wi·h=kehčipenoči.‿

k   ašiči pye·hpahoniči, mehtekwi e·h=mehkawišiniči,‿

l   i·tepi e·h=ineče·škaminiči.

m   "nepanahoko·pi=meko," e·h=išite·he·či.

n   e·h=mama·toma·či.|

o   "ka·ta‿nešihke·ko.

p   kemenwito·to·nepwa=kohi·='yo·we,"| e·h=iči.

q   e·h=apahapane·nemekoči.

r   i·ni='pi ne·wasomečini, ‖ "nakisa·no=wé·na.

15 a   pwa·wi-=ke·h=-nakisa·yane, ki·h=pa·pakamenepena," e·h=ikoči.

b   kwayahkwi=meko e·h=nakisa·či,| e·h=matakwisahoči,

c   e·h=kosa·či.

d   e·h=tetepa·kwapiniči.

e   i·ni=ke·h=meko e·h=inehinehtawa·či.

f   a·neta‿e·h=či·peči·peče·sahekoči.

g   wi·na=ke·hi, "či·payaki=meko," e·h=išite·he·či.

h   kapo·twe| e·h=mama·toma·či wi·h=ketemina·koči.

i   i·ni='pi, "ki·h=awanenepena=ma·h=meko," e·h=ikoči i·niye·ne.

j   "i·noki=ke·hi pwa·wi‿ma·čišinane,

k   i·ni=meko wi·h=pa·pakamena·ke," e·h=ikoči neniwa.

l   e·h=pa·hki·kwe·neki kakišaši·pye.

m   e·h=wa·se·ya·niki=či·hi,

n   e·h=me·nešite·he·či.

o   "nahi´, pe·hki·='nahi kano·šina·ke wi·h=išihišimiwa·ke·ni," e·h=inekoči ‖ i·nihi ihkwe·wahi.

16 a   kekimesi=či·h=meko še·škesi·he·hahi,

b   kekimesi=meko e·h=owi·wiči,

c   meta·swi kotwa·šika še·škesi·hahi.

d   i·ni=ke·hi='pi e·h=nešike·či,

e   nešihka wi·na e·h=nekoto·ke·či.

f   o·ni owi·wahi, e·h=asipike·niči=meko.

g   šwa·šika wi·kiya·pye·ni e·h=ahte·ki.

h   owi·wahi=ke·hi='pi=meko·='nihi,

i   o·ni=wi·na| ša·ka·nameki owi·ki i·na| neniwa.*

j   kekimesi=meko| e·h=na·ni·šo·ke·niči owi·wahi.

k   pe·na·winikini='pi kehč‿o·te·wenika·ni=meko e·h=owi·kiwa·či.| †

l   e·h=pwa·wi-=ke·h=meko -ačihkwiniči.|

---

*/ša·ka·nameki/: AK ⟨šakanemeki⟩.

†/pe·na·winikini='pi/: AK ⟨.penawinikini.pi.⟩.

g When he looked back, sure enough they were coming on the run.
h Surely it was his late wives.
i Now he was really scared, to hear the tale.
j And he was slowly losing his ability to run really fast.
k When they came running closer, they stumbled on a stick,
l and they kicked it at him.
m "Missed me!" he thought.
n And he begged them.
o "Don't kill me.
p I did treat you well," he said.
q And they laughed at him.
r Then one being outraced by the others shouted at him, "At least stop running!
15 a And if you don't stop running, we'll club you to death!"
b He decided he'd better stop running, so he threw himself down and covered up,
c as he was afraid of them.
d They sat around him in a circle.
e And here, he kept hearing them the same way.
f Some kept poking him with their feet.
g And here, *he* was thinking they were ghosts.
h At some point he begged them to take pity on him.
i Then the same one as before said to him, "Listen, we're going to take you home."
j "And if you don't move now,
k we'll club you to death on the spot," she told the man.
l He uncovered his face, slowly and reluctantly.
m He could see then that it was daytime,
n and he was ashamed.
o "Alright, now you can speak to us normally about anything you want," those women told him.
16 a He learned they were all virginal young teenagers.
b And he married every one of them,
c sixteen maidens.

d Another thing, he then lived alone, the story goes,
e staying alone in a house by himself.
f And as for his wives, they lived all clustered together.
g There were eight houses.
h And those were his wives, the story goes.
i And that man's own house was the ninth.
j His wives all lived two to a house.
k And in the summers everyone lived together in a large summer house.
l And another thing, they were not pregnant.

m kapo·twe‿e·h=mi·na·we·netaki owi·yawi e·h=pwa·wi|-kaški-ačihkwiha·či.

n kapo·twe=meko‿če·wina·h=meko e·h=ačihkwiniči. ‖

17 a kapo·twe‿e·h=no·še·niči če·wina·h=mekoho.

b kekimesi=meko‿kwi·yese·he·hahi.

c a·hpene=meko e·h=išihišina·kosiniči.

d wi·na=meko e·šina·kosiči‿e·h=išihišina·kosiniči.

e ki·ši-=meko -menw‿a·ya·nekino·hiniči,

f i·ni=ʼpi=na·hkači mehtose·neniwaki e·h=a·hkwamatamowa·či.[*]

g wi·na=meko=na·hkači e·h=ča·kine·niči‿owi·wahi.

h o·ni=kohi·=ʼna neniwa še·ški e·h=a·hkwamataki| kenwe·ši.

i o·ni oni·ča·nesahi e·h=pwa·wi-a·hkwamataminiči.

j kotakaki=wi·na apeno·haki e·h=ča·kine·wa·či.‖

18 a wi·na=meko nešihka oni·ča·nesahi e·h=ne·se·niči.

b ki·ši-menwi-pema·tesiči, e·h=na·kwa·či oni·ča·nesahi e·h=awiničini,

c e·h=ki·wa·pama·či.|

d a·hpene=ke·h=meko inekineniči.[†]

e ki·ši-=ča·h| -ki·ki·wa·pama·či, e·h=mya·šite·he·či i·na| neniwa.

f o·ni=ʼpi| e·h=owi·ke·hiwa·tehe e·h=a·či.

g i·ni=ʼpi=pe·hki e·h=ta·taši‿mi·hkeče·wi·nitehe owi·wahi e·h=ne·taki,

h e·h=asahase·hke·niči,

i na·hkači e·h=ta·taši-paškwahwa·niči| asayahi.[‡]

j i·ni=ʼpi e·h=mayo·či.

k e·h=ma·wačipahoniči oni·ča·nesahi, ‖

19 a e·h=wawi·kimekoči.

b meše=mekoho e·h=inekihkwika·pa·niči.| [§]

c masa·či=meko e·h=mehkwinawe·mekoči.

d "ši·ˊ‿ke·htena," e·h=ina·či.

e i·ni=ʼpi e·h=wa·wiya·wima·či e·hpi·hči-te·pihekoči e·h=mehkwinawe·mekoči.

f i·ni=ke·h=mo·hči=ʼpi=meko kete·=ʼnahi e·h=nenehke·nema·či ihkwe·wahi.

g i·ni=ke·hi·=ʼpi·=ʼnihi| e·šimekoči oni·ča·nesahi,

h we·či-=ča·hi -mehkwinawe·mekoči.

i kapo·twe| e·h=pye·nota·koči okye·ni.

j "mani=ma·h=wi·na e·šawičiki? ši·ka·wiwaki?" e·h=ineči.

k e·h=mi·na·wa·patisoči, e·h=pwa·wi-=či·hi -ši·ka·wiči. ‖

20 a aškači=meko we·teškwe·se·heminičihi e·h=te·pi-pa·ni·hekoči.

b ki·h‿ki·ši-pa·nipa·ni·či,| e·h=we·pi-mi·ša·tesiči meše=meko.

c "nahi·ˊ, i·ni wi·h=owi·wiya·ni," e·h=išite·he·či.

---

[*]/i·ni=ʼpi=na·hkači/: AK ⟨.inipi|nakači.⟩.

[†]inekineniči: AK ⟨inekineniči⟩ with the first letter an ⟨e⟩ with a dot; cf. 2*i*.

[‡]/-paškwahwa·niči/: AK ⟨.paškwakwaniči|⟩, with ⟨kwa⟩ written over erased ⟨ikx⟩.

[§]/e·h=inekihkwika·pa·niči/: AK ⟨eninekikwikapaniči⟩, with ⟨či⟩ changed from ⟨ni⟩.

m　Sometime later he noticed that he hadn't been able to make them pregnant.
n　And sometime later, at exactly the same time, they got pregnant.
17 a　And sometime later they gave birth, at exactly the same time.
b　They were all little boys.
c　And they all looked exactly alike.
d　They all looked exactly the way *he* looked.

e　　After they were pretty good-sized,
f　then this time the people got sick, the story goes.
g　And this time again, it was *his* wives that all died.
h　And the man *was* only sick for a long time.
i　And his children did not get sick.
j　But the other children all died.
18 a　Only *his* children survived.
b　　After he was healthy again, he went to the places where his children were,
c　going around to see them.
d　Now, they were all just the same size.
e　Well, after having gone around to see them all, the man felt sad.
f　　And then he went to where he and his wives had lived, the story goes.
g　He saw the actual places where his wives had worked,
h　tanning hides,
i　and also the places where they had scraped the hair off hides.
j　　Then he wept, the story goes.
k　And his children came running and gathered together,
19 a　and they spoke to him to comfort him.
b　They stood in a fair-sized group.
c　And with some difficulty they brought his thoughts back with their words.
d　　"Gee, that's true," he told them.
e　Then he thanked them for how pleased they had made him in bringing his mind back.
f　　What's more, his thinking even shifted all the way back to women, the story goes.
g　Now, that's how his children's words had affected him,
h　and how come his thinking had been shifted by them.
i　　At some point his mother came to visit him.
j　"Say, but are ones like this widowers unreleased from mourning?" he was asked.
k　He took a look at himself and suddenly realized he was not in mourning garb.

20 a　　After some time he got his release from strict mourning from the girls' parents.
b　And after becoming a widower released from mourning, he was free to begin dressing up.
c　"Alright, now I'm going to get married," he thought.

d   eˑh=šaˑšiˑšaˑči.|

e   kapoˑtwe‿eˑh=ayiˑhkwiči.|

f   keˑkoˑh=meko eˑh=kosekweˑnetaki otaˑsiyaˑneki.

g   eˑh=wiˑkeˑtaˑsiyeˑnoči=ʼp=aˑpehe, kweˑhčipa=mekoho.

h   kapoˑtwe=peˑhki=meko eˑh=ayiˑhkwihekwiči,

i   eˑh=šekišekišiki.

j   mehtoˑči=meko eˑh=mamaˑčiˑniči owiyeˑhani, eˑh=išiteˑheˑči. ‖

21 a   keyeˑhapa=keˑh=wiˑna=ʼpiˑ=ʼni iˑni| owiˑnakayi.

b   iˑtep=eˑh=inaˑpiči, eˑh=taši-saˑsaˑkinaniweˑniči manetoˑwani.

c   eˑh=pemi‑ketoˑteˑniči.

d   meˑmeˑčiki=meko manetoˑwani,

e   aˑhpene=meko eˑh=inekihkwaˑhkosiniči.|

f   kiˑši-=meko -čaˑki-wepoˑteˑniči, eˑh=kehkeˑnetaki eˑh=maˑčikanweˑči.

g   peˑhki=meko eˑh=kiˑšaˑkoči-=meko -nešiwi-ahkoniki.

h   meše=ʼnah=meko niˑšwi taˑtwaˑhkiwani eˑh=tahkatahkamaˑhkwiseniki iˑni owiˑnakayi,

i   eˑh=manetoˑwi‑ketakikaniki, ‖

22 a   eˑh=makomakočeˑškaˑniki.

b   "šihihyeˑ´," eˑh=išiteˑheˑči.

c   "wiˑh=išawiwaˑneˑni=ʼnah=mani," eˑh=išihišiteˑheˑči.

d   iˑni=ʼpi kapoˑtwe eˑh=wepi‑kaˑkiˑwi‑poˑni-maˑčikanweˑči,

e   eˑh=poˑni-maˑčikanweˑči=kapoˑtwe.

f   eˑh=wepi-ataˑhpahoˑtoˑči,

g   aˑwasi=meko eˑnehpapiči eˑh=inehpaˑkwateˑniki owiˑnakayi.

h   "šihihyeˑ´," eˑh=išiteˑheˑči.

i   eˑh=pwaˑwi-=meko -poˑniteˑheˑči.|

j   eˑh=pwaˑwi-=keˑh=meko -kehkeˑnetaki wiˑh=inaˑhpenatoˑkweˑni.

k   kapoˑtwe=meko=ʼpi=naˑhka eˑh=maˑčikanweˑči.

l   tepinaˑh=ahpemeki eˑh=inehkweˑnaki,

m   eˑh=pemi‑niˑmeˑškaˑniki. ‖

23 a   wiˑna=keˑhi eˑh=aˑhtawaˑšiki.|

b   nanoˑpehka=čiˑhi eˑh=ahkoniki.

c   kapoˑtwe‿eˑh=pyeˑtaˑnemateniki.

d   iˑni=ʼpi eˑh=kawaˑseniki,

e   eˑh=kiˑšaˑkočinakayeˑšiki.*

f   kapoˑtwe‿eˑh=neˑtaki nekoti ihkweˑwa miˑnakayi.

g   keˑkoˑh=meko| eˑh=išiteˑheˑči naˑhinaˑhi neˑtaki,

h   eˑh=meˑšenaki.

i   kwiˑyena=ʼyo=keˑh=meko| eˑhkoniki naˑhinaˑhi eˑh=neˑtaki.

j   kenaˑči=meko| eˑh=kiˑwi-meˑmeˑšenaki.|

k   kapoˑtwe=meko eˑh=ayoˑči.

l   eˑh=šeˑškesiˑhiči=ʼyo=keˑhi, kiˑhkiˑhki=meko| eˑh=ayoˑči.

m   kiˑši-ayoˑči, neniwani=čiˑh eˑh=neˑwaˑči,

---

*The translation follows HL.

^d He was hunting.
^e And at some point he felt tired.
^f He thought there was something heavy in his breechcloth.
^g And he would straighten out his breechcloth, repeatedly, the story goes.
^h And at some point it really made him tired.
ⁱ He was lying down,
^j and he thought it was as if some creature was moving around.
21 a And it turned out that what it was, after all, was his penis, the story goes.
^b And when he looked in there, he saw a snake flicking out its tongue.
^c And it crawled out.
^d It was definitely a snake,
^e and it was uniformly the same size around.
^f After it had all crawled out, he was aware that he had an erection.
^g It was really absolutely incredibly long.
^h That penis of his stretched right on across two ravines, one and then another,
ⁱ and it was spotted like a snake
22 a and kept swelling up.
^b "Oh my!" he thought.
^c "I wonder what I should do now," he kept thinking.
^d And then at some point he began to cease to have an erection,
^e and at some point his erection was gone.
^f He started hauling it in.
^g His penis was piled up higher than he was as he sat.
^h "Oh my!" he thought.
ⁱ He couldn't stop thinking about it.
^j And he had no idea what to do with it.
^k And at some point he had an erection again.
^l He guided it to go straight up,
^m and it began rising.
23 a Now, *he* was lying on his back.
^b And he could see it was tremendously long.
^c At some point the wind came up.
^d And then it was blown over.
^e And his penis landed hard and hurt him.
^f At some point a certain woman saw the penis.
^g She was having thoughts at the time she saw it,
^h and she touched it.
ⁱ Now, it was exactly as long as when she saw it.
^j She slowly touched it in places.
^k And at some point she made use of it.
^l Now, she was a virgin, and she went ahead anyway and used it.
^m After she used it, she suddenly saw a man,

n   e·h=pi·nešiha·či. ‖

24 a   "natawa·či=meko ki·h=owi·weti·pena," e·h=išiwe·či ihkwe·wa.

b   "hao·?,"| e·h=ineči.

c   wi·na=ke·hi·='niya neniwa e·h=mi·ša·te·nemoči=meko.|

d   ne·ya·pi e·šikitehe e·h=išikiči,

e   e·h=očiwena·či.

f   ma·wači=ke·h=meko| e·h=we·wenesiniči i·nini še·škesi·he·hani.|

g   ča·ki=meko e·h=iši_we·wenesiniči.

h   o·ni·='pi e·h=a·mi·wa·či,

i   i·nini e·h=ni·ši·hiwa·či owi·we·hani,

j   oni·ča·nesahi e·h=ča·kiwena·či.

k   kapo·twe=meko='pi=na·hkači| i·niye=meko e·h=išawiči,

l   kekeni=mekoho ‖ e·h=nana·hapiči.

25 a   kwayahkwi| we·či_pye·či·we·pote·wa·či e·h=ina·samapiči.

b   apina=meko e·h=keši·pinakaye·či,*

c   i·ya·h=meko e·h=ahko·nwe·či we·či·wa·či.

d   pe·hki-=meko=na·hkači -še·škesi·he·ha i·ni e·h=ne·taki.

e   kapo·twe=meko| e·h=ki·sa·čisahto·či.†

f   e·h=pwa·wi_kaški-ketenaki.

g   e·h=po·ni-=ke·h=meko -kehke·netaki.

h   aškači e·h=kehke·netaki,

i   i·nini=či·hi e·h=taši_manekoči neniwani.‡

j   e·h=mayo·hka·noči.

k   "natawa·či ki·na=meko ki·h=ona·pe·mene," e·h=ikoči.|

l   "hao·?," e·h=ina·či.

m   e·h=owi·wiči,

n   e·h=ni·šo·hkwe·we·či,

o   še·škesi·he·hahi=mekoho. ‖

26 a   meše=meko=na·hka·='nihi e·h=taši-owihowi·wiči.

b   kapo·twe_e·h=kehke·netaki wi·h=ma·no·hkwe·we·či.

c   ke·waki=meko kapo·twe| e·h=ni·peniki.

d   ni·penike=ke·hi·='pi·='ni wi·h=ma·no·hkwe·we·či.

e   kapo·twe| še·škesi·he·haki=meko,| "mo·šaki pehkiwe·hehke·yakwe," e·h=iyowa·či.

f   e·h=pehkiwe·hehke·wa·či, ne·htawi=meko.

g   pe·hki-=meko -oškinawe·haki pemičinawe e·h=anemiha·wa·či na·wanonehkwe·wa·čiki.

h   wi·na=ke·hi·='na e·h=ši·ša·či.

i   kapo·twe=meko_i·niye e·h=išawiči| e·šawitehe.

j   owi·nakayi| e·h=kenoška·niki, pe·hki=mekoho. ‖

---

*/e·h=keši·pinakaye·či/: /ye·/ from HWB; AK ⟨ya⟩.

†Translation: HWB.

‡/e·h=taši_manekoči/: AK ⟨etačimanekoči⟩.

ⁿ and she needed no encouragement to speak up to him.

24 a 　　"We might as well go ahead and get married," she said.

b 　　"Alright, let's do that," was the reply she got.

c 　　Meanwhile, that man was quite delighted himself.

d His bodily form was back to what it had been,

e and he took her with him from there.

f Now, that young teenager was the prettiest of all,

g and she was pretty in every aspect.

h 　　And then they went to camp,

i just he and his wife together,

j and he took along all his children.

k 　　Then some time later the same thing happened to him as before, the story goes,

l and he quickly sat down.

25 a He decided it would be better to sit facing the direction they all moved there from.

b His penis even itched,

c and it reached all the way back to where they had come from.

d 　　Once again a true young virgin saw it.

e And at some point she shoved it in and got it stuck,

f 　and she was unable to get it out.

g What's more she lost consciousness.

h A while later she came to,

i and discovered that that man was fucking her.

j She pretended to weep.

k 　　"I might as well go ahead and marry *you*," she told him.

l "Alright, let's do that," he told her.

m And he married her,

n and he had two wives,

o young teenage girls.

26 a 　　Again he went along contentedly being married to *them*.

b And at some point he became aware that he would have many wives.

c It was still sometime in summer.

d And in summer was when he was going to marry many wives, the story goes.

e 　　Soon after that some young maidens said, "Let's go pick cherries by ourselves."

f And they went to pick cherries in a separate group alone.

g 　　Some unmarried young men went along off to one side in pursuit of women.

h 　　Meanwhile that man was hunting by himself.

i And at some point the same thing happened to him as before.

j His penis grew longer, really long.

27 a   "šihihye·´," e·h=išite·he·či,

b   e·h=se·kesiči=meko.

c   "wi·h=išawiwa·ne·ni·='nah=mani," e·h=išite·he·či.

d   i·ni='pi·ye·toke e·h=wani·hke·tehe otaša·ti·hani.|

e   e·h=na·wanone·hokoči| owi·wani nekoti,|

f   e·h=awata·koči i·nini| aša·ti·hani.

g   i·ya·h=wi·na| ihkwe·wa peno·či_pye·hpahoči,_

h   me·yo·ničini e·h=ka·škehtawa·či,

i   i·tepi e·h=ihpahoči.

j   i·ya·hi ašiči_pye·hpahoči,_ona·pe·mwa·wani=či·hi e·h=apihapiniči.

k   ašiči_pye·ya·či,_ke·ko·henikwe·ni| e·h=anemi_wa·sewa·sehka·niki.[*]

l   e·h=ne·taki=ke·h=meko_ke·ko·hi e·h=anemi_ketaka·hkwiseniki.[†]

m   po·si=meko| kehčine pye·ya·či, ‖ e·h=ne·wokoči ona·pe·mwa·wani.

28 a   "pya·no," e·h=ikoči.

b   "me·kwe·h=koh=meko ke·ko·h=netešawi," e·h=ikoči.

c   "mani wa·patano," e·h=ineči ihkwe·wa._

d   "i·niye=ke·hi e·nemi_wa·sewa·sehka·ki e·h=owi·šiwiki," e·h=ineči.

e   a·yahpi·hčina·h=meko e·h=anemi|-peškapeška·še·niki e·h=owi·šiwiniki.

f   e·h=peno·mikateniki=ke·h=meko,|

g   e·h=kekeni·mikateniki=meko.

h   še·škesi·he·haki=ke·hi waninawe=meko e·h=ki·wi·tana·si·wa·či,

i   e·h=mamahkenamowa·či pehkiwe·hani.

j   kapo·twe kekimesi=meko e·h=meta·či·kwe·piwa·či,|

k   ke·ko·h=meko e·h=iši-nenehkite·he·wa·či če·wina·hi. ‖

29 a   e·h=ni·šo·piwa·či=ke·hi·'pi, "kaši=ča·h=ki·na ketešawi," e·h=iti·wa·či.

b   "ke·ko·h=ča·h=meko ni·na netešawi," e·h=iti·wa·či.

c   e·h=mi·na·we·neti·wa·či=meko kekimesi.

d   kapo·twe='pi=mekoho če·wina·h=meko e·h=po·ni|-kehke·netamowa·či.

e   kekimesi=meko·='ni| e·h=kehkičikenamowa·či mi·nakayi,

f   e·h=awanekwiwa·či.

g   kapo·twe_e·h=kehke·netamowa·či.

h   "mehtekwi=meko| nekekye·nenama·hkwi,"| e·h=išite·he·wa·či.

i   waninawe·='yo=ke·hi·'yo·we ahpemeki e·h=apihapiwa·či,|

j   ahpemeki e·h=wi·šikenama·hkwi·wa·či=meko.

k   kapo·twe e·h=kano·neči.

l   "i·ni=yá·pi e·h=meči-ka·šinakaye·niye·kwe," ‖ e·h=ineči.

30 a   waninawe e·h=taši-me·nešite·he·wa·či_še·škesi·he·haki.|

b   wi·nwa·wa=meko e·h=kano·na·wa·či.

c   "i·ni=we·=ye·toke=mani natawa·či wi·h=ona·pe·mena·ni," e·h=ikoči i·nihi,[‡]

____

[*]/ke·ko·henikwe·ni|/: AK ⟨kekoenikwe|⟩.

[†]/ka·/: AK ⟨kya⟩.

[‡]/=mani/: AK ⟨.mani.⟩.

27 a   "Oh my!" he thought.

b   He was quite scared.

c   And he had no idea what to do then.

d   And then, it seems, he had forgotten his stone-tipped arrows.

e   And one of his wives went to catch up to him,

f   taking the arrows to him.

g   When the woman got some distance from there on the run,

h   she heard someone weeping,

i   and she ran towards him.

j   And nearing the place on the run, she could see their husband sitting there.

k   And coming close, she saw an unrecognizable object flashing as it went away.

l   What's more, she saw the thing extending away all spotted,

m   And when she got even closer, their husband saw her.

28 a   "Come here," he told her.

b   "I really think there's something the matter with me," he told her.

c   "Look at this," the woman was told.

d   "And at that thing that's going away flashing on the head end," she was told.

e   It could be seen lighting up every now and then on the head end as it went off.

f   And it departed,

g   going fast.

h   Meanwhile, the young maidens were climbing around all over,

i   picking cherries.

j   At some point, they all had looks of delight cross their faces as they sat,

k   as there was something everyone of them had thoughts of at the same time.

29 a   And they sat in pairs, the story goes, and asked each other, "So, what's happening to *you*?"

b   And they told each other, "Well, something's happening to *me*."

c   Everyone noticed about the others.

d   And at some point, all at the same time, they lost consciousness.

e   Every one of them had both arms wrapped around that penis,

f   and it carried them away.

g   Some time later they came to.

h   Each of them thought she was hanging on to a tree for support.

i   Now remember, they were sitting there all over up above.

j   They were holding on tight up above.

k   And at some point they heard a voice speaking to them.

l   "Say, you're all making my penis quite sore now by holding on to it," they were told.

30 a   On all sides the young maidens felt embarrassed.

b   And *they* spoke to *him*.

c   "Well, given this, I guess I might as well *marry* you now," they told him,

d ne·nekoti=ke·h=wi·na=meko e·h=iši-kano·nekoči.
e   e·h=pwa·wi-=’yo=ke·hi=’pi -kehke·netamowa·či wa·wočiwenečini.
f i·ni=’pi-=’ni we·či-’nowe·wa·či.
g a·kwi=ke·hi=’pi| i·ni=meko iši_nahkomečini i·niki| še·škesi·haki.
h   o·ni·=’na we·na·pe·mita._
i   “pena´,_nahkomi.
j kekimesi=ma·hi·=’niki še·škesi·haki.
k ki·h=owi·wi-=ča·h=meko,” e·h=ikoči| i·nini owi·wani.|
l   “hao·ʔ,” i·ni=ča·hi·=’pi e·h=išiwe·či. ‖ *
31 a wi·na=ke·hi·=’na·=’ni·=’pi_neniwa_pe·hki| e·h=ša·ši·ša·či.
b i·niki=ke·hi·=’pi| še·škesi·haki e·h=se·kahkamikateniki e·h=awiwa·či,| †
c e·h=akisowa·či.
d   e·h=waniha·wa·či_mo·šaki=meko| we·še·škesi·hemičiki.
e   e·h=natone·hoči.
f ahpene·či=meko e·h=ma·mahkate·wi·wa·či mehtose·neniwaki.

g   kapo·twe,_ki·ši-=meko| -mama·ne·hto·wa·či owi·ya·si,
h “nahi´, nawači-na·na·kwa·ko,” e·h=ina·či.
i “wanihenaka·kwe,” e·h=ina·či.
j   “kwayahkwi-=’h-=we·=meko kekimesi ki·h=na·kwa·pena,” e·h=iniči| oke·hta_owi·wahi.
k   e·h=penowa·či,
l i·ya·h=e·h=pya·wa·či kekimesi i·niki še·škesi·haki=’yo·we._
m   e·h=mi·ša·te·nemowa·či we·še·škesi·hemičiki=’yo·we. ‖

32 a   i·nihi-=’pi-=’ni kekimesi=meko| e·h=wi·či-kehkye·ma·či.
b ma·wač_ahkowi_ke·hkya·ničini e·h=wi·či-kehkye·ma·či._
c e·h=pwa·wi-=ke·h=meko_nana·ši=na·hkači -oni·ča·nesiči.

d   i·ni=’pi e·šawiči a·mano·neniwa,|
e ašawaye-=meko -mehtose·neniwa.|
f aškači i·ni e·h=aški|-ča·ko·hkawoči_mehtose·neniwaki.
g mana, aye=meko·-’n_anašawaye e·h=ki·ši-=mani=_’šawiči.
h mana ma·wač_ahkowi ma·no·hkwe·wa·ta.
i ni·šwa·pitaki=ke·hi·=’nihi| nye·wi e·h=tašiniči owi·wahi.‡
j mo·šaki=meko_še·škesi·hahi mana_i·nihi_owi·wahi.

---

*The usual word order would have the “hao·ʔ” before /e·h=/; the fronting of the quote is
 emphatic.

†Discontinuous locative clause: i·niki .. še·škesi·haki .. e·h=awiwa·či ‘where those maidens
 were’.

‡/ni·šwa·pitaki/ ‘twenty’: probably should be /neswa·pitaki ‘thirty’. Twenty-seven wives are
 enumerated (9+16+1+1), and no number is given for the final set. If this set had seven, the total
 would be thirty-four, not twenty-four.

^d speaking to him one at a time, in fact.

^e   Now, those maidens did not know the places they had been taken from, the story goes.

^f That's why they all said that.

^g But the girls' proposals were not accepted right away.

^h   And then the man's wife weighed in.

ⁱ   "Why don't you say yes to them?

^j I mean, they're all virgins, every one.

^k So, you should marry them," his wife told him.

^l   So then he said yes.

31 ^a   And then that man, for his part, hunted seriously all the time, the story goes.

^b   And meanwhile, people were frightened where those girls lived,

^c as their whereabouts was unknown.

^d   Those that had nothing but girls felt their absence.

^e   And they were searched for.

^f   The people fasted all the time.

^g   Some time later, after they each had lots of meat,

^h he told them, "Alright, it's time for all of you to go back home."

ⁱ He told them, "You might be missed."

^j   And his original wives said, "Or why don't we *all* just go ahead and go back."

^k   And they went back,

^l and all of those that had been virgins arrived back there.

^m   Those whose young girls they had been were glad.

32 ^a   And then he grew old along with all of them, the story goes.

^b He grew old with the oldest of them all.

^c And he never had any more children.

^d   That's the story told of Lady-Killer,

^e who was a person of long ago.

^f It was later on that the people were first ganged up on by everyone.

^g This man had already done this a long time before then.

^h This man was the last one to have many women.

ⁱ Those wives that he had, to be precise, were twenty-four in number.   (See note ‡.)

^j And those wives this man had were nothing but virgins.

ᵏ   iˑni| eˑhkwiči.

k   That's the end of his story.

wîtekôwani kêteminâkota nashawaye-nenôtêwa

An Indian of Long Ago who was Blessed by an Owl

wîtekôwani kêteminâkota nashawaye-nenôtêwa
Alfred Kiyana[*]

1 a   wiˑtekoˑwani keˑteminaˑkota| našawaye_nenoˑteˑwa.[†]

b   nekoti=keˑhi=’pi našawaye_nenoˑteˑwa_eˑh=naweˑnineniˑheˑhiči,

c   eˑh=menwaˑpeˑwesiči.

d   miˑškota eˑh=kehtweˑwesiči,

e   eˑh=noˑhkihaˑči mahkwahi,| pešekesiwahi.

f   meše=weˑ=mekoˑ=’nahi keˑkoˑhi eˑh=noˑhkihtoˑči.

g   oˑniˑ=’pi eˑh=miˑneči ihkweˑwani, šeˑškesiˑheˑhani.

h   noˑmakeˑwe=meko eˑh=owiˑwiči,

i   eˑh=neškinaˑkoči| iˑnini ihkweˑwani.

j   eˑh=aˑnomeči=keˑh=meko_iˑtepi ayaˑpami| wiˑh=aˑči_ihkweˑwa.[‡]

k   “aˑkwi,” eˑh=iči=meko iˑna| ihkweˑheˑha,

l   eˑh=aˑčimoči.|

m   “neneškinawaˑwa=kohi,” eˑh=iči=meko waˑwosaˑhi ihkweˑwa.

n   eˑh=aˑnwiˑhkawoči=meko iˑtepi wiˑh=aˑči| ihkweˑwa,

o   eˑh=šaˑkweˑnemoči=meko.

p   keˑkeyaˑh=meko ‖ otaweˑmaˑwani eˑh=weˑpi-kiˑškatahokoči.|

2 a   eˑtaswi-=meko -kanoˑnečini, eˑh=kiˑškatahoči ihkweˑwa.

b   “aˑkwi=maˑhi_kanaˑkwa,” eˑh=inaˑči otaweˑmaˑwani.

c   oˑni=yeˑtoke naˑhka=meko atenaˑwi eˑhpiˑhtesiˑhiničini šeˑškesiˑheˑhani| eˑh=miˑneči.

d   iˑtepi=meko eˑh=išiweneči iˑna šeˑškesiˑheˑha eˑh=awiniči iˑnini keˑhtweˑwesiničini.

e   naˑhka=’pi=meko noˑmakeˑwe eˑh=onaˑpeˑmiči iˑna ihkweˑwa iˑnini neniwani.

f   naˑhinaˑh=meko eˑh=naˑkwaˑči,

g   eˑh=aˑhpeči_naˑkwaˑči.

h   iˑni=’pi=meko=neˑhiˑ=’na| eˑh=aˑnomeči wiˑh=naˑkwaˑči| ayaˑpami iši.

i   “nahiˊ, aˑpečiˊ,| iˑtepi=’haˑno,” eˑh=ineči.

j   keˑkeyaˑh=meko, “oˑˊ, aˑkwi=čaˑhiˑ=’tepi_iˑh=aˑyaˑnini,” eˑh=iči._

k   eˑh=mayoˑči| iˑna ihkweˑwa.

l   eˑh=aˑnwiˑhkawoči=meko,

m   eˑh=šaˑkweˑnemoči.

n   oˑni=yeˑtoke naˑhka=meko eˑh=miˑneči kotakeˑhani, ‖

3 a   naˑhka=meko šeˑškesiˑheˑhani.

b   “kaˑta=wiˑna=kiˑna iˑni išawihkani,” eˑh=ineči iˑna miˑnetiˑka.

c   “aˑkwi=čaˑhi iˑni wiˑh=išawiyaˑnini,” eˑh=iči.

---

[*]The manuscript is NAA 1879.15; it has 23 pages. The English version by Ida Poweshiek
 (NAA 1879.17) expands loosely on a few parts of Kiyana’s text but omits most of it.

[†]Title; written on three lines at the top of the page.

[‡]/=meko_iˑtepi/: AK ⟨mekoiitepi.⟩.

An Indian of Long Ago who was Blessed by an Owl
Translated by Ives Goddard

1 a   An Indian of Long Ago Who Was Blessed by an Owl.

b   Now, the story is told of a certain Indian of long ago who was a handsome youth,
c with a nice bodily build.
d On top of that he was an excellent hunter,
e who easily killed bears and deer.
f In fact he easily killed anything.
g   And then, the story goes, he was given a woman, a young girl.
h He was married to her only a short time,
i and the woman didn't like him.
j   Moreover, the woman firmly refused to go back to him.
k The woman said no emphatically.
l Explaining herself,
m the woman even said firmly, "I *do* not like him."
n The woman could *not* be persuaded to go there,
o being quite unwilling.
p Finally, her brother set to whipping her.
2 a Every time the woman was spoken to, she was whipped.
b "See, there's no way," she told her brother.

c   And then, it seems, another, even younger girl was given to him.
d   That young girl was taken right to where that good hunter lived.
e This time as well, the story goes, the woman was married to the man for only a short time.
f And when she did leave,
g she left for good.
h They say she, too, instantly refused to go back.
i   "Alright, come on, go!" she was told.
j Finally she said, "Well, I'm not going."
k And the woman cried.
l She could *not* be persuaded,
m being quite unwilling.

n   And then, it seems, he was given yet another one.
3 a Again it was a young girl.
b   "Don't *you* do that," the one given was told.
c   "Well, I won't do that," she said.

^d "ka·ta| kehkinawa·pamiye·kani i·niki ihkwe·waki.
^e a·kwi=ma·hi·='niki menwawiwa·čini,
^f i·niki i·ni e·h=išawiwa·či," e·h=ineči.
^g "a·kwi=ča·hi·='ni wi·h=išawiyanini," e·h=ineči.
^h "nehki=meko pe·mi_nahe·nemikwe·ni i·ni=nehki wi·h=pemi_wi·čawiwaki," e·h=iči.[*]
ⁱ e·h=mi·ša·te·nemowa·či we·teškwe·se·hemičiki i·ni e·h=inowe·niči.
^j i·ya·h=e·h=pye·neči,
^k kwi·yena=meko e·h=a·pi|-ši·ša·niči.
^l i·ya·h=kwi·yena| pye·neči,
^m e·h=pye·tašiniči.
ⁿ "šihihwi·´," e·h=išite·he·či| ihkwe·wa.
^o e·h=awaneči mahkwa.
^p (mahkwani='yo='pi pye·ne·wa_i·nina·hi.)
^q ni·šokoni='pi| e·h=ona·pe·miči,
^r e·h=na·kwa·či| e·h=owi·kiwa·či.
^s i·ni='pi=meko e·h=ša·kwe·nemoči ‖ ne·ya·pi wi·h=a·či.
^{4 a} ke·keya·h=meko_e·h=we·pi-neški-kano·neči.
^b o·ni, "nahi·´, ma·maya=meko ki·h=we·ši·ho·to=ki·yawi,"| e·h=ikoči o·sani.[†]/[‡]
^c e·h=we·ši·hoči=meko to·hki·či.
^d "na·hina·h=meko i·tepi e·ya·wane·ni i·ni wi·h=wi·seniyani,"| e·h=ineči.
^e "i·noki=ke·hi i·tepi iha·yane, i·ni=meko wi·h=wi·seniyani," e·h=ineči ihkwe·wa.
^f " 'a·kwi·='tepi·='h=a·ya·nini,' nesi=ma·hi," e·h=iči ihkwe·wa.|
^g "o=meše=meko. ki·na=koči=meko," e·h=ikoči o·sani.
^h "ki·h=nano·či-=meko -pahkihte·pene,[§]
ⁱ pwa·wi-_i·tepi -iha·wane·ni," e·h=ineči ihkwe·wa.
^j "a·kwi=meko ke·ko·hi," e·h=iči| wa·natohka.
^k "ki·nwa·wa=koči=meko," e·h=ina·či| omeso·ta·nahi.
^l "ki·nwa·wa=koči ki·h=ki·wi-pa·pakikawini·kwe·pipwa_kete·='nahi.
^m ni·na='h=we·=ke·h=meči[!?]| ni·h=kehke·neta=manahka,[!?]|[¶]
ⁿ ki·ši-pi·ke·pene·hiye·kwe,"‖ e·h=ina·či omeso·ta·nahi.
^{5 a} meše·='nah=meko ma·nokoni e·h=pwa·wi-=meko -ame·či,|
^b e·h=pwa·wi-_šahkwapene·či.
^c pe·hkote·nikini, "nahi·´, i·tepi·='nahi_iha·no," e·h=ina·wa·či.
^d ke·keya·h=meko e·h=po·ni-_kano·nekowa·či.
^e meše·='nah=nekotenwi_tepehki to·hki·či metemo·he·ha,
^f e·h=taši-mayakehtawa·či.
^g e·h=mi·na·wehtawa·či=meko ota·neswa·wani,
^h e·h=to·hkisaha·či ona·pe·mani.

---

[*]/pe·mi_nahe·nemikwe·ni/: AK ⟨peminaanemikweni⟩.
[†]/ki·yawi/: AK ⟨kiyaw|⟩.
[‡]Painting the face with charcoal indicated that one was fasting and should not be offered food.
[§]/ki·h=nano·či-=meko/: ⟨no⟩ changed from ⟨ko⟩.
[¶]/manahka/: AK ⟨nanaka⟩.

d   "Don't model your behavior on those women.
e   See, they didn't behave right,
f   when they did that," she was told.
g   "So, you mustn't do that," she was told.
h   "For as long as I'm the one he wants I'll stay married to him," she said.
i   The parents of the girl were delighted when she said that.
j   When she was brought over there,
k   he was just getting back from hunting.
l   She was just brought there
m   when he came with a load on his back.
n   "Goodness!" thought the woman.
o   A bear was taken home.
p   (For they say he'd brought back a bear at that time.)
q   It's said that she was married for two days
r   and went back home.
s   And right away, she was unwilling to go back.
4 a   Before long she was chastised.
b   And her father told her then, "Alright, early tomorrow you must paint yourself.
c   And she did paint herself when she woke up.   (See the note ‡.)
d   "At the time you go there you shall eat," she was told.
e   "For example, if you go there now, you'll eat right away," the woman was told.
f   "You know I said that I won't go there," the woman said.
g   "As you like. It's up to you, of course," her father told her.
h   "You'll end up starving to death,
i   if you don't go there," the woman was told.
j   "It doesn't matter," she said, indifferently.
k   "It's up to *you*, of course," she said to her parents.
l   "It's *you*, of course then, that'll be sitting with tears running down your faces.
m   *I* obviously won't be aware of anything at *that* time,
n   after you've made me starve to death," she said to her parents.
5 a   For a good many days she didn't budge at all,
b   and she wasn't weak from hunger.
c   Every night they said to her, "Alright, *now* go there."
d   And in time they no longer spoke to her.
e   One night when the old lady woke up,
f   she heard something strange from her.
g   She listened closely to their daughter
h   and shook her husband awake.

ⁱ   to·hki·či pašito·ha,| e·h=pehtawe·či.

^j   e·h=to·hkena·či| metemo·ka,

^k   e·h=mesimesiwe·ška·niči,

^l   me·mečine·h=meko e·h=kehči‗ne·moniči ota·neswa·wani.

^m   ke·htena=meko e·h=pahkihte·pene·ha·či neniwa ota·nesani.

ⁿ   e·h=kehči‗mayo·wa·či kete·=’nahi, če·wi·šwi=meko.

^o   o·ni=’pi·=’na e·h=na·kwa·či neniwa ne·škineškina·kota ihkwe·wahi.[*]

^p   atehči·me·h=meko ‖ e·h=mawi-owi·kiči.

^{6 a}   e·h=we·pi‗ma·mahkate·wi·či,|

^b   e·h=natawe·netaki wi·h=owi·naka·či.

^c   e·h=čakinakaye·hiči=’yo.

^d   i·ni=’pi we·či-ne·neškina·koči| ihkwe·wahi.

^e   ki·ši-=meko -kehke·nemekočini, e·h=neškina·koči.

^f   i·ni=ča·hi=’pi e·h=ma·mahkate·wi·či.

^g   meše=nekotenwi| e·h=taši-mayo·či,

^h   e·h=pye·či-pakišiniči wi·teko·wani meše=na·hina·hi,

ⁱ   e·h=neškinawa·či.

^j   ke·keya·h=meko kehčine‗e·h=pye·či-pakišiniči.

^k   ke·keya·h=meko e·h=kano·nekoči.

^l   “a·kwi=ma·hi·=’ni ke·ko·hekini e·taši-kwe·hta·ni|-mayo·hekwiyani,” e·h=ikoči.|

^m   “ki·nakayi=’yo we·twe·we·kesiyani,” e·h=inekoči.|

ⁿ   “kana·h=mata či·nawe·mečiki nepo·hiwa·te,|

^o   taši-mayomayo·ne·ha,”| e·h=ikoči. ‖

^{7 a}   “nahi´, noši·hi, i·noki pehkote·hike i·ya·h=ni·h=pya.

^b   ka·ta=ča·hi wi·h=apane·niyani| nenehke·netakani.

^c   ni·h=awato‗mi·nakayani,” e·h=ikoči.|

^d   pe·hkote·niki e·h=pya·niči| omešo·mesani.

^e   pye·či|-pi·tike·niči, e·h=ki·ša·koči‗ma·no·škaminiči| mi·naka·hani.

^f   ke·kya·ta=meko e·h=kwaya·ši‗kehč‗apane·niči,

^g   e·h=mi·ša·te·nemoči‗na·mite·he mehtose·neniwa.

^h   e·h=kano·neči.|

ⁱ   “ši·´,‗noši·hi, ta·ni=ča·h=wi·h=inekihkwa·ki,” e·h=ineči.

^j   “o·´,‗mani=ča·hi,” e·h=iči.

^k   “maneto·ketate·haki e·nekihkwitepe·wa·či| wi·h=inekihkwikwe·ya·wi,” e·h=ina·či
omešo·mesani.[†]

^l   “hao·?,” e·h=ikoči.

^m   “ni·na=koči kewe·we·ne·netamwihene,” e·h=ineči neniwa.

ⁿ   “aša·šiko·ha ke·škihkesota| natone·hwi,

^o   šo·škwikesita,”| e·h=ineči neniwa.

^p   e·h=mehkawa·či. ‖

____

[*]/ne·škineškina·kota/: AK ⟨neškinaškinakota⟩.

[†]/wi·h=inekihkwikwe·ya·wi/: AK ⟨wiinikikwikweyawi⟩.

<pre>
i   When the old man woke up, he lit a fire.
j   The old lady touched her to wake her,
k and, stretching this way and that,
l their daughter took one last, deep breath.
m   Sure enough, the man starved his daughter to death.
n And now instead they wept loudly, both of them.

o   And then, the story goes, that man that women always disliked went away.
p He went to live some distance off.
6 a And he began regular fasting,
b seeking to get a penis.
c For the penis he had was small.
d That was why women always disliked him, the story goes.
e After they'd known him intimately, they didn't like him.
f So, he was fasting then, the story goes.
g   One time he was weeping,
h and an owl came and landed not far away,
i and he didn't like it being there.
j Before long it came and landed nearby.
k And before long it spoke to him.
l "You know, what's making you weep so very much is nothing," it told him.
m   "Here it's your penis that's the reason you're wailing," it told him.
n   "Now, if a person's *relatives* die, something like *that,*
o they should be weeping," it told him.
7 a   "Alright, grandson, tonight I'll come there.
b And don't think of smiling.
c I'll bring some penises," it told him.
d   That night his grandfather came back.
e When he came in, he was wearing on his body a huge number of small penises.
f The human almost couldn't help a big smile,
g being delighted inside.
h   And he was spoken to.
i "Well now, grandson, so how big is it to be?" he was asked.
j   "Well, here's how big," he said.
k   "It's neck should be the size of the heads of spirit-otters," he told his grandfather.
l   "So it shall be!" was the reply he received from him.
m   "*I'll* put you in charge, of course," the man was told.
n   "Go look for a seasoned piece of slippery elm,
o a smooth shaft," the man was told.
p   And he found one.
</pre>

8 a   apina=meko e·h=ša·šakesiniči i·nini e·h=nematawoči.*

b   i·niye=ke·hi owi·naka·hi e·h=takwako·to·weči.|

c   "a·kwi=ke·hi owiye·ha wi·h=kaški|- ke·ko·hi -to·tawačini," e·h=inekoči i·nini
wi·teko·wani.

d   e·h=na·kwa·či._

e   kwi·yena=meko e·ški-mi·nečini e·h=ne·wa·či.

f   e·h=aški-ne·wa·či atehči_taši.

g   e·h=kwi·či-=meko -anwa·či·či_ke·ko·hi_wi·h=to·ta·koči.

h   "kekeni=pena´,"_e·h=išiwe·či_ihkwe·wa.

i   "keči·kwani=ma·h=me·kwe·he ketayo," e·h=ineči neniwa.

j   e·h=wa·pato·neči.

k   apina=meko e·h=oški·šekowa·pataki ihkwe·wa.

l   "hwi·´," e·h=iči,

m   e·h=pemi_pasekwi·čisa·či.

n   "šihihwi·´," e·h=ina·či,

o   e·h=mawinana·či.

p   e·h=pwa·wi-'pi=meko ke·ko·hi_nana·ši=na·hka ke·ko·hi kaški-to·tawa·či owiye·hani.

q   e·h=pe·we·nemoči,_

r   ne·ya·pi| e·h=a·či. ‖

9 a   meše=meko menwinehki i·ya·hi e·h=awiči e·h=pye·nota·koči omešo·mesani,

b   e·h=pye·to·niči=meko ka·hkami_mi·nakayi.

c   "koči·h=ye·toke we·či|- ayo·hi -taši-te·wate·wa·ko·tameki," e·h=ikoči.

d   "nahi´,_ni·na=meko·='ni.

e   me·ta·kwe·neta·kwahki=meko ayo·hi ki·h=nemato·pena," e·h=ineči.

f   e·h=sa·keniki='pi.

g   apina=meko mamahkikaniwi,

h   e·h=maka·ke·ya·niki.†

i   o·ni| e·h=na·kwa·či.

j   i·niye·ne=meko na·hka e·h=menehtami-_ke·ko·hi -išawiwa·či.

k   ana·ki·ša·koči=meko e·h=iši-me·meta·ča·hiči| ihkwe·wa.

l   apina=meko e·h=mayo·či.

m   i·ni='pi=meko kekimesi iši|-ne·nekotenwi e·h=pemi|- ke·ko·hi_-to·tawa·či.

n   (apina a·neta mayo·waki.)

o   ki·ši-_ke·ko·hi -išawiwa·čini ‖ ihkwe·waki,

10 a   wi·h=wi·čawiwa·wa·či=meko e·h=išite·he·wa·či.|

b   še·ški=ke·h=meko ne·nekotenwi i·ni e·h=pemi_to·tawa·či owi·wahi='yo·we.|

c   ki·ši-ča·ki- i·ni_-išawiči,

d   o·ni='pi e·h=owi·wiči| kotake·hani še·škesi·he·hani.|

e   waninawe=meko še·ški e·h=taši-a·hkwe·wa·či ihkwe·waki.

f   e·h=ki·ša·koči-=meko -menwa·ko·ma·či we·na·pe·mita.

---

*/nemat-/, *lit.* 'stand (it) up', used for planting a post or tree.

†/e·h=maka·ke·ya·niki/: would mean 'it had a big brim' if referring to a hat.

8 a It even curved back when it was planted on him.

b And here, his now former small penis was hung with the others.

c "Now, you won't be able to have sex with anyone," the owl told him.

d And he went back.

e And he just happened to see the first one he'd been given.

f It was the first time he'd seen her off someplace.

g And at this perfectly bad time she showed a willingness for him to have sex with her.

h "O.K. now, quickly!" the woman said.

i "I guess you're using your knee, obviously," the man was told.

j It was shown to her.

k The woman even thought she saw eyes on it.

l "Oh my!" she said,

m and she leapt to her feet.

n "Goodness!" she said to him,

o attacking him.

p He was never able to have any sex again with anyone, the story goes.

q He gave up

r and went back to the same place as before.

9 a A short time later his grandfather came to him where he was staying,

b straightaway bringing a penis.

c "To be honest, it's likely a source of some discomfort here," (the owl) told him.

d "Alright, now *I'll* do it.

e Here's where we'll plant the entertainment package," he was told.

f They watched it sprout up, the story goes.

g The rod was even bumpy,

h and it had a long foreskin.

i And then he went back.

j And he first had sex again with that one from before.

k The woman enjoyed it immensely.

l She even wept.

m Right away he had sex one time each with all of them, the story goes.

n (Some even wept.)

o After the women had sex,

10 a they thought that they would be married to him.

b And here, it was only one time each that he had sex with his former wives.

c After doing all that,

d he then married another young girl, the story goes.

e On all sides women were simply in a rage.

f The one who married him liked his ways a great deal.

^g　o·ni=’pi owi·hka·nani e·h=a·čimoha·či| e·šawiči.

^h　i·ni=’yo=ke·hi=’pi| e·šiki·hiči i·na_neniwa.|

ⁱ　e·h=po·si-=ča·h=meko -peseše·či e·na·čimoweči.

^j　na·hina·h=ča·hi=’pi e·h=we·pi_šahkašahkaniki,|

^k　e·h=mawi-mahkate·wi·či, e·h=ina·čimoči.

^l　meše=meko·=’nahi nekotahi ta·twa·hki·heki e·h=owi·ke·hiči.

^m　e·h=po·si-=meko -aša·šiko·himišihkiwiniki ‖ e·h=owi·kiči.

^{11 a}　meše·=’nah=nekotenwi e·ški_pehkote·hiniki,

^b　e·h=ketoniči wi·teko·wani.

^c　pa·pekwa·=’nahi e·h=nana·hpinohtawa·či.

^d　ke·htena=meko kehčine, ke·keya·h=meko kepiškwa·te e·h=taši|-ketoniči,

^e　e·h=kano·nekoči.|

^f　“we·kone·hi=’yo=ča·h,=noši·hi we·či_natomiyani,”| e·h=ikoči.

^g　i·nah=meko e·h=oči_kano·na·či.

^h　“wi·h=owi·naka·ya·ni=ča·hi.

ⁱ　wi·h=owi·naka·ya·ni nenatawe·neta,” e·h=ina·či.

^j　“o·´,_noši·hi, ki·h=ašihto·ne,” e·h=ikoči.|

^k　“šewe·=ka·ta apane·nemihkani pemi_pi·tike·yane.

^l　apahapane·nemiyane=ke·hi, če·wi·šwi=meko_ki·h=nepepena,” e·h=ineči.

^m　“wi·šiki·no=ča·hi| wi·h=pwa·wi-apane·nemiyani,” e·h=ineči neno·te·wa.

ⁿ　“meči=’hi=’yo=ke·h^{!?},=nemešo, wa·wosa·hi^{!?} ki·h=wapasa·ye·nemene!?” ‖ e·h=išiwe·či
neno·te·wa.[*]

^{12 a}　“wah´, noši·hi. i·ni=kohi´,” e·h=išiwe·či wi·teko·wa.

^b　“nahi´, wi·šiki·kwe·ška·no·=’nahi,” e·h=ineči neno·te·wa.|

^c　“i·ni=yá·pi wi·h=pi·tike·ya·ni,”| e·h=ineči.

^d　e·h=a·hkwe·wite·he·či,|

^e　e·h=pwa·wi-=ke·hi -wa·pama·či.|

^f　“nahi´,_noši·hi, wa·wa·patano·=’nahi wi·h=inekihkwa·kwe·ni,” e·h=ineči.

^g　man=e·ši_wa·pama·či, nano·pehka_e·h=ahkwi_meškikwe·ka·pa·niči.

^h　i·ni=’pi=meko, “hahahaha·´,” e·h=iči.

ⁱ　e·nika·wi=meko e·h=iši-a·htawa·sa·wa·či,|

^j　a·yaka·mete·we e·h=ki·wa·kwasowa·či.

^k　o·ni e·h=mawa·pama·či we·sese·hita.

^l　i·ya·h=e·h=pya·či,

^m　pe·mi|-pi·tike·či, “hao·?,” e·h=iči.

ⁿ　aye=či·h=meko osese·hani| e·h=išina·kosiniči,

^o　našawe·me·h=meko e·h=nepenitehe.

^p　e·h=pwa·wi-=ke·hi -mi·na·wa·piči, ‖

^{13 a}　e·h=na·kwa·či.

^b　i·ya·h=pye·ya·či, “nepo·hikwe·ni,” e·h=ina·či| omeso·ta·nwa·wahi.

―――――――――――――

[*]/ki·h=wapasa·ye·nemene/: AK ⟨.kiwapasa‖yenemene.⟩.

g   And then he told his friend what he had done.

h   Now, that man was small in that way.

i   So, he listened intently to what was recounted.

j   And at the time when everything was starting to thaw,

k   he declared that he was going somewhere to fast.

l   He camped someplace or other in a ravine.

m   There were many slippery elm trees where his lodge was.

11 a   One time when it was first dark

b   an owl hooted.

c   And right away he imitated it.

d   Sure enough, it hooted nearby, and eventually at the door,

e   and it spoke to him.

f   "So, what's the reason you called me, grandson?" it said to him.

g   He spoke to it there.

h   "Well, to have a penis.

i   I seek to have a penis," he told it.

j   "Ah, grandson, I shall make one for you," it told him.

k   "But don't smile at me when I walk in.

l   What's more, if you laugh at me, we both shall die," he was told.

m   "So, try your hardest not to smile at me," the Indian was told.

n   "Come on, grandfather, it's hardly likely that I'd laugh derisively at you!" the Indian
declared.

12 a   "I hope not, grandson! That's excellent," said the owl.

b   "Alright, now set your face firmly," the Indian was told.

c   "O.K. now, here I come," he was told.

d   He felt offended,

e   to the point of not looking at (the owl).

f   "Alright, grandson, now you can pick what size it will be," he was told.

g   As soon as he looked at (the owl), he saw it standing there with the head of its penis
greatly exposed.

h   Instantly, he laughed, "Ha-ha-ha-ha!"

i   They both fell backwards in opposite directions,

j   and they lay there dead across the lodge from each other.

k   And then his younger brother went to see him.

l   He arrived over there,

m   and when he walked in, he said, "Hello!"

n   And here he saw his older brother looking like he'd been there a while

o   and had died quite a long time ago.

p   And without looking closely,

13 a   he went back.

b   When he got back, he told their parents, "He died."

c   i·tepi e·h=a·wa·či_mehtose·neniwaki.
d   we·wi·hka·nita, "apahapane·neme·toke," e·h=išite·he·či.| *
e i·ni=meko e·h=anemi-'šite·he·či.
f   i·ya·h=pe·kamose·či,
g "wi·teko·wani=koči aka·mete·ki ki·wa·kwasoniwani," e·h=iyoweči.
h e·h=pwa·wi_kehke·nememeči e·šawinikwe·ni.
i   ke·keya·h=e·h=a·čimoči.
j "mani=ma·h=ye·toke mana e·šawiči:
k ma·hani wi·teko·wani me·mešihka apahapane·neme·toke
l e·h=neno·te·wikiho·noniči.
m me·mešihka| wi·h=ketemina·kotehe='yo·we,"| e·h=išiwe·či.
n e·h=pwa·wi-=meko -te·pwe·htawoči,|
o a·wasi=meko wi·h=nesemeči e·nowa·čiki.
p   "pwa·wi-=ye·toke=mana| -mešahkwa·šone·ha," e·h=iči. ‖
14 a "a·kwi=kana·kwa=meko."

b   ke·keya·hi='pi e·h=po·ta·na·či wi·teko·wani i·na ke·temina·kota='yo·we._
c   "nahi´,_wi·teko·we=ni·hka, a·čimono e·šawiwe·kwe·ni," e·h=ina·či.
d   "hao·?," e·h=iči| wi·teko·wa,
e e·h=we·pi_a·čimoči.
f   "e·h=ketoya·ni,
g nenana·hpinohta·kwa," e·h=ina·či| i·nini.
h   "kena·či=meko| ašiči nepye·notawa·wa.|
i ke·keya·h=meko ayo·hi_kepiškwa·te_netaši-keto.
j nenana·hpinohta·kwa=meko," e·h=iči._
k   "o·ni e·h=kano·naki.
l mani e·naki:
m 'we·kone·hi='yo=ča·h,=noši·hi_we·či|-natomiyani,' netena·wa.
n o·ni, 'wi·h=owi·naka·ya·ni=ča·hi,'_e·h=iči.
o o·ni e·h=mama·tomaki wi·h=pwa·wi_apahapane·nemiči.
p o·ni,_'wa·wosa·h=ye·toke!?, nemešo, wi·h=wapasa·ye·nemena·ni!?' e·h=išiči.†
q 'wah´, i·ni=koh,=noši·hi,'_netena·wa," ‖ e·h=iči wi·teko·wa.
15 a   o·ni,| "neta·čimoha·wa=meko| wi·h=išawiya·ke.
b 'ki·hpene| apahapane·niyane,_
c ki·h=nepepena=meko če·wi·šwi,'| netena·wa._
d mani=meko e·ši-pemi_pi·tike·ya·ni,
e a·kwi_ke·htena apane·ničini.
f kwi·yena=ča·h=meko wi·h=nematawakehe| ne·tawe·netaki,
g i·ni e·h=apahapane·niči.
h 'hahahaha·´,' e·či=meko,_ni·na e·h=ni·me·sahoya·ni.
i mehto·či=meko·='ni e·h=pa·pakami·namekehe," e·h=iči wi·teko·wa.

---

*/apahapane·neme·toke/ (cf. 13*k*): AK ⟨apaapanenematoke⟩.
†/e·h=išiči/ (IG): AK ⟨einači⟩.

c   People went there.

d   His friend thought, "He must've laughed at him."

e   As he went along, he thought exactly that.

f   When he arrived over there,

g   people said, "Incidentally. he has an owl lying dead across the lodge from him."

h   It wasn't known what had happened to him.

i   Eventually he explained.

j   "See, this is what seems to have happened to him:

k   He probably must've laughed at this owl.

l   It took on human form.

m   It probably had blessed him previously," he said.

n   He was *not* believed,

o   but rather some who said he had to have been killed were.

p   "I wonder why he wouldn't've been scalped," he said.

14 a   "It's not possible."

b   Eventually, the story goes, the one who had been blessed by the owl blew on it.

c   "Alright now, owl, tell what happened to the two of you," he said to it.

d   "O.K.," said the owl,

e   and it began his account of things.

f   "When I hooted,

g   he imitated me," it told him.

h   "I slowly came near to him.

i   Eventually, I hooted at the door here.

j   And he *imitated* me," it said.

k   "And then I spoke to him.

l   This is what I said to him:

m   'So tell me, what's the reason you called me, grandson?' I said to him.

n   And then he said, 'Well, it's in order for me to have a penis.'

o   And then I implored him not to laugh at me.

p   And when he said to me, 'It's hardly likely that I'd laugh derisively at you!'

q   I told him, 'I hope not! That's excellent, grandson!'," said the owl.

15 a   And then, "I explained to him what would happen to us.

b   'If you ever *do* laugh at me,

c   we both shall definitely die,' I told him.

d   Right when I walked in,

e   he didn't really smile.

f   So, I was just about to plant what he wanted on him,

g   and then he laughed.

h   And right when he laughed, 'Ha-ha-ha-ha!', *I* shot up in the air.

i   It was as if we'd then been clubbed to death," the owl said.

^j   ača·hmeko e·h=te·pwe·htawoči neno·te·wa menehta_a·čimota,_
^k   menehta_ke·temina·kota.

^l   o·ni=na·hka nekoti, "ni·na=wi·na awita=meko a·mi-'ši-apane·nema·wake·ni," e·h=iči.
^m   aškači e·h=neškimekoči omeso·ta·nahi.
ⁿ   kaka·čiči=meko, "i·ni=koh=meko ‖ a·mi-'šawiya·ni!?" e·h=ina·či.[*]
^{16 a}   e·yi·ki-'yo=ke·h=meko e·h=owi·hka·niči e·pahapane·neke·moničini.
^b   o·ni e·h=a·hpeči-=meko -nenehke·nema·či| owi·hka·nani.
^c   meše=nekotenwi_ši·ša·či,
^d   peno·či=meko e·h=taši_nesa·či pešekesiwani,
^e   e·h=menwi_'nekino·hiniči.
^f   "wi·h=iši-=pena´ mana_te·po·ma·wake·ni| e·h=owi·ke·hiya·ke," e·h=išite·he·či.
^g   e·h=wi·ke·čiwanehke·či=meko.
^h   ki·ši-=meko -menwiwanehke·či, e·h=na·kwa·či.
ⁱ   e·na·kwi·hiniki, wi·teko·wani e·h=ketoniči.
^j   e·h=nana·hpinohtawa·či.
^k   e·h=pemehka·či=ke·h=meko.
^l   ke·keya·h=meko kehčine e·h=tanwe·taminiči.
^m   e·h=a·kwapiči,
ⁿ   e·h=aneškenana·či| oto·hpwa·kanani.
^o   ki·ši-pahte·hčike·či, e·h=na·kwa·či._
^p   pa·pekwa=na·hka e·h=ketoniči,
^q   e·h=nahkoma·či=meko.
^r   wi·na=ke·hi ‖ e·h=anemi_mama·ki-pekešawe·či.
^{17 a}   ke·keya·h=meko wi·h=anemiha·či e·h=mawi-pakišiniči_kaškiški.
^b   tepina·h=pe·mehka·či,
^c   "nawači_naki·no, noši·hi," e·h=ikoči.
^d   e·h=naki·či.
^e   "we·kone·h=ča·h=we·či_natomiyani," e·h=ikoči.
^f   "a·kwi=ča·h=ni·na natomena·nini," e·h=ina·či.
^g   "o·´,_ni·na=wé·na, 'wi·h=atame·hiči=ye·toke,' netešite·he."
^h   "a·kwi," e·h=ina·či.
ⁱ   "nahi´,_noši·hi, mi·ši·hino=ta·ni nese·ma·wa wi·h=atama·ya·na," e·h=ikoči.
^j   "ni·na=ma·h=e·yi·ki me·mečine·h=meko ni·h=anaškenačike," e·h=ina·či.
^k   "a·kwi| wi·h=kaški_mi·nena·nini,"| e·h=ina·či.
^l   na·hka, "ne·hihkame·henokwe·na a·mi|-natotamawata,"_e·h=ina·či.
^m   wi·teko·wa_e·h=kehč_a·hkwe·či,
ⁿ   e·h=pem_anisa·či._
^o   "na·hina·h=meko e·h=po·našiwane·ni, ‖ [†]
^{18 a}   i·nina·h=meko wi·h=nepeyani," e·h=ineči we·wi·wašita.
^b   "ši·´,_ki·na=ni·hk=e·yi·ki,

---

[*] !? (IG).

[†] /e·h=po·našiwane·ni/: ⟨na⟩ resembles ⟨ne⟩ with an open loop.

j   Only then was the Indian who had first given the explanation believed,
k   the one it had blessed first.

l   And then someone else said, "There's no way *I* would laugh at him."
m   Later his parents admonished him.
n   And he persisted, saying to them, "*That* is certainly not something I would do."
16 a   Now, he was also a friend of the one that had laughed.
b   And then he was always thinking about his friend.
c   One time when he went out to hunt,
d   he killed a deer quite far away,
e   a good-sized one.
f   "O.K. now, I wonder how I'm going to be able to carry this home," he thought.
g   He carefully bundled it together for carrying.
h   And after he had a nice bundle for his back, he set out.
i   Early in the evening an owl hooted.
j   He imitated it.
k   And he kept walking right along.
l   Before long it hooted nearby.
m   He sat down to rest
n   and filled his pipe.
o   After he'd gotten it going, he continued on.
p   Right away it hooted again.
q   And he *answered* it.
r   Now, he for his part was sending up great clouds of smoke as he went.
17 a   And before long it went and landed in the way where he was going.
b   When he went by the spot,
c   it said to him, "Stop for a while, grandson."
d   And he stopped.
e   "So, why did you call me," it said to him.
f   "Well, *I* didn't call *you*," he told it.
g   "Oh, *I* thought you were probably going to give me a smoke."
h   "No," he told it.
i   "Alright, grandson, give me a bit of tobacco to smoke, if you could," it said to him.
j   "See, *I'll* only be able to fill my pipe one more time as well," he told it.
k   "I won't be able to give you any," he told it.
l   And he also said to it, "Whoever taught you to smoke is who you should ask for it."
m   The owl was very angry
n   and flew away.
o   "At whatever time you put your load down,
18 a   right then you will die," the one carrying the load was told.
b   "Well, you too,

c   na·hina·h=meko e·h=pakišinowane·ni,

d   i·nina·hi wi·h=nepeyani," e·h=ineči wi·teko·wa.

e   e·h=wa·wa·či-=meko_-se·kiti·wa·či.

f   neno·te·wa, nehkanitepehkwe=meko e·h=ki·ki·watahokoči.|

g   i·na·ka=na·hka wi·teko·wa,| nehkanitepehkwe=meko e·h=ki·wisa·či.

h   ke·tawi-=meko| -wa·pano·hiniki,

i   e·h=ayi·hkwiči| wi·teko·wa,

j   e·h=na·wanone·hwa·či_neno·te·wani.

k   wi·na=ke·h=e·yi·ki_neno·te·wa e·h=ayi·hkwiči=meko ki·ša·koči._

l   wi·teko·wa=na·hkači.|

m   "noši·hi," e·h=išiwe·či wi·teko·wa.

n   (e·hkwiniči=ke·h=meko ahkihki·me·hi e·h=pemi|-tašisa·či.)

o   "meše·='nah=po·našino," e·h=išiwe·či| wi·teko·wa.

p   "a·kwi=ča·h=natawi-po·našiya·nini," e·h=ineči. ‖

19 a   "a·kwi=ča·h=wi·h=nepeyanini po·našiyane," e·h=išiwe·či,

b   kakišaši·pye=meko.

c   " 'a·kwi,'_ketene=ma·hi.

d   a·kwi=we·=nenoše·yanini?

e   'a·kwi,'_ketene=ma·hi,"| e·h=ina·či.

f   "nahi´,_noši·hi,_ki·h=ketemino·ne=ča·hi._

g   meše=meko e·š_aka·wa·tamowane·ni," e·h=išiwe·či_wi·teko·wa.

h   i·ni=ke·hi='pi=meko| e·h=pemi_ta·kita·kinekwe·sa·či_ahki·ki.

i   "ohoho·´, nahi´,_ni·h=po·naši," e·h=ineči.

j   "ki·na=wi·na e·yi·ki=meko meše·='nahi ki·h=pakišine," e·neči_wi·teko·wa.

k   ahki·ki=meko e·h=pakišino·hiči,

l   e·h=ki·ša·koči-ayi·hkwiči.

m   no·make·piči,_e·h=a·nwi|-neneškinekwe·ška·či,

n   e·h=či·pačiseniki onekwi·kanani wi·teko·wa.|

o   meše·='nah=meko nehkaniki·šekwe e·h=apihapiwa·či.

p   aškači='pi wi·teko·wa, "apina=ni·hka kenana·hi='yo·we -mayakimene,"‖ e·h=išiwe·či
wi·teko·wa.|

20 a   "ki·hki·hki-=ke·h=po·našiyanehe,

b   awita_ke·htena ke·ko·hi išawihkapa.

c   awita nepo·hihkapa," e·h=ineči neno·te·wa.

d   "aše=meko='yo·we, 'wi·h=išawikwe·ni,' e·h=ine·nemena·ni we·či- i·ni| -inena·ni."

e   "ši·´,_ni·na=ma·h=ne·hi aše=meko='yo·we ketešimene.

f   ki·hki·hki-=ke·hi pakišinanehe,

g   awita_ke·ko·hi_išawihkapa,"_e·h=ineči_wi·teko·wa.

h   e·h=wa·wa·či-=meko -se·kiti·wa·či.

i   "o·´,_ki·na=wi·na i·ni=meko| a·mi_išawiya·ni e·šimiyani," e·h=išiwe·či wi·teko·wa.

j   "kemaneto·wipwa_a·wasi e·h=mehtose·neniwiye·kwe," e·h=išiwe·či wi·teko·wa._

k   "i·ni=ča·h=ni·na_we·či_kwe·hta·ni-kehči-se·kimiyani," e·h=išiwe·či wi·teko·wa.

l   " 'maneto·wiwaki=kohi ‖ anemi_mehtose·neniwaki,' neteko·p=a·pehe,

^c at whatever time you land,

^d you shall die," the owl was told.

^e They frightened each other by exchanging curses.

^f In the Indian's case, all night long he went around with the load on his back.

^g And meanwhile in the owl's case, all night long he flew around.

^h When it was almost daybreak,

ⁱ the owl was tired

^j as he went following after the Indian.

^k What's more, the Indian also, for his part, was extremely tired.

^l As was the owl.

^m "Grandson," the owl said.

ⁿ (Now, it was flying along a little below (the man's) height.)

^o "Feel free to put down your load," the owl said.

^p "Well, I'm not planning to put down my load," it was answered.

19 a "Well, you won't die if you put down your load," it said,

^b with considerable reluctance.

^c "I told you no, obviously.

^d Do you actually not understand?

^e I told you no, obviously," he told it.

^f "Alright, grandson, so I'll bless you.

^g Anything you desire to do," the owl declared.

^h Now, right then, the story goes, its wings were brushing the ground as it flew along.

ⁱ "Oh I see! Alright! I'll put down my load," it was told.

^j And when the owl was told, "But, you, as well, are free to land,"

^k the poor thing landed right on the ground

^l and was extremely tired.

^m After sitting a short while, the owl was unable to spread its wings,

ⁿ as its wings were stiff.

^o The two of them sat there most of the day.

^p Some time later, the story goes, the owl spoke, saying, "Actually, I said something odd to you back then that I shouldn't have.

20 a "To be clear, if you'd gone ahead anyway and put down your load,

^b nothing would actually have happened to you.

^c You wouldn't have died," the Indian was told.

^d "I said that to you just for the heck of it, wondering what would happen to you."

^e "Well, listen, I *also* said what I said to you just for the heck of it.

^f To be clear, if you'd gone ahead and landed,

^g nothing would have happened to you," the owl was told.

^h They frightened each other by exchanging curses.

ⁱ "Oh, but exactly what *you* told *me* would have happened to me," the owl said.

^j "You humans are more powerful," the owl said.

^k "So, that's why you really frightened me terribly saying that," the owl said.

^l "'The People-to-Be are powerful,' I was always told,

21 a eˑyeˑh-pyeˑči-apenoˑheˑhiyaˑni," eˑh=iniči iˑnini wiˑtekoˑwani.*

b "eˑyeˑh-=weˑ=yeˑtoke -pyeˑči-panašaˑheˑhiyani," eˑh=inaˑči.

c "eheˑhe," eˑh=iči wiˑtekoˑwa.

d eˑh=kosehkyeˑči=meko keˑkoˑhi| wiˑh=inoweˑči wiˑtekoˑwa.

e "niˑna=maˑh=neˑh=aˑpehe iˑni=meko kwiˑyena eˑšihišimiki.

f 'čaˑki=kohi_owiyeˑha manetoˑwiwa,' netekoˑp=aˑpehe.

g eˑh=neˑwonaˑke=naˑhka, 'kemešoˑmeswaˑwaki,' netekoˑpen=aˑpehe eˑh=apenoˑhiyaˑke,†

h meše=maˑh=mekoˑ='nahi eˑtaswi-=meko -neˑwonaˑkini.

i meše-='nah=keˑh=wiˑn=aˑpehe ketehkweˑhipwaˑtoke," eˑh=inaˑči.|

j "eheˑhe, keˑhtena=meko," eˑh=iniči.

k "niˑnaˑna='yo aˑhpene=meko ketenaˑpamenepena.

l niˑnaˑna=naˑhka_iˑni=meko ‖ eˑnaˑpamiyaˑke=yeˑtoke.| ‡

22 a aˑhpene=meko ketenaˑpamipenaˑtoke," eˑh=ikoči| wiˑtekoˑwani.

b "eheˑhe," eˑh=inaˑči.

c eˑnemi_pehkoteˑniki, wiˑtekoˑwa eˑh=kokweˑči-šoˑškinekweˑškaˑči,

d eˑh=aˑnawihtoˑči=meko.

e eˑh=čiˑpačeˑweˑšiki=meko kiˑšaˑkoči.

f keˑkeyaˑhi='pi eˑh=weˑpi_šašawenaˑči wiˑna=meko.

g kwiˑyena=meko waˑpanoˑhiniki eˑh=kiˑši-šašawenaˑči.

h "nahíˑ, niˑh=naˑte| wiˑh=miˑčiyakwe," eˑh=ikoči.|

i eˑh=anisaˑniči.

j eˑh=pyeˑtoˑniči kehči-nasikani,

k (noˑmake=keˑh=meko eˑh=ineˑteniči.)

l eˑh=kehči|-wiˑseniči.

m "šiˑhčeˑˊ," eˑh=išiteˑheˑči,

n eˑh=kiˑhpočeˑči.|

o naˑwahkweˑniki eˑh=naˑkwaˑči,

p eˑh=awanaˑči=meko opešekesiˑmani.

q iˑyaˑh=keˑhi='pi eˑh=wanisotehe_keyeˑhapa‖ weˑčiˑči.

23 a kwiˑyena=meko| nekotenwi eˑh=aˑpi-natoneˑhoči, eˑh=pyaˑči.

b oˑni| eˑh=aˑčimohaˑči omesoˑtaˑnahi.

c eˑh=nanakwiˑkweˑči eˑh=aˑwinoˑhokoči| oˑsani.

d "peˑhki=koh=meko,| nekwiˑhi, kekiˑšaˑkoči-waˑwaneškaˑhi," eˑh=ineči.

e "mehtoˑči=keˑh=niˑhka-='yoˑwe keneškimene," eˑh=ineči.

f eˑh=nanaˑhi-=meko -kehči_neškimeči,

g eˑh=nakanakapehkweˑpiči.

h eˑh=seˑkimekoči oˑsani.

i naˑmiteˑhe=meko eˑh=seˑkimekoči,

j naˑhka eˑh=aˑhkweˑči=meko.

---

*/eˑyeˑh-pyeˑči/: AK ⟨.|eye.pyeči⟩.

†/eˑh=neˑwonaˑke=naˑhka/: ⟨ke⟩ changed from ⟨ka⟩.

‡/eˑnaˑpamiyaˑke=yeˑtoke/: AK ⟨‖enapamiyake.yetoke|⟩.

21 a   while I was yet a child," the owl said.

b   "Rather, while you were yet a fledgling, probably," he said to it.

c   "Yes," said the owl.

d   The owl was afraid to say anything.

e   "In my case too, you understand, that's exactly what *I* always used to be told.

f   'Every creature truly has power,' I would be told.

g   And also when we saw you, we were always told when we were children, 'They're your grandfathers,'

h   I mean, any time we saw you.

i   Although you always probably could have been females," he told it.

j   "Yes, it's true," it said.

k   "After all, *we* see *you* as all alike.

l   That's also probably just how *you* see *us*.

22 a   You must see us as all just alike," the owl told him.

b   "Yes," he said to it.

c   As soon as it was getting dark, the owl tried straightening its wings

d   but just couldn't do it.

e   It still had extremely stiff muscles.

f   Eventually, the story goes, he set about limbering up the owl himself by rubbing it.

g   Exactly at daybreak he had it completely limbered up.

h   "Alright, I'll go after something for us to eat," it told him.

i   And it flew off.

j   It brought back a large roasting stick of meat.

k   (Now, it was gone only a short time.)

l   He ate a lot.

m   "Oh my!" he thought,

n   as he was full.

o   At noon he left,

p   taking home his deer.

q   Now, back where he came from it turns out he had been though to be lost.

23 a   And just when one party was back from searching for him, he arrived.

b   And then he told his parents about what had happened.

c   And his father pointed right in his face.

d   "You've really behaved extremely badly, son," he was told.

e   "And it's as if I scolded you before," he was told.

f   He got severely scolded anyway,

g   sitting there with his head down.

h   His father frightened him by what he said.

i   He frightened him deep inside.

j   And he was quite angry.

[k]   na·hina·hi=ʾyo=ča·hi=ʾpi mi·ka·ti·wa·či aša·hahi,
[l]   mehta·hkwi=meko i·tepi_e·h=a·či.
[m]   i·ya·h=meko e·h=taši-neseči.
[n]   kete·=ʾnahi=ʾpi pašito·he·ha e·h=kehči-mayo·či,
[o]   ina·čimop=a·pehe.|

[p]   i·ni. ‖

^k   So then, at the time when they fought the Siouxs,
^l he went there ill-equipped.
^m And he was killed over there.
ⁿ   Now the old man wept loudly instead,
^o so the story is always told.

^p   That's all.

mênetôwita metemôhêha

The Older Woman Who Had Manitou Power

mênetôwita metemôhêha

Alfred Kiyana[*]

1 a   me·neto·wita_metemo·he·ha.[†]

b   našawaye=ʼpi nekoti_metemo·he·ha e·h=maneto·hkwe·wiči=meko ta·taki.

c   e·h=naha·piči=meko.

d   e·h=maneto·wi-metemo·he·hiči=meko.

e   e·h=nekotiha·či=ke·hi=ʼpi ota·nesani.

f   e·h=ki·ša·koči-=meko| -nawe·nihkwe·he·hiniči i·nini ota·nese·hani.

g   e·h=aški-=meko -ki·šiki·hiniči.

h   pe·hki=meko e·ši-natawe·nememeči ihkwe·wahi e·h=išawiniči i·nini ota·nese·hani.

i   apina=ʼpi e·h=asa·witepe·niči, e·h=wa·peškihkwe·winiči. ‖

2 a   e·h=mahkwa·tesiniči=meko ki·ša·koči.|

b   e·h=pwa·wi-=ke·h=wi·na=meko -nahi- ke·ko·hi=-ʼši-neškima·či,

c   ašewe·na e·h=mahkwa·či-=meko -še·škesi·hiniči.

d   ahpene·či=meko e·h=a·nawiha·wa·či oškinawe·haki.

e   mahkwa·či=ke·h=meko e·h=neškimeči oškinawe·he·haki kwe·či-mi·hkemehkwe·wa·čini.

f   e·h=pwa·wi-=meko -nasata·wi-_ke·ko·hi=-ʼši-kano·neči.

g   mahkwa·či=ʼpi=mek-a·pehe e·h=kano·neči.

h   mahkwa·či=meko| e·h=a·čimoheči e·h=wa·wana·hpenana·wa·či. ‖

3 a   wi·h=kehči-neškimekowa·či e·h=ine·nema·wa·či,

b   mahkwa·či=meko e·h=neškimekowa·či.

c   a·neta=ʼpi ihkwe·wahi e·ši-aniwe·neke·moniči e·h=kehke·netamowa·či na·tawino·ni.

d   i·ni=ča·hi=ʼpi wi·h=ayo·tena·wa·či e·h=išite·he·wa·či

e   we·či-natawe·nema·wa·či wi·h=kehči-neškimekowa·či i·nini še·škesi·he·hani.

f   mehto·či=ʼpi=meko i·ni e·h=iši-nekoti·hiniči še·škesi·he·hani| e·h=ahpi·hčite·he·wa·či| oškinawe·he·haki.

g   e·h=pwa·wi-=ke·h=meko ‖ owiye·ha -kakano·neti·hekoči.

4 a   o·ni metemo·he·ha ke·keya·hi i·nini ota·nesani,

b   "ši·´,_pwa·wi-=wi·na=-ʼna me·nwe·nema·kwe·hini -kakano·neti·he·wa?" e·h=ina·či ota·nesani.[‡]

c   "a·kwi=ča·h=menwe·netama·nini še·ški wi·h=taši-kakano·neti·haki neniwaki.

d   neme·nese·neta," e·h=ina·či okye·ni.

e   "ki·h=nekoti-=ča·h=meko -wi·te·ma·petoke wi·h=ona·pe·miwane·na,"| e·h=ineči i·na_ še·škesi·he·ha.[§]

f   "a·kwi=ča·h=ni·na| nana·ši wi·h=ona·pe·miya·nini," ‖ e·h=ina·či okye·ni.

5 a   "a·kwi pešeke·netama·nini owi·weti·weni.

---

[*]The manuscript is NAA 2788; it has 49 pages.

[†]/me·neto·wita/: AK ⟨manetowita⟩; 'older woman': *lit.*, 'young old woman'.

[‡]A criticism tempered by being couched in the third person; 'this girl': *lit.*, 'that one'.

[§]/e·h=ineči/: AK ⟨einači⟩.

The Older Woman who had Manitou Power
Translated by Ives Goddard

1 a   The Older Woman Who Had Manitou Power.

b   Long ago, the story goes, there was an older woman who was sort of a manitou woman.

c   Indeed, she could see things.

d   She was indeed a manitou lady.

e   Now, she had one daughter, the story goes.

f   Her young daughter was as beautiful as she could be.

g   And she had only recently reached womanhood.

h   Her young daughter was everything women are desired to be.

i   She even had blond hair and a fair complexion, to hear the tale.

2 a   And she was quiet as could be.

b   What's more, she never scolded her at all,

c   and still she was a quiet young girl.

d   Young men always failed with her.

e   Actually, whenever young men tried to pay court, they were calmly admonished.

f   They were not spoken to crossly at all.

g   It's said they would always be spoken to quietly.

h   It was calmly explained to them that they had no chance with her.

3 a   They expected that she would scold them severely,

b   and they were admonished calmly.

c   Some are said to have known medicine, by using which, women become admiring.

d   So, because that is said to be what they were thinking of using on her,

e   they looked for that young maiden to scold them severely.

f   They say it's as if the young men believed she was the only young maiden there was.

g   And what's more, she never had conversations with any of them.

4 a   Eventually the older woman (confronted) her daughter,

b   saying to her daughter, "Gee, so *why* doesn't this girl have conversations with one she likes?"

c   "Well, it's only that I don't like to be having conversations with men.

d   I'm embarrassed by it," she told her mother.

e   "So, what you'll probably do is go with one you may marry just once, and that will be that," the young girl was told.

f   "Well, *I'm* never going to get married," she said to her mother.

5 a   "Marriage holds no attraction for me.

b   a·kwi menwe·netama·nini wi·h=taši- ke·ko·hi -to·tato·tawiwa·či neniwaki,” e·h=ina·či
     okye·ni.
c   “nahi´, neta·nese, ona·pe·miyane=ma·hi ki·h=menwawi.
d   i·ni=wi·na| e·šite·he·yani a·kwi paši-menwikekini,”| e·h=ina·či.
e   “nahi´, nekwaya·ši-=koh=meko -me·nešite·he,
f   wi·h=pwa·wi-=meko owiye·ha -kehke·nemiči, -išite·he,” e·h=ina·či okye·ni.
g   “o·´, neta·nese,| sanakato·pani e·šite·he·yani,” ‖ e·h=ina·či ota·nesani.
6 a   “a·kwi=ke·hi nana·ši| wi·h=po·ni·hko·hkini oškinawe·he·haki.
b   kapo·twe=meko ki·h=mayakite·he.
c   (ki·h=metwite·he=’h=we·na manihi wi·h=išite·he·yani.)*
d   kapo·twe=meko ki·h=meme·sačite·he.
e   če·w_ahpi·hčite·he pi=ya·pi neniwaki,” e·h=ina·či.
f   “ki·hpene=ča·hi, neta·ha, me·me·sačite·he·wane·ni=ki·hpene,
g   ki·h=nekoti-=meko| -ačihkwiheko·pi.
h   ki·h=nenehke·neta=’yo-wi·na·=’ni ne·škinamani e·na·čimoyani.
i   ma·mahka·či=meko i·ni wi·h=anemiha·yani.
j   ta·tepi ‖ wi·h=oči-konakwi·yani.
7 a ketehkwe·wi=manihi.
b   me·me·čiki=ča·h=meko ki·h=oni·ča·nesi,” e·h=ineči.
c   “aše išikihiwe·wa maneto·wa| wi·h=oči_a·naha·nehkwikiweči
     wi·h=anemi-’ši|-ašihašiheti·weči.
d   a·kwi=kehi e·h=wa·waneška·hiki oči- i·ni -išahišawikini,
e   mehteno·h=meko e·h=ona·pe·miki,
f   e·h=wa·wi·če·noti·ki=ča·hi.
g   i·ni| e·šiwe·pikeki-=’ni e·taši_neškinamani e·na·čimoyani.
h   aše ki·na·na_ketešikiha·sopena e·h=ihkwe·witehka·soyakwe i·ni| wi·h=to·toto·to·nakwe ‖
     neniwaki.
8 a wi·na=na·hka neniwa, aše=meko| i·ni e·ne·nemekoči maneto·wani,†
b   we·či- i·ni meše·=’nahi -anemi_to·to·nakwe wena·pe·ma·ko·makwini,
c   we·či- meše·=’nah=meko| i·ni -anemi_to·to·nakwe.
d   “ni·na=’yo ni·šenwi nepye·či-ona·pe·mi.
e   a·kwi=ča·h=ni·na=mani ke·ko·hi išawiya·nini.‡
f   šewe·=wi·na ke·htena i·ni=meko iši_ni·šwi ke·hke·nemiwa·či neniwaki.
g   ke·htena a·kwi| owiye·ha e·h=mi·hkemiči i·ni to·tato·tawičini.
h   mehteno·h=meko na·hina·hi ‖ pye·tehkwe·wa·šikini wi·kiya·peki, meše·=’nahi·=’nahi.§
9 a a·kwi menehta_i·ni to·tawiwa·čini pye·či-ona·pe·miya·niki.
b   ki·ši-=meko -pye·šiwa·čini wi·kiya·peki,
c   i·ni e·h=anwa·či·ya·ni.
d   i·ni=ni·na pye·či-išawiya·ni, neta·ha.

---

*/manihi/: AK ⟨mani.i.⟩.

†/neniwa/ ‘man’, representative singular.

‡/ni·na=mani/: AK ⟨nina|mani⟩.

§/wi·kiya·peki/ ‘to the family house’, *lit.*, ‘to the house’ (also in 9*b*); cf. the use as ‘main house’.

^b I don't like to think that men will be having sex with me," she told her mother.
^c "Listen, my daughter, you'll be doing the right thing by getting married, you realize.
^d But what you're thinking of doing is not right at all," she said to her.
^e "Listen, I'm already truly ashamed
^f and have already decided that no one will know me intimately," she said to her mother.
^g "Oh, my daughter, what you intend to do sure is hard," she said to her daughter.
^{6 a} "And what's more, the young men will never leave you alone.
^b And all at once you'll have a funny feeling.
^c (After all, it's about time you were through thinking *these* thoughts!)
^d All at once you'll have a randy feeling.
^e Let me tell you, our feelings are as intense as men's," she told her.
^f "And once that happens, my daughter, once you do have those randy feelings,
^g you'll right away be made pregnant, and that will be that.
^h As you *will* think about the thing you say you hate.
ⁱ You won't avoid going down that path.
^j What way would you go to escape?
^{7 a} Here, you're a woman.
^b So I'm sure you will have a child," she was told.
^c "The manitou made us as we physically are simply to be the way we would continue
making each other, as the means for us to go on from generation to generation.
^d What's more, we don't do that because we're wicked,
^e only because we're married,
^f and so we enjoy each other's company.
^g That's the significance of the thing you're saying you hate.
^h We, who bear the name of 'women', were given our bodies just so men would do that us.
^{8 a} And for *men* also, that's just what the manitou intended them to do,
^b which is why they may go on doing that to us whenever we make them our husbands,
^c why they are free to continue doing that to us.
^d "I, for example, have had two husbands.
^e And in the present circumstances I don't do anything.
^f But those were truly the only two men who knew me intimately.
^g And the truth is that no one was doing that to me when he courted me.
^h Only at the times when I was taken to the family house as a bride, then he could.
^{9 a} The husbands I've had didn't do that to me the first thing.
^b After they had brought me to the family house,
^c then I was willing.
^d That's what I have done, my daughter.

^e   "a·kwi ma·mani·nina·hi wi·h=pešekwa·hiya·ni nenehke·netama·nini.

^f   mehteno·h=meko ne·po·hiwa·čini wi·čihe·hiya·niki i·ni e·h=po·ni-wi·čawiwaki.

^g   na·hkači a·kwi| nahi-anohka·nakini.

^h   na·hkači meše=meko ‖ ki·wi‗ta·taši-ma·mi·hkemehkwe·we·waki.

^{10 a}   a·kwi=ni·na| ke·ko·hi inahinakini na·hkači mi·hkema·wa·čini.

^b   a·kwi wi·h=mya·ne·nemaki na·hka‗wi·čawiwakiki ke·hke·nemakini
          mi·hkemehkwe·we·wa·čini.

^c   o·ni=pe·hki e·h=me·menwihta·ke·ya·ni ke·ko·hi mi·ša·tesiweni.

^d   a·kwi=ča·hi nahi|-pakišikini.

^e   a·neta | ma·haki kene·wa·waki e·hpi·hči-we·wenesiwa·či.[*]

^f   i·n=a·pehe| e·hpi·hči-we·wenesiwa·či mi·hkemečiki.

^g   kapo·twe·='nah=a·pehe po·ni·hkawa·petoke.

^h   "ni·na=ke·hi ‖ meše=meko še·ški netaši-ma·mi·hkeče·wi·hi.

^{11 a}   a·yaškač=a·pehe nepye·nota·ko·pi.

^b   pye·notawikini,| a·kwi, 'mani=pena´ nawači-iši·hta·no,' a·kwi ihkye·ya·nini.

^c   "a·kwi=na·hka| taši-kehteniwe·ya·nini.

^d   meše=meko.

^e   mi·škota če·wi·šenwi we·na·pe·miya·niki a·maha·mano·neniwikwe·hiki.

^f   i·ni=meko| če·wi·šenwi pye·či|-išawiwa·či.

^g   i·ni=ke·h=me·kwe·h=meko wa·wota·hpene·wa·či pye·či|-wi·čawiwakiki.

^h   ihkwe·wahi e·h=asa·mi‗aniwi·hkawa·wa·či. ‖

^{12 a}   i·ni=me·kwe·h=meko wa·woči-nepowa·či," e·h=ina·či ota·nesani.[†]

^b   "ki·na we·yo·siyana‗pe·hki a·wasi e·ši-aniwi·hkawa·ta ihkwe·wahi.

^c   ki·na=ča·h=mani kekehči-=meko -mayakite·he·petoke e·h=neškinawači neniwaki,

^d   wi·h=pwa·wi-=meko -kehke·nemehki e·h=išite·he·yani.

^e   keki·ša·koči-=meko| -sanake·netamo·ne i·ni=ye·toke e·h=išite·he·yani."

^f   "ehe·he, i·ni=koh=meko e·ši|-me·nešite·he·ya·ni kwaya·ši.

^g   wi·h=pwa·wi-=mekoho ‖ -kehke·nemiwa·či neniwaki netešite·he," e·h=ina·či=meko okye·ni.

^{13 a}   "o·´‗kemenwawi,| neta·nese, i·ni e·h=išite·he·yani,

^b   i·ni e·h=ine·netamani ki·yawi," e·h=ina·či ota·nese·hani.

^c   (e·h=ki·ša·koči-='yo=ke·hi -mano·kihkwe·we·hiniči,

^d   e·h=ki·ša·koči-=meko -menwa·pata·niniči ota·nesani.)

^e   o·ni meše=nekotenwi e·h=pena·winiki.

^f   (wi·sahke·hani='yo=ke·hi e·h=wi·čikamikesi·ma·wa·či.

^g   meše=meko na·hina·hi e·h=owi·kiči wi·sahke·ha,

^h   ke·no·te·hi e·h=owi·kiči.) ‖

^{14 a}   o·ni·='na metemo·he·ha e·h=akiha·či ota·nesani.

^b   nye·wokoni='pi| ki·h‗pwa·wi‗pya·niči,

^c   e·h=we·patone·hwa·či.

^d   e·h=ki·wi-nana·toma·či wi·kiya·pihki·ki ota·nesani.

---

[*]/ma·haki/ 'these' for 'these women'.

[†]/ota·nesani/: ⟨sa⟩ changed from ⟨se⟩.

e   "I didn't consider getting divorced from time to time.

f   Only when the ones I lived with died did I cease to be married to them.

g   And I also never gave them orders.

h   And also, they were free go around chasing other women.

10 a   And I also never said anything to them when they chased women.

b   Also, my husbands didn't chase women so I'd dislike them when I found out.

c   And I used to make them some really nice things for fancy clothing.

d   So, I was never divorced.

e   You see how pretty some of these (women) are.

f   That's how pretty the ones that were chased after would be.

g   And pretty soon they'd always seem to be given up.

h   "Meanwhile, *I* just happily went ahead and did my work.

11 a   From time to time they would come to me.

b   And when they came to me, I wouldn't say, "Could you first do *this*?"

c   "And I also didn't hold my husbands back.

d   It didn't matter.

e   On top of that, the ones I married both times must have been naturally hot-blooded men.

f   That's just what they were like both times.

g   What's more, I think that's why the husbands I've had died.

h   They were too preoccupied with women.

12 a   I think that's why they died," she told her daughter.

b   "The one whose daughter you are was the one really more concerned with women.

c   So, under the circumstances, it's a very odd feeling *you* seem to have, to be hating men,

d   to be not wishing them to know you intimately.

e   I think it's a great difficulty for you that you apparently think that."

f   "Yes, that's certainly exactly what I'm unalterably ashamed to do.

g   I *don't* want men to know me intimately," she told her mother firmly.

13 a   "Oh, you do well, my daughter, in wishing that,

b   in thinking of yourself that way," she told her daughter.

c   (Now, her daughter had a perfect womanly form,

d   and she was as fine-looking as she could be.)

e   And then at a certain time it was summer.

f   (Now, another thing, they lived in the same settlement with Wisahkeha.

g   Wisahkeha had his lodge a short distance away,

h   and his lodge was a longhouse.)

14 a   And the older woman didn't know where her daughter was.

b   After she hadn't come back for four days, the story goes,

c   she began searching for her.

d   She went around the settlement asking for her daughter.

e eʰ=pwaˑwi-=meko -mehkwatomaˑči.

f keˑkeyaʰ=meko, "nekwisa=čaˑhi!ʔ waˑwaneˑnemaˑsa!ʔ eˑšawinikweˑni okiˑhani!ʔ" eˑh=išiteˑheˑči.

g oˑni, "iˑtepi niˑh=mawi|-nanaˑtohtawaˑwa_nekwisa," eˑh=išiteˑheˑči.|

h neseˑmaˑwani| eˑh=awatawaˑči,

i iˑtepi eˑh=aˑči.

j iˑyaʰ=pyeˑyaˑči, nanakoteˑki ‖ keˑkoˑhi eˑh=maˑtakwahaˑteˑniki.

15 a eˑh=awatenamawaˑči neseˑmaˑwani.

b "nekwiˑhi, wiˑsahkeˑčaˑkwe, netaˑneseˑha=kohi eˑh=wanihaki,

c weˑči|-pyeˑči-nanaˑtohtoˑnaˑni.

d 'waˑwaneˑnemaˑsa='hi='yo!ʔ nekwisa wiˑsahkeˑčaˑkwa!?' netešiteˑhe.

e iˑni=čaˑhi_weˑči-pyeˑči-nanaˑtohtoˑnaˑni eˑšawiˑhikweˑni netaˑnesa,"| eˑh=inaˑči.

f "oˑhoˑ´, weˑnahi_iˑni.

g mana='yo=nekoti ihkweˑwa.*

h keˑnemaˑpi=mana_wiˑh=otaˑnesiyani," eˑh=ikoči.

i eˑh=paˑhkiˑkweˑnaˑči.

j kaši´, otaˑnesani=čiˑhi. ‖

16 a iˑni=keˑhi=ʾpi=meko eˑh=weˑpweˑweˑhikeˑniči.

b metemoˑheˑha eˑh=pemi_weˑpekaˑči.

c eˑh=šaˑwanoˑwekaheči.

d peˑhki=meko eˑh=kiˑšaˑkoči-kehči|-niˑmiči metemoˑheˑha.

e eˑyeˑniwe=meko eˑh=ahpiˑhtekaˑči.

f eˑh=pwaˑwi-=meko nanaˑši -poˑnekaˑči.

g ahpeneˑči=meko ayeˑniwe eˑh=ahpiˑhtekaˑči iˑna metemoˑheˑha.

h eˑh=pyeˑmačinoˑhiči| ohkoneˑheˑhi.

i mahkwayi=ʾpi| ohkoneˑhiwa.

j eˑh=teˑhteˑpipiweˑsaˑki mahkwayi.|

k mešeˑ=ʾnah=meko nyeˑwokoni ayeˑniwe=meko eˑh=ahpiˑhtekaˑči| metemoˑheˑha. ‖

17 a nyeˑwokonakateniki, "ihihyaˑ´.

b iˑni=niˑhka| eˑh=ayiˑhkwiyaˑni eˑh=niˑmihenaˑni, nekiˑhe.

c iˑni=čaˑhi eˑh=anihiyani.

d menehta=niˑna netaškinekweˑsa,

e naˑhka=menehta netayiˑhkwi eˑh=nakamoyaˑni," eˑh=iniči.

f "iˑni=čaˑh=mana| ketaˑnesa wiˑh=awanači," eˑh=ikoči.

g eˑh=pasekwiˑtenemeči.

h eˑh=kiˑšaˑkoči-=keˑh=wiˑna=meko=ʾyoˑwe -paˑsaneneniči,†

i naˑhinaˑhi peˑsekwiˑtenemeči, eˑh=pwaˑwi-=meko keˑkoˑhi| -inaˑpataˑniniči.

j neˑyaˑpi=meko eˑh=inekinoˑhiniči.

k "mani=kohi=ʾyoˑwe ‖ weˑči- iˑni_-toˑtawaki:

18 a nesiˑmeˑha wiˑna wiˑh=otehkweˑmitehe eˑh=ineˑnemaki.

b iˑni=ʾyoˑwe weˑči-pahkihteˑwi_-niˑmihaki," eˑh=ineči| metemoˑheˑha.

---

*/mana='yo=nekoti/ (IG, AW): AK ⟨manayone|nekoti.⟩.

†/-paˑsaneneniči/: AK ⟨.epasane|neniči.⟩.

e	And her inquiries did not turn her up.
f	Finally she thought, "Well, my nephew would hardly fail to know what happened to his aunt."
g	And then she thought, "I'll go to my nephew's and ask him."
h	She took tobacco for him
i	and went there.
j	When she got there, she saw something covered up in the middle of the lodge.
15 a	And she handed him tobacco.
b	"My nephew Wîsahkêchâkwa, I've surely lost my daughter,
c	which is why I have come to ask you a question.
d	I thought, 'My nephew Wîsahkêchâkwa can hardly fail to know about her.'
e	So that's why I've come to ask you what could have happened to my daughter," she said to him.
f	"Oh, I see, so that's it.
g	Well, this is one woman.
h	I don't know whether this one is your daughter," he said to her.
i	And she uncovered her face.
j	And what do you know, it *was* her daughter.
16 a	And at that, the story goes, he began to drum.
b	And the old lady began to dance.
c	The Shawnee Dance was drummed for her.
d	The old lady really danced as hard as she could.
e	She danced steadily at the same speed.
f	And she never stopped dancing.
g	That old lady always danced at the same steady speed.
h	And she had her robe tied around her middle.
i	Her blanket was a bearskin, the story goes.
j	And the pile of the bearskin moved in waves.
k	The old lady danced on for four days at the same speed.
17 a	After four days he said, "Wooh!
b	Darned if I'm not tired from drumming for you, my aunt!
c	So, now you beat me.
d	*My* arms got tired first,
e	and I got tired singing first.
f	"So, now you can take your daughter here home," he said to her.
g	And the girl was raised to her feet.
h	Even though she had been completely bloated from rotting,
i	when she was raised to her feet, she showed no visible effects at all.
j	She was back to the size she had been.
k	"And let me tell you the reason why I did that to her:
18 a	it's because I wanted my younger brother to have her as his own sister.
b	That's why I made her dance till she died," the old lady was told.

^c "i·ni=’yo·we e·ne·nemaki mana keta·nese·ha.

^d mani=ke·hi we·či·-=’ni -ine·nemaki:

^e ke·htena=meko mahkwa·či e·h=iškwe·se·hiči,

^f i·noki=na·hkači mahkwa·či=meko e·h=še·škesi·he·hiči,

^g e·h=pwa·wi-=meko| owiye·hani -kehke·nemekoči.

^h i·ni=ča·hi we·či- i·ni -ine·nemakehe=’yo·we.

ⁱ "i·noki=ča·hi ki·h=awana·wa=meko=wi·na.

^j asa·mi=ni·hka keme·neši-ayi·hkwihi," ‖ e·h=ineči metemo·he·ha.

^{19 a} "ši·´, kakata·ni=’hi=’yo, nekwi·hi.

^b i·ni=koh=meko| e·ši-nekotihe·hiya·ni manaha neta·nese·ha.

^c a·kwi na·htaswihakini neni·ča·nesaki.

^d i·ni=meko e·ši-nekotihe·hiya·ni neta·nese·ha."

^e še·šketo·he·hani e·h=mi·neči i·na| še·škesi·he·ha,

^f na·hkači na·tawino·ni.

^g no·še·hčikani e·h=mi·neči.

^h "ki·h=na·no·še·ha·waki ki·či-ihkwe·waki," e·h=ineči i·na še·škesi·he·ha.

ⁱ e·h=na·kwa·wa·či.

^j i·ya·h=aya·pami e·h=pye·neti·wa·či,

^k aya·pami owi·kewa·ki.

^l i·ya·h=na·hkači ‖ ki·ši-pya·wa·či,

^{20 a} "nahi´, neta·nese, natawi-=’škwe| -ona·pe·mino.

^b i·ni=ya·pi-ye·hapa ča·ki maneto·waki e·h=kehke·nemehki e·h=še·škesi·he·hiyani," e·h=ina·či we·ta·nesita.

^c e·h=we·pi-=na·hkači -memye·ška·čimoha·či.

^d o·ni wa·paniki, "na·pi=wi·na| wi·kopihke·yakwe," e·h=ina·či,

^e e·h=na·kwa·wa·či.

^f o·ni ši·ša·ta i·ya·h=nekotahi i·nihi e·h=ne·wa·či.*

^g kwi·yena=meko e·h=pye·čiha·niči meše e·h=ahkwikaniki e·h=ki·wa·kwate·niki pemitasakatwi e·h=pepikwe·ya·niki. ‖

^{21 a} e·h=pi·to·te·či,

^b ta·htapako·ni wa·wi·tawi e·h=oči-kepiseto·či,

^c e·h=kepaškahoči.

^d kwi·yena=meko i·nahi e·h=pye·či-nana·hapiniči.

^e e·h=we·pi|-a·ya·čimohemeči| še·škesi·he·hani.

^f "nahi´, neta·ha, ki·h=wi·tamo·ne e·šikeki mani ne·škinamani ona·pe·miweni.

^g neniwa e·h=wi·čawiwoči nekoti,| e·h=menwito·tawoči,

^h ki·ša·koči-=meko -menwito·ta·ke·wa," e·h=ineči.

ⁱ "na·hkači neniwaki menamena·škonohiwe·waki.

^j ki·na·na=mani e·h=mo·šaki-ihkwe·wiyakwe a·kwi nekotenwi| wi·h=kaško·hpenato·hiyakwini ‖ ‘mi·čipe·he·hi’ e·tameki.| †

---

*/i·ya·h=nekotahi/: AK ⟨.|iya.nekotai.⟩.

†/mi·čipe·he·hi/: AK ⟨‖mičipiei.⟩.

c   "That's what I intended to happen to your daughter.

d   And here's why I wanted that to happen to her:

e   Because she was truly a quiet girl

f   and is also at present a quiet young maiden, indeed,

g   and because no one has known her intimately.

h   So, that's why I did intend that to happen to her.

i   "So, now you may indeed take her home, though.

j   You sure did shame me much in tiring me out," the old lady was told.

19 a   "Say, that's great, my nephew.

b   You must know, my daughter here is my only child.

c   I don't have several children.

d   My daughter is the only one I have."

e   The young maiden was given a little kettle,

f   and also medicine.

g   She was given childbirth medicine.

h   "You'll be a midwife to the other women," that young maiden was told.

i   And they left.

j   The two of them went back home together,

k   back to their house.

l   After they had gotten back again,

20 a   the older woman said to her daughter, "Alright, my daughter, it's time you got married.

b   Look, it turns out that all the manitous know that you're a virgin."

c   And she began again to instruct her confusedly.

d   And then the next day she said to her, "How about if we at least get basswood bark."

e   And they set out.

f   And there was a hunter that saw them over there someplace.

g   The way they were coming led right to where there lay a hollow log of medium length.

21 a   And he crawled inside

b   and set leaves blocking both ends,

c   shutting himself in.

d   He heard them come right there and sit down.

e   And the instruction of the young girl began.

f   "Alright, Daughter, I'm going to tell you about nature of this marriage that you hate.

g   When finally we marry a man, he treats us well.

h   He treats us extremely well," she told her.

i   "And also men furnish us with fresh meat.

j   We women who live alone have not once been able to kill what is called 'game'.

22 a mehteno·h=ye·toke ma·haki či·nawe·me·hiyakwiki| pe·hkihenakwini i·ni wi·h=mena·škono·hiyakwe," e·h=ina·či ota·nese·hani.
b "mani=ča·h:|
c keki·sa·či-=meko -išite·he·petoke$^{?}$
d wi·h=pwa·wi-=meko owiye·ha -kehke·nemehki$^{?}$ e·h=išite·he·yani?[*]
e a·kwi=ni·na| menwe·netamo·na·nini i·ni e·h=išite·he·yani,
f i·ni e·h=ine·netamani ki·yawi.|
g "mani=ke·hi·=’ni e·šiwe·pikeki ne·škinamani:
h wi·h=waniwani·hkama·ki ki·šišino·hikini.[†]
i i·ni·=’ni| we·či-išikihiwe·či ‖ maneto·wa_ki·šihiwa·ta.|
23 a pwa·wi-=’h=we·na$^{!?}$ -ča·ki-neniwine·ha!?
b ‘a·kwi=pena´ ma·haki wi·h=kehke·neti·wa·čini,’ ine·neti·ke,
c i·ni_a·mi-̲’šawiki.
d šewe·na na·hina·h=meko ča·kine·ke,|
e awita·=’nahi na·hkači nekotahi oči-̲sa·kine·ha.
f "mani=wi·na| e·h=ihkwe·wiki:
g ke·htena=meko naha·pata·nipi.[‡]
h "na·hkači mo·šaki-=meko -ihkwe·wike,
i i·ni=meko a·mi-̲’šawiki.
j awita=nana·ši owiye·ha oni·ča·nese·hisa.
k "i·ni=ke·hi me·nese·netamani,
l ne·so·nameki i·ni to·to·hke neniwa, ‖
24 a i·n=a·mihtahi_kehke·netamani e·hpi·hči-̲me·meta·ča·hiki.
b ki·ša·koči=meko me·meta·ča·hiwi e·h=wa·wa·čišineki neniwaki.
c apina=meko mehto·či sayasaya·wanasite·pi inamata·pi.
d i·ni we·či-pwa·wi- a·neta -kaškihto·wa·či wi·h=pešekwa·hiwa·či
e ki·ši-̲anehkawa·wa·čini nekoti neniwani.
f a·neta meše=meko·=’nahi i·ni anemi-̲to·ta·ko·ki neniwahi.
g "ke·htena=koči=wi·na| ki·ša·koči=meko| me·meta·ča·hiwi.
h mo·hči i·nahi ‖ e·h=tašinehke·šinowa·či,
25 a koči·h ke·htena=meko e·h=še·škesi·hiki,
b ki·ša·koči=meko saya·wesipi i·nahi we·či-ihkwe·wiki.
c na·hkači e·h=aški-=meko i·ni -to·ta·ke·wa·či,
d saya·wihiwe·waki=meko.
e "šewe·na_no·make=meko i·ni=meko e·h=ki·ši-anehkawoči e·h=ona·pe·miki.
f ki·ši-anehkawočini, meše·=’nah=meko e·ka·wa·tamekini i·ni ina·pi,
g ‘mani=pena´_išawita·we,’ ina·pi e·h=ona·pe·memeči," e·h=ina·či ota·nesani. ‖
26 a "a·kwi=meko ke·ko·hi iši|-kosetawočini.
b i·ni·=’ni e·šikeki owi·weti·weni," e·h=ina·či.
c e·h=pwa·wi-=meko| nana·ši ke·ko·hi -inowe·či še·škesi·he·ha.

[*]Interrogative intonation: IG.
[†]/wi·h=wani/: AK ⟨.wiwani.⟩.
[‡]⟨pa⟩ changed from ⟨pe⟩.

22 a It seems that the only times we'll have meat are when our relatives give us a share," she told her daughter.

b   "So consider this:

c Are you maybe having second thoughts

d in thinking you don't want anyone to know you intimately?

e I don't think it's good for you to be thinking that,

f to be thinking that about yourself.

g   "And this is the significance of the thing you hate:

h so we can have a diversion after we lie down.

i That's the reason why the manitou that made us made our bodies that way.

23 a How come we're not all men, after all?

b If we think, 'O.K. now, they're not going to know us intimately,'

c that's what we'd be.

d But at the time we all die,

e we wouldn't then spring up out of the ground again from someplace else.

f   "Here's the thing about us women, though:

g the truth is we look good.

h   "And also, if we women live alone,

i the same thing would happen.

j No one would ever have any children.

k   "And as for the thing you're ashamed of,

l the third time a man does that to you,

24 a you'd know how much fun it is.

b When we lie face-to-face with men it's more fun than anything.

c It's like we even feel a tingling in the soles of our feet.

d That's why some are unable to live as divorced women

e after they've gotten used to a certain man.

f Some let men continue doing that to them.

g   "But it truly is a whole lot of fun, you know.

h Even when they have their hand there,

25 a no matter if we're still truly virgins,

b we get a terrific thrill there in our womanly part.

c And also when they first do that to us,

d they really make us tingle.

e   "But it doesn't take that long to get used to the man we're married to.

f After we get used to him, we can ask him to do that whenever we crave it,

g and we can say to him, 'Come, let's do it,' when we're married to him," she said to her daughter.

26 a   "We're not shy with him at all.

b That's how marriage is," she told her.

c   And the young maiden never said anything.

^d   "ki·na=ʼyo=mani, ma·ne=meko ki·wi-tašite·he·waki ki·yawi," e·h=ina·či.

^e   o·ni, "mehto·či=meko wa·wa·pamiye·kapa wi·h=ona·pe·miwane·na.

^f   ke·htwe·wesita=meko a·mi|-ona·pe·miyana.

^g   ma·haki še·ški we·ta·se·waki awita ke·ko·hi_iši-nahkomiye·kapa.

^h   ke·htwe·wesikwe·na=ča·h=meko a·mi-ona·pe·miyana," ‖ e·h=ina·či ota·nese·hani.

27 ^a   "ni·na=ʼyo=wi·na ahpene·či=meko nemya·nehka·hi.

^b   ahpene·či=meko| nenatawe·neta nepo·pi_wi·h=meno·hiya·ni.

^c   ni·h=metwi-=ʼh=we·=mani| -taši-ma·mya·nehka," e·h=išima·či ota·nesani.

^d   a·kwi·ʼpi=meko ke·ko·hi ikočini nana·ši.

^e   "na·hkači meše·=ʼnah=meko kapo·twe| ki·h=ačihkwi.

^f   a·kwi owiye·ha wi·h=kehke·nemačini taši- ke·ko·hi -to·toto·to·hke maneto·waki.|

^g   meše·=ʼnah=meko ki·h=taši-manamaneko·ki.

^h   wi·h=iši-=meko -me·nešihehki ki·h=to·ta·ko·ki.

ⁱ   a·kwi=ke·hi·=ʼnahi ‖ wi·h=kehke·nemačini," e·h=ineči še·škesi·he·ha.

28 ^a   i·na=ke·hi neniwa a·yahpi·hčina·h=meko e·h=maki-kotaki osehkwiweni.

^b   "šihihwi·´," e·h=išite·he·či.

^c   "pe·hki=ni·hka=meko taši-me·mehta·čimoha·pi," e·h=išite·he·či.

^d   aškači=meko ki·ši-a·ya·čimoheči še·škesi·he·ha,

^e   "nekwaya·ši-=koh=meko -mečime·nemo_i·ni wi·h=išawiya·ni neniwaki.

^f   no·hkomesa=ma·hi| e·h=a·ya·čimohiči,

^g   ʻneponepo·hi·paniki na·no·ša·čiki,ʼ netekwa=ʼyo·we.

^h   i·ni=ča·h| we·či-kehči-‖ kohtama·ni i·ni_wi·h=to·tawiwa·či neniwaki.

29 ^a   ʻanašaša·pwi·=ʼnahi i·ni=ni·na išawihka,ʼ e·h=išite·he·ya·ni

^b   we·či-=meko -ki·ša·koči-mečime·nemo·hiya·ni," e·h=ina·či okye·ni.

^c   "na·hkači, ʻa·neta neniwaki pa·pahkihte·hwe·waki ihkwe·wahi,ʼ netekwa,

^d   ʻma·ma·kinakaya·čiki.

^e   a·neta mama·kimi·nakaye·waki,ʼ netekwa=koh=a·pehe no·hkomesa.[*]

^f   "na·hkači, ʻe·h=ašk_ona·pe·miki, a·kwi nahi_menwi|-nepe·hiwe·wa·čini.

^g   ahpene·či=meko ‖ e·taswi-pehkote·nikini mehta·ne·šike·mowaki,ʼ netekwa=koh=a·pehe_
       no·hkomesa.

30 ^a   ʻki·hpene e·h=nepo·te·wesiwa·či,

^b   ahpene·či=meko·=ʼni e·h=maneti·ki.

^c   meše·=ʼnah=meko na·htasenwi mašiwe·waki,ʼ

^d   netenahina·čimohekwa=kohi_no·hkomese·ha mani we·pa·totamawičini a·mano·weni,"
       e·h=ina·či okye·ni.

^e   "o·ho·´, ke·htena,| neta·ha.[†]

^f   aše=kohi=ʼyo·we e·h=ka·ki·ša·koči-mya·nehka·ya·ni
       we·či- wi·h=ona·pe·me·hiyani ‖ -inena·ni.[‡]

---

[*]/mama·kimi·nakaye·waki/: AK ⟨.mamaki.|minakayewaki|⟩.

[†]/ke·htena/: or /ke·htena^ʔ/ ʻReally?ʼ

[‡]/aše=kohi=ʼyo·we/: AK ⟨.ašekoi.|yowe.⟩.

<table>
<tr><td>d</td><td>"For, in your case now, there are many that have you in their thoughts," she said to her.</td></tr>
<tr><td>e</td><td>And then she said to her daughter, "It's as if you'd be selecting who you're going to marry.</td></tr>
<tr><td>f</td><td>Who you should marry is a good hunter.</td></tr>
<tr><td>g</td><td>You shouldn't say 'yes' about anything to these others that are just warriors.</td></tr>
<tr><td>h</td><td>So, whoever is indeed a good hunter is who you should marry.</td></tr>
<tr><td>27 a</td><td>"For, speaking for myself, I rather crave meat all the time.</td></tr>
<tr><td>b</td><td>I always want soup to drink.</td></tr>
<tr><td>c</td><td>In fact, as it is I've about had it with craving meat!" she declared to her daughter.</td></tr>
<tr><td>d</td><td>And she said nothing in response to her at all, to hear the tale.</td></tr>
<tr><td>e</td><td>"And also, you could get pregnant sometime.</td></tr>
<tr><td>f</td><td>You won't know anyone intimately if manitous are having sex with you.</td></tr>
<tr><td>g</td><td>They'll just be screwing you at will.</td></tr>
<tr><td>h</td><td>They'll do it to you as a way of shaming you.</td></tr>
<tr><td>i</td><td>It's just that in that event you won't know them intimately," the young maiden was told.</td></tr>
<tr><td>28 a</td><td>Meanwhile, that man every now and then took a big swallow of spit.</td></tr>
<tr><td>b</td><td>"Jeepers," he thought.</td></tr>
<tr><td>c</td><td>"She's really getting a damn clear explanation," he thought.</td></tr>
<tr><td>d</td><td>Sometime after the young maiden had been instructed, she said to her mother,</td></tr>
<tr><td>e</td><td>"There's no doubt that I'm firmly reluctant to do that with men.</td></tr>
<tr><td>f</td><td>I mean, that time when my grandmother instructed me,</td></tr>
<tr><td>g</td><td>she told me then that women do definitely die in childbirth.</td></tr>
<tr><td>h</td><td>So that's why I'm very much afraid to have men do that to me.</td></tr>
<tr><td>29 a</td><td>Because I think it might be just my luck to be the one that happened to then,</td></tr>
<tr><td>b</td><td>I am extremely reluctant."</td></tr>
<tr><td>c</td><td>"And she also told me that some men kill women when they have sex with them,</td></tr>
<tr><td>d</td><td>the ones with big penises.</td></tr>
<tr><td>e</td><td>My grandmother was certainly always telling me that some of them have large penises.</td></tr>
<tr><td>f</td><td>"And you should know, my grandmother was also always telling me, that when we first get married, they never let us have a good night's sleep.</td></tr>
<tr><td>g</td><td>Every night they're always laying us down with our privates bare.</td></tr>
<tr><td>30 a</td><td>And in cases where they have strong sexual desires,</td></tr>
<tr><td>b</td><td>then we're screwing every time.</td></tr>
<tr><td>c</td><td>They may screw us several times.</td></tr>
<tr><td>d</td><td>So my grandmother did use to instruct me whenever she undertook to tell me about sex," she told her mother.</td></tr>
<tr><td>e</td><td>"Oh, I see! That's right, Daughter.</td></tr>
<tr><td>f</td><td>It's actually just because I always have a great craving for meat that I told you to get married.</td></tr>
</table>

31 a keˑhtena=čaˑh| kiˑh=teˑpihto=kiˑyawi iˑni iši-aˑhpeči-tepaˑnate weˑči-ihkweˑwiyani.*

b naˑhkači kiˑh=anohanohkaˑnaˑwa wiˑh=šaˑšiˑšeˑnotamoˑnakwe iˑna weˑči-ihkweˑwiyani,” eˑh=inaˑči otaˑneseˑhani.

c peˑhki=meko eˑh=kiˑšaˑkoči-=meko -kehč_aˑhkweˑči,

d eˑh=aˑnawimaˑči wiˑh=onaˑpeˑminiči.

e eˑh=naˑkwaˑwaˑči.

f iˑyaˑh=meko pyeˑyaˑwaˑči, metemoˑheˑha eˑh=nanaˑhišiki,

g eˑh=šekišekišiki.†

h “kaši=’škwe=mana ‖ išikiˑtoke weˑči-mečimeˑnemoči wiˑh=onaˑpeˑmiči,” eˑh=išiteˑheˑči iˑna| metemoˑheˑha.

32 a aˑkwi=’pi=meko poˑniteˑheˑčini iˑni eˑh=išiteˑheˑči.

b ahpeneˑči=meko iˑni eˑh=ineˑnemaˑči iˑnini otaˑneseˑhani.

c mešeˑ=’nah=kapoˑtwe eˑh=penaˑwiniki eˑh=kehči_nepaˑniči.

d (oˑni wiˑh=niˑmiheti weči=’yo=keˑhi eˑh=iyoweči.)

e aye=čaˑhi=’pi maˑmaya=meko kiˑwi-wiˑhkoweˑwaki wiˑhkowaˑčiki.

f iˑni=’pi-=’na| metemoˑha eˑh=kehkeˑnemaˑči ‖ eˑh=kehči_nepaˑniči otaˑnesani.

33 a eˑh=katawi-=meko -meškišiniči,

b eˑh=kiˑšaˑkoči-šašahkipwaˑmeˑwinaˑkosiˑhiniči.

c seseˑsi=meko eˑh=mawi-kokweˑčipwaˑmeˑnaˑči,

d eˑh=nanaˑpaˑči|-meškišimaˑči.

e eˑh=kotenaˑči.

f “taˑniˑ=’nahi neniwiyaˑne.

g manenakaˑha,” eˑh=inaˑči.

h eˑh=nawači-kiˑmenoči.

i kiˑši-kiˑmenetisoči, eˑh=kiˑmenaˑči otaˑnesani.

j eˑh=nowiˑči.

k wiˑhkowaˑta=wiˑna| peˑmi-piˑtikeˑči,

l eˑh=nepaˑtaˑkwasoniči šeˑškesiˑhani. ‖

34 a peˑhki=meko eˑh=waˑpamaˑči metemoˑka,|

b aˑšowi eˑh=waˑwosaˑpamaˑči.

c kapoˑtwe=meko eˑh=kiˑmenemeči.

d kapoˑtwe eˑh=toˑhkeneči ihkweˑwa,

e šeˑški| eˑh=wiˑpwisahoči.

f metemoˑka meše=naˑhinaˑhi eˑh=oči_pyeˑči-sesosesotaki,

g eˑh=pemi-piˑtikeˑči.

h waˑnatoˑhka=meko nanakoteˑki eˑh=kiˑwi|-nemasoniči wiˑhkowaˑničini.

i “aye=meko kiˑši-maˑtakwisahowaneˑni.

j šeˑški=’yoˑwe nepemi|-nowi eˑh=nepaˑtaˑkwasoyani.

k kekiˑšaˑkoči-=meko=’yoˑwe ‖ -meškaˑkwaso.

---

*In 31a-b the object is a participle with a head that is an oblique (and hence necessarily inanimate) but is construed as having the animate gender of /kehketena/ ‘your vagina’.
†/eˑh=šekišekišiki/: AK ⟨.ešeki.šeki|šiki.⟩.

31 a   So, you'll really do yourself good if you always hold back your womanly thing like that.

b   And you can also start ordering that womanly thing of yours to hunt for us," she said to her daughter.

c   She was really extremely furious,

d   as she had failed to persuade her to get married.

e   And they went back.

f   When they got back home, the old lady went to her bed

g   and lay there.

h   "I wonder what her body could be like that would explain her reluctance to get married," the old lady thought.

32 a   She couldn't get the thought out of her mind when she thought that, the story goes.

b   She had that thought about her daughter all the time.

c   One time in the summer her daughter was sleeping soundly.

d   (Now, she had heard it said that there would be a dance.)

e   So, early in the morning, the story goes, inviters were going around inviting people.

f   And the old lady knew that her daughter was sleeping soundly then.

33 a   She saw her lying almost exposed.

b   And she looked like she had extremely soft thighs.

c   She hurried over and tried out different positions for her thighs,

d   laying her so that she was utterly indecently exposed.

e   And she felt her.

f   "I wish I were a man.

g   I would fuck you," she said to her.

h   She paused to feel herself up.

i   And after feeling herself up, she felt up her daughter.

j   And she went out.

k   And when an *inviter* stepped in the door,

l   here was a young girl sprawled out indecently.

34 a   The old lady watched them closely,

b   watching from the other side (of the wall).

c   Pretty soon the girl was felt up.

d   And soon she was awakened by the touching,

e   and she merely clapped her legs together.

f   The old lady approached from nearby coughing

g   and walked in.

h   And here was the inviter nonchalantly standing around in the middle of the lodge.

i   "You must have thrown the covers over yourself earlier.

j   I simply walked out when you were sprawled indecently.

k   You were sprawled in an extremely exposed posture.

35 a 'mana=wi·na=ne·hi,' ketene=še·ški,

b e·h=pemi_nowi·ya·ni.

c i·ni=ča·h=meko=mana_me·ša·pamehka wi·h=ona·pe·miyani," e·h=ina·či.

d "keki·sa·či-='yo=wi·na=meko| manaha -meša·pamekwa.

e keki·sa·ta·pamekwa='yo=wi·na manaha.

f i·ni=ča·h=meko wi·h=ona·pe·miyani," e·h=ineči.

g "pehkote·ke ki·h=pya ayo·hi," e·h=ineči i·na| oškinawe·ha,

h e·h=ikoči i·nini metemo·he·hani.

i pe·hkote·niki neniwa| i·tepi e·h=a·či.

j me·h-=meko ‖ -nana·hišinikwe i·ya·hi e·h=pya·či e·ka·wa·na·so·hani e·h=awiniči.

36 a e·h=anemi|-mi·ša·te·nemoči=meko.

b a·yahpi·hčina·h=meko e·h=anemi-e·nikite·he·či.

c "ši·hče·´,| i·ni=ni·hka e·h=owi·wiya·ni še·škesi·he·ha," e·h=anemi_'šite·he·či.

d "nemena·ni-=ni·hka=mekoho -kaškiho·hi," e·h=išite·he·či.

e i·ya·hi e·h=pya·či,

f e·h=pwa·wi-=meko -nakesiči.

g e·h=apihapiniči=meko e·h=mawi-nana·hapiči,

h e·h=nana·hišiniči.

i mani wi·h=iši-nana·hišikehe, ‖

37 a "ši·´,_ka·ta=wi·na ayo·hi| nana·hišikani," e·h=ineči.

b "pena´, na·kwa·no," e·h=ineči.

c a·kwikana·kwa=meko.

d ke·keya·h=meko e·h=a·čimoha·či metemo·hani.

e " 'na·kwa·no,' netekwa=ya·pi=manaha," e·h=ina·či o·hkomani=ta·taki.

f ke·keya·h=meko e·h=we·pi-kekye·htena·mi-pakameči.

g aškači=meko e·h=pemi_nowi·či.

h o·ni,| "neki·ši-owi·wi," e·h=ki·wi-ina·čimoči.

i "aše=ča·h=meko| ni·na neša·kwe·nemo,"_e·h=ina·či oškinawe·hahi.

j "metemo·ka ‖ neki·ša·koči-menwe·nemekwa," e·h=išiwe·či='p=a·pehe.

38 a še·ški=meko e·h=ki·wi_taši-owi·wehka·soči.

b kapo·twe='pi, "nahi´, ni·h=ona·pe·mi='škwe_natawa·či," e·h=ina·či okye·ni.

c "ni·na='h=we·na¹? ki·h=neškimene!?

d 'ši·´,_kakata·ni='hi='yo,'_ni·h=išite·he=ma·h=ni·na ona·pe·me·hiyane," e·h=ina·či.

e "we·ne·h=ča·hi me·nwe·nemata," e·h=ina·či_ota·nese·hani.*

f e·h=a·čimoniči.

g e·h=mya·ši-=meko -kehčineniwiniči_ke·hkahwa·ničini.

h "i·na=ča·h=me·kwe·he mehteno·hi ke·htwe·wesita," e·h=iniči. ‖

39 a ke·htena=ke·h=meko i·nini e·h=kehtwe·wesiniči.

b i·ni=meko='pi iši|=nekoti ča·ki=meko| ke·ko·hi no·hkihto·niči,†

c meše=meko iši|-mi·čipe·hi.

---

*/e·h=ina·či/: ⟨na⟩ changed from ⟨ne⟩.

†/no·hkihto·niči/ (IG, AW): AK ⟨.enokitoni|či.⟩.

35 a I simply said to you, 'Look at you, now!'

b as I walked out.

c So now, you must marry this one that saw your privates," she said to her.

d   "As this one has put you in a bind by seeing your privates.

e He's seen you, and you're stuck with that.

f So, now you must marry him," she was told.

g   And the young man was told, "You must come back here tonight."

h So the old lady told him.

i   That night the fellow went there.

j Before the object of desire even lay down he arrived where she was.

36 a He was delighted indeed as he went.

b Every once in a while along the way he laughed to himself.

c   "How great! Now I'm marrying a young maiden," he thought as he went.

d   "It's damn strange, indeed, how I managed to do it," he thought.

e   He got there

f and proceeded without delay.

g He went and sat down right where she was sitting,

h and she lay down.

i Just as he was about to lie down,

37 a he was told, "Hey, don't lie down here.

b   "You'd better leave," he was told.

c He got nowhere.

d   Finally he told the old lady.

e "Now she's telling me to leave!" he said to his would-be mother-in-law.

f Eventually he started being hit seriously.

g And after a while he walked out.

h   And then he went around reporting that he had gotten married.

i   "Well, it's just that I didn't want to," he told other young men.

j   "The old lady really likes me a lot," he would declare.

38 a He went around just pretending to be married.

b   Sometime later, the story goes, she said to her mother, "Alright, I've decided to go ahead and get married after all."

c   "Well, I'm not going to scold you, obviously!

d I mean, *I'm* going to think, 'Gee, that's great,' if you get married," she said to her.

e   "So, who's the one you like?" she asked her daughter.

f She told who it was.

g And the one she named was rather an older man.

h   "Well, I think he's the only good hunter," she said.

39 a And it was true that he was a good hunter.

b They say he was the only one who could easily kill everything,

c any kind of game.

d   "o·´,‿we·nahi·='na.‿

e   ke·htena=koči·='na kehtwe·wesiwa," e·h=ineči še·škesi·he·ha.[*]

f   o·ni·='na neniwa e·h=mawi-natawiheči.

g   kapo·twe=meko e·h=kehke·nema·či i·nini še·škesi·he·hani e·šite·he·niči mehto·či.

h   i·ni=meko='pi e·h=we·pi|-mi·hkemehkwe·we·či.

i   mani=meko e·ši‿kano·hkye·či, e·h=kaškowe·či wi·h=owi·wiči, ‖

40 a   e·h=awatehkwe·we·či.‿

b   e·h=awatehkwe·wa·soči| i·na‿še·škesi·he·ha.

c   e·h=ki·ši-ona·pe·miči.

d   pe·hki=meko ke·hčita·wesiničini e·h=kehč‿ona·pe·miči| i·na še·škesi·he·ha='yo·we.

e   e·h=ki·ša·koči-=meko -kya·we·niči.

f   e·h=ne·neseči.|

g   kete·='nah=meko='pi e·h=a·hkwaha·hkwe·či we·ta·nesita.

h   e·h=ne·neškinawe·heči we·pi-nesemečini ota·nesani.

i   " 'menwikenwi e·h=ona·pe·miki,' keteši=koči='yo·we," e·h=inekoči='p=a·pehe.

j   "e·h=menwawiwa·či=kohi neniwaki," e·h=ina·či='p=a·pehe| še·ški.[†]

41 a   kapo·twe·='nahi, "meše·='nah=meko pakiši.

b   meše·='nah=meko owiye·ha kotaka| ki·h=ona·pe·mi,"‿e·h=ineči.| [‡]

c   e·ye·ši-=ča·hi='pi=meko -ona·pe·miči, kotakani e·h=ona·pe·miči neniwani.

d   ki·ši-ona·pe·miči,

e   kete·='nah=meko='pi i·nini e·h=menwawiniči we·wi·wetama·ka·ničini owi·yawi.

f   i·niya=ke·hi='pi| neniwa e·h=pwa·wi-=meko kete·='nahi o·hkomani -po·ni·hkawa·či,

g   wi·h=ne·ya·pi-=meko -owi·wiči| e·h=išihišima·či. ‖

42 a   wa·wosa·h=meko='pi i·nahi e·h=ne·nepa·či| e·h=awiwa·tehe

b   (e·h=naha·kanihkwe·winiči=ke·hi='pi i·nini ihkwe·wani.)

c   ke·keya·h=meko='pi,| "nahi´, še·ški=ča·h=meko nekotenwi ni·h=nawači-wi·hpe·ma·wa," e·h=ina·či o·hkomani='yo·we.[§]

d   "kana·kwa.

e   a·kwi=ni·na we·we·ne·netamawakini owi·yawi.

f   wi·na=koh=meko we·we·ne·netisowa," e·h=ina·či='pi onekwanani='yo·we.

g   ke·keya·h=meko wi·na=meko wi·h=wi·hpe·ma·či e·h=išimekoči metemo·ka.

h   e·h=mya·ši-=meko ‖ -pana·čiheči.

43 a   kapo·twe=meko metemo·ka,| "ši·´,‿na·pi=we·na=ni·na| ki·h=wi·hpe·mi," e·h=išiwe·či.

b   o·ni metemo·ka e·h=wi·hpe·či.

c   e·škačitepehki·niki e·h=kehči|-ana·soči onekwanani='yo·we.

d   (ota·nesani=ke·hi='pi i·nahi tahpinawapahkwe e·h=taši-pesepeseta·kowa·či.)|

e   na·hka=meko onekwanani kapo·twe e·h=po·ni|-pakana·moniči.

---

[*]/e·h=ineči/: AK ⟨.e|iniči.⟩.

[†]/neniwaki/: AK ⟨.neniwa‖ki.⟩.

[‡]/kotaka| ki·h=ona·pe·mi/: AK ⟨.kotakaki|kionapemi⟩.

[§]/=ča·h=/ (EK): AK ⟨ta⟩.

d   "Oh, is *he* the one.

e   It's true that he's a good hunter, of course," the young maiden was told.

f   And then that man went to be sounded out.

g   It didn't take him long to know what the young maiden seemed to have in mind.

h   And right away, the story goes, he set to courting.

i   No sooner were the words out of his mouth than his proposal of marriage was accepted,

40 a   and he took home a bride.

b   The young maiden was taken away as a bride.

c   She had gotten married.

d   The young-maiden-that-was got married in a big way to a man who was fully an adult.

e   And he was extremely jealous.

f   She was beaten repeatedly.

g   The young woman's mother, with they say her attitude completely changed, was furious every time.

h   It made her angry every time her daughter underwent a beating.

i   "You told me marriage is a good thing, remember," (her daughter) would tell her.

j   And all she would say to her was, "Because, I promise you, men are good."

41 a   Then finally the young woman was told, "Oh, just divorce him.

b   You can marry someone else."

c   So, while still married, she married another man, the story goes.

d   After she had married him,

e   the one who had married her as the wife of another man was, quite the opposite they say, well behaved.

f   Meanwhile, that other man, the story goes, never stopped pestering his now regretful mother-in-law,

g   asking to marry his former wife again.

42 a   He went so far as to sleep in the place the two of them used to have, the story goes.

b   (For they say the younger woman was living with her in-laws.)

c   Eventually, the story goes, he said to his former mother-in-law, "Alright, so I only want to have one more chance to sleep with her."

d   "No way.

e   I have no say over her body.

f   As you must know, she has the say over herself," she's said to have told her former son-in-law.

g   Eventually, he suggested to the older woman that *she* sleep with him.

h   And she was somewhat bewitched.

43 a   Soon after the old lady said, "Say, why don't you sleep with *me*."

b   And then the old lady had a bedmate.

c   And late at night she had a great tussle with her erstwhile son-in-law.

d   (Meanwhile, the story goes, her daughter was there listening to them through the wall.)

e   And again her son-in-law suddenly fell silent.

f metemo·ka, "nenemači·neki očipwa·me_wi·šiki-pepye·tekonino," e·h=ina·či.*/†
g aškači, "kaši='yo=ki·na ketenamata,"| e·h=išiwe·či ‖ metemo·ka.
44 a "ni·na='yo=wi·na apina=meko nemya·ši-šekiwamata," e·h=išiwe·či| metemo·ka.
b ("nahi´,_na·kwa·ta·we='škwe," e·h=ina·či| ona·pe·mani i·na| ihkwe·wa.‡
c e·h=po·ni-=meko i·tepi -iha·wa·či.)

d ke·keya·h=koči='pi=meko wi·na i·nini ona·pe·miwa onekwanani='yo·we.|
e ki·ši-mehči_ona·pe·miči,
f e·h=we·pi-pya·niči ota·nesani.
g kete·='nah=ke·hi·='pi=ne·hi·='na ihkwe·wa na·we·neme·wa i·nini| ona·pe·me·hani.
h i·nini=meko a·wasi| mač·owiye·hani ‖ e·h=me·mehkwe·nema·či i·na ihkwe·wa.
45 a kapo·twe i·tepi e·h=a·či i·na ihkwe·wa,
b e·h=nesapiniči i·nini neniwani.
c e·h=pana·teška·koči okye·ni ona·pe·mani.§
d ke·keya·h=meko e·h=kehke·nemekoči okye·ni.
e pye·ya·čini, ahpene·či=meko e·h=pemi_nowi·niči.
f ahpene·či=ke·h=meko e·h=me·meta·ča·hiwa·či.|
g ke·keya·h=meko='pi e·h=a·hkwe·htawa·či pi·neši i·nini ona·pe·mani i·na
   še·škesi·ha='yo·we,
h okiki e·h=a·či.
i i·ya·hi_e·h=mawi-‖ki·wita·či okiki.
46 a še·ški=meko kenwe·ši e·h=taši-wa·wi·čiha·či okye·ni.
b kapo·twe='pi·='ni e·h=mehči-=meko_i·ni| -išahišawiči i·nini neniwani.|
c e·h=pwa·wi-=meko -kahkiso·htawa·či okye·ni.
d e·h=menwe·netaminiči.
e kapo·twe=meko e·h=ni·šo·hkwe·wa·sowa·či.
f i·nini okye·ni e·h=owi·to·šiči.
g e·h=ne·neso·šinowa·či| ahpene·či.
h e·h=po·ni-=ke·h=meko ke·ko·hi -iši|-kya·we·niči i·nini neniwani.
i pe·hki='pi ‖ e·h=ša·ši·ša·niči.
47 a ahpene·či i·nini ona·pe·mwa·wani e·h=ki·ša·koči-=meko -menwito·ta·kowa·či.|
b wi·nwa·wa=na·hkači e·h=menwito·tawa·wa·či.¶
c na·hkači e·h=pwa·wi-=meko -mya·ne·neti·wa·či i·niki owi·to·šeti·haki.
d e·h=ki·ša·koči-=meko -mana·tesiwa·či,
e e·h=neno·te·wi-mana·tesiwa·či i·niki ni·šo·hkwe·wa·sočiki.
f (e·h=ahpi·hči-=ke·h=meko -kokwe·či_-mi·hkemekowa·či neniwahi.
g a·kwi=ke·hi='pi·='nini pe·hki ‖ nawe·ni-neni·he·hiničini e·taši|-ni·šo·hkwe·wa·nekowa·čini.)
48 a e·h=pwa·wi-=meko ke·ko·hi -ine·neti·wa·či.

---

*/očipwa·me_wi·šiki-/: AK ⟨.očipwa|mewiši.ki.⟩.
†/e·h=ina·či/: AK ⟨.einiči.⟩.
‡/na·kwa·ta·we/: ⟨ta⟩ changed from ⟨te⟩.
§/e·h=pana·teška·koči/: AK ⟨etanateskakoči⟩; *pana·teškaw- TA is a conjecture (IG).
¶/e·h=menwito·tawa·wa·či/: AK ⟨.|emenwitotakowa|či.⟩.

f   And the old lady said to him, "Bend my left leg up tight."

g   And after a while the old lady said, "What do *you* feel?"

44 a   And the old lady said, "I mean, *I* actually even kind of felt like I was going to pee."

b   ("Alright, already! Let's leave," the woman said to her husband.

c   And they stopped going there.)

d   Eventually, to be sure, she married her former son-in-law herself, the story goes.

e   And after she was openly married to him,

f   her daughter started coming over.

g   Now, that younger woman, having changed her mind too, they say, did not think much of her husband.

h   It was more the mean one that that woman kept remembering.

45 a   And the time came when that woman went there,

b   and that man was home by himself.

c   And she succumbed to the advances of her mother's husband.

d   Before long, her mother knew about her.

e   Whenever she came, (her mother) always stepped out.

f   And always they had fun together.

g   And before long, the story goes, that erstwhile maiden got mad at her husband unprovoked

h   and went to her mother's.

i   She went over to her mother's to stay.

46 a   And for a long time she was living only with her mother.

b   And the time came, the story goes, when she would do that openly with that man.

c   She did not conceal herself from her mother.

d   And her mother was fine with it.

e   And the time came when the two of them were wives together.

f   Her mother was her co-wife.

g   The three of them slept always three to a bed.

h   What's more, that man was not jealous at all anymore.

i   And he really hunted, the story goes.

47 a   Their husband always treated them extremely well.

b   And for their part *they* also treated *him* well.

c   Also, those co-wives had no dislike of each other.

d   They were extremely well-off,

e   well-off in the Indian way, the two wives of the man.

f   (Now, men were constantly trying to pay court to them.

g   And moreover, that one whose wives they both were was not really handsome, it is said.)

48 a   They had no bad thoughts towards each other.

^b   meše=nekotenwi nekoti| ne·tawi-mi·hketama·ka·ta i·ya·hi ašiči| tahpinawapahkwe
e·h=nenye·masoči,*

^c   e·h=taši-pesepesetawa·či| i·nihi owi·weti·hahi.

^d   (pepehči·me·hi=’yo=ke·h=meko e·h=owi·kiwa·či| i·niki ni·šo·hkwe·wa·sočiki.)

^e   e·h=a·maneniči.

^f   ke·keya·h=meko po·si či·kapahkwe| e·h=mawi_nenye·masoči.

^g   metemo·kani mehto·či=’pi=meko ‖ e·škiki·he·hani.

^{49 a}   a·wasi=meko e·h=iši-e·škiki·hi·hka·soniči,|

^b   mehto·či=meko=’pi iškwe·se·he·hani.

^c   “če·wi_’nenina·ke=meko,” e·h=išiwe·či ihkwe·wa,|

^d   meškemo·ka=’h=we·na.|

^e   če·wina·hi=’yo=ča·hi=’pi neseko·ki aša·hahi.

^f   e·h=anawiwa·či=’pi,

^g   i·ya·hi·=’ni e·h=taši-neseči i·niki owi·weti·haki.

^h   ki·ša·koči-=meko=’pi| meso·nwe·kwe·ni i·na| neniwa._

ⁱ   i·niki=ke·hi=’pi ihkwe·waki nešinešiwana·čiki·hiwaki,_

^j   ina·čimopi=we·n=a·pehe._

^k   i·ni. ‖

---

*/tahpinawapahkwe/: ⟨ta⟩ changed from ⟨te⟩.

^b   One day, someone seeking to court a married woman was standing nearby on the other side of the wall,

^c   listening to those married folks.

^d   (Now, the two wives had their dwelling a little ways from the others.)

^e   And they were having sex.

^f   Before long, he went and stood right up close to the wall.

^g   The older woman was just like she was a young person, to hear the tale.

49 ^a   She was pretending to be younger,

^b   just like a little girl, to hear the tale.

^c   "Hold us both the same way," the woman said,

^d   or rather the old gal.

^e   And actually, the story is, they were killed by Siouxs all at the same time.

^f   The story is that they went on a hunt,

^g   and then those married folks were killed out yonder.

^h   It's said that the man had an extremely large penis.

ⁱ   And the anatomies of the women are said to have been rather deformed, as well,

^j   or at least so the tale is always told.

^k   That's it.

kîyamowêwani ihkwêwani wêwîwita

The Man who Married a Giant Woman

kîyamowêwani ihkwêwani wêwîwita

Alfred Kiyana[*]

1 a   ki·yamowe·wani ihkwe·wani| we·wi·wita.

b   o·ni=wi·na=’pi mehtose·neniwaki e·h=ma·wa·seto·wa·či,[†]

c   e·h=ma·ne·wa·či.|

d   o·ni nekoti neniwa| e·h=kehči-=meko -neniwiči.

e   e·h=oškinawe·hiči=ke·h=wi·na,

f   e·h=aka·wa·taki wi·h=owi·wiči.

g   e·h=ma·mi·neči=ke·h=wi·na ihkwe·wahi,|

h   šewe·na e·h=neškinawa·či=meko.

i   e·h=pwa·wi-=ke·hi·’pi -nawači|-wi·hpe·ma·či.

j   e·h=pe·we·nemoči=’pi wi·h=ke·ko·h_=to·tawa·či ihkwe·wahi,

k   e·h=meša·niki=’pi owi·nakayi.|

l   mehto·či=’pi=meko e·h=neso·pwa·me·či.

m   e·h=wi·ša·hekoči=ke·hi·’pi a·pehe ke·ko·hi wi·h=to·tawa·či.[‡]/[§]

n   e·nwa·či·čini=’pi, “keči·kwani=ma·hi·=’ni ketayo,” e·h=ikoči·’p=a·pehe ihkwe·wahi.

o   e·h=wa·pato·na·či·’pi, ‖

2 a   kaškipwa·wi-=’pi=mek=a·pehe,| “šihihwi·´,” -iničini.

b   e·h=se·kesiwa·či·’pi=mek=a·pehe ihkwe·waki.

c   apina=’p=a·pehe e·h=pye·miškwihkwe·kane·ko·te·niki, i·ni me·ša·ki.

d   i·ni=ča·hi=’pi·=’na ki·wa·čihekwiči neniwa,

e   e·h=pwa·wi|- ke·ko·hi -kaški_=to·tawa·či ihkwe·wahi.

f   kapo·twe=’pi=meko=’pi·=’ni e·h=na·kwa·či,

g   meše=meko·=’nahi e·h=a·či.

h   a·yaškači=ke·h=meko=’pi e·h=nawači-a·kwapiči,

i   na·hka a·yaškači=meko e·h=wi·seniči.|

j   mama·nokoni=meko=’pi a·kwi wi·seničini.| [¶]

k   meše·=’nah=meko nye·wawahi·me e·h=anemehka·či.

l   kwi·yena=meko nye·wawahi·makateniki e·h=pye·notaki kehčikami·wi.

m   e·h=pwa·wi-=meko ‖ -te·pa·pataki e·nekihkwaka·maki·nikwe·ni.[*]

3 a   še·ški=meko nepi e·h=ne·taki o·ni_ki·šekwi.

b   mehto·či=meko e·h=takwikeniki e·h=ina·pataki.

c   “ši·hče·! e·nekihkwaka·maki·kwe·ni=ni·hka,” e·h=išite·he·či.

d   “a·mi_-’ši-=tike -akwa·čime·wa·ne·ni,”| e·h=išite·he·či.

---

[*]The manuscript is NAA 2655.1:1-23; it has 23 pages.

[†]/o·ni=wi·na=’pi/: Kiyana’s “Fox Clan” (K-FC) begins with these words used similarly.

[‡]/e·h=wi·ša·hekoči/: AK ⟨ewišeekoči⟩.

[§]/=’pi a·pehe/: or edit as /=’p=a·pehe/.

[¶]/mama·nokoni/: or /ma·ma·nokoni/.

[*]/-aka·maki·-/: HWB.

The Man who Married a Giant Woman
Translated by Ives Goddard and Horace Poweshiek

1 a   The Man Who Married a Giant Woman.

b   Then in another story, the people were living in a village,

c   and there were many of them.

d   And there was then a certain man who was a large man,

e   although he was a young man,

f   and he wanted to get married.

g   And although he kept being given women,

h   still he just had no use for them.

i   What's more, they say he didn't sleep with them before deciding.

j   He was reluctant to have sex with the women, the story goes,

k   because his penis was extra large.

l   It was as if he had three thighs.

m   They would always try their best to get him to have sex with them, the story goes.

n   And when he consented, the women would tell him, "Why, you're just using your knee for it."

o   They say he would let them look at it,

2 a   and they could never help exclaiming, "Wow!"

b   The women would always get quite scared, the story goes.

c   They say it would even always hang down with a twisted neck, that huge thing.

d   So, that's what made the man so sad, the story goes,

e   because he couldn't have sex with women.

f   At some point, the story goes, they say he then set out,

g   going just anywhere.

h   And what's more, they say he would stop to rest only at long intervals,

i   and also he would only eat at long intervals.

j   For many days at a time they say he didn't eat.

k   And for as long as four years he traveled on.

l   After exactly four years' time he reached the ocean.

m   And he couldn't see how far it was to the other side.

3 a   He saw nothing but water and sky.

b   It looked to him as if they were connected together.

c   "How strange! Gosh, I wonder how far it is to the other side," he thought.

d   "I wonder how I could swim to the shore," he thought.

e   kapo·twe| e·h=koči-čapo·kenaki| meši-pemitasakatwi,

f   e·h=po·siči.

g   "manahka_oteče," e·h=iči, we·či·či.

h   kena·či=meko| e·h=we·pa·nemateniki.

i   e·škami=meko e·h=ina·nemateniki.

j   ke·keya·h=meko pe·hki e·h=ki·ša·koči-aniwa·nemateniki.

k   "šihihwi´," e·h=iči='p=a·pehe.

l   e·h=ateko·wa·ška·niki.

m   wa·natohka=meko e·h=anemi_šekišiki nanawa·pye·ki.| *

n   tepina·hi='yo=ke·h=meko| e·h=ihpoko·te·niki. ‖

4 a   kapo·twe_e·h=pye·notaki_wi·h=oči-te·pa·pataki| ahki,

b   e·h=sese·site·he·či wi·h=kekeni-i·ya·h=-pya·či.|

c   meše·='nah=meko na·htasokoni e·h=anemipoko·te·niki e·yo·či.†

d   i·ya·h=pye·ya·či ača·hmeko e·h=nenwapene·či,

e   e·h=we·wi·tepešihaki.

f   mi·škota e·h=čakeši·hiniči pišikisi·he·hani ne·sa·čini.‡

g   meše·='nah=meko·='nini e·h=katawi_ča·kama·či pešekesi·he·hani.|

h   meše·='nah=nekotenwi e·h=ne·wa·či neniwani_ši·ša·ničini,| §

i   e·h=kakano·neti·či.

j   "ta·tepi=ča·h=we·či·yani," e·h=ikoči._

k   "we·či|-kesi·ya·ki=ča·h=ota·hkwe| kotakeki ahki·ki," e·h=ina·či.

l   "ši´,_či·hče·´," e·h=ikoči.

m   "nahi´, e·h=owi·ke·hiya·ke iha·ta·we," e·h=ikoči. ‖

5 a   e·h=oči-wi·te·ma·či| i·nini,

b   e·h=meša·niki wi·siyaškwika·ni e·h=ahte·niki.¶

c   "o´, e·nawi·haki," e·h=išite·he·či, ki·ši|-nenaki wi·siyaškwika·ni.

d   e·h=pi·tike·wa·či.

e   a·yaka·mete·we e·h=apihapiniči ihkwe·wahi,

f   e·h=mi·na·wa·pamekoči.

g   e·h=wača·heči.

h   e·h=mama·kihkwe·winiči i·nihi ihkwe·wahi.

i   wa·paniki e·h=ši·ša·či.

j   o·ni='pi·='na e·h=kano·na·či otehkwe·mani.

k   "nahi´, ona·pe·mino=ma·hiya," e·h=ineči ihkwe·wa.

l   e·h=še·škesi·hiči=ke·hi.

---

*/nanawa·pye·ki/: elsewhere /nanawepye·ki/; cf. /na·ma·pye·ki/, /na·mepye·ki/ 'under the water'.

†'The log he was on': AK /e·yo·či/ 'what he was using'.

‡/pišikisi·he·ha/ 'cute little Bambi': affective hyper-distortion of /pešekesi·he·ha/ 'little deer'.

§/meše·='nah=nekotenwi/ 'one time': implying that some time has passed.

¶/wi·siyaškwika·ni/ 'grass-lodge' (diminutive in K-M 54e): phonemic transcription conjectured.

e After a while he tried putting a large log in the water
f and got on it.
g "Let the wind blow from over there," he said, meaning the way he came from.
h The wind slowly began to pick up,
i growing stronger and stronger.
j And eventually the wind was blowing really hard.
k "Wow," they say he kept saying.
l The waves were rolling.
m And he went along calmly lying there out in the middle of the water.
n Now, the log was floating straight across with him.

4 a At some point he got to where he could see land from,
b and he was impatient to get there quickly.
c The log he was on kept floating on for several more days.
d When he got there, for the first time he felt pangs of hunger,
e and he hurriedly set out to hunt.
f But to make matters worse, the cute little Bambi he killed was a small one.
g He ate up pretty nearly that whole deer.

h One time he saw a man who was hunting,
i and he struck up a conversation.
j "So, where did you come from?" the other man asked him.
k "Well, from in the north, on the other land," he told him.
l "Gee! How strange!" he said to him.
m "Alright, let's go to our house," he said to him.
5 a And he went from there with that man,
b to where there was a large grass-lodge.
c "Oh, they're hunters," he thought, after he recognized the grass-lodge.
d And they went in.
e Women were sitting there on opposite sides of the lodge,
f and they looked at him closely.
g And a meal was cooked for him.
h Both women had large womanly frames.

i The next day he went out to hunt.
j And then, the story goes, that man spoke to his sister.
k "Alright now, marry this guy," the woman was told.
l Now, she was a young girl who had never been married.

m   "ši·´,_nahe·nemite='yo, ni·h=wi·čawi·kwa," e·h=iniči,

n   e·h=anwa·či·niči.

o   wi·na=ke·hi e·h=pye·tašiči.|

p   mahkwani e·h=nesa·či,|

q   sa·kiči e·h=po·našiči.

r   "wihihwi·´," e·h=iči| neniwa. ‖

6 a   "we·kone·h=ča·h=kwe·hta·ni|-makwe·we·seto·yani," e·h=ina·či.

b   "mahkwa," e·h=ina·či,

c   keye·hapa=ke·hi='pi| owi·hta·wani.

d   "ašake·mono=wi·nó!" e·h=ineči ihkwe·wa,[*]

e   e·h=ašake·moči.

f   "nahi´, nahe·neme·hiyane| mana netehkwe·me·ha,

g   wi·čawiwiye·kapa," e·h=ineči neniwa,

h   e·h=mi·neči še·škesi·hani.

i   "o·´, nah=we·=me·kwe·he.

j   ine·nemite='yo, i·ni ni·h=išawipena," e·h=ina·či.

k   "ni·na=wi·na_netanwa·či=meko," e·h=iči.

l   e·h=ni·šo·piči,

m   e·h=makenehkwe·we·či.

n   pe·hkote·niki=koči='pi apina=meko| e·h=nowiwehkye·či.

o   e·h=mawi-sa·kiči·či e·h=inwa·soči,

p   e·h=wi·te·mekoči owi·wani.

q   i·ya·h=ke·ko·hi e·h=taši-to·tawa·či.

r   meme·nawi=meko e·h=išawiniči. ‖ [†]

7 a   "ši·´,_či·hče·´," e·h=išite·he·či.

b   e·h=menwa·ko·ma·či,

c   wi·na=na·hka e·h=menwa·ko·mekoči ki·ši-nakačinawi·mekoči.[‡]

d   aškiča·h=ke·h=wi·na e·h=a·nemiha·či=meko,

e   ki·ši-=meko -nakate·nemekoči, e·h=ki·ša·koči-=meko -tepa·nekoči i·nini ihkwe·wani.

f   meše·='nah=kapo·twe_e·h=na·kwa·wa·či,

g   e·h=ča·ki-=meko -penowa·či.

h   wi·na=ke·hi e·h=wi·če·we·či.

i   kehčine_pye·ya·wa·či, e·h=te·te·pehtawa·wa·či ahkohko·ni.

j   kwi·yena=meko e·h=ma·mata·nahkiwihto·nitehe i·nihi mehtose·neniwahi, e·h=pya·wa·či.

k   e·h=mata·kwa·pamekoči.

l   "kaši='yo_netešina·kosi," e·h=ina·či.|

m   "e·taswi-=ma·h=meko -ne·wakini mehtose·neniwaki, ‖

8 a   neki·ša·koči-=meko| -mata·kwa·pameko·ki," e·h=ina·či.

---

[*] /=wi·nó/: /ó/ is a short, lower high vowel on a lower pitch than the preceding /o/ (EK).

[†] 'She took him quite easily': *lit.*, 'she had plenty of room (for him)'.

[‡] /nakačinawi·m-/ TA 'get used to moving (the body) with': AK ⟨.nakači.nawim⟩ (untranslated by HP), presumably based on /-inawi·/ AI 'move the body by wiggling, flexing, etc.'.

^m "Gee! Well, if he *likes* me, he can marry me," she said,
ⁿ being willing.
^o Now, *he* came back with a load of game on his back.
^p He had killed a bear,
^q and he dropped it down outside.
^r "Well, well!" the man exclaimed.
6 a "So, what did you put down with such a fearsome great noise?" he asked him.
^b "A bear," he told him,
^c told his brother-in-law, as it turned out, the story goes.
^d "How about giving our guest a meal!" the woman was told,
^e and she served the meal.
^f "Alright now, if you like my little sister here,
^g you could marry her," the man was told,
^h being given a virgin.
ⁱ "Oh, alright then, I guess.
^j Well, if she *wants* to with me, we'll do that," he told him.
^k "But *I'm* quite willing," he said.
^l And he sat as one of a couple,
^m married to a large wife.
ⁿ That night he actually even took a woman outside, the story goes.
^o He made as if going out to urinate,
^p and his wife went with him.
^q Out there he had sex with her.
^r And she took him quite easily.
7 a "Wow! How sweet!" he thought.
^b He liked her ways very much,
^c and she also liked *his* ways after she got used to how to move with him.   (See note ‡.)
^d Even though at first he was too much for her,
^e after she had gotten used to him, the woman loved him very dearly.

^f After a while they went back from their camp,
^g all going home.
^h And *he* went along as well.
ⁱ When they got near, they started hearing a drum.
^j They arrived just when those people were having a celebration.
^k And *they* found him fascinating to look at.
^l "Tell me, what do I look like?" he asked her.
^m "I mean, every time I see people,
8 a they're looking at me with great fascination," he said to her.

b   "o=meše=ke·h=newe·wenesipetoke,"| e·h=ina·či.
c   "ši·´, pe·hki=ma·hi keki·ša·koči_we·wenesi," e·h=ikoči owi·we·hani.
d   "mekoč=ayo·h=meko kete·hi tana·ške·hiwi," e·h=ikoči.
e   "ši·´, wa·´, e·htani·hka," e·h=iči.
f   "ayo·h=ke·h=wi·na ma·haki we·to·te·weničiki,
g   kekimesi=meko ahpemeki| ahte·niwani ote·hwa·wani," e·h=iniči.*
h   "kohtamo·ki=meko e·h=ki·wawiwa·či ote·hwa·wani," e·h=iniči owi·wani.
i   "i·ni=ča·hi we·či|-mečimečima·pamehki ne·wohkini,
j   e·h=ki·wawiyani kete·hi," e·h=ineči neniwa._
k   "mekoč=ayo·h=meko ako·te·hiwi kete·hi," e·h=ineči.
l   e·h=kehči_‖apane·niči.
9 a   "a·kwi=ma·h=ni·na·='ni nete·hi owi·ya·siwikini.
b   owi·ya·siwike=mata i·n=a·mi_'šawiya·ni," e·h=ina·či owi·wani.
c   "ki·h=wa·pata,"| e·h=ina·či,
d   e·h=wa·pato·na·či, e·h=ketenaki.
e   kohkoseni=či·hi.
f   "hwi·´," e·h=išite·he·či ihkwe·wa.
g   na·hka na·waškote=meko e·h=ahto·či,
h   e·h=meškwano·te·niki.
i   ki·ši·=meko -meškwano·te·niki, e·h=nahiseto·či.
j   wa·natohka=meko e·h=ki·wi_'šawiči.|
k   "ya·´, nena·pe·ma!†
l   we·nahi, maneto·wa=we·=meko," e·h=išite·he·či.

m   meše·='nah=meko aškači| e·h=ma·wačimeči neniwaki,
n   wi·na e·h=takwi_natomeči.
o   ke·no·te·hi e·h=ašihto·weči.‡
p   wi·na=ke·hi nekotahi e·h=apihapiči.
q   aškači=meko e·h=ča·ki_‖pya·niči mehtose·neniwahi.
10 a   ki·ši_ča·ki_pya·niči, nanakote·ki e·h=ana·hkahamoweči,
b   e·h=či·tapiheči i·na neniwa.
c   e·h=a·čimoweči ahpemeki wi·h=mawi-ahtawoči ote·hi.
d   e·h=ča·ki-=meko -menwe·netaminiči neniwahi.
e   o·ni=wi·na, "a·kwi=kana·kwa," e·h=ina·či.
f   "a·kwi=kana·kwa i·ni ni·na wi·h=išawiya·ni,"| e·h=ina·či.
g   "mani=koči e·šikeno·hiki nete·he·hi," e·h=ina·či.
h   meše·='nah=meko e·h=ketenaki.
i   aseni=či·hi, kohkoseni,
j   e·h=nešiwiwanakateniki.
k   meše·='nah=meko=na·hka·='nahi e·h=taši_meškwano·saki.|

---

*Giants put their hearts away in their houses (C-Giants 23*x*).

†/nena·pe·ma!/: pronounced with exaggerated high pitch on /pe·m/.

‡/ke·no·te·hi/ 'longhouse': "a large long shaped wickiup" (HP).

^b "Or I guess I must be very beautiful," he said to her.

^c "Gee! Mind you, you're really extremely beautiful," his dear wife told him.

^d "Your heart can clearly be seen beating right here," she told him.

^e "Gee! Oh my! What have I gotten myself into!" he said.

^f "After all, in the case of the people who live in this town,

^g everyone's hearts are put somewhere up high," she said.   (See note *.)

^h "They're afraid to have their hearts with them," his wife said.

ⁱ "So, that's why they keep staring at you when they see you,

^j because you have your heart with you," the man was told.

^k "Your heart can clearly be seen hanging in here," he was told.

^l And he laughed hard.

9 a "*My* heart has no meat on it, you understand.

^b If it *did* have meat on it, I'd do that," he said to his wife.

^c "Take a look at it," he told her,

^d and he let her look at it, taking it out.

^e And here, it was a flint rock.

^f "Oh my!" the woman thought.

^g Next he placed it right in a fire,

^h and it became red hot.

ⁱ After it got red hot, he put it back in place.

^j And he seemed completely unaffected.

^k "Oh my, look at my husband!

^l Why, he's actually a manitou!" she thought.

^m A while later the men were all called together.

ⁿ And *he* was called along with them.

^o A longhouse was made for them.

^p And here *he* was, sitting there someplace.

^q Sometime later, all the people came.

10 a After they all had come, something was spread on the ground in the center,

^b where that man was made to sit.

^c It was declared that his heart should be taken somewhere and put up high.

^d The men all liked the idea.

^e Then it came to *him*, and he told them, "It's not possible.

^f "It's not possible for *me* to do that," he told them.

^g "Just look at what my heart is like," he told them.

^h And he proceeded to take it out.

ⁱ And here it was a rock, a flint rock,

^j and it was terrifically heavy.

^k And he proceeded to make it red hot again there.

l   e·h=se·kesiwa·či e·taso·škene·wa·či.

m   "šihihwi·´," e·h=iyowa·či.

n   keki-=meko ‖ -meškwano·te e·h=nahiseto·niči i·ni_mete·hi.[*]

11 a   wa·natohka=meko| e·h=išawiniči.

b   ača·hmeko e·h=kosa·wa·či| i·nini mehtose·neniwani.

c   o·ni_nekoti e·h=maneto·wiči=meko.

d   "ni·na=mata,| nešiye·ka·ha=meko," e·h=išiwe·či.

e   e·h=kehke·nemeči='yo=ke·hi e·h=nahi-mahkate·wi·či.

f   e·h=a·čimoheči neno·te·wa,

g   "nesenesa='pi,"| e·h=ineči.

h   "wi·to·hkawake='yo, nešisa," e·h=iči.

i   "wi·na=ke·hi, 'ni·h=nesa·wa,' ine·nemake, nešiye·ka·ha=meko,"| e·h=iči.

j   i·ni=meko e·h=mačina·ti·wa·či.

k   "o·´,_wa·pake na·wahkwe·ke ni·h=neseti·pena,"| e·h=iči me·čina·ka·ta.

l   e·h=mawi-a·čimoheči ‖ neno·te·wa.

12 a   "wi·na=koči=meko," e·h=iči.|

b   "wi·na=koči wi·h=we·we·ne·netamwa,"_e·h=iči.

c   owi·wani=ke·hi='pi e·h=neškimekoči. [†]

d   "nahi´, meše·='nah=pena´.

e   ka·ta_mi·ka·ti·hkani," e·h=ikoči.

f   "a·kwi=ma·h wi·h=nešičini," e·h=ina·či.

g   "ke·htena?" e·h=išiwe·či ihkwe·wa.[‡]

h   o·ni_wa·paniki e·h=na·kwa·či neno·te·wa.

i   atehči·me·hi_e·h=mawi-taši_meškwano·saki ote·hi.

j   meškwa·wa·hkwani e·h=pehtawe·či.

k   na·wahkwe·niki i·tepi e·h=a·či wi·h=taneneti·či.

l   aye=či·h=meko e·h=ki·šihto·wetehe nepise·hi.

m   e·h=mawi-nana·tohta·koči.

n   "o·´, ne·nye·wenwi.

o   ki·h=taši·hka·ti._

p   a·kwi| wi·h=nana·hkoneti·yakwini," ‖ e·h=iči neno·te·wa.[§]

13 a   o·ni·='na e·h=mi·ša·te·nemoči.

b   "o·´,_we·ne·h=ča·h=menehta wi·h=taši·hka·ka·ta," e·h=iči me·čina·hkwa·ta.

c   "o·´, ki·na| menehta," e·h=ineči,

d   e·h=nana·hena·či.

e   e·h=čapo·keneči neno·te·wa.|

f   mani e·ši-mo·hki·čini, wa·natohka=meko| e·h=ki·wi·_šina·kosiči.

g   aškači e·h=tepi- nye·wenwi -čapo·keneči.

---

[*]/e·h=nahiseto·niči/: AK ⟨.enaiseteniči.⟩.

[†]/owi·wani=ke·hi='pi/: AK ⟨owiwani.keipi.⟩.

[‡]/e·h=išiwe·či/ 'asked out loud', *lit.* 'said (to someone)'.

[§]/a·kwi/: ⟨A⟩ replaces erased ⟨px⟩.

l   All who filled the lodge were frightened.

m   "Wow," they said.

n   And while it was still red hot they saw him put the heart back in place.

11 a   And he was completely unaffected.

b   After that they were afraid of that human being.

c   And there was one who did have manitou powers.

d   And he declared, "Let *me* try, and *I* could kill him."

e   Now, he was known as one who fasted.

f   It was reported to the Indian.

g   "He said he could kill you," he was told.

h   "Well, if I let him, he could kill me," he said.

i   "And then, if I want to kill him, I could kill *him*," he said.

j   Right away they challenged each other.

k   "Well, tomorrow at noon, we shall try to kill each other," said the challenger.

l   The word was sent to the Indian.

12 a   And he said, "It's up to him, of course."

b   And he said, "It's his call, of course."

c   Now, his wife got after him, the story goes.

d   "Now, please let it go!

e   Don't fight," she said to him.

f   "He won't slay me, you understand," he said to her.

g   "Are you sure?" the woman asked out loud.

h   And then the next day the Indian went out.

i   He went a little ways away and heated his heart red hot.

j   He made a fire with cedar wood.

k   At noon he went there to where they were to fight.

l   And he found that a small pond had already been made.

m   The other one came to ask him what the deal was.

n   "Well, four times each.

o   You'll give it a try.

p   And we won't fight back against each other," the Indian said.

13 a   And the other fellow was quite pleased.

b   "Well, so who'll give it a try against the other first?" the challenger asked.

c   "Well, you first," he was told.

d   And he grabbed hold of him.

e   The Indian was put under the water.

f   Each time he came up, he looked completely unaffected.

g   And after a while he had been put under the water the full four times.

h   "me·mečine·hi," e·h=iči.

i   "a·kwi," e·h=ineči.

j   mani wi·h=iši|-mawinahkye·tehe,

k   e·h=nahkohoči mete·hi.

l   i·ni=meko e·h=iši-peškone·či.

m   e·h=sahkasoči i·niya me·čina·ka·ta neniwa.|

n   i·ni=ča·hi=ʾpi e·h=se·kesiwa·či neniwaki.

o   e·h=kosa·wa·či.

p   ote·hi=meko ‖ e·h=ayo·či, e·h=pakačike·či.

14 a   na·hina·h=ke·hi=ʾpi pe·kačike·čini, e·h=sesekeše·niki=meko i·ni| ote·hi.[*]

b   "šihihwi´," e·h=iyowa·či i·niki mehtose·neniwaki.

c   "we·nah=a·kwi aše=meko mehtose·neniwičini," e·h=ina·wa·či.

d   "we·nah=maneto·wi·hapa," e·h=ina·wa·či i·niki mehtose·neniwaki.

e   na·hina·h=no·ta·ke·či| we·na·pe·mita,

f   "nese·wa=ʾpi mi·ka·ti·čini," e·neči ihkwe·wa,

g   e·h=nawatena·či še·šketo·he·hani.|

h   we·nekwanita=ke·hi e·h=ata·hpena·či oto·hpwa·kanani,

i   e·h=atama·či ača·hmeko.

j   mečemo·ka=ke·hi e·h=ni·senaki e·šihto·či maškimote·hi.

k   ke·htena ma·ne=meko oškinawe·hahi e·h=pye·či-wi·če·we·niči. ‖

15 a   e·h=pye·či-ma·ne·niči.

b   e·h=mi·ša·te·nemoči we·na·pe·mita,

c   na·hka i·niki ke·hkya·haki.

d   "ma·ne=meko, neta·ha, wača·nota·no," e·h=ina·či we·ta·nesita pašito·ha.

e   na·hina·hi pe·kamose·niči,

f   ma·ne=meko e·h=keta·wana·či meškohpwa·kanahi| pašito·ha,

g   e·h=atame·hiwe·či.

h   oškinawe·hahi e·h=kehč-atame·ha·či.

i   ki·šese·hkwe·či ihkwe·wa, e·h=ana·škahike·či.

j   asayani wa·peškye·kiničini e·h=ana·škahike·či,

k   e·h=otato·hposo·niwa·či.

l   e·škikiničini e·h=ana·škahike·či.

m   we·ča·hoči=ke·hi| pešekesiwi-owi·ya·si,|

n   na·hka takwaha·ni, wa·pikonani maškoči·sani e·h=wa·wiya·keswa·či.

o   o·ni mehtekoki ‖ we·či-kečika·niki si·sepa·hkwi e·h=wi·škopanohike·či.

16 a   wi·nwa·wa=pe·hki=meko e·h=ki·ša·koči-menwisenye·wa·či.

b   o·ni i·na ihkwe·wa omeso·ta·nahi.

c   "na·pi=wi·na we·či·kwe·ni iha·ye·kwe," e·h=ineči.[†]

d   "hao·ʔ," e·h=ineči| ke·hkya·haki.

e   "i·nina·h=kohi kwi·nomeko·toke omeso·ta·nahi," e·h=ineči ihkwe·wa.

---

[*]/=ke·hi/: a second hand adds ⟨i⟩ before this.

[†]Syntax of 16*b-c* accepted as is by AW.

h   "One last time," (the man) said.

i   And he was told, "No."

j   And just as he had been about to attack,

k   he was intercepted and brought to a halt by the heart.

l   And immediately he went up in a blaze.

m   The man who had made the challenge was burned up.

n   So, then the men were scared, they say.

o   They were afraid of him.

p   It was his heart he used in striking the blow.

14 a   What's more, they say, when he struck a blow, that heart of his gave off flashes of sparks.

b   "Wow," those people said.

c   "Look, he isn't just an ordinary person," they said about him.

d   "Look, it's clear that he's a manitou," those people said of him.

e   The moment the wife heard the news,

f   when the woman was told, "They say he's slain the one he fought with,"

g   she took up the cooking pot.

h   And the father-in-law picked up his pipe

i   and smoked for the first time in a while.

j   And the old lady took down the bag she was making.

k   Sure enough, many young men came along.

15 a   They came in numbers.

b   The wife was quite pleased,

c   and the old folks as well.

d   "Cook for a lot of people, Daughter," the woman's father said to her.

e   When the crowd arrived,

f   the old man got out lots of redstone pipes

g   and gave people a smoke.

h   He afforded the young men a great deal of smoking.

i   After the woman finished her cooking, she spread out a floor-covering.

j   She spread out a white buckskin,

k   and they used it as a tablecloth.

l   It was a new skin that she spread out.

m   And what she cooked was venison,

n   and also corn mush, cooking in pumpkins and beans.

o   And then she sweetened the food with sugar that oozed out of trees.

16 a   *They* enjoyed a really nice meal.

b   The woman's parents (had something to say) next.

c   "The two of you ought to go to wherever he came from," she was told.

d   "Yes, I agree," was the reply to the old folks.

e   "His parents must certainly be missing him by now," the woman was told.

f   o·ni ona·pe·mani i·ni e·h=ina·či.

g   "šihihwi·´," e·h=iniči.

h   "ši·´, pe·hki=ma·hi nešiwi=na·hina·hi netoči," e·h=ina·či.|

i   "manahka=ma·hi we·či‑kesi·ya·ki netoči.

j   aka·mi‑kehčikami·we| netoči," e·h=ina·či owi·wani.

k   "i·ni wi·h=inači," e·h=ina·či owi·wani.

l   "peno·či=ma·h=netoči.

m   'peno·či='pi‿oči·wa.

n   asa·mi=na·hina·hi,' ‖ ki·h=ina·waki kemeso·ta·naki," e·h=ineči| ihkwe·wa.

17 a   e·h=a·čimoha·či omeso·ta·nahi.

b   "asa·mi=ma·hi='pi·='na peno·či oči·wa," e·h=ina·či.

c   "i·ni=ma·h=ki·na e·šawiwa·či neniwaki.

d   na·nano·pehka=na·hina·hi| oči·wene·waki ihkwe·wahi," e·h=ineči.

e   "kaši=we·na=mani ni·h=išawipena nakašiya·ke.

f   meše·='nah=meko ki·h=nakašipena," e·h=ineči.

g   "ki·h=na·kwa=meko," e·h=ineči| ihkwe·wa.

h   "mani=ke·hi:

i   e·taši‑pe·we·nemowe·kwe·ni wi·h=a·šo·hkame·kwe kehčikami·wi,

j   ki·h=we·we·ne·neta·pwa=meko wi·h=anemiha·we·kwe·ni," e·h=ineči.

k   "ahpemeki išite·he·ye·kwe, ahpemeki,

l   ahkwitepye·ki išite·he·ye·kwe, ahkwitepye·ki ‖ ki·h=anemiha·pwa," e·h=ineči ihkwe·wa.

18 a   "i·ni=ča·h=ki·h=ina·wa," e·h=ineči.|

b   pe·hkote·niki ihkwe·wa| e·h=pye·ma·hkohowe·či,

c   e·h=kehkitehkwe·nike·či=ke·h=ahpeme.

d   e·h=a·čimoha·či ona·pe·mani.

e   " 'mani=ke·hi:

f   e·taši‑pe·we·nemowe·kwe·ni wi·h=a·šo·hkame·kwe kehčikami·wi,

g   meše=meko ki·h=we·we·ne·neta·pwa wi·h=anemiha·we·kwe·ni,' " e·h=ineči neniwa,

h   "neteko·pi," e·h=ikoči owi·wani.

i   "o·´, meše=wi·na=ke·hi ki·h=na·kwa·pena," e·h=ineči ihkwe·wa.*

j   "šewe·na| aškači·me·hi," e·h=iči| neniwa.

k   te·kwa·kiniki| e·h=na·kwa·wa·či,

l   ahkwitepye·ki e·h=anemiha·wa·či.|

m   aka·me·heki ki·ši‑pya·wa·či, e·h=a·čimoha·či owi·wani.

n   "a·kwi=ke·h=mani ‖ a·ya·nekinowa·čini| ihkwe·waki," e·h=ina·či.

19 a   "meše=meko.

b   i·ni=ke·hi wi·h=inekinowane·ni,| †

c   i·ni=meko ni·h=inekine," e·h=iči ihkwe·wa.

d   e·h=wa·pama·či e·h=nemasoniči,

____

*/meše=wi·na/: AK ⟨meše.wi·na⟩.

†/i·ni .. wi·h=inekinowane·ni/ 'if you're going to be that size': "if I have to be that size" (HP).

f   Then she told her husband that.

g   And he said, "Gosh!

h   "Oh boy! See, I've really come a terribly long way," he told her.

i   "See, I came from way up north.

j   I came from the other side of the ocean," he told his wife.

k   "That's what you must tell them," he told his wife.

l   "See, I came from far away," he said.

m   "You must tell your parents, 'He says he came from far away,

n   too long a distance,' " the woman was told.

17 a   And she explained it to her parents.

b   "See, he says he came from too far away," she told them.

c   "Well see, that's what men do.

d   They get women from great distances away," she was told.

e   "After all now, what do you think will happen to us if you leave us?

f   You can just go ahead and leave us," she was told.

g   "You *have* to go," the woman was told.

h   "And here's another thing.

i   If you two are reluctant to cross the ocean,

j   you may have your choice of what way to go," she was told.

k   "If you want it to be up in the air, it will be in the air,

l   and if you want it to be on the water, you'll go on the water," the woman was told.

18 a   "So, you must tell him that," she was told.

b   That night the woman wrapped her legs around

c   as well as giving a neck hug.

d   And she explained to her husband.

e   " 'And here's another thing:

f   if you two are reluctant to cross the ocean,

g   you may have your choice of whichever way to go,' " the man was told,

h   "So I was told," he was told by his wife.

i   "Well, so if that's what you want, we'll go," the woman was told.

j   "But after a while," the man said.

k   That fall they headed out,

l   going on top of the water.

m   After they got to the other side, he explained to his wife.

n   "Now, the women are not large like you here," he told her.

19 a   "That's fine.

b   And if you're going to be that size,

c   I shall be the same size," the woman said.

d   He looked at her as she was standing there,

e   " 'i·ni,'| ki·h=i," e·h=ikoči.[*]

f   e·škami=meko e·h=anemi|-čakeška·hiniči,

g   e·škami=ke·h=meko e·h=iši-we·wenesiniči.|

h   kapo·twe e·hkwiči atena·wi e·h=ahkwi·hiniči,|

i   e·h=ki·ša·koči-=meko| -we·wenesiniči owi·wani.

j   ke·ko·hi_e·h=išawiwa·či, meme·nawi=meko e·h=išičinowa·či.

k   e·h=ašihta·koči owi·naka·hi i·nini ihkwe·wani.

l   e·h=menwi-inekihkwa·hkwateniki,

m   e·h=po·si_čake·netamo·hiči.

n   e·h=we·weneteniki. ‖

20 a   i·na·hi e·h=pya·wa·či,[†]

b   ača·hmeko e·h=nana·tohtawa·či e·ši_mehtose·neniwinikwe·ni.|

c   "neki·yamowe·wi,"_e·h=iniči.

d   "ki·yamowe·waki=ma·hi·='niki e·h=a·pi_tanaha·kapiyani," e·h=ikoči owi·wani.|

e   "o·ho·´," e·h=ina·či.

f   "meše=ča·h=ni·na_wa·natohka| i·ya·hi neta·pi·tanaha·kapi."

g   "a·kwi=we·na·='niki_kehke·nemačini? e·h=a·hpeči_mena·škonowa·či?" e·h=iniči.|

h   "a·kwi=ča·h=meko mi·na·we·nemakini," e·h=iči.

i   "ki·yamowe·waki=ča·hi,"_e·h=ikoči.|

j   "o·ho·´," e·h=ina·či i·nini owi·wani.

k   ča·ki-=ne·peh=meko -ke·ko·he·hi e·h=awato·niči ihkwe·wimine·hani.

l   me·no·hkami·niki e·h=ahčike·wa·či. ‖

21 a   ni·peniki_na·hina·hi,| e·h=ki·šikeniki=meko| ča·ki_ke·ko·hi,

b   e·h=ma·mi·čiwa·či.

c   o·ni_mehtose·neniwaki e·h=mi·neči wi·h=ahčihahčike·wa·či.

d   e·h=ma·wači-=meko -we·wenesiniči owi·wani.|

e   e·h=pwa·wi-=meko -kehke·nema·wa·či we·čiwenema·te·ni oškinawe·haki.

f   wa·wosa·h=meko a·neta e·h=mahkate·wi·wa·či,

g   e·h=natokwawa·wa·či ihkwe·wahi oškinawe·haki.

h   a·kwi=ne·pehe-='pi| nana·ši oni·ča·nesiha·čini.[‡]

i   aškači, "metemo, kaši-ni·hka ketešawipena·toke

j   e·h=pwa·wi-oni·ča·nese·hiyakwe," e·h=ina·či.

k   "hwi·´," e·h=iči ihkwe·wa.

l   i·ni=ča·hi='pi, ‖ "na·piwe·na ki·h=oni·ča·nesi," e·h=ikoči,|

22 a   kete·-='nah=meko e·h=ačihkwiniči owi·wani.[§]/[¶]

b   no·še·niči, kwi·yese·he·hani e·h=oni·ča·nese·hiwa·či.

---

[*]'i·ni,'| ki·h=i; *lit.*, You must say, 'That's it.'

[†]/i·na·hi/: /a·/ confirmed by AW.

[‡]"He never made a child for her." (HP), but the more usual interpretation is implied by 21*l*.

[§]/kete·='nah=meko/: this seems preferable to /ke·htena=meko/ "surely" (HP).

[¶]/owi·wani/ 'his wife': translated in 21*l*; the Meskwaki syntax foregrounds the man.

e   and she told him, "Say when."

f   She gradually became smaller and smaller,

g   and she became more and more beautiful besides.

h   Before long his wife was a little shorter than he was

i   and was very beautiful, indeed.

j   When they had sex, they fit together with plenty of room.

k   The woman made a little penis for him.

l   It had a diameter of proper size,

m   and he thought it was rather too small.

n   It was a nice one.

20 a   As they arrived over there,

b   he asked her for the first time what kind of person she was.

c   "I'm a giant," she said.

d   "I mean, they're all giants where you've been living as a son-in-law," his wife told him.

e   "So *that's* it!" he said to her.

f   "So, *I've* just been freely living over there as a son-in-law as if it were nothing!"

g   "Didn't you know, after all, that they eat meat all the time?" she asked.

h   "Well, I never gave them that much thought," he said.

i   "Well, they're giants," she told him.

j   "So *that's* it!" he said to his wife.

k   Oh, and she had brought along with her all kinds of seeds.

l   That spring they planted.

21 a   And that summer, as everything matured,

b   they ate them.

c   And then the people were given seeds for them all to plant.

d   His wife was the prettiest,

e   and the young men had no idea where she had been brought from.

f   Some of the young men went so far as to fast,

g   seeking women in their dreams.

h   Oh, and she never gave him a child.

i   And after a while he said to her, "Say, old girl, I wonder what the heck's wrong with us

j   that we can't have a child."

k   "Oh my!" the woman said.

l   So then, the story goes, he was told by his wife, "Alright then, you shall have a child,"

22 a   and now, with her thinking changed, she got pregnant.

b   And when she gave birth, they had a little boy.

c e·h=ki·ša·kote·nememeči oni·ča·nesani,
d e·h=tepa·nekosiniči.
e meso·te·wi=meko e·h=tepa·tamawoči.

f ki·h-=meko -ki·šiki·hiniči,|
g aya·pami e·h=a·wa·či,
h e·h=wi·te·ma·wa·či okwiswa·wani.
i i·ya·h=pye·ya·wa·či, e·h=asipi-=meko| -me·nawa·nemeči.
j "šihihwi·´, pe·hki=ni·hka_ma·haki mama·kekino·ki,"| e·h=iči i·na oškinawe·ha.
k o·ni e·h=owi·wiči okima·hkwe·wi-še·škesi·hani.
l ki·ši-owi·wiči, e·nekihkwa·pe·wesi·hiči| atena·wi=meko e·h=inekihkwa·pe·wesiniči i·nini ‖
   ihkwe·wani.
23 a meše·='nah=meko nešiwana·či| taswawahi·me i·ya·hi e·h=awiwa·či.
b kapo·twe okwiswa·wani e·h=kano·nemeči wi·h=okima·winiči,*/†
c e·h=anwa·či·niči,
d e·h=okima·winiči.

e o·ni=wi·nwa·wa| e·h=na·kwa·wa·či na·hka,|
f e·h=a·čimowa·či okwiswa·wani e·h=okima·winiči.
g menwinehki=meko i·nahi e·h=awiwa·či.

h o·ni omeso·ta·nahi e·h=awana·či i·tepi iši.
i meše=meko e·h=anemi-_papa·ma·tesiwa·či.
j aškači i·tepi e·h=pya·wa·či,
k ki·yamowe·na·ki e·h=awiwa·či.
l e·h=pwa·wi|- nana·ši i·ya·hi_aya·pami_-pya·wa·či.

m i·ni e·hkwiči. ‖

---

*'Was approached': lit., 'was spoken to'.
†'A chief' (HP in 23*b*, 23*d*, and 23*f*).

c   Her child aroused deep feelings
d   and was dearly loved.
e   Her child was universally loved.

f   After their son was just grown up,
g   they went back,
h   taking him along.
i   And when they got there, everybody admired him.
j   "Wow! These people are really big," the young man said.
k   And then he married the young daughter of the chief.
l   And after he married her, that woman became smaller than the smaller size he was.
23 a   They went right on living over there for a good many years.
b   And at some point their son was approached to become a chief,
c   and he was willing,
d   and he became a chief.

e   And then *they* went back again,
f   and they reported that their son was a chief.
g   They stayed there a good while.

h   And then he took his parents to that place.
i   They traveled along, taking their time, living from place to place.
j   And after a long time they arrived in the giant country,
k   and they stayed there.
l   They never came back across again.

m   That's the end.

ashkotênêsiwa manetôwahi êh=ashihekochi

When the Spirit of Fire was Made by the Manitous

ashkotênêsiwa manetôwahi êh=ashihekochi

Alfred Kiyana[*]

1 a   aškote·ne·siwa maneto·wahi e·h=ašihekoči.[†]

b   meše=wi·na=ʼpi ma·haki nekotayaki e·h=owi·ke·hiwa·či,

c   e·h=aški-=meko -owi·weti·hiwa·či.

d   če·wi·šwi=meko e·h=ketema·kesi·hiwa·či.

e   če·wi·šwi=meko e·h=pwa·wi-omeso·ta·niwa·či.|

f   ihkwe·wa še·ški e·h=omešo·hiči.

g   i·nini=ke·h=meko=ʼpi mehteno·hi či·nawe·me·hičini.

h   a·kwi·=ʼnahi=ʼpi owiye·hani| kotakani či·nawe·ma·čini.

i   i·nini=meko mehteno·hi pašito·he·hani.

j   ašewe·na=ʼpi a·kwi wa·waneška·hičini.

k   mahkwa·či=meko=ʼpi iškwe·se·hiwa.[‡]

l   i·nini=ke·hi=ʼpi=meko mehteno·hi wi·čiha·čini.

m   a·kwi·=ʼnahi=ʼpi nekotahi mawi|-nepa·čini,

n   a·ye·niwe=meko.

o   o=i·na=na·hka pašito·he·ha e·h=mahkwa·tesiči=meko,|

p   e·h=pwa·wi-wa·waneška·hi|-pašito·hiči.

q   e·h=ki·ša·koči-=meko -menwi-=pemena·či o·šisemani. ‖

2 a   mahkwa·či=meko e·h=pemena·či.

b   a·kwi=ke·hi=ʼpi ke·ko·hi e·h=iši-nepo·te·wi-=to·tawa·či.

c   mahkwa·či=meko e·h=iškwe·se·he·hiniči=meko oči-pye·či e·h=pemena·či.

d   keša·či=meko e·h=iši-pemena·či o·šisemani.|

e   e·h=pwa·wi-=ke·h=meko nana·ši -kehči-neškima·či.|

f   mahkwa·či=meko e·h=kano·na·či.

g   na·hka e·h=pwa·wi|-kokwiya·na·či,

h   mehto·či=meko e·h=ki·hki·čiha·či o·šisemani.

i   ahpene·či=meko manahka=meko e·h=po·si-iškwe·se·he·hiniči| oči-pye·či
e·h=pwa·wi-=mo·hči nekotenwi-kokwima·či.

j   na·hka e·h=pwa·wi- nana·ši -ki·ški·škatahwa·či.

k   e·h=pwa·wi-=ke·hi -nahi-wi·hpe·ma·či e·h=čakeši·he·hiniči.

l   e·h=tanehkwe·hiči=ʼp=a·pehe e·h=nepa·hiniči.

m   ke·keya·h=meko e·h=ki·šiki·hiniči e·h=iši-‖menwi-to·tawa·či.[§]

3 a   o=i·na=na·hka e·h=mi·na·we·netaki owi·yawi še·škesi·he·ha.

---

[*]The manuscript is NAA ms. 1875.16; it has 112 pages.

[†]At the top as a title, below "No 1". A second hand adds: 112 − 6 ½ + 10. This is apparently
Michelson's calculation of 112 pages times 6 ½ cents a page, plus 10 cents.

[‡]A divider was added at the end of the sentence.

[§]Translation: AW.

When the Spirit of Fire was Made by the Manitous
Translated by Ives Goddard

1 a   When the Spirit of Fire was Made by the Manitous.

b   There was this married couple living by themselves wherever it was, the story goes.
c   The young folks were recent newlyweds.
d   Neither of them had anything.
e   Neither of them had their parents living.

f   The woman had just a grandfather.
g   And he was the only relative she had, the story goes.
h   She didn't have any other relative.
i   Only that old man.
j   But it's said she wasn't wild.
k   She was a quiet girl.
l   What's more, it's said he was the only one she stayed with.
m   She never went anywhere else to sleep,
n   just always in the same place.
o   And that old man, also, had a quiet nature.
p   He was not an old rascal.
q   He took extremely good care of his grandchild.
2 a   He took care of her in a calm and quiet way.
b   And it's said that he didn't in any way behave lewdly toward her.
c   From when she was a young girl he took care of her calmly and quietly.
d   In a kindly way is how he took care of his grandchild.
e   What's more, he never scolded her severely.
f   He spoke to her quietly.
g   Also, he never snapped at her.
h   He treated his grandchild with almost solicitous reserve.
i   The whole time beginning back when she was a very little girl he'd never spoken sharply to her even once.
j   Also, he never took a switch to her.
k   And another thing, he never slept with her in his bed when she was small.
l   It's said that she would sleep at his head.
m   In time she was grown up, and he treated her well yet.
3 a   And that young girl for her part took notice of her life.

^b e·h=ki·ša·koči-=meko -menwi_pemena·soči.*

^c e·h=ki·ša·koči-=meko -tepa·na·či omešo·mesani.

^d e·h=aya·wi_-’šimekoči=meko_omešo·hani,

^e e·šimekočini=meko e·h=iši_-mehtose·neniwiči.

^f e·h=wa·pataki=’pi=mehto·či owi·yawi.

^g ke·htena=meko e·h=pešikwi-še·škesi·he·hiči.|

^h ma·mi·hkemehkwe·wa·čiki=ke·hi| e·h=pwa·wi-=meko -we·te·wi·hka·nowa·či.

ⁱ a·neta=’pi| ki·ši-a·nawesiwa·čini e·h=kehči-ki·hka·ma·wa·či i·nini oškinawe·haki.

^j a·kwi=ke·hi=’pi i·nina·hi ke·ko·hi ki·šete·niki| ma·mi·čiwa·čini.

^k meše·=’nah=meko e·h=aškeniki, e·h=mi·čiwa·či=meko.

^l a·kwi=’pi nahi_-wača·howa·čini. ‖

^{4 a} e·h=aškeniki=meko ke·ko·hi e·h=mi·čiwa·či.

^b na·hka a·kwi=’pi nahi-awasowa·čini.

^c i·ni=’pi e·šawiwa·či i·nina·hi.

^d o·ni=na·hkači oškinawe·ha mahkwa·či=meko e·h=oškinawe·hiči.

^e e·h=pwa·wi-=meko ihkwe·wahi -nenehke·nema·či,

^f mahkwa·či=meko.

^g na·hka me·meta·ča·hi e·h=pwa·wi|-nenehke·netaki, a·mano·weni.

^h e·h=pwa·wi-=we·=meko -kehke·netaki wi·h=mi·hkemehkwe·we·či.

ⁱ mehteno·h=meko=’pi| o·hkomese·hani e·h=wi·čiha·či, e·h=o·hkomese·hiči.

^j e·h=keša·či neniwiči.|

^k mo·hči=meko=’pi apeno·he·hahi ne·wa·čini, e·h=keše·moči=meko.

^l mahkwa·či=meko e·h=keše·moči.

^m ihkwe·wahi=na·hka mahkwa·či=meko e·h=kakano·netisoči.

ⁿ e·h=pwa·wi-=ke·hi -mi·hkemehkwe·we·či.|

^o ke·keya·h=meko=’pi ‖ e·h=anemi-_pe·hki -ki·šiki·hiči.

^{5 a} e·h=a·šimemeči owi·yawi še·škesi·he·hahi,

^b e·h=pwa·wi-=meko -wi·kwa·na·či.

^c mo·hči=’pi e·h=pi·nešihekoči,

^d e·h=pwa·wi-=meko -wi·kwa·na·či.|

^e a·neta=’pi ki·ši-a·nawihekočini e·h=kehči-ki·hka·mekoči.

^f ke·keya·h=meko=’pi| ihkwe·wahi ‘kečinešiwa’ e·h=ikoči.

^g i·ni=ča·hi=’pi e·šitehka·nekoči ki·mo·či ihkwe·wahi.

^h ‘kečinešiwa’| išitehka·nekwa=’pi ihkwe·wahi.

ⁱ e·yi·ki=meko=’pi·=’na o·hkomese·hani e·h=takwitakwimeči.†

^j i·na=ne·hi=’pi a·kwi=’pi_nana·ši o·hkomese·hani kehči-_neškimekočini.

^k mahkwa·či=meko e·h=kano·nekoči,

^l e·h=ki·ša·koči-=meko -menwi_-to·ta·koči.

^m mo·hči=meko=’pi nekotenwi a·kwi nasata·wi|-kano·nekočini.

---

*⟨so|⟩ is written over an erased ⟨či⟩.

†/o·hkomese·hani/: ⟨.okoneseani.⟩.

b She was taken care of extremely well.
c And she was extremely fond of her grandfather.
d Her granddad told her just what to do,
e and she lived her life in the ways he told her to.
f They say it was as if she minded herself.
g She was truly a proper young girl.
h   What's more, the ones who chased after girls had no success at all.
i Some of the young men, when they failed, are said to have reproached her severely.

j   Now, it's said that at that time they didn't eat things that were cooked.
k They had to put up with them being raw and eat them anyway.
l It's said that they never cooked them.
4 a Things were just raw when they ate them.
b And it's said, too, that they never warmed themselves by a fire.
c That's how it was for them at that time.

d   And the young man also was a quiet young man.
e He didn't think about women,
f just calm thoughts.
g And he didn't think about "fun" either, about sex.
h In fact, he didn't at all understand that he was going to court women.
i He lived with just his grandmother, the story goes, having just a grandmother.
j He was kind.
k When he saw babies, they say he would even stroke them and speak soothingly,
l doing it quietly.
m And with women, also, he would converse quietly.
n Remember, he didn't go courting.
o   In time, the story goes, he became quite grown up.
5 a He was urged on young girls,
b and he paid no attention to them.
c They even just approached him boldly,
d and he paid no attention to them.
e It's said that some of them, after they failed with him, reproached him severely.
f Eventually, they say women called him a gelding.
g So that was the name women used for him secretly.
h The women used "the Gelding" as his name.
i They would also whisper about him and his grandmother, they say.
j   Also in his case, they say his grandmother never scolded him severely.
k She spoke to him quietly,
l and she treated him extremely well.
m They say she never spoke to him crossly even once.

n   kena·či=meko e·h=a·ya·čimohekoči, ‖ we·pi-a·ya·čimohekočini.
6 a na·hka=’pi a·kwi nana·ši pakamekočini o·hkomese·hani.
b   i·nini=ke·hi=’pi=meko mehteno·h·ne·hi·=’na či·nawe·me·hičini.
c   e·h=ki·ša·koči-=ča·h·wi·na=meko -nawe·ni|-neni·he·hiči.*
d   kekimesi=meko iškwe·se·haki, i·nini=meko=’pi me·nwe·nema·wa·čini—
e   mehteno·hi=’pi pe·hki-ihkwe·waki.
f   a·kwi=’pi=meko paši-we·te·we wi·h=mi·hkemekowa·či.
g   a·neta=’pi e·h=koči-=meko -pi·nešiha·wa·či ihkwe·waki,|
h   še·škesi·he·haki=’h=we·na,
i   e·h=pwa·wi-=’pi=meko -kaški·hkawa·wa·či.
j   e·h=pwa·wi-=ke·h=meko=wi·na·=’na -kehke·netaki a·mano·weni,
k   e·h=pwa·wi-=meko -kehke·netaki e·ši-me·meta·ča·hiniki.†
l   ke·htena=meko e·h=kekye·htena·mi|-mahkwa·tesiči. ‖

7 a o·ni we·yo·šisemita kapo·twe=meko e·h=nana·tohtawa·či o·šiseme·hani, metemo·he·ha.‡
b   “’šina·kwa, noši·he, owiye·ha·wi·na=ki·na kemi·hkema·wa?” e·h=ina·či.
c   “kaši=ya·pi_ni·h=išawi mi·hkemake owiye·ha,” e·h=ikoči wa·natohka.
d   e·h=apahapane·nema·či o·šisemani.
e   “’šina·kwa=wi·na=mana.
f   ke·htena=we·=meko| te·pima·petoke, ‘kečinešiwa’ e·h=ineči,” e·h=ina·či o·šisemani.
g   e·h=pwa·wi-nenoše·či e·šiwe·pima·te·ni oškinawe·ha.
h   “kaši=’yo_ketešiwe·pimi, ano·hko,” e·h=ina·či_o·hkomesani.
i   “ši·=’ni=ča·h=e·neči pwa·wi-_mi·hkemehkwe·wa·čiki,” e·h=ina·či o·šisemani
    metemo·he·ha.
j   na·hka=meko, “kaši=ya·pi išawipi e·h=mi·hkemehkwe·we·ki,” e·h=ikoči o·šisemani. ‖
8 a “a·kwi=we·na? nahi-nenehke·nemačini? ihkwe·waki?” e·h=ina·či.
b   “a·kwi=ča·h=meko nenehke·nemakini,” e·h=ina·či| o·hkomesani.
c   “kaši=ya·pi| ni·h=išawi nenehke·nemake i·niki ihkwe·waki,” e·h=ina·či.
d   e·h=na·mo·či-=meko -se·kesiči metemo·he·ha.
e   “ke·nema·pi=’h=we·na katawi|-e·ye·hkwe·wite,” e·h=išite·he·či,
f   e·h=ine·nema·či o·šiseme·hani.
g   kočike·hkwi=ke·h=wi·na e·h=ne·nesa·niči pešekesiwahi,
h   e·h=kehtwe·wesiniči.

i   na·hka i·nina·hi: a·kwi=’pi| nahi-mahkate·wi·wa·čini neno·te·waki.

j   o·ni·=’na pašito·he·ha o·šisemani, “noši·he,” e·h=ina·či.
k   “na·pi=wi·na ki·či-_ke·tema·hena·na ona·pe·me·hiyane.|
l   neša·kwe·nemo_wi·h=men-_ona·pe·me·hiyani,” e·h=ina·či.§

____

*/koči-=ča·h=/: ⟨kočiči|⟩, with second ⟨i⟩ changed to ⟨a⟩ by a second hand.
†/=meko/: ⟨.meko.|⟩.
‡/we·yo·šisemita .. metemo·he·ha/ ‘grandparent .. old woman’ for ‘grandmother’.
§/mo/: ⟨no⟩.

n   She instructed him patiently, when she began instructing him.
6 a Also, they say his grandmother never struck him.
b   Now, also in his case, *she* was his only relative, the story goes.
c   Well, but he was a strikingly handsome youth.
d   For all the girls, it's said that *he* was the only one they liked—
e   speaking of only the really mature ones.
f   And they say, there was no way that he would court them.
g   Some women are said to have tried simply approaching him boldly,
h   or rather young girls,
i   and they got nowhere with him.
j   But here, he knew nothing about sex.
k   He didn't know what fun it was.
l   He was truly seriously reserved in his nature.

7 a   And at some point the grandmother asked a question of her grandchild.
b   "Say, grandson, are *you* courting anyone, though?" she asked him.
c   "So tell me, what will I be doing if I *court* someone?" he answered, unconcerned.
d   She laughed at her grandson.
e   "What's with this one!
f   They must really have it right after all when they call him 'the Gelding,'" she said to her
     grandson.
g   The young man didn't understand the meaning of the name used for him.
h   "Tell me, what does the name you're calling me mean, grandma?" he said to his
     grandmother.
i   "Gee! So that's a name given to ones who don't court women," the old lady told her
     grandson.
j   And again her grandson asked her, "So tell me, what does someone do when they court
     women?"
8 a   "You mean you actually don't ever think about women?" she said to him.
b   "Well no, I *don't* think about them," he said to his grandmother.
c   "Please tell me, what will I be doing if I court the women?"
d   The old lady was secretly apprehensive.
e   "I wonder if he might be about to become a berdache," she thought,
f   thinking about her grandson.
g   Although he did kill deer,
h   having a knack for getting game.

i   Another thing about that time: they say the Indians never fasted for spiritual power.

j   And then that old man said to his granddaughter, "Granddaughter,
k   it would be good a good thing if you married the one who's poor, like us.
l   I'm against you marrying someone well-off.

^m   "čeˑw‗ahpiˑhči‑=čaˑh=meko ‑ketemaˑkesiˑhiyeˑkwa ‖ wiˑčawiweˑhiyane kiˑh=menwawi,"
eˑh=inaˑči oˑšisemeˑhani.

^{9 a}   oˑniˑ‑='na šeˑškesiˑheˑha, "aše=yeˑtoke=meko.

^b aˑnahaˑnawiheˑwaki=keˑh=wiˑna moˑhči| weˑwenesičiki iˑnini," eˑh=inaˑči omešoˑmesani.

^c   oˑniˑ‑='na šeˑškesiˑheˑha omešoˑmesani,

^d   "iˑtepi=keˑh=meko niˑh=a," eˑh=inaˑči omešoˑmesani.

^e   "iˑna=koči=yeˑtoke aˑšimiyana," eˑh=inaˑči.

^f   "eheˑhe," eˑh=išiweˑči pašitoˑha.

^g   eˑh=weˑpi‑nana henoči šeˑškesiˑheˑha.

^h kiˑšiˑhtaˑči, eˑh=naˑkwaˑči.

ⁱ   —neˑpehe, omešoˑhani,

^j "kekyeˑhkinawaˑči onaˑpeˑmiyaˑne aˑkwi waˑpake wiˑh=pyaˑyaˑnini," eˑh=inaˑči
omešoˑmesani.

^k   "hawoˑʔ," eˑh=inaˑči oˑšisemani.—

^l   oˑni=yeˑtoke iˑna| šeˑškesiˑha iˑyaˑh=eˑh=pyaˑči,|

^m eˑh=nesapiniči metemoˑheˑhani.

ⁿ   (eˑh=šiˑšaˑtehe_iˑna| oškinaweˑha.)

^o   ana=kiˑšaˑkoči=mekoho ‖ eˑh=iši‑weˑwenesiniči| šeˑškesiˑheˑhani pyeˑyaˑničini
metemoˑheˑha.

^{10 a} eˑh=kehkeˑnetaˑkosiniči=keˑhi iˑnini eˑh=kiˑšaˑkoči‑mahkwaˑtesiniči.

^b meše=meko eˑh=apihapiniči mahkwaˑči.

^c   aškači, "kemaˑmataˑkwi‗kiˑyokiˑyoseʔ, nošiˑhe," eˑh=inaˑči metemoˑheˑha.

^d   "eheˑhe.

^e nemešoˑmesa=kohi,

^f 'iˑna=wiˑna naˑpi onaˑpeˑmeˑhiyane oškinaweˑha,' netekwa=kohi_nemešoˑmesa," eˑh=inaˑči
metemoˑheˑhani.[*]

^g   "iˑni=čaˑhi weˑči|‑pyaˑyaˑni," eˑh=inaˑči.

^h metemoˑheˑha naˑmoˑči eˑh=miˑšaˑteˑnemoči oˑšisemani eˑh=pyeˑnotawomeˑči.

ⁱ   "šiˑšeˑwa=čaˑhi‑'yoˑwe.

^j anaˑkwike wiˑh=pyeˑwa," eˑh=inaˑči| šeˑškesiˑhani.

^k   "anikaˑne=koči eˑh=apiči, akaˑmeteˑki, iˑh=apihapiyani," eˑh=inaˑči.

^l   iˑni=wiˑna='piˑ='na eˑh=mawi‑nanaˑhapiči akaˑmeteˑki ‖ šeˑškesiˑheˑha.

^{11 a} "šihihwiˑ´," eˑh=išiteˑheˑči iˑna šeˑškesiˑheˑha.

^b   aškači eˑnaˑkwiˑhiniki saˑkiči eˑh=poˑnašiniči.

^c   metemoˑka eˑh=pemi‗nowiˑči.

^d   "'na=maˑmataˑkwi=niˑhka noˑhkomeseˑha pyeˑči‗nowiˑwa,

^e keˑkoˑh=yeˑtoke eˑh=iši‗nanaˑhkawehtaˑkeˑči noˑhkomesa," eˑh=inaˑči oˑhkomesani.

^f   metemoˑka eˑh=tepasišimoˑhiči aˑčimoˑči.

^g   "'šinaˑkwa, nošiˑhe; kepyeˑnotaˑkwa=maˑh=kiˑna šeˑškesiˑheˑha," eˑh=inaˑči.

^h "iˑni=čaˑhi wiˑh=owiˑwiyani, nošiˑhe," eˑh=inaˑči oˑšisemani.

---

[*]/iˑna=wiˑna/: ⟨ina.wina⟩ with divider erased.

^m So, if you're married to someone equally poor, you'll do nicely," he told his
granddaughter.

9 a   And then that young girl said to her grandfather, "I guess just to be doing it.
b   After all, even the pretty ones fail with him."
c   And then to her grandfather that young girl said,
d   "And *there* I shall go," she told her grandfather.
e   "I can obviously see he's the one you're urging on me," she said to him.
f   "Yes," was the old man's reply.
g   The young girl set to getting herself in order.
h   And after she finished dressing, she left.
i   —Oh, I forgot, her granddad,
j   she told her grandfather, "It will mean I'm married if I don't come back tomorrow."
k   And he told his granddaughter, "Alright."—

l   And then, it seems, that girl arrived over there
m   and found the old lady home alone.
n   (That young man had gone hunting.)
o   It was an exceptionally pretty young girl that the old lady had come to her.
10 a   What's more, it was one known to have an extremely quiet nature.
b   She let her sit there quietly.
c   And after a while, the old lady said to her, "Are you out enjoying a walk,
granddaughter?"
d   "Yes.
e   Actually my grandfather,
f   well my grandfather *did* say to me, 'It would be a good thing if you married *that* young
man,'" she told the old lady.
g   "So that's why I've come," she told her.
h   The old lady was secretly glad that someone had come to her grandson.
i   "Well, he went hunting.
j   He'll come back this evening," she told the girl.
k   "Over where he sits, of course, on the other side, is where you'll be sitting," she told
her.
l   And it was only *then*, the story goes, that the young girl went and sat on the other side
of the lodge.
11 a   "Oh my!" that young girl thought.

b   After a while, in the early evening, someone was heard dropping a load of game outside.
c   The old lady walked out.
d   "What a pleasant surprise that my grandmother has come out.
e   My grandmother must have heard some wicked tale," he said to his grandmother.
f   The old lady lowered her voice when she told her news.
g   "Listen, grandson! See now, a young girl has come to you," she told him.
h   "So, now you'll have a wife, grandson," she told her grandson.

i e·h=po·si_pepehči·me·hi-iši|-ki·hkika·pa·či.

j "kaši=ya·pi| ni·h=išawi owi·wiya·ne,| ano·hko.

k a·kwi=ma·hi kehke·netama·nini a·mi_-'šawiwa·ne·ni owi·wiya·ne,"| e·h=ina·či
o·hkomese·hani.|

l "'šina·kwa_ki·h=wi·hpe·ma·wa=ma·hi·='na i·noki pehkote·ke," e·h=ina·či o·šisemani.‖

12 a "o·´,_i·ni_ni·h=išawi," e·h=ina·či o·hkomese·hani.

b e·h=menwite·he·či metemo·he·ha.

c "ka·ta| nasata·wi-išawihkani,"| e·h=ina·či.

d e·h=na·kwa·či metemo·he·ha,

e e·h=a·čimoha·či ihkwe·wani.

f "neta·čimwiha·wa=koči no·šisema e·h=pye·notawači.

g wi·h=pwa·wi-=ča·hi -mya·ne·netaki we·či-a·pi-a·čimohaki," e·h=ina·či o·šisemani.

h (e·h=o·šisemiči='yo=meko=ne·hi·='nini še·škesi·hani.)

i neniwa_pe·mi_-pi·tike·či,

j e·h=nahkwi-apane·nemekoči i·nini wi·h=owi·wičini.

k e·h=nana·hapiči,

l e·h=taši-mečime·nemoči ke·ko·hi wi·h=iši-kano·na·či i·nini ihkwe·wani.

m o·ni mečemo·ka e·h=we·pi-a·ya·čimoči.

n e·h=a·ya·čimoha·či i·nihi e·šk_-owi·weti·ničihi wi·h=iši-pemeneti·niči ‖ če·wi·šwi.

13 a "mani:

b kemahkwa·tesipwa," e·h=ina·či.

c ke·htena=ke·h=meko pe·hki e·h=peseta·koči če·wi·šwi.|

d e·na·či=meko na·na·kači e·h=peseta·koči.

e o·ni| pe·hkote·niki e·h=we·pi-na·katawe·nema·či wi·h=išawinikwe·ni mečemo·ka.|

f e·h=maneto·wi-='yo=meko -mečemo·kiči i·na metemo·he·ha.

g e·h=nana·hišiniči, e·h=wi·hpe·niči o·šisemani.

h kete·='nah=meko pe·hki e·h=nepa·niči če·wi·šwi.

i mahkwa·či=meko e·h=nepa·niči.

j e·h=pwa·wi-=meko ke·ko·hi -iši-wa·waneška·hi_-to·ta·ti·niči,

k na·hka e·h=pwa·wi-=meko -kakano·neti·niči.

l i·ni=meko e·h=iši-nepanepa·niči če·wi·šwi.

m e·h=kehke·nema·či=meko e·šawiniči.| *

n wi·na=ke·hi·='na oškinawe·ha, "mahkwa·či=meko," e·h=ineči, ‖

14 a e·h=pwa·wi-=meko ke·ko·hi| -to·tawa·či i·nini wi·hpe·ma·čini.

b o·ni wa·paniki ihkwe·wa e·h=na·kwa·či,|

c omešo·heki e·h=a·či.

d i·ya·h=pye·ya·či omešo·meseki,

e "e·h=ki·ši-wi·čawiwači,? ihkwe·se," e·h=ineči.

f "ehe·he," e·h=iči.†

g "i·ya·h=kohi nenepe·wowe," e·h=ina·či omešo·mesani.

____

*/či.|/: a dot was added to make the dot of the ⟨i⟩ a divider.

†/ehe·he/: ⟨.e.e.|⟩.

ⁱ He went and stood a little further away from the lodge.

^j "So tell me, what will I do if I have a wife, grandma?

^k I obviously don't know what I should do if I have a wife," he said to his grandmother.

^l "Why, you'll sleep with her tonight, obviously," she told her grandson.

12 a "Oh, I'll do that," he told his grandmother.

^b The old lady was glad.

^c "Don't be unfriendly," she told him.

^d The old lady went back in

^e and spoke to the woman.

^f "I told my grandson that you've come to him, of course.

^g It's just so he won't get angry over it that I've informed him," she told her granddaughter.

^h (For that girl was *also* her grandchild.)

ⁱ When the man walked in,

^j the one he was to marry greeted him with a smile.

^k And he took his seat,

^l hesitating to speak any words to the woman.

^m And then the old lady began speaking.

ⁿ She instructed the newlyweds in how they should each take care of the other.

13 a "Here's the thing:

^b you both have quiet natures," she said to them.

^c Now, both of them truly listened really closely to her.

^d They followed what she said to them exactly, as they listened to her.

^e And then that night the old lady set about keeping track of what they would do.

^f After all, that little old lady was an old woman with manitou powers.

^g They lay down, her grandson sharing his bed.

^h But, disappointingly, they actually both slept..

ⁱ And they slept nice-and-quietly.

^j There was no naughty behavior of any kind between them.

^k And also they didn't talk with each other.

^l Both slept on just like that.

^m And she *did* know what they did.

ⁿ And as for that young man, "quiet" was the word for him..

14 a He didn't do anything to his bedmate.

^b And the next morning the woman left,

^c going to her granddad's.

^d When she arrived over at her grandfather's,

^e she was asked, "Are you married now, girl?"

^f "Yes," she said.

^g "I did, indeed, spend the night over there," she told her grandfather.

ʰ   eˑnaˑkwiˑhiniki, "nahiˊ,‿noši·hi, natawi|-naˑkwaˑno," eˑh=inekoči omešoˑmesani.
ⁱ   eˑh=naˑkwaˑči.
ʲ   iˑyaˑh=eˑh=pyaˑči eˑnaˑkwiˑhiniki,
ᵏ   eˑh=nepeˑwoweˑči.
ˡ   šeˑški=meko naˑhka eˑh=nepaˑwaˑči.
ᵐ   eˑh=pwaˑwi-=keˑh=meko keˑkoˑhi -išiteˑheˑči| neniwa.
ⁿ   naˑhkači ihkweˑwa iˑni=meko eˑh=išawiči.
ᵒ   mahkwaˑči=meko eˑh=išiteˑheˑwaˑči.
ᵖ   waˑpaniki,‿eˑh=naˑkwaˑči ihkweˑwa.

 q   oˑni metemoˑheˑha eˑh=nanaˑtohtawaˑči oˑšisemeˑhani.
ʳ   "šiˊˊ,‿noši·he," ‖ eˑh=inaˑči.
15 a   "taˑni=ča·h=eˑšawiči, wiˑh=šeˑškesiˑhiči=keˑhi," eˑh=inaˑči oˑšisemani.
ᵇ   "kepwaˑwi-=niˑhka -nanaˑtohtawaˑwa," eˑh=inaˑči oˑhkomesani.
ᶜ   "aˑkwi=ʼh=weˑna meˑh-=keˑkoˑhi -toˑtawačini!?" eˑh=inaˑči oˑšisemani.*
ᵈ   "kaši=ča·h=wiˑh=toˑtawaki," eˑh=ikoči.
ᵉ   (eˑh=kehkeˑnemaˑči=keˑh=wiˑna| eˑh=pwaˑwi- keˑkoˑhi -toˑtaˑtiˑniči.)
ᶠ   "ʼšinaˑkwa, mani=koči| eˑšawiwaˑči weˑwiˑwetiˑčiki:
ᵍ   kehkeˑnetiˑwaki eˑšikiwaˑči.
ʰ   ihkweˑwaki onaˑpeˑmwaˑwahi kehkeˑnemeˑwaki,
ⁱ   oˑni neniwaki owiˑwaˑwahi kehkeˑnemeˑwaki eˑšikiniči.
ʲ   aˑyahpiˑhčinaˑh=meko kiˑšišiničini owiˑwaˑwahi, čiˑkakoˑteˑneˑwaki," eˑh=inaˑči oˑšisemani.
ᵏ   "ši-=ʼnoki=ʼyo=keˑhi ketanaˑčimohipena mahkwaˑči=meko ‖ wiˑh=wiˑčawiˑtiˑyaˑke,"
         eˑh=ineči mečemoˑka.
16 a   "eˑh=aˑčihaˑčimohiyani=ʼyo=keˑh=aˑpehe,
ᵇ   'ihkweˑwaki menaˑkosiwaki,' keteš=aˑpehe, eˑh=aˑyaˑčimohiyani,
ᶜ   oˑ=ʼni=naˑhka wiˑh=kehkeˑnemaki=meko eˑh=išimiyani maˑhiya‿niˑwa,"| eˑh=inekoči‿
         oˑšisemani| metemoˑheˑha.
ᵈ   "iˑni=maˑh=kiˑna‿weˑči-owiˑwiwaˑči neniwaki,
ᵉ   eˑh=metaˑteˑnetamowaˑči eˑh=maˑmayaki‿toˑtawaˑwaˑči owiˑwaˑwahi," eˑh=inaˑči.
ᶠ   "kiˑna=ʼyo=mani peˑhki=meko ketoškinaweˑhi," eˑh=inaˑči oˑšisemani.
ᵍ   "keˑnemaˑpi=ʼh=weˑna katawi-eˑyeˑhkweˑwite," eˑh=išiteˑheˑči naˑmoˑči,|
ʰ   oˑšisemani eˑh=ineˑnemaˑči.

ⁱ   oˑni peˑhkoteˑniki, "meˑmeˑčiki=meko·=ʼni," eˑh=išiteˑheˑči,
ʲ   eˑh=ineˑnemaˑči| iˑnihi weˑwiˑwetiˑhiničihi.
ᵏ   eˑh=aˑči-pwaˑwi‿nepaˑči metemoˑheˑha. ‖
17 a   waˑnatohka=meko eˑh=kehči‿nepaˑniči čeˑwiˑšwi.
ᵇ   "kaši=ʼškwe| mana išawiˑtoke weˑči|-pwaˑwi- keˑkoˑh=meko -toˑtawaˑči," išiteˑheˑči,†
ᶜ   eˑh=ineˑnemaˑči.
ᵈ   eˑh=weˑpi-mamiˑnaˑwiteˑheˑči metemoˑka.|

---

*/keˑkoˑhi toˑtaw-/ 'do something to' (also in 25*h,k*) is the polite euphemism for 'have sex with'.
†/išiteˑheˑči/: a colloquialism (of a type rare in Kiyana's writing) for /eˑh=išiteˑheˑči/.

h Early that evening her grandfather said to her, "O.K., granddaughter, it's time for you to go."

i And she left.

j She arrived over there in the early evening

k and spent the night.

l And again, all they did was sleep.

m What's more, the man thought nothing of it.

n And the woman, also, was the same way.

o Their thoughts were calm.

p The next morning the woman left.

q And then the old lady asked her grandson a question.

r "Say, grandson," she said to him.

15 a "So, how is she, as to being a virgin, specifically?" she asked her grandson.

b "Why don't you ask her?" he said to his grandmother.

c "Haven't you 'done something' to her yet?" she asked her grandson.

d "Well, what am I supposed to do to her?" he answered her.

e (But in fact, she knew that they hadn't "done something" together.)

f "Why, here's what married people do, of course:

g They know about how each other's bodies are.

h Women know about their husbands' bodies,

i and men know about their wives'.

j Every so often, after their wives are in bed, they push their skirts up," she told her grandson.

k "Gee! Remember, you've been telling us now to stay together nice-and-quietly," was the reply to the old lady.

16 a "And remember, when you're always telling me about things,

b you always say to me, 'Women smell bad,' when you explain things to me.

c And now you're also telling me to know all about my wife who was here," the old lady's grandson told her.

d "See, that's why men get married,

e because they think it pleasant when they do odd things to their wives," she told him.

f "But as it is, I'm sorry to say, *you're* a virgin young man," she told her grandson.

g "I wonder if he's about to become a berdache," she thought secretly,

h thinking about her grandson.

i And then that night she thought, "I'm sure of it,"

j thinking about the ones who were married.

k Again the old lady didn't sleep.

17 a The others both slept soundly, as if nothing was amiss.

b "What in the world could be the matter with him that he doesn't 'do something' to her," she thought,

c thinking about him.

d The old lady began giving it serious thought.

e   "me·kwe·he='škwe=meko no·šisema| nenešiwana·čiha·wa," e·h=išite·he·či.

f   e·h=we·pe·nema·či.

g   meše·='nah=meko ma·nokoni e·h=we·pi-na·katawe·nema·či e·ši-mehtose·neniwiniči,

h   ahpene·či=meko.

i   e·šišimoniči=ke·hi e·h=na·katawe·nema·či.

j   ke·keya·h=meko metemo·ka| ki·šišikini e·h=we·pi-mayo·či.

k   i·ni=meko ahpene·či| e·h=išawiči.

l   ki·šišikini=meko e·h=mayo·či.

m   na·mo·či=meko='pi e·h=taši|-mayo·či.

n   e·h=pwa·wi-=ke·h=meko nana·ši -kehke·nema·či o·šisemani ke·ko·hi
wi·h=iši-meme·satesiči. ‖

18 a   ke·keya·h=meko metemo·he·ha| e·h=we·pi-ana·hpawa·či,
o·šisemani wi·h=meme·satesiniči=meko e·h=ine·nema·či.

b   ki·ši-=meko -ana·hpawa·či, e·h=to·hki·niči o·šisemani.

c   "i·ni=yá·pi," e·h=išite·he·či metemo·he·ha.

d   e·h=kwa·škwisahoniči=či·hi.

e   "ano·hko," e·h=ikoči,

f   "a·kwi=ki·na katawi-sa·kiči·hiyanini?" e·h=ikoči=či·hi o·šisemani.

g   "nekatawi-=ča·h=-sa·kiči," e·h=ina·či.

h   e·h=ni·šiwa·či o·hkomesani,

i   e·h=ni·šo·piwa·či, e·h=sa·kiči·wa·či.

j   mečemo·ka e·h=nešiwi-maki_-ni·škiša·či.

k   o·ni neniwa nešiwi-na·hina·h=meko e·h=ahkwa·škahwe·či.

l   "ano·hko, pe·hki=ni·hka-ki·na kenešiwe·we·ša," e·h=ina·či o·hkomesani.

m   "ši·´, meči='h=we·na netaškiki!ʔ wi·h=čaka·ška·hiki!ʔ" e·h=ina·či.

n   "ano·hko, ‖ ta·ni=ya·pi wi·h=išawiya·ni meme·satesiya·ne," e·h=ina·či o·hkomesani.

19 a   "we·ta='hkwe·´,| noši·he.

b   nahi´, ki·h=wi·tamo·ne.

c   kete=ke·hi kekekye·pa·čihene," e·h=ina·či.

d   "o·´, i·ni=ma·h=ki·na ka·hkami wi·h=išimiyanehe," e·h=ikoči| o·šisemani.

e   "nahi´, po·si=meko pepehči·me·hi iha·ta·we," e·h=ina·či o·šiseme·hani.

f   meše=meko na·hina·hi e·h=a·wa·či.

g   "nahi´, a·kwi=ke·hi| nahi-a·čimokini," e·h=ina·či o·šisemani.

h   "mani=koči wi·h=išawiyani," e·h=ina·či.

i   "ayo·hi oči·kwanapino," e·h=ina·či,

j   e·h=oči·kwanapiniči.

k   e·na·samapiniči e·h=mawi-šowika·šiki.

l   "nahi´, či·kakonano·='nahi neko·te·hani," e·h=išiwe·či.

m   oko·te·hani e·h=či·kakonamawoči metemo·ka.

n   "nahi´, ketenano·='nahi ki·nakayi," e·h=išiwe·či. ‖

20 a   e·h=ketenaminiči!ʔ

b   "ki·h=me·meta·ča·hi=ké·hi," e·h=ina·či.

e   "Oh, I probably messed up my grandson," she thought,

f   as she set to pondering about him.

g   For a good many days she undertook to keep an eye on how he conducted his life,

h   all the time.

i   She paid careful attention to what his voice was like, for example.

j   Eventually, the old lady got to the point of weeping after she was in bed every night.

k   It was always the same thing with her.

l   After she was in bed every night, she wept.

m   And she wept deep in her heart, to hear the tale.

n   And here, she never knew that her grandson would get in any way randy.

18 a   Eventually the old lady got to the point of invoking her dream power,

b   and with her mind she willed her grandson to get randy.

c   After she had invoked her dream power, her grandson woke up.

d   "Here we go!" thought the old lady.

e   And suddenly here he was, leaping down from the platform.

f   "Grandma," he said to her.

g   And here was her grandson saying to her, "Don't *you* have to go pee a little?"

h   And she said to him, "Well, I do have to go pee,"

i   He and his grandmother went together,

j   and squatted down together, and peed.

k   The old lady let out a terrifically wide stream.

l   And the man let fly a terrifically great distance.

m   "Grandma, you really make a terrible, great noise when *you* pee," he said to his grandmother.

n   "Gosh! Well, I'm obviously not a young thing for it to be flowing small!" she told him.

o   "Grandmother, now tell me, how will I be when I'm randy," he said to his grandmother.

19 a   "Oh my goodness, grandson.

b   Alright, I'll tell you.

c   But it's on you that I make a fool of you," she told him.

d   "Oh, see, that's what I was going to say to you right from the start," her grandson told her.

e   "Alright, let's go a little further away from the lodge," she told her young grandson.

f   They went some little distance.

g   "Alright, another thing, it's never talked about," she told her grandson.

h   "This is what you must do," she told him.

i   "Kneel down here," she told him,

j   and he knelt down.

k   She went and lay down in front of where he knelt with her legs spread.

l   "Alright, now push up my skirts," she said.

m   The old lady's skirts were pushed up.

n   "Alright, now pull out your prick," she said.

20 a   And he didn't pull it out!

b   "You're gonna have *fun*!" she told him.

c   "we·kone·h=ya·pi·='ni ki·nakayi," e·h=iniči.

d   "ši·´,‿mani='škwe.

e   ni·na=ta·ni´| ki·h=ketaho·to·ne," e·h=ina·či.

f   e·h=ketenamawa·či.

g   "ši·´, mahkwa·či=ni·hka," e·h=ikoči.|

h   "'šina·kwa='škwe, pena=ki·na| mahkwa·či," e·h=ina·či.

i   "keta·čimohene=ma·hi," e·h=ina·či.

j   ke·taho·to·či,|

k   ota·hi·hemeki e·h=sahkenaki.|

l   kapo·twe e·h=aniška·niki,

m   e·h=ki·ša·koči-=meko| -maka·hkwateniki.

n   ki·ši-=meko -wi·šiki-nemate·niki,

o   e·h=pi·tenaki.

p   "nahi´,| ašita·hkwinawi·no," e·h=ina·či o·šisemani,

q   e·h=ašita·hkwinawi·niči.

r   e·h=a·čimoha·či wi·h=išisahoniči.

s   kapo·twe='pi,| "nekatawi-‿šeki," e·h=iniči.|

t   "ši·´,‿meše·='nah=ma·h=meko i·nah=ki·h=šeki," e·h=ina·či| metemo·he·ha. ‖

21 a   kenwe·ši=meko e·h=taši-me·meta·ča·hiniči.

b   metemo·ka e·h=ki·ša·koči-=meko apina -no·no·škamataki,

c   e·h=aški-paši·škičima·či.

d   "i·ni=ma·h=ki·na wi·h=to·tawači," e·h=ina·či.

e   "ki·h=me·meme·meta·ča·hipwa=ke·hi," e·h=ina·či.

f   e·h=na·kwa·wa·či.[*]

g   i·ya·h=meko no·make·-‿pya·wa·či,

h   e·h=we·pi-meme·sačiha·či owi·wani.

i   še·škesi·ha e·h=pwa·wi-=meko -kehke·netaki wi·h=išišinokwe·ni.

j   nano·škwe=meko e·h=išišiki.

k   mani e·ši-nana·hakonamoweči, e·h=we·pi-pye·mipye·misahoči.

l   ke·keya·h=meko| e·h=kaški-mahkwa·čišiki.|

m   masa·či=meko e·h=kaški-‿pe·hki -maneči.

n   na·htasenwi i·ni e·šawiči, e·h=we·pi-pi·nepi·nešihto·či ‖ i·ni wi·h=išawiči.

22 a   e·h=ki·ša·koči-=meko -mata·kwe·netamowa·či če·wi·šwi.

b   ahpene·či=meko i·ni| e·h=išawiwa·či i·niki| owi·weti·he·haki.

c   "me·mečine·h=pena´," e·h=iči='p=a·pehe ihkwe·wa.

d   i·niya=ke·hi·='pi metemo·he·ha mehteno·h=meko e·h=kohkahkye·neči e·h=kaški-kohkišiki.

e   e·h=kokwi-=meko -metemo·he·hiči,

f   e·h=kokwi-=meko -nešiwana·tesiči.

g   kapo·twe=meko='pi e·h=nepo·hiči.

h   e·h=kwe·hta·nite·he·či we·yo·hkomese·hita ki·ši-nepo·hiniči.

---

[*] /kwa·/: ⟨kwe⟩.

^c "But tell me, what's the yaprik?" he said.
^d "Oh, here!
^e Why don't I haul it out for you myself," she told him,
^f pulling it out for him.
^g "Say, take it easy!" he told her.
^h "Well now, *you* should take it easy," she told him.
ⁱ "I mean, I explained to you," she told him.
^j After hauling it out,
^k she put the tip up to her thing.
^l Soon, there it was swelling up,
^m and it was extremely large.
ⁿ And after it was standing up firmly,
^o she put it inside.
^p "Alright, slide up," she told her grandson.
^q And he slid up.
^r She explained to him about shoving himself.
^s And suddenly he said, "I have to pee."
^t "Well, you must go ahead and pee in there, of course," the old lady told him.
21 a And he was a long time having fun.
^b The old lady even experienced extremely delicate feelings,
^c as she peeled the lad back for the first time.
^d "See, that's what you must do to her," she told him.
^e "And you two will have fun and more fun!" she told him.
^f And they went back.

^g After they quickly got back,
^h he began to get randy towards his wife.
ⁱ The girl didn't know which way to lie.
^j She lay the way she guessed was it.
^k As soon as her skirts were arranged, she began squirming.
^l Before long she was able to lie calmly.
^m And she could, with difficulty, be properly fucked.
ⁿ After doing that several times, she began taking the lead to do it.
22 a They both enjoyed it immensely.
^b Always when the young couple did that,
^c the say the woman would say, "Just one more time!"

^d And the next thing was that the old lady of the tale could only roll over when she was
helped to turn over.
^e She became old abruptly.
^f Abruptly she became completely decrepit.
^g And soon, the tale goes, she died.
^h The grandson was heartbroken after she died.

i   "nemešo·heki=pena´ mawi-ki·wita·ta·we," e·h=išiwe·či ihkwe·wa.

j   "hawo·ʔ," e·h=ineči.

k   e·h=mawi-naha·kapiči| neniwa.

l   pe·hki=ʼyo=ke·h=meko=ʼpi e·h=kehke·netaki na·tawino·ni i·na| pašito·he·ha.

m ki·ši-wi·čiha·či ‖ i·nihi owi·weti·he·hahi, e·h=we·pi-a·ya·čimoha·či| i·ni e·šikeniki na·tawino·ni.

23 a e·h=wi·ke·či-=meko -mahkwa·či-wi·tawi·tamawa·či o·šisemahi.

b (e·h=o·šisema·ko·ma·či=ʼyo i·nini neniwani.)

c   e·h=mi·ša·te·nemoči na·hina·hi we·pi-ša·ši·ša·niči onekwanani pašito·he·ha.

d   meše·=ʼnah=kapo·twe e·h=meša·pama·či o·šiseme·hani e·h=nepa·niči.

e e·h=meškekwa·meniči o·šisemani.

f e·h=ki·ša·koči-=meko -mama·kipwa·me·niči,*

g e·h=mešihketene·niči.

h (e·h=ašenoniči=ke·hi we·wi·winičini,

i e·h=neši|-nepa·niči.)

j aškiča·h=wi·na·=ʼpi e·h=pasi-=meko -wa·pama·či.

k ke·keya·h=meko e·h=wa·pama·či| kehčine·he.

l   "ohohwa·´," e·h=išite·he·či.

m ke·keya·h=koči·h=meko=ʼpi ‖ e·h=mawi-=meko -ki·mena·či o·šisemani,

24 a wa·natohka=meko e·h=ka·škiko·hiniči.

b ke·keya·h=meko e·h=koči-_pe·hki -šowika·na·či.

c wa·natohka=meko e·h=kehči|-ka·škiko·hiniči o·šisemani.

d   ki·ši-=meko -menwišima·či,

e e·h=koči-memekwisaha·či.

f wa·natohka=meko e·h=kehči_-nepa·niči.

g   kapo·twe=meko e·h=pemi-nana·heškawa·či.

h   o·ni·=ʼna ihkwe·wa e·h=a·mano·wa·hpawa·či.

i e·h=ki·ša·koči-=meko -ma·mata·kwi-a·mano·wa·hpawa·či.

j   i·na·ka=ke·h=pašito·ha ke·keya·h=meko| pe·hki e·h=po·ni-kena·sehkawa·či.

k ki·še·wi·či, aka·mete·ki e·h=mawi-nana·hišiki.

l   kwi·yena=meko ki·ši-menwišiki, e·h=to·hki·niči.

m e·h=kano·na·či,

n "we·ne·h=ča·hi·=ʼniya," ‖ e·h=ina·či, wa·natohka=meko.

25 a "nemešo, a·kwi-ma·h=meko paši-kehke·nemakini,"| e·h=ina·či.

b "ta·ni·ča·h=nehki ayo·h=e·wiči," e·h=ina·či.

c   "našawe·me·h=ča·h=meko pi·tike·wa," e·h=ina·či.

d   "e·h=taši-wa·wane·netamo·hka·noyani.

e kekehke·nema·petoke=ke·h=wi·na.

f aše=meko ketenowe·petoke," e·h=ina·či o·šisemani.

g   "a·kwi, meškišimi·ke·ni=ma·hi," e·h=iniči.

h   "me·kwe·h=ke·hi ke·ko·h=meko to·tawikwe·ni," e·h=ina·či omešo·hani.

---

*⟨pwa⟩ changed from incomplete ⟨pwe⟩.

i   "Let's go live at my grandfather's, why not," the woman said.

j   "Alright," was the response.

k   And the man went to be one living with in-laws.

l   Now they say that old man really knew medicine.

m   And after he had that young couple living with him, he began telling them about the nature of that medicine.

23 a He would carefully tell his grandchildren about it quietly.

b   (For the man was a relative he called grandchild.)

c   The old man was delighted when his son-in-law began hunting.

d   One day he caught sight of his young granddaughter's snatch as she slept.

e   His granddaughter was sleeping with her private area exposed.

f   Her thighs were extremely large,

g   and she had big twat.

h   (Now, the husband was away,

i   and she was sleeping alone.)

j   They say he just shot a quick glance at her at first.

k   And before long he looked at her up close.

l   "Mercy me!" he thought.

m   And before long, they say, even though he went over and felt his granddaughter's pussy,

24 a she snored unperturbed.

b   And before long he tried spreading her legs fully apart.

c   His granddaughter snored loudly, unperturbed.

d   After putting her in a good position,

e   he tried shaking her.

f   Unperturbed, she slept soundly.

g   Then at some point he went on to get her set under him.

h   And the woman, for her part, was having an erotic dream.

i   She was having a most unusual and delightful erotic dream.

j   That old man, meanwhile, eventually stopped going slow with her and got on with it properly.

k   After he was finished, he went and lay down on the other side of the lodge.

l   Just after he got settled, she woke up.

m   And he spoke to her,

n   asking her, quite casually, "So, who was that?"

25 a   "Why, granddad, you understand, I have no idea who," she told him.

b   "So, how long was he here?" she asked him.

c   "Well, he came in quite a while ago," he told her.

d   "Here you're acting like you don't know.

e   Although you *must* know who it was.

f   You must just be fibbing," he told his granddaughter.

g   "No, listen, I was spread open, apparently," she said.

h   "And I think he had sex with me," she told her grandfather.

ⁱ   e·h=neškima·či o·šisemani.

^j mani=wi·na: e·h=me·nešite·he·či na·mo·či.|

^k   "ya·´,_ we·nahi´, ke·ko·h=meko_to·tawi·ke·ni," e·h=ina·či=meko omešo·hani.

^l   "mehto·či=ni·hka a·kwi nepa·yanini," e·h=ina·či.

^m   "a·kwi, nemešo.

ⁿ a·kwi=koh=meko paši-kehke·nemakini," ‖ e·h=ina·či omešo·hani.|

^{26 a} wa·paniki, "noši·he," e·h=ina·či,

^b "a·kwi=ma·hi ke·ko·hi wi·h=išawiya·nini," e·h=ina·či.

^c "mo·hči=’še=ke·hi a·čimoya·ne, ki·na=meko ki·h=me·me·nešimeko·pi,"| e·h=ina·či
o·šisemani.*

^d "aše=ma·hi ketešikiha·sopwa_i·ni wi·h=išahišawiye·kwe," e·h=ina·či.

^e "ni·na=’yo=wi·na a·kwi=meko| ke·ko·hi wi·h=inena·nini," e·h=ina·či o·šisemani.|

^f "aše=koh=a·pehe e·h=mya·na·totama·ni asa·mi_-taswi| i·ni wi·h=to·ta·ke·wa·či neniwaki.

^g i·ni=kohi we·či_-mya·ne·netama·ni," e·h=iniči.

^h "aše=koh=mek=a·pehe ketešihišimene.

ⁱ mahkwa·či wi·h=awihawiyani ine·nemena·ni we·či- i·ni -inehinena·ni," e·h=ina·či.†

^j "na·hka kemenwe·nemeko·toke=meko, we·či·=meko ‖ i·ni -to·to·hki,"_e·h=ina·či.‡

^{27 a} "te·pwe·wane·ni," e·h=ina·či.

^b "meči=’h=we·=ke·hi wa·wosa·hi pahkwe·honesa!?, ke·htena| i·ni e·to·to·nokwe·ni!?"
e·h=ina·či.

^c "ši·´, ke·htena=ma·h=meko mašikwe·ni e·h=nepa·ya·ni," e·h=ina·či omešo·mesani.

^d "wa·wosa·h=meko kekehč_-a·nwe·hto·ne ni·na,"| e·h=ina·či.§

^e "ke·htena=koh=meko.

^f anwa·či·yane=’hkwe, pye·či-=meko meše·=’nahi -kotenihkapa.

^g e·h=a·nwe·htawiyani=ma·h we·či- meše·=’nahi i·ni -inena·ni," e·h=ina·či omešo·mesani.

^h "wa·wosa·h=ča·h| ša·kwe·nemohka·ha, i·ni išiyane," e·h=ina·či o·šisemani.

ⁱ "ši·´,_nah=pena´,_pya·no,"_e·h=ikoči.

^j e·h=pemi_-pasekwi·či neniwa.

^k "i·ni=yá·pi," e·h=išite·he·či,

^l i·tepi e·h=a·či.

^m "’šina·kwa," e·h=iči_pašito·ha,

ⁿ e·h=anemi|-a·nemi·ne·moči. ‖

^{28 a} "ši·´,_wa·wosa·h=we·=wi·na=ke·h=ki·na ke·ko·hi to·tawihkapa!?"_e·h=ineči.

^b e·h=anwehanwe·we·tepe·hoči paškwahikani.

^c apina=’pi e·h=papo·hkwiseto·niči meškwa·wa·hkwi-paškwahikani.

^d natawa·či=meko pašito·ha e·h=nowa·moči.

^e nano·škwe=meko e·h=a·či.

^f e·h=me·nešite·he·či.

---

*/o·šisemani/: ⟨ma⟩ changed from ⟨me⟩.

†/ine·nemena·ni/: AK ⟨.ineneinenani.⟩; for /e·h=ine·nemena·ni/.

‡/e·h=/: ⟨e⟩ over undotted ⟨i⟩(?).

§/kekehč_-a·nwe·hto·ne/: ⟨e⟩ in ⟨nwe⟩ is over two strokes.

i   He chided his granddaughter.

j   But the thing is: inside he was ashamed.

k   "Oh my! Listen, someone had sex with me," she told her grandfather.

l   "It seemed like you weren't asleep," he said to her.

m   "No, granddad.

n   I do *not* have any idea who he was," she told her grandfather.

26 a   The next morning, "Granddaughter," he said to her.

b   "I won't do anything, obviously," he told her.

c   "But even if I tell anyway, it's *you* who'll be embarrassed by it," he told his granddaughter.

d   "I mean, you women are just made to be doing that," he told her.

e   "But in this case *I* certainly won't say anything about you," he told his granddaughter.

f   "I just always say it's truly bad for men to do that with someone too much.

g   That's why I definitely think it's bad," he said.

h   "I just always tell you that, certainly.

i   I say that to you because I want you to stay nice-and-quietly," he told her.

j   "And he must like you, why he did that to you," he told her.

27 a   "Assuming you're telling the truth," he said to her.

b   "After all, he'd hardly chop a piece off you, if he really did do that to you," he told her.

c   "Well, he truly must have fucked me while I slept, obviously," she told her grandfather.

d   "As you might guess, *I* really don't believe you," he told her.

e   "It's definitely *true*.

f   If you're agreeable, you could go ahead and come right here and feel me.

g   Understand, it's because you don't believe me that I'm going so far as to tell you that," she said to her grandfather.

h   "Well, I'd hardly refuse, if you ask me to do that," he said to his granddaughter.

i   "Well, come on! Come!" she told him.

j   The man got right to his feet.

k   "Here we go," he thought,

l   going to her.

m   "Well now," the old man said,

n   breathing heavily as he went.

28 a   "Now, who would have thought that, after all, it would be *you* that had sex with me!" were the words he heard.

b   And he was cracked repeatedly on the head with a beaming tool.

c   She even had the cedar beaming tool break into pieces, to hear the tale.

d   The old man lost no time fleeing out the door.

e   He went he knew not where.

f   He was ashamed.

g   ke·htena=ke·h=meko i·ni e·h=išawiči we·či-=meko_-po·si|-ki·ša·kota·moči.

h   wa·paniki we·wi·wita e·h=pya·či.
i   "ta·tepi=ča·h=a·piha·yani," e·h=ikoči owi·wani.
j   "o·´, newa·pawa·pama·waki wi·če·noti·čiki.
k   mešihke·ha ma·mahkese·hiwa wa·pitena·hkwani.
l   a·kwi=ča·h=nana·ši aniheti·wa·čini," e·h=ina·či.
m   "nehkanitepehkwe=meko nemata·kwa·pama·waki,"| e·h=ina·či owi·wani.

n   (i·nina·h=ke·h=meko='pi ‖ mešihke·ha e·h=kašketiči,[*]
29 a   masa·či=meko e·h=kaški_-mi·si·či,
b   kenwe·ši=meko='pi a·nwi-mi·si·wa| mešihke·ha.)

c   ki·ši-nepa·či,| na·hina·h=meko to·hki·či, e·h=a·čimohekoči owi·wani.
d   "nahi´, nena·pe·me, e·šawiya·ni ki·h=a·čimohene.
e   ki·h=pešikwi-=meko -wi·tamo·ne,
f   wi·h=iši-=na·hka=ki·na -te·pwe·htawiwane·ni," e·h=ina·či ona·pe·mani.
g   "tepehkoki e·h=nepa·ya·ni meškišinowa·ne·ni," e·h=ina·či.
h   "keye·hapa=ke·hi ke·htena=meko me·šikehe.
i   maši·ke·ni='yo| e·h=nepa·ya·ni," e·h=ina·či ona·pe·mani.
j   "nemešo·ha=ke·hi·='niya.
k   tepehkoki=meko nekehči_-nesa·wa," e·h=ina·či.
l   "nemya·ši-=meko -ahtena·wa," e·h=ina·či.
m   "mani we·či-ahtenaki:
n   ateškawi=meko netaši|-išimekwa," e·h=ina·či. ‖
30 a   "awita=ke·hi·='na aše=meko išimenesa e·nenokwe·ni.
b   ke·htena=meko te·pwe·hi·toke e·šimenokwe·ni."
c   "'šina·kwa, mani=ča·h=e·šiči.
d   ke·htena=koči=meko=wi·na newi·tama·kwa,
e   neta·čimohekwa.
f   'we·ne·ha=ča·hi·='nahi we·či_-nowi·ta,' netekwa,
g   e·h=nana·tohtawiči.[†]
h   'a·kwi=ča·h=kehke·nemakini,' netena·wa.
i   i·ni=meko a·čipanakiči e·h=we·pi-išimiči.
j   ke·keya·h=meko, 'a·nwe·htawiwane·ni=koči=wi·na,
pye·či-=meko meše·='nahi -kotenihkapa,'_e·h=inaki.
k   i·ni=ča·hi e·h=taši-wa·waneška·he·nemaki," e·h=ina·či.
l   "kete·='nah=meko ayo·hi pana·či_-ne·mowa," e·h=iniči owi·wani.
m   "ayo·h=meko pye·či-pana·či|-ne·moči, e·h=we·patahwaki.
n   nepaškwahikani nahmeko netayohayo·tena·wa," ‖ e·h=ina·či ona·pe·mani.

---

[*]/=meko/: ⟨neko⟩.

[†]/e·h=nana·tohtawiči/ 'asking me' (accepted by EK): AK ⟨enanatotawaki⟩ 'I asked him'.

g　　　And it was because he really had done that that he ran off at full tilt.

h　　　The next morning the husband came back.
i　"Where have you been?" his wife asked him.
j　　"Oh, I was watching the players.
k　Turtle played the moccasin game with Whooping Crane.
l　Well, they never defeated each other," he told her.
m　"I enjoyed watching them all night long," he told his wife.

n　　　(Now, at that time Turtle was constipated.
29 a　He could barely ease himself.
b　For a long time Turtle was unable to take a crap.)

c　　　After he had slept, when he first woke up, his wife told him what happened.
d　　"Listen, my husband, I'll tell you what happened to me.
e　I'm going to tell you straight out,
f　and in a way that *you* must believe me," she told her husband.
g　　"Last night as I slept I must have had my legs spread apart," she told him.
h　　"And I later realized that I had actually been fucked.
i　I mean, I was fucked as I slept," she told her husband.
j　　"What's more, my grandfather was the one.
k　Last night, in fact, I beat him severely," she told him.
l　　"I pretty much have to blame him," she told him.
m　"Here's why I blame him:
n　He was giving me all kinds of explanations," she told him.
30 a　　"Now, he wouldn't lie to you in whatever he said to you.
b　He must have really pretty much told the truth, whatever he told you."
c　　"Well, so here's what he said to me.
d　You know, he told me *himself*.
e　He informed me.
f　'So, who was there and went out?' he said to me,
g　asking me.
h　'Well, I don't know who it was,' I told him.
i　Right away he started saying all kinds of things to me.
j　Finally I said to him, 'But you know, if you don't believe me, you're free to come and feel me.'
k　So, that's when I knew he was being wicked," she told him.
l　　"Here a change came over him and he was struggling to breathe," his wife said.
m　　"When he came right *here* struggling to breathe, I thrashed him.
n　Then and there I used my beaming tool on him a few times," she told her husband.

31 a　　“i·ni=ča·h=meko e·h=taši-nešiwana·te·nemaki,[*]

b　　e·h=pye·či- apina -neneki_ne·moči.

c　　‘meše·=’nah=ke·h=ye·toke i·ni=mana e·to·tawiči,’ e·šite·he·ya·ni=meko, e·h=we·patahwaki.

d　　nenano·či-=meko -ča·ki-pekihkiseto i·niye meškwa·wa·hkwi|-paškwahikani,” e·h=iči.

e　　“pe·hki=ni·hka=meko ma·mahka·či!? kwe·htakwe·hta·natahwa·wate·ni!? kemešo·mesena·na!?” e·h=ina·či owi·wani.

f　　“a·kwi menwikekini i·ni ke·htena e·to·tawa·wate·ni,” e·h=ina·či.

g　　“a·kwi=ye·toke=meko nenehke·netamanehe e·ši-pemenehki.|

h　　kotake·hiyanehe=’yo=wi·na,| e·ši-=meko na·na·kači| -pye·či_’ši_pemenenokwe·ni wa·patakapa._

i　　‘nemenwi-to·ta·kwa nemešo·mesa,’_kesi=’y=a·pehe,” e·h=ina·či. ‖

32 a　　“na·hka ke·htena=meko keki·ša·koči-še·škesi·he·hi| e·ški_wi·čawi·ti·yakwe.

b　　wa·waneška·hite, awita| i·ni paši-iši-še·škesi·hihkapa,” e·h=ina·či owi·wani.

c　　“mehto·či=meko kehči|-pešekwa·ha išikihkapa ayo·nina·hi·=’noki,” e·h=ina·či.

d　　“i·ni a·mi_’šite·he·yanehe, nenehke·nematehe kemešo·mesena·na,” e·h=ina·či.

e　　“a·kwi=ni·na i·na| i·ni ine·nemakini,” e·h=ina·či.

f　　“wi·ša·wi=mata| mešihke·hi·toke.

g　　mešihke·ha| pe·hki=meko wi·saki-kenwe·ši a·pi-sa·kiči·wa,”| e·h=iči.

h　　“kašketiwa, ina·čimowa,” e·h=iči.

i　　“masa·či=meko_kaški|-mi·si·wa,” e·h=iči.

j　　“me·kwe·h=ča·h=meko mešihke·hi·toke i·na me·nenokwe·na.

k　　i·na=wi·na kemešo·mesa awita| i·ni kaški-‖to·to·nesa,” e·h=ina·či.

33 a　　“aše=meko kemešo·hena·na| kekehči_nese·hipetoke.

b　　i·na=ke·h=wi·na me·nwi_ki·šikenehka.

c　　we·či-mehtose·neniwiyani mehto·či e·h=menwi-ašamehki.

d　　ayo·nina·hi·=’nahi mehto·či kepye·či-očisaha·wa kemešo·mesena·na,” e·h=ina·či| owi·wani.

e　　“wi·h=menwi-=ke·h=meko=wi·na=’yo·we -to·tawatehe kemešo·mesena·na,” e·h=ina·či_owi·wani.

f　　kete·=’nahi e·h=mayo·mekoči ihkwe·wa.

g　　e·h=mya·šinawe·mekoči ona·pe·mani ihkwe·wa.

h　　“nahi´, po·nwe·kesino=ni·hka,” e·h=iko·či.

i　　(meči=’h=we·na ke·ko·hi owiye·hani to·ta·kwa!?)

j　　“ki·na=meko mehto·či e·h=ahtenači we·či- i·tepi nano·škwe_-iha·či e·ya·kwe·ni kemešo·hena·na,” e·h=iči neniwa.|

k　　“kemya·šitana·wa.” ‖

34 a　　e·h=otahama·či=meko i·nini pašito·he·hani neniwa.[†]

b　　i·ni=ča·hi=’pi_meše=na·hina·hi| e·h=mawi_po·ni·hiwa·či i·niki owi·weti·he·haki.|

c　　omešo·hwa·wani e·h=akiha·wa·či kete·=’nah.

d　　kete·=’nah=meko=’pi e·h=a·hpetwe·kesiči ihkwe·wa.

---

[*]/na·/: ⟨ne⟩.

[†]/pašito·he·hani/: AK ⟨.pašitoea.⟩.

31 a   "So, there was where I had a bad feeling about him,

b   when he even came with quivering breath.

c   And when I thought, 'I guess maybe that's what *he* did to me,' I thrashed him.

d   I kept at it till I had that cedar beaming tool all in pieces," she said.

e   "Golly! It was *really* not necessary for you to give our grandfather such a severe beating," he told his wife.

f   "It's not good if you really did that to him," he told her.

g   "I guess you didn't think about how he took care of you.

h   If you'd been someone *else*, you'd have considered how he brought you up exactly the right way all through the years.

i   As you always say, 'My grandfather treated me well,' " he told her.

32 a   "And it was truly the case that you were a complete virgin when we were first married.

b   If he's wicked, you wouldn't at all have been a virgin like that," he told his wife.

c   "You'd have an outfit like an old divorcée now," he told her.

d   "That's what you'd have realized, if you'd thought about our grandfather," he told her.

e   "*I* don't think *he* did that," he told her.

f   "It's likely that it was rather Turtle.

g   Turtle has been really straining to ease himself for a painfully long time," he said.

h   "He's reported to be constipated," he said.

i   "He's barely able to take a crap," he said.

j   "So, I think Turtle must be the one who fucked you.

k   But that grandfather of yours wouldn't have been able to do that to you," he told her.

33 a   "It seems you beat up our poor old grandfather for no reason.

b   Even though he was the one who raised you nicely.

c   The reason you have life, as it were, is because he fed you well.

d   Now with that, it's as if you came and threw our grandfather out," he told his wife.

e   "And here, you were *supposed* to have treated our grandfather nicely," he told his wife.

f   The woman's thinking changed, and his words made her cry.

g   The woman was made to feel bad because of what her husband said.

h   "Alright, stop crying," he told her.

i   (Nobody *"did something"* to her! Don't be ridiculous!)

j   "It's like you blamed our grandfather for not going the right way to where he was going," the man said.

k   "You treated him ill."

34 a   The man really stood up for the old man.

b   So then that young married couple went and camped some distance away.

c   Their fortunes had changed with the loss of their grandfather.

d   And the woman had changed and wept all the time.

^e   e·h=ma·ne·wa·či ne·tone·hwa·čiki i·nini| pašito·he·hani.*

^f   meše·=ʼnah=meko| kenwe·ši e·h=pemi_natone·hwa·či.

^g   e·h=natomeči pe·seše·hiwa·ta,†

^h   e·h=peseše·či.

ⁱ   e·h=pwa·wi-=meko nekotahi| -kehke·nema·či e·ya·nikwe·ni.

^j   ke·keya·h=meko wa·pitena·hkwa e·h=natomeči wi·h=te·pa·piči,

^k   e·h=te·pa·piči.

^l   "o·´,_i·ya·ma·h=ča·hi ki·wa·kwasowa," e·h=iči.

^m   e·h=anohka·neči ateška·ha,

ⁿ   e·h=na·kwa·či.

^o   ke·htena=či·hi ayo·hi e·h=ki·wa·kwaso·hiniči.

^p   e·h=mayo·wa·či.

^q   e·h=anohka·neči ni·šwi,

^r   masakahkwa, mo·na·ne·ha. ‖ ‡

35 a   i·ni e·h=iši_ni·šiwa·či.

^b   masakahkwa, mo·na·ne·hani e·h=anohka·neči.

^c   i·ya·h=ke·h=meko e·h=apiniči e·h=mawi_taši_pi·tahwa·wa·či.|

^d   o·ni·=ʼniki=ʼpi pe·hki=meko e·h=nešike·hiwa·či owi·weti·he·haki.

^e   kapo·twe·=ʼpi wi·čike·ma·wa·čihi e·h=a·mi·heti·niči,

^f   o·ni wi·nwa·wa i·nah=meko a·ye·niwe| e·h=owi·ke·hiwa·či.

^g   "nahi´,| metemo, na·hina·h=meko we·ni·ča·nesiwakwe·ni, i·ni wi·h=a·mi·yakwe,"
     e·h=ina·či owi·wani.

^h   "pwa·wi-=ke·h=meko nana·ši -oni·ča·nesiyakwe, ayo·h=meko a·ye·niwe
     ki·h=owihowi·ke·hipena," e·h=ina·či owi·we·hani.

ⁱ   "anwa·či·yane·=ʼh=we·na.

^j   ša·kwe·nemoyane=ke·hi, meše·=ʼnah=meko ki·h=na·kwa.

^k   e·h=awiwa·či| i·niye·ka iši_na·kwa·hkapa," e·h=ina·či‖ owi·wani.

36 a   "keki·ši-=ma·hi_a·čimo wi·h=išawiyakwe,"| e·h=ikoči.

^b   "a·kwi wi·h=kaški|-na·kwa·ya·nini."

^c   "o·´,_kemenwawi," e·h=ina·či ihkwe·wani,| owi·we·hani.§

^d   wi·seniwa·čini=ʼpi mehtose·neniwaki,| e·h=nešiwi-=meko -meškowa·naketone·piwa·či.

^e   kekaški=meko e·h=mi·čiwa·či ke·ko·hi,

^f   šewe·na·=ʼpi| a·kwi nahi-mya·neška·kwiwa·čini ke·ko·hi._

^g   meše=meko·=ʼnahi e·h=mi·čiwa·či=meko.

^h   o·ni ni·šwa·pitaki e·taswi_pepo·niki, ača·hmeko ihkwe·wa| e·h=aški-ačihkwi·hiči.

ⁱ   meše·=ʼnah=meko meta·swawahi·me e·h=pemi_ačihkwiči.

---

*/pa/: ⟨|pi⟩.

†/pe·seše·hiwa·ta/ 'one who makes people listen': AK ⟨pesešiiwata⟩.

‡/mo·/: AK ⟨|ma⟩.

§/e·h=ina·či/: AK ⟨.eineči.⟩.

e   There were many who searched for the old man.

f   For a long time they kept on searching for him.

g   A clairvoyant was asked,

h   and he listened.

i   He couldn't tell anything about where he had gone.

j   Eventually Whooping Crane was asked to look clairvoyantly.

k   And he saw him clairvoyantly.

l   "Oh, well, he's lying around dead over yonder," he said.

m   Kingfisher was sent,

n   and he left.

o   Sure enough, there he found him, lying there dead.

p   They wept.

q   And two were sent,

r   Badger and Woodchuck.

35 a   It was just the two of them.

b   Badger and Woodchuck were sent.

c   And they went and buried him right where he lay.

d   And then, the story goes, that young married couple lived all by themselves.

e   And at some point the ones they were camping with moved away.

f   And they then continued living in that same place by themselves.

g   "Alright, Wife, whenever we have a child, we'll move," he told his wife.

h   "What's more, if we never have a child, we'll keep living right here in the same place,"
he told his young wife.

i   "I mean, if you're willing.

j   Now if you're *not* willing, you're free to leave.

k   You could go away to where those others are," he told his wife.

36 a   "You've said what we shall do, obviously," she told him.

b   "Nothing will make me leave."

c   "Ah, you're doing the right thing," he told the woman, his young wife.

d   It's said that, when people ate, they sat with horribly bloody mouths.

e   They ate things raw.

f   But it's said that things never disagreed with them.

g   They went right ahead and ate them.

h   Only after twenty years did the woman become pregnant for the first time.

i   And her pregnancy lasted for a full ten years.

j kwi·yena=meko neswa·pitaki taswawahi·me nehki pe·m‗owi·weti·wa·či, e·h=no·še·či ihkwe·wa.

k saka·ki=meko e·h=kaški-‖no·še·či.

37 a (i·ni=’yo=ke·h=meko e·h=iši‗ni·ši·hiwa·či.)

b e·h=no·še·ha·či nano·škwe‖owi·wani.

c e·h=pwa·wi-=meko -kehke·netamowa·či‖ wi·h=išawikwe·hiki.

d saka·ki=meko e·h=nahi-mehtose·neniwiči ihkwe·wa.

e kwi·yese·he·hani=’pi e·h=oni·ča·nese·hiwa·či.

f e·h=čaki-kwi·yese·he·hiniči.

g kapo·twe e·h=pya·niči metemo·he·hani.

h e·h=a·čimoheči wi·h=to·tawa·wa·či‖ i·nini apeno·he·hani.

i “ki·h=ašihto‗tehkina·kani wi·h=tehkineči,” e·h=ineči.

j “ka·hka·we·himiši‗ki·h=pahkwe·ha,” e·h=ineči.

k “i·nini‖ pe·hki=meko me·menwa·keške·wani na·wi·kwe·ho·nani.

l e·h=ašihto·wa·či‖ neniwaki a·tanasite·piso·nani,” e·h=ineči‖ neniwa._*

m e·h=taši-=meko‖ -kekye·hkimekoči i·nini metemo·he·hani. ‖

38 a wi·h=to·tawa·wa·či=meko‖ e·h=taši‗kekye·hkimekowa·či.

b nye·wi-pepo·nwe·niči, e·h=nahehkwe·pi·hiniči‖ ača·hmeko.

c šwa·šika‖ e·taswi-pepo·nwe·niči,‖ e·h=nahose·hiniči,

d e·h=ki·yoki·yose·niči.

e e·h=mačowiye·hiniči.

f meše·=’nah=meko=’pi e·h=anemi-=meko -nesa·niči ki·yo·te·neniwahi.

g menehta=meko pi·si·owiye·he·hahi e·h=anemi-=meko -amwa·niči.

h meše=meko ke·ko·hi e·h=mi·čiči=meko.

i meše=ke·h=meko e·h=ina·towe·či.

j maneto·wahi, ča·ki-=meko -iši-neno·te·waki e·yi·ki=meko, e·h=nenohtawa·či=meko,

k meše=meko·-’nahi.

l meše nekotenwi e·h=a·čimoheči.†

m kwi·yena=meko o·sani e·h=ki·wi-wi·te·ma·či e·h=ši·ša·niči. ‖

39 a “wi·h=mawi-tepowe·yani,”‖ e·h=ineči.

b e·h=a·čimoha·či o·sani.

c “ano·se,‖ ni·h=mawi-=ma·hi=’pi -tepowe,” e·h=ina·či.

d “nepye·či‖-natomeko·pi,” e·h=ina·či o·sani.

e “a·kwi=ča·h=kana·kwa wi·h=wi·to·hko·na·ni,”‖ e·h=ina·či we·kwisita.

f “a·kwi nekotahi nešihka wi·h=a·yanini,” e·h=ina·či okwisani.

g e·h=pwa·wi-=ke·hi‖ -kehke·nema·wa·či e·h=ča·ki-nenohtawa·niči ayo·h=meneseki taswi‖ e·winiči,

h meše=meko·-’nahi e·h=na·no·taminiči ke·ko·hi.

i neno·te·wahi e·taswayakesiniči=meko ayo·hi‖ meneseki e·winičihi‖ e·h=ča·ki-=meko -nenohtawa·či.

____

*/a·tanasite·piso·nani/ (AW): AK ⟨.atanesite·pisonani.⟩.

†⟨ne⟩ changed, perhaps from ⟨me⟩.

j And when they'd been married for exactly thirty years, the woman gave birth.

k And she was able to give birth only with difficulty.

37 a (Remember, it was just the two of them.)

b He served as his wife's midwife without really knowing what he was doing.

c They had no idea what they should do.

d The woman barely lived.

e They had a baby boy.

f He was a little boy.

g Soon they had an old lady arrive.

h They were told what to do with that baby.

i "You must make a cradleboard to put him on," the man was told.

j "You must chop some bark off a hackberry tree," he was told.

k "Those cradle-board bows are really nice and flexible.

l And men make footrests," he was told.

m The old lady was teaching him.

38 a She was teaching them what to do with the baby.

b When he was four years old, he was able to sit up for the first time.

c When he was eight years old he was able to walk,

d and he would go walking around.

e He was cruel.

f It's said they would let him kill snakes.

g And at first he would eat small creatures.

h He ate just anything.

i And what's more, he spoke any language.

j Spirits, and Indians of every kind as well, he could understand,

k any of them.

l One time he received an instruction.

m Just at that time he was going around with his father, hunting.

39 a "You're to go to council," he was told.

b And he informed his father.

c "Father, just to let you know, I'm told I have to go to council," he told him.

d "They came to invite me," he told his father.

e "Well, there's no chance I'd allow you to," the father told his son.

f "You're not to go anywhere by yourself," he told his son.

g Now, they didn't know that he understood all who dwelt on this island,

h and he always heard anything.

i As many tribes of Indians as there were on this island, he understood them all.

j o·ni maneto·wahi na·hka na·mahkamiki e·napiničihi, e·yi·ki=meko,

k na·hka| na·mepye·ki, ‖ mo·hči=meko neme·sahi, e·h=ča·ki-=meko nenohtawa·niči.

40 a na·hka kehči‑maneto·wani e·yi·ki=meko e·h=nenohtawa·niči.

b ahpemeki e·winičihi e·yi·ki=meko e·h=nenohtawa·niči.

c meše=we·=meko·=’nahi iši‑maneto·wani e·h=nenohtawa·niči.

d o·ni·=’na e·h=mi·na·wimekoči kehči‑maneto·wani kwi·yese·ha,

e e·h=pešeke·nemekoči.

f meše=meko·=’nahi e·h=ina·towe·niči,*

g a·ye·niwe=meko e·h=inehtawa·či.

h i·ni=ke·h=meko e·na·towe·ničini e·h=ina·towe·či i·na kwi·yese·ha.

i kapo·twe| e·h=aka·wa·nekoči=meko| wi·h=ne·wokoči kehči‑maneto·wani.

j menehta i·ni| e·h=ine·nemekoči i·nini kehči‑maneto·wani.

k o·ni ahkowi wi·sahke·hani i·ni ‖ e·h=ine·nemekoči.

41 a o·ni| wi·sahke·ha e·h=mawi‑wa·pama·či owi·hka·nani keše·maneto·wani.†

b i·ya·h=e·h=pya·či ahpemeki wi·sahke·ha,

c e·h=we·pi‑kakano·neti·wa·či i·nini keše·maneto·wani.‡

d e·h=a·čimoha·či owi·hka·nani wi·sahke·ha.

e “’šina·kwa, ni·hka·ne, nekoti=mana anemi‑mehtose·neniwa nekehči‑menwe·nema·wa wi·h=awa·soči.

f kekimesi=me·kwe·h=meko kenenohta·kona·na,” e·h=ina·či owi·hka·nani.

g “o·´, nekehke·nema·wa.

h i·ye·me·h=meko nekehke·nema·wa.

i i·ni=ča·h=meko| ne·h=ni·na e·ne·nemaki| e·ne·nemači mana| ko·šisemena·na.

j a·mi·’ši‑anwa·či·kwe·ni netene·nema·wa.

k šewe·na e·h=natomeči, o·sani| a·kwi wi·to·hka·kočini=’pi,” ‖ e·h=iči kehči‑maneto·wa.|

42 a “ ‘me·kwe·h=meko pečimekosa!?| o·sani!?’ netešite·he,” e·h=iči.|

b “o=me·mešihka=ke·h=wi·na awita kaški- ke·ko·hi -ikosa,”| e·h=išiwe·či wi·sahkeča·hkwa.§

c “o=mani=ke·hi išawiyakwe:

d tepowe·yakwe nawa·či,

e taswi=meko ‘maneto·wa’ e·nenakwe tepowe·yakwe.

f kekimesi=ča·h=meko| i·ni išite·he·yakwe, i·n=a·mihtahi,

g ke·htena=meko i·ni išite·he·yakwe,” e·h=iti·wa·či.

h “menehta ayo·hi.

i ahkowi| i·n=a·mihtahi i·ya·h=meko e·h=owi·kiyani taši‑pahkowe·yakwe,” e·h=ineči wi·sahke·ha.

j “menehta=meko ayo·hi ahpemeki e·wičiki.

---

*/e·h=ina·towe·niči/: AK ⟨.einatoweči.⟩; obviative /ni/ added to agree with verbs in 40*de* and 40*g*.

†/keše·maneto·wa/, in origin the name of the Christian God borrowed (most likely) from Potawatomi, is used as a synonym of /kehči‑maneto·wa/ ‘the Great Spirit’ (40*adij*); note 41*a-k*.

‡/e·h=we·pi‑kakano·neti·wa·či/: ⟨no⟩ changed from ⟨mo⟩.

§/me·mešihka/: AK ⟨nenešika⟩.

j   And also the manitous stationed under the earth, those as well,

k   and also under the water, even the fish, that he understood them all.

40 a   And also the Great Spirit, that he understood him as well.

b   And the ones above, that he understood them as well.

c   In fact that he understood any kind of manitou.

d   And then that boy was singled out for mention by the Great Spirit,

e   as he thought he was cute.

f   When he spoke any language,

g   he understood him all the same.

h   What's more, the boy *spoke* the same languages he *spoke*.

i   At some point the Great Spirit had a desire to see him.

j   First the Great Spirit thought that about him.

k   And next Wîsahkêha thought that about him.

41 a   And then Wîsahkêha went to see his friend God.

b   Wîsahkêha arrived up there,

c   and began talking with God.

d   Wîsahkêha explained to his friend.

e   "Well, my friend, I very much want this certain one of the People-to-Come to be given a task.

f   I think he understands every one of us," he told his friend.

g   "Oh, I know him.

h   I knew him a while back.

i   So, *I* think the same thing *you* do about this grandson of ours.

j   I want him to do whatever he's willing to.

k   But when he was invited, his father wouldn't let him, I heard," the Great Manitou said.

42 a   "I thought it was hardly likely that his father would forbid him!" he said.

b   "Or maybe *he* couldn't manage to say anything to him," Wîsahkêha said.

c   "Or what if we do this:

d   first have a council.

e   All of us called 'manitou' have a council.

f   So, if every one of us thinks the same, that would be it.

g   If we really think that way," they said to each other.

h   "First here.

i   Afterwards then we would declare our decision over at your place," Wîsahkêha was told.

j   "First the ones who live up here.

^k　ahkowi=ča·hi i·ya·hi e·wičiki e·h=awiye·kwe," e·h=ineči| wi·sahke·ha.

^l　　"ta·ni=we·=mani wi·h=išawiwa·či wi·h=anemi-mehtose·neniwičiki.

^m　a·kwi_ke·ko·hi nana·ši wi·h=ayo·wa·čini," ‖ e·h=iyowa·či.

43 a　　"o·´,_ni·h=anohka·na·wa nekwisa wi·h=ma·wačima·či ayo·hi," e·h=iči keše·_-maneto·wa.

^b　　o·ni| okwisani e·h=anohka·na·či,

^c　či·šešani, keše·maneto·wa oči·pay_-okwisani.

^d　　i·na=ča·hi='pi e·nohka·neta| wi·h=ma·wačima·či.

^e　　o·ni ki·ši·-=meko -ma·wači·wa·či, ahpemeki e·h=a·wa·či.

^f　nye·wenwi e·h=pi·hto·keniki mani ki·šekwi| e·h=a·wa·či.

^g　a·kwi=meko='pi| kana·kwa.

^h　e·h=ka·škehta·kowa·či=meko i·nini kwi·yese·hani.

ⁱ　　e·h=a·čimoha·či omeso·ta·nahi.

^j　"newe·pi-=ni·hka=meko -tepowa·neko·ki maneto·waki," e·h=iči,

^k　e·h=ina·či omeso·ta·nahi.|

^l　　"i·noki='yo e·h=mawi-taši|-tepowa·šiwa·či manahka.|

^m　nye·wo·nameki e·h=pi·hto·keniki mani ki·šekwi i·ni e·na·waneti·wa·či," e·h=ina·či ‖ omeso·ta·nahi.

44 a　　e·yi·ki=ke·h=meko e·h=mya·ši-=meko_-we·pesi·he·nemekoči i·nihi| omeso·ta·nahi.[*]

^b　e·h=a·nweha·nwe·hta·koči e·nahina·čimoha·či.[†]

^c　i·ni='yo=wi·na='pi| e·h=a·nwe·hta·koči=meko e·na·čimoha·či, ahpemeki e·h=taši-tepowa·neči e·h=ina·čimoči.

^d　　"me·kwe·h=ma·hi_we·pesi·hiwiwa," e·h=iyowa·či we·ni·ča·nesičiki.

^e　e·h=we·pi-=meko -mami·na·wi-iši-na·katawe·nema·wa·či okwiswa·wani.[‡]

^f　　i·ne·ke=wi·na te·powa·čiki maneto·waki, ki·h_-ki·ši-=meko -ma·wači·wa·či,

^g　e·h=nana·hika·pa·či wi·sahke·ha nanakote·ki.

^h　e·h=mehčinameške·či, še·ški e·h=ota·siya·niči,

ⁱ　e·h=omehte·hiči,|

^j　še·ški e·h=omahkese·hiči,

^k　e·h=ni·maškahike·či wi·sahke·ha.

^l　　"nahi´, e·neniwiyane, i·noki=mana e·h=ma·wačimena·kwe ‖ ka·ka·nwi-mi·šihkwiya·ta.[§]

45 a　'aše=meko nema·wači·pena·toke,' ketešite·he·pwa·toke.

^b　a·kwi.|

^c　a·kwi aše=meko ma·wači·yakwini," e·h=iči.

^d　　"mani we·či_-ma·wači·yakwe:

^e　wi·h=aškote·ne·siwihakwe nekoti| anemi-mehtose·neniwa," e·h=iči wi·sahke·ha.

^f　　"kekimesi=meko wi·h=nenohtawakwa,|

^g　wi·na=na·hka wi·h=nenohto·nakwa," e·h=iči wi·sahke·ha.

^h　　o·ni| nekoti e·h=kano·nekoči.|

---

[*]/mya·ši/: ⟨a⟩ is squeezed in.

[†]⟨.enai⟩: ⟨na⟩ changed from ⟨ne⟩.

[‡]/na·katawe·nem-/: ⟨ta⟩ changed from ⟨te⟩.

[§]⟨nwi.⟩: divider added later.

^k And then the ones who live where you people live," Wîsahkêha was told.

^l   "After all, as it is now, what will the future people do?

^m They won't ever have anything to use," they said.

43 a   "Oh, I'll send my son to call them together here," said God.

^b   And then he sent his son,

^c Jesus, God's son that died.   (*Lit.*, his ghost son.)

^d   So, he is said to have been the one sent to call them together.

^e   And then after they were assembled, they went above.

^f They went to the fourth level of this sky.

^g It was no use, to hear the tale.

^h That boy could still hear them.

ⁱ   He told his parents.

^j "Gee, the manitous are setting about to council over me," he said,

^k telling his parents.

^l   "As they're now going yonder to council over me.

^m The fourth level of this sky is where they're all heading off to," he told his parents.

44 a   Now, another thing is, his parents thought he was kind of crazy.

^b They didn't use to believe the things he told them.

^c And in this case, it is said, they didn't believe what he told them when he reported that he was being counciled over up above.

^d   "He's likely crazy, you understand," the parents said.

^e And they began keeping a close eye on their son.

^f   But meanwhile, after those manitous who were counciling had all assembled,

^g Wîsahkêha went and stood in the middle of the lodge.

^h He was naked except for a breechcloth,

ⁱ and he had a bow

^j and just moccasins,

^k and he had something stuck in his hair, Wîsahkêha did.

^l   "Alright men, today this one with long chin-whiskers has called you together.

45 a I imagine you think we're probably getting together just for the heck of it.

^b No.

^c We're not getting together just for the heck of it," he said.

^d   "Here's why were getting together:

^e For us to make one of the People-to-Come the Spirit of Fire," Wîsahkêha said.

^f   "One that every one of us will understand,

^g and who will understand us," Wîsahkêha said.

^h   And then one of them addressed him.

i   "ohoho·´,‿wi·sahke·ha=wi·na anemi|-mehtose·neniwani=meko,"| e·h=iko·či.*

j   "nana·ši=wi·na| ki·na·na⁈ nekotahi ki·h=kehkahokona·na⁈ taswi 'maneto·wa'
    e·nenakwe⁈

k   we·kone·hi·='na wi·h=kehke·netaki anemi-mehtose·neniwa,"| e·h=iči nekoti maneto·wa.

l   e·h=me·nešite·he·či keše·maneto·wa.

m   (i·nini='yo=ke·h=wi·na='pi nekoti ki·šiha·čini keše·maneto·wa.)|

n   na·hka=meko ‖ wi·sahke·ha e·h=pemi‿pasekwi·či.

46 a   "nahi´, e·neniwiyane, i·noki=mana keno·tawa·pwa e·nowe·či.

b   ni·na·na=ke·h=mani| keki·ši-mama·či·henepena," e·h=ina·či.

c   "a·wasi=ča·h=meko ahpi·hte·netisowa| e·hpi·hčawi·hiya·ke," e·h=iči.

d   "awita‿i·ni kaški-ahpi·hčawihkapa e·hpi·hčawiwa·či anemi‿mehtose·neniwaki,"
    e·h=ina·či,

e   e·h=sakihta·hpe·saha·či,

f   e·h=nowa·hke·či wi·sahke·ha.

g   kwi·yena=meko e·h=ki·ši‿kemiya·hiniki.

h   nano·škwe e·h=pemi‿we·po·te·či| tepowe·neni·ha='yo·we.

i   "i·ni=kohi wi·h=išawi·hiyani.

j   'kahka·hkači·ha' ki·h=iko·ki nešise·haki, neki·haki.

k   e·h=ne·wohkini=meko ki·h=taši-pa·pakameko·ki," e·h=ina·či.

l   "ki·h=neškina·ko·ki=meko.

m   i·noki=mani e·nowe·yani='yo·we i·ni‿wi·h=oči|-kehči‿neškino·hki," e·h=ina·či wi·sahke·ha. ‖

47 a   e·h=anemi-=meko -menwe·netamowa·či kotakaki| maneto·waki.

b   a·hpene=meko e·h=iši-menwe·netamowa·či.

c   meše·='nah=meko nye·wa·pitaki taswawahi·me| e·h=taši-te·tepowe·wa·či.

d   i·nah=meko ča·ki=meko ke·ko·hi e·h=nana·hiseto·wa·či wi·h=išihiši-keteminawa·wa·či
    o·šisemwa·wahi.

e   "ki·h=o·šisemipena anemi-mehtose·neniwaki," e·h=iyowa·či.

f   "taswi=meko 'maneto·wa' e·nenakwe, ki·na·na.†

g   mana=wi·na wi·sahke·ha ošise·hahi anemi‿mehtose·neniwahi,

h   na·hka ihkwe·wahi a·hpene=meko oki·hahi.

i   i·ni=wi·na e·na·ko·ma·či mana‿wi·sahke·ča·kwa.

j   ki·na·na=ke·hi a·hpene=meko ki·h=o·šisemipena," e·h=iči kehči‿maneto·wa.

k   "ki·h=keteketeminawa·pwa=ke·hi," e·h=ineči maneto·waki.

l   "ni·na='yo ni·h=o·šisemi. ‖

48 a   a·hpene=meko‿ni·h=o·šisemi| anemi‿mehtose·neniwaki,"| e·h=iči keše·maneto·wa.

b   o·ni ote·hi e·h=ketenaki.

c   e·h=pahkwe·šaki ki·ši-ketenaki,

d   e·h=awatenamawa·či wi·sahke·hani.

e   "kaši-ča·h=mani| išiwe·pi," e·h=ineči wi·sahke·ha.

f   "'šina·kwa, ma·hani=ča·h wi·h=oto·kima·miwa·čini," e·h=iči.

---

*⟨|o.o.o⟩, with dots as dividers.

†/ki·na·na/: AK ⟨.kinanana.⟩.

ⁱ "So that's it! Wîsahkêha and the People-to-Come," he said to him.

^j   "But he'll never name any of *us*, who are called manitous, of course!

^k What will that Person-to-Come know?" said one manitou.

^l   God was ashamed.

^m (Even though it's said that in this case he was one that God had made.)

ⁿ   Again Wîsahkêha got to his feet.

46 a "Alright, men, you heard now what this man said.

^b But we for our part have given you life," he told them.

^c   "So, he thinks he's greater than we are," he said.

^d   "You wouldn't be able to be greater that the People-to-Come will be," Wîsahkêha told him,

^e and he grabbed him by the scruff of the neck,

^f and threw him out the door.

^g   Right then it had started raining a little.

^h   The whilom councilor began crawling in no particular direction.

ⁱ "That's just how you will be.

^j My uncles and my aunts will call you a salamander.

^k Wherever they see you, they'll club you to death," he told him.

^l   "They'll really hate you.

^m They'll hate you a lot because of what you just said now," Wîsahkêha told him.

47 a   The other manitous were pleased as things went on.

^b They were all pleased alike.

^c They were counciling for some forty years.

^d Right there they put everything in place about how they would bless their grandchildren.

^e   "The People-to-Come will be our grandchildren," they said.

^f   "Of all of *us* who are called 'manitou'.

^g But the People-to-Come are maternal uncles of Wîsahkêha here,

^h and the women, uniformly, his maternal aunts.

ⁱ That other way is how Wîsahkêchâkwa here is related to them.

^j And in *our* case, though, they'll uniformly be our grandchildren," the Great Spirit said.

^k   "What's more, you'll bless them," the manitous were told.

^l   "They'll be *my* grandchildren, for example,

48 a The People-to-Come will uniformly be my grandchildren," said God.

^b   And then he took out his heart.

^c He cut a piece off it after taking it out,

^d and handed it to Wîsahkêha.

^e   "What does this signify?" Wîsahkêha was asked.

^f   "Well, this will be their chief," he said.

^g "ehe·he, i·ni=kohi," e·h=iči keše·maneto·wa.*

^h "ke·htena kenepwa·hka, ni·hka·ne," e·h=inekoči owi·hka·nani wi·sahke·ha.

ⁱ e·h=asipi-=meko -menwe·nemeči neno·te·wa| wi·h=aškote·ne·siwiheči,
^j kekimesi=meko i·nihi te·powa·ničihi.[†]

^k o·ni nye·wa·pitaki e·taswawahi·makateniki, e·h=na·na·kwa·wa·či.
^l ne·nye·wawahi·me| e·h=na·na·kwa·wa·či.

^m o·ni wi·sahke·heki e·h=a·či keše·maneto·wa ne·sokonakateniki. ‖
^{49 a} wi·sahke·ha=ke·hi e·h=šekišekišiki, e·h=pya·či i·ya·hi owi·hka·neki.

^b "o·´, e·htameko kenehtonehto·mišino·hi," e·h=ineči wi·sahke·ha.

^c "aše=koh=meko| nešekišekišine e·h=ayi·hkwi|-tepowe·ya·ni," e·h=ina·či wi·sahke·ha
owi·hka·nani.

^d "nahi´, ni·hka·ne, mani=kohi| we·či-sese·si-pya·ya·ni," e·h=ina·či.

^e "owiye·ha ke·hte·koni| natoma·wasote.
^f kekehke·nema·petoke e·niwisa·kwe·na.
^g meše=ča·h=meko e·h=pehkote·nikwe·ni nepe·wowe·sa," e·h=ina·či owi·hka·nani.

^h "ši·´, ke·htena=ma·h=meko.
ⁱ a·kwi=meko i·ni iši-mi·na·wite·he·ya·nini," e·h=ina·či owi·hka·nani wi·sahke·ha.

^j "šepawi·hta=ča·hi i·ni iši|-mi·na·wite·he·wane·ni ki·na," e·h=ina·či.[‡]

^k "wa·wotami·='nahi.

^l "ano·hko, we·ne·ha='yo a·mi-anohka·naka| wi·h=ki·watoke·moči,"| e·h=ina·či
o·hkomesani. ‖

^{50 a} "awahi·ma=ča·h=na·pi=meko nahipaho·hiwa ša·watesiwa," e·h=ikoči o·hkomese·hani.

^b "i·na=ča·hi a·mi|-anohka·nata.
^c i·nini=koči='yo we·i·niya ko·sa omami·ši·heme·hani," e·h=ina·či.[§]

^d "o·´, i·na=ča·h=ye·hapa.|
^e nahi´, ni·h=nawači-natoma·wa.
^f ki·h=we·pi-wača·hipena=meko, ano·hko," e·h=iči.

^g e·h=we·pi-wača·hoči| mečemo·ka.

^h wi·sahke·ha| no·make=meko e·h=ine·teki,
ⁱ aya·pami e·h=pya·či e·h=owi·ke·hiwa·či.

^j aškači·meki·hi e·h=pya·či ša·watesiwa.

^k i·nah=či·h=wi·na keše·maneto·wani e·h=apihapiniči.

^l ki·ši-wi·seniwa·či,

^m "nahi´, ki·h=ki·wi|-a·čimoha·waki ki·či|-maneto·na·naki ayo·h=wi·h=ma·wači·yakwe,
ⁿ ayo·hi e·h=owi·ke·hiya·ni.

^o wa·pake očiwe·pi wi·h=ma·wači·yakwe," ‖ e·h=ina·či wi·sahke·ha.

^{51 a} " 'wi·sahke·ha='pi e·h=owi·kiči wi·h=ma·wači·yakwe,' ki·h=ina·waki," e·h=ineči
ša·watesiwa.|

---

*/ehe·he/: AK ⟨.e.e.e.⟩, with dots between the ⟨e⟩'s.

†/kekimesi/: AK ⟨kekinesi⟩.

‡/mi·na·wite·he·-/: /mi·/ (AW), ms. ⟨ni⟩.

§/omami·ši·heme·hani/: /mi·/, ms. ⟨ni⟩.

g   "Yes, exactly," said God.

h   "You are truly wise, my friend," Wîsahkêha was told by his friend.

i   It was approved by all together that an Indian be made the Spirit of Fire,

j   by every one of those councilors.

k   And then after forty years they departed in groups.

l   They departed at four-year intervals.

m   And God went to Wîsahkêha's three days later.

49 a   Now, Wîsahkêha was lying around, when he arrived over at his friend's.

b   "Oh how pensively you lie!" Wîsahkêha was told.

c   "You should know, I'm just lying around because I'm tired from counciling,"
Wîsahkêha told his friend.

d   "Alright, my friend, I must tell you why I've hurried to come," he told him.

e   "What if someone does the inviting the day before.

f   You must know a fast runner.

g   So, he could sleep as a guest wherever he was when night falls," he told his friend.

h   "Say! Why, sure enough.

i   I did *not* think of that," Wîsahkêha told his friend.

j   "So, it's lucky *you* thought of that," he told him.

k   "What a bother, now.

l   "Say, grandma, so who should I ask to go around inviting people?" he asked his
grandmother.

50 a   "Well, that South Wind is a good runner, at least," his grandmother told him.

b   "So, *he's* one you could to do it.

c   He was your late father's messenger, of course," she told him.

d   "Oh yes, I guess he'd be the one.

e   Alright, I'll first invite him.

f   You must set to cooking for us, grandma," he said.

g   The old lady began cooking.

h   Wîsahkêha was away for a short while

i   and came back to their house.

j   A little later, South Wind arrived.

k   And he found God sitting there.

l   After they had eaten,

m   "Alright, you must go around and tell our fellow manitous that we're to all meet here,

n   in my house.

o   We're to meet together starting tomorrow," Wîsahkêha told him.

51 a   "You must tell them, 'We're supposed to meet at Wîsahkêha's house,'" South Wind was
told.

^b "kekimesi=meko ki·h=wi·tamawa·waki," e·h=ineči.

^c "e·h=pehkote·nemiwane·ni=ča·h=meko nepe·wowe·hkapa," e·h=ineči ša·watesiwa.[*]

^d "hawo·?,"| e·h=iči.

^e mani=meko e·ši|-nowi·či, e·h=pemipenoči.|

^f no·make=meko e·h=ine·teki.

^g aya·pami_e·h=pye·či_-pi·tike·niči omami·ši·hemani wi·sahke·ha,

^h "'šina·kwa, keki·we," e·h=ina·či.

ⁱ "a·kwi.

^j i·ni=ča·h=meko e·h=ča·k_-a·čimohaki.

^k kekimesi=meko newi·tamawa·waki," e·h=iči ša·watesiwa.

^l "ahpemeki=ča·hi,_neta·pi·=ča·hi e·yi·ki -a·čimoha·waki,"_e·h=iči.

^m "na·mahkamiki=ča·hi e·yi·ki,| neča·ki·=koh=meko -wi·tamawa·waki.

ⁿ mo·hči| na·mepye·ki ‖ e·wičiki, e·yi·ki=meko newi·tamawa·waki."

52 a "ta·ni=ča·h e·šihiši-kano·nehki."

^b "o·´,_mahkwa·či=ča·h=meko, 'hawo·?,' iwaki.

^c a·kwi owiye·ha mya·ši-kano·šičini.

^d kekimesi=meko| nemenwi_-kano·neko·ki,"| e·h=iči.

^e "o·´,_i·ni=kohi we·čitawi," e·h=iči wi·sahke·ha.

^f "i·ni me·nwikeki," e·h=iči.|

^g e·h=ki·hkenaki owi·ki.

^h e·h=ki·ša·koči-=meko -meši|-wi·kiya·piki wi·kiya·pi.

ⁱ e·h=ki·ša·koči-=meko -menwina·kwahki pi·tike.

^j e·h=we·pi-pya·niči wa·paniki na·wahkwe·niki,

^k e·h=ča·ki-ma·wači·niči,

^l e·h=po·ni_-pya·niči.

^m wi·nwa·wa=ke·hi e·hkwa·te·meki| e·h=nani·šo·piwa·či owi·hka·nani, wi·sahke·ha keše·maneto·wani.

ⁿ ki·ši-ma·wači·niči, e·h=nana·hika·pa·či keše·maneto·wa.|

^o "nahi´, 'maneto·wa' ‖ e·neneke, e·neniwiyane,|

53 a 'we·kone·h=ča·h=ye·toke we·či|-ma·mata·kwi-ma·wačimi·nameki,' ketešite·he·pwa·toke.

^b mana=ča·hi nekoti ko·šisemena·na anemi-mehtose·neniwa wi·h=aškote·ne·siwihakwe netene·nema·pena| ni·na·na mana me·hčimehčinameške·pita, e·h=ni·šiya·ke," e·h=iči keše·maneto·wa.[†]

^c "o·´,_we·nahi·='ni,"| e·h=iyowa·či.

^d a·neta,_"nemenwe·neta·pena=ča·h=wi·na ni·na·na," e·h=iniči,

^e e·h=ča·ki-=meko -menwe·netaminiči.

^f na·hka=meko nye·wa·pitaki taswawahi·me| e·h=pemi_-tepowe·wa·či maneto·waki.

^g o·ni kekimesi=meko e·h=menwe·netamowa·či maneto·waki.[‡]

^h e·h=natomeči we·ni·ča·nesičiki.

---

[*]/ni=ča·/: AK ⟨čiča⟩.

[†]/keše·-/: ⟨kečikeše⟩; AK started to write /kehči-maneto·wa/ instead of /keše·maneto·wa/.

[‡]/kekimesi/: ⟨.e|kekimesi⟩; /e·h=/: AK ⟨e⟩ added later.

b   "You must tell everyone," he was told.

c   "And if you're overtaken by nightfall, you should spend the night as someone's guest,"
South Wind was told.

d   "Alright, I'll do that," he said.

e   As soon as he went out he sped away.

f   He was gone for only a short time.

g   When Wîsahkêha had his messenger come back in,

h   he said to him, "Well, you turned back."

i   "No.

j   So, I've now informed all of them.

k   I told everyone," South Wind said.

l   "So, up above, so I've been to inform them also," he said.

m   "And under the earth as well, I've indeed told them all.

n   Even the ones under the water, I told them as well."

52 a   "So, how did they reply to you?"

b   "Oh, well, they calmly said, 'Alright.'

c   No one spoke unkindly to me.

d   Everyone spoke to me nicely," he said.

e   "Oh, that's really excellent," said Wîsahkêha.

f   "That's the right thing," he said.

g   He made his house be longer.

h   And the house was an extremely large house.

i   And it looked extremely nice inside.

j   He had them arriving starting the next day at noon.

k   And he had them all assembled

l   and no more coming.

m   Now, he and his friend were sitting there together at the far end of the lodge, Wîsahkêha
and God.

n   After the others were assembled, God stood to speak.

o   "Alright, you men who are called 'manitou',

53 a   you're probably wondering why you've been called to this unusual assembly.

b   Well, *we*, I together with this one sitting here naked, have in mind for all of us to make a
certain grandchild of all of ours of the People-to-Come be the Fire Spirit," God said.

c   "Oh, so that's it," they said.

d   Some were saying, "Well, *we* are pleased, though,"

e   as they all liked the idea.

f   Again the manitous counciled for forty years.

g   And then every one of the manitous was pleased.

h   And the parents were summoned.

ⁱ   če·wi·šwi=meko, ihkwe·wa na·hka| neniwa, e·h=natomeči.
^j   e·h=natomekowa·či ‖ ša·watesiwani.
54 a   e·h=na·kwa·wa·či.
^b   mehto·či=meko e·h=kehčine·to·hiniki wi·sahke·hani e·h=owi·kiniči.
^c   nahmeko=meko e·h=pya·wa·či i·ya·hi.
^d   e·ški=či·h=meko neniwahi=meko ne·htawi e·h=tepiki·škiči·kwane·ška·ti·niči.
^e   keye·hapa=ke·hi=’pi maneto·wahi=meko ne·htawi.
^f   e·h=we·pi-a·ya·čimohekowa·či keše·maneto·wani, mahkwa·či=meko.
^g   na·hka wi·sahke·hani mahkwa·či=meko e·h=a·ya·čimohekowa·či.
^h   kotake·hahi a·kwi=’pi wi·to·hkawomečini.
ⁱ   i·nini=meko mehteno·hi keše·maneto·wani o·ni wi·sahke·hani.
^j   i·ni=meko iši‿ni·šwi e·h=a·ya·čimohekowa·či.
^k   ne·nye·wenwi a·čimohekowa·či, e·h=we·pi-a·čimoheči wi·h=išawiniči okwiswa·wani,
^l   wi·h=ka·kike·neniwiniči=meko. ‖
55 a   na·hka=meko wi·nwa·wa e·šawiwa·či e·h=a·čimoheči.
^b   “ahpene·či=ke·h=meko ki·h=ne·wa·pwa‿kekwiswa·wa,” e·h=ineči.|
^c   “na·hka ahpene·či=meko wi·h=awa·sowa.
^d   a·kwi‿nana·ši wi·h=po·ni-nenehke·nemekočini anemi-mehtose·neniwahi,” e·h=ineči
        we·kwisičiki.
^e   “mani=ke·hi we·či|-mehkwe·nemeči,
^f   we·či-mehkwe·nemakeči:
^g   kekimesi=meko nenohtawe·wa maneto·wahi ayo·h=mani meneseki e·winičihi.‿
^h   kekimesi=meko| kakano·neti·ha·sa.‿
ⁱ   mo·hči=meko wi·škeno·he·hahi, kakano·neti·sa=koh=meko.[*]
^j   ča·ki=meko e·šikiničini ne·wa·te, kakano·neti·ha·sa=koh=meko,” e·h=ina·či
        kehči‿maneto·wa we·ni·ča·nesiničihi.‿
^k   o·ni e·h=nawači-po·nimeči.
^l   “no·make·we nawači-na·kwa·ko,” e·h=ineči. ‖
56 a   e·h=na·kwa·wa·či i·niki owi·weti·he·haki.
^b   i·nini=ke·hi okwiswa·wani meše=meko e·h=ahpi·hčiki·hiniči,
^c   e·h=oškinawe·he·hiniči=meko.
^d   e·h=nešiwi-=ke·h=wi·na=meko -ma·nwipepo·nwe·niči.
^e   i·ya·h=pye·ya·wa·či, e·h=apahapane·nemekowa·či okwiswa·wani.
^f   “keteši‿pwa·wi-=ni·hka -nahkoma·pwa,”‿e·h=ineči,
^g   e·h=ikowa·či okwiswa·wani.
^h   “a·kwi=ke·hi wi·h=menwi-mehtose·neniwiya·nini a·hpeči|-ša·kwe·nemoye·kwe.
ⁱ   me·me·čiki=meko ni·h=nepe.
^j   i·ni=wi·na aškote·ne·siwiya·ne,|
^k   ahpene·či=meko ke·htena ni·h=menwi‿-pemenekwa wi·h=anemi-mehtose·neniwita,”|
        e·h=iniči.
^l   “a·kwi=ke·hi wi·h=nepo·hiya·nini,” e·h=iniči.[†]

---

[*]/kano·/: ⟨no⟩ changed from start of ⟨mo⟩.
[†]/a·kwi=/: AK ⟨.akwi.⟩, with dividers added.

i Both of them, the woman and the man, were summoned.

j They were summoned by South Wind,

54 a and they set out.

b It was as if where Wîsahkêha lived was very near.

c And in a flash they arrived over there.

d And here was nothing but men, sitting cross-legged side-by-side with knees touching.

e In fact, it turned out, to hear the tale, it was nothing but manitous.

f They had God begin talking to them, quietly.

g And they had Wîsahkêha quietly talk to them.

h It's said that others were not allowed to.

i Only God and Wîsahkêha.

j Those were the only two that talked to them.

k After they were spoken to by them four times each, they began to be told what their son would do,

l that he would be an immortal.

55 a And they were also told about their situation.

b "Now, you will always see your son," they were told.

c "And he will always have a task assigned to him.

d The People-to-Come will never cease thinking of him," the parents of the boy were told.

e "Now, here's why he was thought of,

f why we thought of him:

g He understands every one of the manitous who are on this island.

h He could converse with every one of them.

i Even little birds he could definitely converse with.

j Every kind, if he sees them, he could definitely converse with them," the Great Spirit told the parents.

k Then they were given a break from being talked to.

l "Go home for a while," they were told.

56 a And the married couple went back, just themselves.

b Now, their son was not very advanced in his growth,

c being barely a young man.

d Although he was a huge number of years old in age.

e When they got there, their son laughed at them.

f "Well, why didn't you tell them yes?" they were asked,

g their son asked them.

h "I won't have a good life at all if you persist in refusing.

i I'm sure I'll die.

j But *that* way, if I'm the Spirit of Fire,

k I'll certainly always be well taken care of by the future people," he said.

l "What's more, I won't die," he said.

^m   "ki·nwa·wa=ča·h=meko ki·h=mya·nešihipwa‿a·hpeči-a·nomena·kwe.[*]

ⁿ   tepa·šiye·kwe, ki·h=nahkota·pwa,"‿e·h=ina·či omeso·ta·nahi. ‖

57 a   ihkwe·wa e·h=kano·na·či okwisani.

^b   "ni·na=koh=wi·na| te·pwe·hto·naka·ha.

^c   me·meso·si=ma·hi·='na keše·maneto·wa| i·nahi taši‿wi·či‿tepowe·ke·wa."

^d   "ni·na=ma·h=ne·hi, metemo."

^e   "i·ni=meko e·šite·he·ya·ni," e·h=ina·či okwiswa·wani.

^f   "i·ni=meko išawiko e·nena·kwe," e·h=ina·či| omeso·ta·nahi.

^g   "ši·´‿na·piwe·na," e·h=ikoči=meko okye·ni.

^h   "če·ye·neswi=ke·hi·='noki i·ni wi·h=natoma·kaniwiyakwe," e·h=iniči.

ⁱ   ke·htena nye·wokonakateniki e·h=pye·či-natomeči če·ye·neswi,

^j   e·h=anemehka·wa·či.|

^k   "nahi´, ki·h=nahkota·pwa=meko, nemeso·ta·netike," e·h=ina·či omeso·ta·nahi.

^l   "hawo·?," e·h=iči=meko ihkwe·wa,|

^m   e·h=nahkoma·či=meko okwisani e·na·čimoniči.|

ⁿ   i·ya·h=pye·ya·wa·či, wi·sahke·hani menehta e·h=kano·nekowa·či. ‖

58 a   o·ni keše·maneto·wani e·h=we·petone·moniči.

^b   nešiwi·=meko -kenwe·ši e·h=tana·naketone·moniči.

^c   ki·šetone·moniči keše·maneto·wani, e·h=pemi‿pasekwi·či ihkwe·wa.

^d   "nahi´, ineni·tike, ni·na=koh=wi·na a·kwi ša·kwe·nemoya·nini e·šimiya·ke.

^e   koči·h netepa·na·pena| nekwise·hena·na,

^f   ašewe·na, ineni·tike, kenahkomenepwa=meko ki·hki·hki," e·h=iči ihkwe·wa.

^g   "i·ni=meko| ki·h=išawipwa e·nowe·ye·kwe," e·h=ina·či maneto·wahi.

^h   "wah! i·ni=kohi.

ⁱ   kete·piha·pwa=ma·hi·='na.

^j   nehki=meko e·nemi‿ahkiwinikwe·ni, wi·na=ke·hi wi·h=anemi|-mehtose·neniwiwa.

^k   nehki=ke·h=meko wi·h=anemi|-ka·ki·‿ki·ke·nonikwe·ni mehtose·neniwahi, wi·h=wa·wa·ta·samapiwa.

^l   ahpene·či=meko wi·h=kakano·nekwa ayo·hi ‖ taši-mehtose·neniwahi," e·h=iniči.

59 a   aškači=meko, "'šina·kwa, ki·na=ča·hi^{!?},| pašito," e·h=ineči we·kwisita‿neniwa.

^b   "ši·´‿kanoma·h=ča·h=ni·na ke·ko·hi‿ni·h=ine·neta," e·h=iči.

^c   "o·´‿i·ni=ma·h=ki·na," e·h=ineči.

^d   "nahi´, peninawi·no·='nahi," e·h=ineči,

^e   e·h=ča·ki·=meko -peninawi·či.|

^f   nanakote·ki e·h=no·hka·mehkonameki,

^g   mese·hani ke·hte·kekini e·h=pi·tikato·ki.

^h   e·h=we·pi-we·ši·heči,

ⁱ   e·h=meškwa·hkoneči.

^j   e·h=aniwa·soči=meko e·h=meškwa·hkoneči.

^k   e·h=we·pi-kakano·na·či kehči‿maneto·wa, mahkwa·či=meko wi·h=išite·he·niči.

---

[*]/mya·neših-/ (only here): FM "made him feel bad."

m "So, *you'll* make *me* feel bad if you persist in not being persuaded.

n If you love me, you'll say yes," he told his parents.

57 a The woman spoke to her son.

b "*I* would certainly do what you say.

c I mean, what was extraordinary, God took part in the council there."

d "I, too, obviously, my wife."

e "I'm thinking the same way," (the man) told their son.

f "Do just what they tell you to," he told his parents.

g "Well, alright then," his mother said to him.

h "Another thing, all three of us will receive invitations now," he said.

i Sure enough, four days later someone came to invite all three of them,

j and they went.

k "Alright, you must say 'yes,' my parents," he told his parents.

l "We will," the woman said firmly,

m agreeing to what her son said.

n When they got there, Wîsahkêha spoke to them first.

58 a And then God began talking.

b He went on talking for an incredibly long time.

c After God finished talking, the woman rose to her feet.

d "Alright, men, *I* definitely do not refuse what you ask me to do.

e Although, of course, we love our son,

f still, men, I nevertheless say yes to you," the woman said.

g "You must do what you said," she told the manitous.

h "Oh good, that's the idea.

i I mean, you're doing a good thing for him.

j For as long as the earth may continue to exist, *he* shall continue to live.

k And for as long as people shall continue to celebrate clan-feasts in places, he shall sit facing them.

l He shall always speak to the people here," (God) said.

59 a After some while, "Well, what about you?" the lad's father was asked.

b "Why, well even less will *I* think anything bad of it," he said.

c "Well, there you go!" he was told.   (Addressed to the boy.)

d "Alright, now take your clothes off," he was told,

e and he took all his clothes off.

f In the center of the lodge the earth was softened,

g and old wood was brought in.

h He began to be painted,

i being painted red all over.

j He was shining bright where he was painted.

k The Great Spirit began speaking to him for him to think calmly.

l kapo·twe=meko waninawe e·h=oči‗pemi‗ni·ški‗pekeše·niči.

m kapo·twe=meko e·h=meso·te·wi‗peškone·niči.

n e·h=aniweše·niki.

o e·h=ni·kahkeše·niči, e·h=pehtawe·weči mehteko·ni. ‖

60 a ke·htena=meko e·h=ahkate·niki.

b o·ni=kapo·twe‗kehkeše·wani-'yo·we e·h=ša·kohka·na·pehkowiniki.

c "o·´‗mani=ke·h=meko owi·yawi," e·h=ineči.

d e·h=kwa·pa·hke·či wi·sahke·ha.

e "meše=meko·='nahi nešise·haki, neki·haki wi·h=anemi‖-mehkamo·ki,
   wi·h=ayohayo·wa·či," e·h=iči wi·sahke·ha.*

f "nekoti=mani aškwa·ne·hkete·wi ki·h=awato·pwa‖ na·kwa·ye·kwe," e·h=ineči.

g "o=mani=ke·hi wi·h=oči‖-anemi‗kehke·netama·tisoči‗owiye·ha owi·yawi,‖ †

h mani we·šiwe·ši·hote kehkeše·wi," e·h=ineči.

i e·h=a·čimoheči wi·h=iši·howa·či.‖

j e·h=pwa·wi-=ke·h=meko ke·ko·hi iši-mya·šite·he·wa·či we·ni·ča·nesičiki.

k e·h=na·kwa·wa·či ki·ši-a·ya·čimoheči,

l e·h=awato·wa·či=meko meši-aškwa·ne·hkete·wi. ‖

61 a e·h=owi·ke·hiwa·či pye·ya·wa·či,

b e·h=we·pi-=meko -nasa·hkohesowa·či,

c pešekesiwani e·h=nasa·hkohwa·wa·či.

d kapo·twe='pi e·h=pya·niči i·niye·he a·mi·ničih.

e metemo·he·hani i·niye·ne e·h=pya·niči e·taši-a·ya·čimohekowa·čini.

f "i·nina·hi e·hpi·hčikikwe·ni," e·h=iniči.

g "keye·či·h=ča·h=meko aškote·ne·siwihekwa kehči‗maneto·wani.‖

h mana=ča·hi·='na·='na," e·h=ina·wa·či.

i "'šina·kwá," e·h=iniči i·nini metemo·he·hani.‡

j e·h=aka·wi-=meko -mayo·niči.‖

k ke·htena=meko='pi mehtose·neniwahi e·h=pe·pye·či-na·tešawe·niči.

l meso·te·wi=meko wi·kiya·peki e·h=awiniči.

m e·h=mi·ša·te·nemowa·či we·ni·ča·nesičiki,§

n mesi=meko wi·kiya·peki e·h=awiniči‖ okwise·hwa·wani='yo·we.‖

o e·h=ki·ša·koči-=meko ‖ -sasa·kihto·wa·či mehtose·neniwaki.

62 a "'aškote·ne·siwa'‖ ki·h=išitehka·na·pwa," e·h=ikowa·či we·ni·ča·nesiničihi.

b i·ni=ča·hi·='pi e·šitehka·tamowa·či.

c 'aškote·ne·si·ha' išitehka·tamo·ki='pi i·nina·hi.

d o·ni e·h=we·pi-a·yaha·ya·čimowa·či wi·h=išahišawiniči.

e wi·h=oči-=ke·hi -kehke·netama·tisoniči mehtose·neniwiweni e·h=a·čimoha·wa·či.¶

____

*/nešise·haki/: AK ⟨.nešisea|aki.⟩.

†/owiye·ha/: ⟨o⟩ is over a divider.

‡/'šina·kwá/: AK ⟨.šinakwi.⟩; /metemo·he·hani/: AK ⟨.netemoeani.⟩.

§/nemo/: AK ⟨namo|⟩.

¶/neni/: ⟨neni⟩ changed from ⟨nani⟩.

l   Soon smoke began billowing out of him on all sides.

m   And soon he blazed up all over.

n   The fire rose higher.

o   He broke into hot coals as the sticks were used for the fire.

60 a   And sure enough they burned up.

b   And then at some point what had been pieces of charcoal became flint.

c   "Oh, now this is his body," they were told.

d   Wîsahkêha scattered them abroad.

e   "My uncles and aunts will be able to find it in years to come, as something they will always use," Wîsahkêha said.

f   "Now you can take one firestick with you when you leave," they were told.

g   "Or this will be how anyone in the future shall gain knowledge of themselves,

h when they paint their faces with this charcoal," they were told.

i   They were told how to paint themselves.

j   Another thing, the parents didn't feel bad at all.

k They left after they had been instructed.

l taking a large firestick with them.

61 a   When they got back to their house,

b they started in to roast things on roasting sticks set in the ground,

c roasting a deer.

d   At some point, the story goes, those who had moved away came back.

e And that old lady who had been telling them what to do came.

f   "I wonder how old he is by now," she said.

g   "Well, just a short while ago the Great Spirit made him into the Spirit of Fire.

h So, this is him," they told her.

i   "Goodness me!" that old lady said.

j And briefly she wept.

k   Sure enough, the story goes, they kept having people come to get fire.

l   He was in all the houses.

m And his parents were glad.

n Their son that had been was in all houses.

o   People were extremely careful with it.

62 a The parents told them, "You must call him 'Spirit of Fire'."

b So that's how they named it.

c They named it 'Spirit of Fire' at that time, the story goes.

d   And then they began explaining what the others should do.

e In particular, they told them how they would know about life for themselves.

f　　　　" 'mahkate·wi·wa,' ki·h=ina·pena=ča·hi mani we·ši·hota.

g　　ke·htena=ke·h=meko maneto·wani wi·h=ketemina·kwa mani e·ši‑na·katamokwe·na,"
　　　　e·h=išiwe·wa·či a·ya·čimoha·čiki mehtose·neniwahi.

h　　ke·htena=meko e·h=we·pi‑ma·mahkate·wi·niči| mehtose·neniwahi,

i　　ihkwe·wahi, iškwe·se·hahi, na·hka kwi·yese·hahi.

j　　　　meso·te·we·we·=mekoho ‖ e·h=ma·mahkate·wi·wa·či, mahkwa·či=meko.*

63 a　a·neta=ke·hi e·h=wa·waneška·hi‑=meko ‑mahkate·wi·wa·či.

b　　e·h=we·pi‑ meše=meko‑='nahi ‑awa·wa·či i·nini aškote·ne·siwani.

c　　aškači·meki·hi we·p‑ašihto·ta i·ni| aškote·wi e·h=ča·kesoči.|

d　　i·nini=ke·h=wi·na='pi ne·sekočini aškote·ne·siwani,

e　　e·h=wawi·nwa·soči| e·h=a·hkwateniki aškote·wi.

f　　　　i·ni='pi e·h=kosa·wa·či,

g　　wi·h=wapawapašotamowa·či aškote·wi.†

h　　e·h=ki·ša·koči‑=meko ‑kohtamowa·či ke·ko·hi wi·h=itamowa·či.

i　　　　mi·škota=ke·h=mo·hči='pi e·h=kokwisahto·wa·či aškwa·ne·hkete·wani,

j　　i·ni='pi=meko e·h=atosowa·či,

k　　e·h=ma·mya·hkihekwiwa·či=meko.

l　　ma·ne=meko e·h=mya·hkihekwiwa·či i·ni aškote·wi.

m　　a·neta='pi ‖ e·h=katawi‑=meko ‑ča·kesowa·či.

64 a　aše=ke·h=meko e·h=to·ta·kwiwa·či i·ni| aškote·wi.

b　　　　na·hka te·pwe·htakiki mehto·či=meko e·h=kehke·nemekwiwa·či we·ča·howa·čini,

c　　e·h=kekeni‑=meko ‑ki·ši‑wača·howa·či.

d　　i·ni='pi e·šawiwa·či te·pwe·htakiki i·ni aškote·wi.

e　　　　mo·hči=meko='pi apeno·he·haki e·h=kokwisahto·wa·či| aškwa·ne·hkete·wani,

f　　e·h=pwa·wi‑=meko ‑a·nawe·nemekwiwa·či,

g　　e·h=atosowa·či=meko.

h　　ma·mahka·či=meko e·h=atosoči| owiye·ha ke·ko·hi e·to·taka.

i　　　　na·hka mahkwa·či=meko ke·kano·taka, mo·hči=meko='pi onehkeki e·h=pakiseniki,

j　　e·h=pwa·wi‑kaški·wi·sakesowa·či me·nwi‑to·tawa·čiki aškote·ne·si·hani. ‖

65 a　ma·ne=meko e·h=kehke·nema·wa·či pwa·wi‑kaški|‑atosoničihi.‡

b　　　　na·hka ne·hi‑atosoničihi e·h=ketema·kiha·či mehtose·neniwahi.§

c　　　　omeso·ta·nahi=ke·hi a·ye·niwe·=meko e·h=ahpi·htesiniči.

d　　kenwe·ši=meko e·h=mehtose·neniwiniči.

e　　meše·='nah=mekoho wi·či‑ahpi·htesi·ma·ničihi e·h=ča·ki|‑nepo·hiniči,

f　　wi·č‑ahpi·htesi·ma·wa·čihi.¶

g　　meše·='nah=meko nye·wenwi| mehto·či e·h=ča·kine·niči mehtose·neniwahi.

____

*/meso·te·we·we·=/: AK ⟨mesotawewa⟩.

†63fg: lit., 'they feared him to be making fun of fire'.

‡P. 65 has a damaged right edge, as if it was sticking out from the others for some time.

§/ne·hi/: dividers added.

¶Repeated for the proximate shift.

f   "So, you will say of one that paints their face with this, 'He or she is fasting.'
g   And a manitou will truly bless whoever follows it this way," those instructing the people declared.
h   Sure enough, they saw the people begin fasting,
i   including women, girls, and boys.
j   In fact, they fasted all over, quietly.
63 a   And there were some that fasted in a reckless way.
b   They began using the Spirit of Fire for anything.
c   A little while later, one who ill-used that fire burned up.
d   But in fact, it was the Spirit of Fire that killed him.
e   He had bragged on fire as dangerous.
f   Then, for fear of that spirit, to hear tell,
g   they wouldn't make fun of fire.
h   They were really afraid to say anything about it.
i   What's more, even when they just jerked firesticks out quickly,
j   they burned themselves.
k   It would cause them injury.
l   Many were injured by that fire.
m   And they say some almost burned up.
64 a   But the fire was just toying with them.
b   Also, when ones who heeded it cooked, it was as if it knew who they were.
c   They quickly finished their cooking.
d   That's what the ones who heeded that fire did.
e   Even when children jerked firesticks out quickly
f   it didn't exempt them.
g   They burned themselves.
h   Anyone who did anything bad to it couldn't avoid getting burned.
i   Also, one who spoke to it quietly, even when it landed on their hand,
j   the ones that treated the Spirit of Fire well couldn't be hurt by burns.
65 a   They knew many who couldn't be hurt by burns.
b   And he made the people who kept getting burned suffer.

c   Now, his parents always remained the same age.
d   And they lived long lives.
e   In the course of time those of the same age as they were all died,
f   those of their same age.
g   As time went on it was as if people all died four times over.

h nye·wo·nameki e·h=wi·či-kehkye·ma·wa·či owi·či-mehtose·neni·wa·wahi.[*]

i kekimesi=meko| e·h=kehkya·niči.

j e·h=ma·ne·wa·či ke·hkya·čiki i·nina·hi.

k na·hina·hi ke·hkya·wa·či, owi·či-ke·hkya·hwa·wahi ‖ e·h=ma·ne·niči.

66 a aškači e·h=we·pi-nepeniči owi·či-ke·hkya·hwa·wahi.

b e·škami=meko mehto·či e·h=wi·pwinehkawoči.

c ma·wač-ahkowi=meko wi·nwa·wa e·h=nepo·hiwa·či.

d če·wina·h=ke·h=meko e·h=nepo·hiwa·či ke·hkya·haki.

e ki·ši-nepo·hiwa·či, e·h=ma·takwišimeči.|

f če·wi·šwi=meko e·h=ma·takwišimeči.

g wa·paniki| pa·hkeneči, če·wi·šwi=meko e·h=aseniwiwa·tehe.[†]

h neniwa e·h=ča·ki-=meko -aseniwiči,

i metemo·he·ha po·hkwi e·h=aškw-aseniwiči.

j e·h=okehči·pi·hiči e·h=aškw-aseniwiči,

k ahpemeki='ši e·h=ča·ki-=meko -aseniwiči.

l onehkani e·h=ča·ki-=meko -aseniwiniki,

m ohka·tani=mata·'pi a·kwi me·hi-aseniwinikini. ‖

67 a še·ški='pi e·h=ki·ši-=meko -mayakinameške·ška·či i·na metemo·he·ha.

b e·hpi·hči·hkawoči=meko, e·h=ki·ši-=meko -ča·ki-aseniwiči.

c i·niye·ne=ke·h=meko mehteno·hi='pi oni·ča·neswa·wani aškote·ne·siwani.

d a·kwi·='nahi='pi na·hka oni·ča·nesiwa·čini nana·ši.

e i·ni=meko iši-nekotenwi we·ni·ča·nesiwa·či.

f o·ni mehtose·neniwaki e·h=pwa·wi-kehke·nema·wa·či wi·h=to·tawa·kwe·hiki ki·ši-ča·ki-aseniwiniči.[‡]

g aškači pašito·hani e·h=kanawiniči.

h "'šina·kwa,| owiye·ha=koči mani| e·ši-nepekini, ahpene·či=meko pi·tahwa·pi.|

i i·ni=ča·h=meko wi·h=to·tawiya·ke.

j ki·h=pi·tahwipena," e·h=iči pašito·he·ha. ‖

68 a o·ni=ča·hi='pi e·h=pi·tahoči.

b e·h=mawi-wa·nehke·wa·či wi·h=pi·tahwa·čiki.

c o·ni='pi=na·hka ahki e·h=ki·ša·koči-=meko -wi·šika·waki·niki.

d (e·h=no·hka·waki·hiniki=ke·hi,

e šewe·na i·nina·hi e·h=ki·ša·koči-=meko -nešiwi-wi·šika·waki·niki.)

f masa·či=meko| e·h=ka·ki·ša·nehke·wa·či.|

g če·wina·h=meko e·h=ka·ki·ša·nehke·wa·či.

h če·wina·h=meko e·h=ki·ša·nehke·wa·či,

i e·h=na·kwa·wa·či wi·h=na·na·čiki.

j i·ya·h=pye·ya·wa·či, masa·či=meko e·h=kaški-konepeče·na·wa·či.

k na·hkači e·h=koči-ni·me·na·wa·či,

---

[*]/nye·wo·nameki/: AK ⟨.nyewona.meki.⟩.

[†]/wa·paniki| pa·hkeneči/: AK ⟨.wapani|pakeneči.⟩.

[‡]/wi·h=to·tawa·kwe·hiki/: AK ⟨.witotakwa|kweiki.⟩.

h   And the fourth time they got old along with the other people.

i   Every one of them was old.

j   There were many old people at that time.

k   At the time when they were old, there were many other old people.

66 a   After a while the other old people began dying.

b   It was as if they were being driven further and further into a corner.

c   And last of all *they* died.

d   The old folks died at exactly the same time.

e   After they died, they were covered up.

f   They were both covered up.

g   And when they were uncovered the next day, they had both turned to stone.

h   The man was entirely stone,

i   while the old lady was half not turned stone.

j   At the belt line she left off being stone,

k   while above it she was all stone.

l   Her hands were all stone,

m   but her feet, on the other hand, were not yet stone.

67 a   It's only that the old lady's skin had become strange.

b   And right while she was being tended to, she finished turning completely to stone.

c   Now, that Spirit of Fire was the only child they had.

d   They never had another child again after him.

e   It was only that one time that they had a child.

f   And the people didn't know what to do with them after they turned all to stone.

g   Some time later the old man spoke.

h   "Well, as soon as anyone dies, of course, they're always buried.

i   So, that's what you must do to us.

j   You must bury us," the old man said.

68 a   So, then they were buried, the story goes.

b   The ones who were going to bury them went to dig graves.

c   And another thing, they also say the earth was extremely hard.

d   (Now, it was a place with loose earth,

e   but at that time it was just as hard as it could possibly be.)

f   They were barely able to finish digging the graves.

g   They finished digging the graves at exactly the same time.

h   They finished the grave digging at exactly the same time,

i   and the ones who were going to go get them went back.

j   When they got there, they were barely able to roll them over.

k   Again, they tried lifting them up,

^l   e·h=pwa·wi-=meko a·wa·či meše inehpi -ni·me·na·wa·či.|

^m   o·ni=ʼpi e·h=ča·ko·na·wa·či,

ⁿ   meše=meko na·hina·hi e·h=ahkwiwena·wa·či, ‖

^{69 a}   e·h=a·kwapiwa·či.

^b   na·hka kotakani e·h=na·na·wa·či.|

^c   a·wasi=meko e·h=ahpi·hčiwanakesiniči._

^d   no·make·wi-=meko -awana·wa·či, e·h=a·kwapiwa·či.

^e   mani wi·h=iši-kena·či- mehči·ki wi·h=asa·wa·tehe, meše=meko na·hina·hi e·h=ota·hke·wa·či.

^f   mani_ahki·ki e·ši-pakišiniči, meši_kohkoseni=či·hi i·nahi e·h=ahte·niki,

^g   e·h=meša·niki.

^h   aye=meko ahpi·hte·hkamiki e·h=išina·kwateniki| i·ni aseni.

ⁱ   e·h=ki·ša·koči-=meko -ke·hte·keniki.

^j   e·hkwiwa·či=meko| a·wasi e·h=inehpiseniki.

^k   "šihihwi·ʹ," e·h=iyowa·či.

^l   o·ni kotakani e·h=mawi·hkawa·wa·tehe.

^m   a·č_a·wasi·me·h=meko e·h=inekihkwa·niki i·ni| aseni,

ⁿ   a·wasi=ke·h=meko e·h=išina·kwateniki. ‖

^{70 a}   še·ški e·h=sahkahwe·hto·wa·či,|

^b   kekimesi=meko mehtose·neniwaki.

^c   nye·wawahi·me i·nahi e·h=ahte·niki.

^d   nye·wawahi·makateniki, e·h=ašenoniki, če·wina·h=meko.

^e   e·h=mayo·wa·či=ʼpi mehtose·neniwaki,

^f   e·h=mawitamowa·či i·nini kekye·hči-kohkosenye·ni.

^g   e·h=a·mi·heti·wa·či.

^h   o·ni| i·ni aškote·wi ahpene·či=meko e·h=mya·ši-to·ta·kwiwa·či.

ⁱ   a·neta=ʼpi apeno·he·haki, kete·=ʼnah=meko e·h=ketemina·kwiwa·či, mehteno·hi.

^j   ke·hčikičiki=ke·hi=ʼpi a·kwi=meko| paši-menwi-to·ta·kwiwa·čini.[*]

^k   e·škami=meko e·h=iši_ketema·kihekowa·či i·nini aškote·ne·siwani.

^l   kapo·twe e·h=mi·na·we·nema·wa·či maneto·waki ni·šwi. ‖

^{71 a}   kapo·twe=meko e·h=mawi|-a·čimoha·wa·či wi·sahke·hani.

^b   ki·ši-a·ya·čimoheči wi·sahke·ha, e·h=a·čimoči.

^c   "pa·pekwa=ye·toke| peteki_wi·h=iši-aše·we·nemakwe.

^d   kekwaya·šima·pena=ma·hi,

^e   ʼnehki=meko e·nemi-ahkiwikwe·ni,ʼ e·h=inakwe," e·h=ina·či i·nihi maneto·wahi wi·sahke·ha.

^f   o·ni=na·hka kehči_maneto·wani_e·h=awiniči_e·h=a·wa·či,^{†/‡/§}

^g   e·h=mawi_a·čimowa·či e·ši-ketema·kiha·niči| mehtose·neniwahi.

^h   e·h=ča·ki-=meko -a·čimowa·či.

---

[*]/=meko/: AK ⟨.meko|⟩.

[†]/maneto·wani/: AK ⟨manetowa⟩.

[‡]/e·h=awiniči/: ⟨či⟩ has the usual small dot to the right and a long dash above.

[§]/e·h=a·wa·či/: AK ⟨e|awači.eawači.⟩.

l   and they couldn't even lift them up a moderate distance.

m   Then, the story is, they all lifted one together

n   and carried it a little ways

69 a   and sat to rest.

b   And they went back for the other one.

c   It was even heavier.

d   After carrying it a short while, they sat to rest.

e   Just as they were about to slowly set it down, they tossed it a short distance.

f   And just as it landed on the ground, suddenly a large granite boulder was there,

g   a big one.

h   That stone looked as if it had already been there some time.

i   It was extremely old.

j   And it stood there taller than they were.

k   "Golly!" they said.

l   And then they'd gone to deal with the other one.

m   That stone was even larger.

n   What's more, it looked even bigger than it was.

70 a   They just burned tobacco to them,

b   every one of the people did,

c   They had them there for four years.

d   After four years, they disappeared, both at the same time.

e   They say people wept,

f   mourning the loss of those large granite boulders.

g   And they all moved away together.

h   And the fire always treated them badly.

i   Some of the children, only, it treated another way entirely and blessed, they say.

j   But the grown-ups they say it didn't treat well at all.

k   They were made more and more miserable by the Spirit of Fire.

l   At some point two manitous took notice of him.

71 a   And at some point they went to inform Wîsahkêha.

b   After Wîsahkêha had heard the report, he spoke.

c   "It seems we'd be immediately going back and reversing our plan for him.

d   As you know, we've already given him our irrevocable word,

e   when we told him, 'As long as the earth may last,' " Wîsahkêha told those manitous.

f   And then next they went to where the Great Spirit was,

g   going to report about the way that one was making people miserable.

h   And they reported everything.

ⁱ ki·ši-=meko -ča·ka·čimowa·či,

^j "a·kwi=ča·h=mo·hči=meko nahmeko=meko ayo·nina·hi ke·ko·hi wi·h=ine·neme·hiyakwe.

^k wi·na=meko| we·we·ne·netamwa owi·yawi.

^l ki·na·na a·kwi=meko kana·kwa ‖ ke·ko·hi wi·h=inakwe ayo·nina·hi.

72 a mehteno·h=meko=ye·toke ki·ši-a·čihto·ya·ne_mani ahki,_

^b i·ni=ye·toke_mehteno·hi ke·ko·hi_wi·h=ina·soči,

^c ke·htena i·ni e·šawikwe·ni e·na·čime·kwe.

^d i·noki=wi·na wi·na=meko we·we·ne·netamwa| owi·yawi," e·h=ineči.

^e "a·kwi-kana·kwa=meko ke·ko·hi| wi·h=ikoči owiye·hani.

^f mehteno·h=ye·toke wi·sahke·ha a·mi_kaški-=ke·ko·hi -ina·hpenana·ta,

^g i·na we·we·ne·netaka inahkamikatwi," e·h=ineči.

^h "ni·na a·kwi ke·ko·hi we·we·ne·netamo·hiya·nini,"| e·h=ikowa·či.

ⁱ "mani=ča·hi a·mi-'ši-menwi|-to·tawe·kwe,

^j i·ni ine·neme·kwe, keteminawe·kwe:_

^k še·ški=meko mehtose·neniwaki keteminawe·kwe. ‖

73 a pwa·wi-=meko=wi·na_ke·ko·hi -ine·neme·kwe,*

^b še·ški=meko ko·šisemena·naki a·mi_keteminawe·kwiki.

^c awita=ke·hi ke·ko·hi iši-mya·ši-kano·šiye·ke·koha.

^d mahkwa·či=meko wi·tamawiye·ke·koha e·ši-keteminawa·we·kwe·ni.

^e mahkwa·či=meko| ki·h=a·čimopwa," e·h=ineči i·niki mi·na·we·nečika·čiki._

^f "nahi´, pe·hki=meko meše=meko·-'nahi ki·h=anemi_keteminawa·pena.

^g a·kwi ma·mahka·či_ke·hči-mahkate·wi·čiki,

^h meše=meko·-'nahi,

ⁱ apeno·haki=ke·hi,

^j meše=meko·-'nahi."

^k mi·škota=ke·hi-='niki i·ni=meko e·h=iši|-ni·šo·ke·wa·či maneto·waki,

^l e·h=pwa·wi-a·ya·teši-owi·kiwa·či.

^m e·h=mene·wite·he·wa·či, e·h=a·nwi·hka·sowa·či. ‖

74 a wi·h=a·čihemetehe·ta·taki| aškote·ne·siwani e·h=išiwe·pi-we·činowite·he·wa·či.

^b o·ni e·h=we·pi|-keteketeminawa·wa·či=meko,

^c meše=meko·-'nahi e·h=anemi_keteminawa·wa·či.

^d a·kwi=ke·hi-='pi| ma·mahka·či me·hkate·wi·ničihi.

^e meše=meko·-'nahi e·h=anemi_keteminawa·wa·či.

^f ke·keya·h=meko a·pehtawi e·h=ahkwi-keteminawa·wa·či.

^g e·h=a·čimekowa·či aškote·ne·siwani.

^h aškote·ne·siwa_keše·maneto·wani e·h=a·čimoha·či.

ⁱ o·ni=na·hka wi·sahke·ča·kwani e·h=a·čimoha·či aškote·ne·siwa.

^j e·šawiniči=meko na·na·kači e·h=a·čimoha·či,

^k na·hka taswi ke·teminawa·niči,

^l na·hkači| e·šihiši-keteminawa·niči, ‖

75 a a·ya·taso·no·ki e·ši_keteminawa·niči.

^b e·h=a·čimoči=meko_aškote·ne·siwa.

---

*/pwa·wi-=meko=wi·na/: AK ⟨pwawimeko.wina⟩.

ⁱ After they had given a complete report,

^j "Well, it's not that we would even contemplate anything against him here and now at present.

^k He's the one who has the say over himself.

^l It's not possible for *us* to tell him to do anything at the present time.

72 a I suppose, only after I've remade this earth,

^b only then, I suppose, will he be told to do anything,

^c if he's really doing what you say he is.

^d But for now it's *he* that has the say over himself," they were told.

^e "It's not possible for anyone to tell him to do anything.

^f I suppose only Wîsahkêha is the one who would be able to deal with him.

^g He's the one that has the say over the earth," they were told.

^h "I don't have the slightest say over anything," he told them.

ⁱ "So, this is how you would do them good,

^j if you think of them that way, if you bless them:

^k if you bless only people.   (That is, not other manitous.)

73 a But if you don't plan to do anything else for them,

^b only our grandchildren should be the ones you bless.

^c And you shouldn't speak roughly to them in any way.

^d You should quietly tell them however it is that you bless them.

^e You must speak quietly," those observant ones were told.

^f "Now listen, you must bless anyone with a full blessing.

^g It's not necessary that they be great at fasting,

^h just anyone,

ⁱ including children,

^j anyone."

^k Now, to make things worse, it was just those two manitous living together,

^l and not living apart from each other.

^m And they were disgruntled at having failed to be persuasive.

74 a They imagined it was an easy thing to, as it were, make over the Spirit of Fire.

^b And then they set about blessing them in earnest.

^c They went ahead blessing anyone.

^d And, they say, it didn't have to be ones who fasted.

^e They went on blessing anyone.

^f In time they had blessed half of them.

^g And the Spirit of Fire reported what they were doing.

^h The Spirit of Fire told the Great Spirit.

ⁱ And the Spirit of Fire also told Wîsahkêha.

^j He told them exactly what they did,

^k and also how many they blessed,

^l and the ways they blessed them,

75 a and the amounts of the blessings they conferred on them.

^b The Spirit of Fire gave a full report.

^c   o·ni i·niki owi·hka·neti·haki e·h=ne·woti·wa·či atehči·me·hi.

^d e·h=we·pi-mi·na·wima·wa·či i·nihi,

^e asa·mi| taswi e·h=keteminawa·niči.

^f   me·teno·ški=meko mama·ne e·h=keteminawa·wa·či.

^g   ke·keya·h=meko, "ke·ko·h=meko iši-nahi·hkawate,

^h meše=meko e·to·tawa·wate·ni_to·tawiye·kapa," e·h=ineči| wi·sahke·ha.

ⁱ   "ke·nema·pi,"| e·h=išiwe·či.

^j   "ke·ko·h=meko wi·h=ina·hpenanači, ketene·nemene," e·h=ina·či owi·hka·nani

ke·še·maneto·wa.

^k   "i·ni=we·=meko ki·h=išawi e·nena·ni," e·h=ineči wi·sahke·ha.

^l   "o·´,_meše ni·h=kočawi," e·h=išiwe·či wi·sahke·ča·kwa.‖

76 a   meše=meko na·hina·hi e·h=mawi-ki·wita·či i·ya·hi ašiči neno·te·wahi e·h=awiniči.|

^b   o·ni na·hka e·h=na·kwa·wa·či me·wi-ketemina·ka·čiki.

^c   wi·sahke·ha e·h=anemi-ahko·wa·či.

^d e·h=a·mo·wiči,

^e e·h=pwa·wi-=meko -kehke·nemekoči.

^f wa·natohka=meko e·h=anemehka·niči.|

^g i·ya·hi e·h=pya·niči neno·te·wahi e·h=awiniči,

^h e·h=kehkahama·ti·niči wi·h=taši-ni·šwi|-ketemina·ke·niči,

ⁱ na·ni·šwi=meko wi·kiya·pye·ni e·h=na·sehkaminiči,

^j nya·nanwi| mehtose·neniwahi e·h=mawi-keteminawa·niči.

^k če·wina·h=meko| e·h=ketemina·ke·niči.|

^l   o·ni wi·h=a·niči e·h=mawi-pi·čisa·či,

^m e·h=a·mo·wika·niwihto·či ‖ i·ni wi·kiya·pi.

77 a   a·mo·wa=meko e·h=ahkwa·wišiki i·nahi wi·kiya·peki.

^b   "mani=meko iši|-če·wi·šwi-pi·tike·wa·te, ki·h=mesi-=meko -mawinana·pwa,"_e·h=ina·či.

^c   "ča·ki=meko na·meše ki·h=sakahwa·pwa," e·h=ina·či a·mo·wahi.

^d   "e·h=ohkiwaniwa·či_e·yi·ki=meko ki·h=pi·to·te·pwa,"| e·h=ina·či.

^e   "na·hka mešketonowa·te, ki·h=pi·to·te·sa·pwa=meko,

^f na·meki=meko onakeši·wa·ki wi·h=sakahwe·kwe," e·h=ina·či a·mo·wahi.

^g   o·ni i·tepi e·h=a·wa·či,| ki·ši-ketemina·ke·wa·či.

^h o·ni=nekoti, "na·pi=wi·na na·kwa·hiyakwe," e·h=iči.

ⁱ kenwe·ši=meko e·h=taši·hka·ti·wa·či.

^j   ke·keya·h=meko, "ke·ko·h=meko netene·neta ‖ i·ni wi·kiya·pi," e·h=iči.|

78 a   "nahi´, i·tepi=meko_iha·ta·we," e·h=iyoweči.*

^b   "me·mečine·h=meko, a·kwi=ča·h=na·hka," e·h=išiwe·či| nekoti.

^c   "o·´,_meše ki·na| ki·h=ni·ka·ni," e·h=ineči.

^d   "o·´,_ni·h=ni·ka·ni," e·h=iči,

^e e·h=anemi-=meko -ni·ka·ni·či.

^f   e·h=pemi-=meko -ni·ka·ni·či neniwa,|

^g e·h=anemi-=meko -ahko·woči.

---

*/e·h=iyoweči/: AK ⟨eiyowači⟩.

      ^c And then the two friends met each other some distance away.

^d They launched into a detailed discussion of them,

^e that those two had blessed them too much.

    ^f They were too easily blessing them in large numbers.

    ^g Finally Wîsahkêha was told, "If you can deal with them in some way,

^h you can do whatever you want to them."

    ⁱ "I wonder if I could," he answered.

    ^j "I want you to do something serious to them," God told Wîsahkêha.

    ^k "In fact, you must do what I'm telling you to," Wîsahkêha was told.

    ^l "Oh, if that's what you want, I'll try," Wîsahkêha answered.

  76 ^a He went to stay a little ways away over near where the Indians were living.

    ^b And the ones going to bless people set out again.

    ^c Wîsahkêha went following behind them,

^d becoming a bee,

^e and they didn't know it was him.

^f There they were, walking on with no concerns.

^g And they got to where the Indians were.

^h They decided with each other where they would bless people together,

ⁱ and they approached the lodges jointly,

^j going to bless five people.

^k They bestowed their blessings simultaneously.

    ^l And then he flew into a place where they would be going,

^m making that lodge into a beehive.

  77 ^a Bees filled that lodge.

    ^b "As soon as they both come in, you must all attack them," he told them.

^c "You must all sting them inside the ears," he told the bees.

^d "And you must crawl into their noses, as well," he told them.

^e "Also, if they open their mouths, you must quickly crawl right in,

^f to sting them inside their intestines," he told the bees.

    ^g And then they went there, after blessing some people.

^h And one said, "Why don't we go back?"

ⁱ For a long time they tried to persuade each other.

    ^j Finally he said, "I have my suspicions about that lodge."

  78 ^a "Come on, let's go there," was the response.

    ^b "One last time, no more," the other one said.   (*Lit.*, 'one said'.)

^c "O.K., then, *you* go first," he was told.

^d "Oh, I'll go first," he said,

^e and he went first.

    ^f The fellow walked along in the lead,

^g followed as he went.

h   e·h=pi·tike·wa·či.

i   če·wi·šwi=meko ki·ši|-pi·tike·wa·či, e·h=mawinanekowa·či a·mo·wahi.

j   ča·ki=meko ohtawaka·wa·ki e·h=sakahokowa·či.

k   na·mikome=meko e·h=sakahokowa·či e·yi·ki.

l   na·hka| onakeši·wa·ki e·h=sakahokowa·či.

m   e·h=nowinehka·kowa·či,

n   e·h=anemi-sesosesotamowa·či,

o   e·h=na·kwa·wa·či. ‖

79 a   e·h=anemi-=meko -tanwe·we·ti·wesi·hiwa·či.

b   masa·či=meko e·h=owi·ke·hiwa·či e·h=pya·wa·či.

c   mehto·či e·h=api·hiwa·čini e·h=nananana·hisahowa·či.

d   e·h=taši-mama·twe·wa·či.

e   "ya·´, ya·´, ya·´,| ya·´," e·h=iyowa·či.

f   "ohohya·´,| ohohya·´, ya·´, ya·´," e·h=iyowa·či a·mo·wahi se·kasakahokočiki.

g   wa·paniki e·h=pya·niči wi·sahke·hani.

h   "'šina·kwa, a·hkwamatamowe·kwe·ni," e·h=ikowa·či.

i   "ehe·he," e·h=iči pepe·naki e·šawita.[*]

j   "a·mo·waki=kohi| nenesekona·naki,"| e·h=ina·či.[†]

k   "kaši=ča·h=e·h=teki.

l   kemi·ka·ti·ha·pwa?"| e·h=ikowa·či.

m   "a·kwi, wi·kiya·peki awikwe·hiki,"| e·h=ina·či.

n   "e·h=mawi-='yo·we -keteminawaketehe neniwa,

o   keye·hapa_i·nahi ‖ e·wiwa·tehe wi·kiya·peki.

80 a   i·ni=ča·hi e·h=taši_-nešiyameči," e·h=iči.

b   i·na=ke·hi nekoti e·h=po·ni-=meko -kehke·netaki.

c   še·ški=meko e·h=taneška·či e·h=ne·mo·hiči.

d   wi·sahke·ha e·h=keteminawa·či,

e   a·mo·wi| e·h=ašama·či.

f   e·h=a·čimoha·či,

g   "mani mi·čiye·kwe, ki·h=ne·se·pwa,"| e·h=ina·či.

h   e·h=ašama·či i·nini pepe·naki e·šawi·hiničini,

i   e·h=mi·činiči.

j   ke·htena=meko e·h=ne·se·niči.

k   o·ni a·mo·wa·powi e·h=menaha·wa·či i·nini ke·tawi-=meko -nepo·hiničini.

l   na·hina·h=meko kwe·taminiči, e·h=ne·se·nič _

m   nye·wokoni e·h=wi·čiha·či.

n   ki·h_-ki·ši-=meko -ne·se·niči pe·hki,

o   me·me·čiwi| pe·hki, ‖

81 a   e·h=nana·tohtawa·či.

b   "e·šiwe·pi-sakahokona·kwe·ni."

c   "'šina·kwa, mani=ča·hi e·šawiya·ke:

------

[*]⟨e.e.e.|⟩: the dividers are added small dots.

[†]/e·h=ina·či/ (continuing the proximate subject in 79*i*): AK ⟨einiči⟩; cf. 92*b* and 88*k*.

^h And they went in.

ⁱ After they both had come in, the bees attacked them.

^j They all stung them in their ears.

^k They stung them inside the nose as well.

^l And they stung them in the intestines.

^m They drove them out,

ⁿ and they went off coughing,

^o going back home.

79 a And they were as if quarreling on the way.

^b They barely made it back to their house.

^c It was as if they threw themselves down in their usual spots.

^d And they were moaning away.

^e "Ow! Ow! Ow! Ow!" they said.

^f "Oh mercy! Oh mercy! Ow! Ow!" said the ones who'd been stung by the bees.

^g The next day they had Wîsahkêha arrive.

^h "Well, you must be under the weather," he said to them.

ⁱ "Yes," said the one who was in better shape.

^j "We were definitely murdered by some bees," he told him.

^k "So, how come?

^l Did you pick a fight with them?" he asked them.

^m "No, they must've lived in the house," he told him.

ⁿ "When we had gone to bless a man,

^o it turned out they lived in the house.

80 a So, that's where they murdered us," he said.

^b Now, that other one had lost consciousness.

^c He just went on breathing softly.

^d Wîsahkêha took pity on them,

^e giving them honey to eat.

^f And he explained to them about it,

^g telling them, "If the two of you eat this, you'll get better."

^h He gave it to the one who was in better shape,

ⁱ and he ate it.

^j Sure enough, he got better.

^k And then they gave honey tea to the one who was almost dead.

^l And the moment he swallowed it, he was better.

^m He stayed with them for four days.

ⁿ After they had been cured completely,

^o both of them completely,

81 a he asked them a question.

^b "I wonder just why they stung you."

^c "Well, so here's what we did:

d   ma·haki ko·šiseme·hena·naki nema·mawi-keteminawa·pena.

e   meše=nekotenwi| i·tepi e·ya·ya·ke, i·ni| e·h=nešiyameči a·mo·waki,

f   pi·tike=meko wi·kiya·peki," e·h=iči.

g   "mana=wi·na ni·či-pašito·ha mya·ši-=meko -kohtamo·hiwa," e·h=iči.[*]

h   "nahi=ča·hi·='nahí, ni·h=te·pwe·htawe·hi!?[†]

i   a·čimowa=ke·hi,|

j   'ke·ko·h=meko ni·na neteñe·neta i·ni wi·kiya·pi,' netekwa.

k   pema·či=ča·hi·='nahi ni·h=paši|-te·pwe·htawa·wa!? [‡]

l   neki·hki·hkima·wa=meko i·tepi| wi·h=a·ya·ke.

m   'meše ki·na| ki·h=ni·ka·ni,' netekwa,

n   e·h=ni·ka·ni·ya·ni.

o   wa·natohka=mekoho ‖ netanemi-pi·tike·pena,"| e·h=iči.

82 a   "kapo·twe_newe·pi-sakahokona·naki," e·h=iči.

b   e·h=apahapane·niniči wi·sahke·hani,

c   "ha· ha· ha· ha·," e·h=iniči.[§]

d   "ki·hpene=meko i·ni e·h=išawiki," e·h=iniči.

e   "na·hka=ke·hi pi·tike·ye·kwe neno·te·wi-_wi·kiya·pye·ni,

f   me·mešihka=meko a·wasi·me·hi ki·h=išawipwa,"_e·h=ikowa·či wi·sahke·hani.

g   e·h=kohtamowa·či kete·='nah.

h   o·ni wi·sahke·ha owi·hka·nani e·h=mawa·pama·či, keše·maneto·wani ahpemeki e·winičini.

i   i·ya·h=e·h=pya·či,|

j   "'šina·kwa, ni·hka·ne, neki·ši·hkawa·waki='yo·we," e·h=ina·či.

k   "he·´," e·h=iniči.

l   "o·´,_kemenwi-to·tawa·waki?" e·h=ikoči.

m   "a·hpečinanate, ki·h=menwi-to·tawa·waki," e·h=ikoči.

n   "a·kwi=ča·hi ‖ wa·wosa·hi a·hpečinanakini," e·h=ina·či.

83 a   "še·ški=meko wi·h=iši_kosa·wa·či neto·tawa·waki,"_e·h=ina·či.

b   "o·´,_we·nahi·='ni," e·h=iniči.

c   "ni·na=we·na,| 'a·hpečinane·toke=meko,' netešite·he," e·h=iniči.

d   "a·kwi, na·hka=ča·hi ke·ko·hi| inanohkye·wa·te,

e   i·ni no·make·we wi·h=wa·wana·čihaki," e·h=ina·či.

f   o·ni e·h=na·kwa·či ne·ya·pi e·h=owi·ke·hiči wi·sahke·ha,

g   o·hkomese·heki| e·h=a·či.

h   nye·wawahi·me| wi·sahke·ha e·h=nepa·či.

i   kwi·yena=meko nye·wawahi·makateniki, e·h=to·hki·či.

j   aše=ma·hi·='pi| o·hkomese·hani to·hkinehka·kwa.

---

[*]⟨mya⟩: ⟨a⟩ is over the erasure of the start of ⟨š⟩.

[†]/=ča·hi·='nahí/: intonation from AW; expressive negative intonation conjectured.

[‡]/pema·či/ "sort of" (going with /paši/) (FM); expressive negative intonation conjectured;

[§]⟨.a.|a.a.a.⟩: the dividers in ⟨a.a.a⟩ are added lines.

d   We went to bless some of our grandchildren.

e   When we went to that one place, then the bees murdered us,

f   right inside the lodge," he said.

g   "But this other old fellow here was kind of leery of it," he said.

h   "So, naturally then, I wouldn't even believe him a little!

i   And he explained himself,

j   telling me, '*I* have my suspicions about that lodge.'

k   So, naturally, then I would persist in not believing him at all!

l   I insisted to him that we go there.

m   'Then, *you* go first,' he told me,

n   and I went first.

o   We blithely went right on in," he said.

82 a   "Suddenly, they began stinging us," he said.

b   And here, Wîsahkêha laughed,

c   going, "Ha! Ha! Ha! Ha!

d   "Once that happens to anyone, it'll be forever happening to them," he said.

e   "What's more, if you go into Indian houses again,

f   that will probably happen to you more," Wîsahkêha told them.

g   Now their minds were changed, and they were afraid of doing it.

h   And then Wîsahkêha went to see his friend, God who was in heaven.

i   He arrived there

j   and said to him, "Well, my friend, I dealt with them."

k   "Ah!" he answered.

l   "Oh, did you treat them well?" he asked him.

m   "If you kill them outright, you'll treat them well," he told him.

n   "Well, I didn't go so far as to kill them outright," he told him.

83 a   "I only did enough to them so that they'll steer clear of them," he told him.

b   "Oh, so that's it," he said.

c   "*I* thought you probably killed them outright," he said.

d   "No, so if they do anything again,

e   then I'll make them confused for a little while," he told him.

f   And then Wîsahkêha left for home again,

g   going to his grandmother's.

h   For four years Wîsahkêha slept.

i   After exactly four years he woke up.

j   Mind you, they say his grandmother just decided to roust him from sleep.

k "'šina·´,̮noši·he, kenwe·ši=meko·='ni| e·h=nepa·yani," e·h=ikoči.

l "natawi-=ča·h-=to·hki·yane," e·h=ikoči.

m "ši·´,̮ke·htena=ni·hka," ‖ e·h=ina·či.

84 a e·h=pemi-̮wana·ki·či wi·sahke·ha.|

b "ano·hko, ta·ni-̮nehki| ne·pa·ya·ni," e·h=ina·či.

c "'šina·´,̮noši·hi, i·noki=ča·hi·='ni e·h=nye·wawahi·makateki, kwi·yena=meko," e·h=iniči.

d "o·´,̮we·nahi·='ni,"| e·h=ina·či.

e "i·ni=ča·h wi·h=ki·yoki·yose·ya·ni," e·h=ina·či.*

f "meše=meko·='nahi ni·h=ki·wi-ne·nepe·wa·waki̮ni·či-̮maneto·waki," e·h=ina·či.

g "e·ne·nema·kwe·hiki nešise·hani e·h=aškote·ne·siwiniči," e·h=ina·či o·hkomese·hani.

h "owiye·ha=ke·hi wi·h=mya·ne·nema·či," e·h=ina·či o·hkomese·hani.

i "ki·na='yo=wi·na e·ne·nema·wate·ni."

j "o·´,̮ni·na=wi·na a·kwi=meko̮ke·ko·hi iši-mya·ne·nemakini," e·h=iči metemo·he·ha. ‖

85 a "me·mešihka=koči=meko a·neta̮mya·ne·neme·toke·hiki," e·h=ina·či.

b "ši·´,̮we·ne·h=ki·na wi·h=mya·ne·nema·ta," e·h=ikoči o·šisemani.†

c "mehteno·h=meko=ye·toke po·sesaki wi·h=mya·ne·nema·čiki.

d a·kwi=wi·na." ‡

e "we·ne·haki=ya·pi·='niki po·sesaki," e·h=ina·či.

f "'šina·kwa='škwe=wi·na·='na.§

g wa·waneška·haki=ma·h=ki·na i·niki 'po·sesaki' e·nečiki," e·h=iniči.

h "o·´,̮we·nahi wa·waneška·haki," e·h=ina·či.

i "'ši=we·=towi,"| e·h=iniči.

j "kašina·kwa, natawa·či, kehke·nemake owiye·ha po·sesite, ke·ko·he·hi=meko
ni·h=ina·hpenana·wa,"| e·h=ina·či.

k "wa·wosa·h=ke·hi netawe·ma·waki| ke·ko·hi ki·h=to·tawa·waki!?" e·h=ikoči. ‖

86 a "we·nah=wi·na owiye·ha ketotawe·ma·wi," e·h=ina·či.|

b "mehto·či·='yo=wi·na a·kwi| owiye·ha paši-otawe·ma·wiyanini," e·h=ina·či.

c "ši·´, meso·te·we·='škwe| maneto·waki netotawe·ma·wi," e·h=ina·či o·šisemani.¶

d "o·ho·´," e·h=ina·či.

e "o·´, wa·wosa·hi·='hi='yo| ke·htena," e·h=ina·či,

f e·h=na·kwa·či.

g e·h=aški-=meko̮-pi·tikawa·či meso·swani.

h e·h=ki·ša·koči-=meko -menwihkeše·we·šima·niči.

i e·h=nana·tohtawa·či.

j "o·´,̮nemenwe·nema·wa no·šisema," e·h=iniči.

k "i·ni=kohi´," e·h=ina·či,*

---

*⟨ča.⟩: divider perhaps added.

†AK /o·hkomese·hani/ emended to /o·šisemani/.

‡AW suggested also: "Not *him*."

§Translation follows HP in K-Wâpasaya 139*i*.

¶/meso·te·we·='škwe/: AK ⟨mesotewaškwe|⟩.

*⟨na⟩: ⟨a⟩ over flat ⟨a⟩.

k   "Well, grandson, you slept for a pretty long time," she told him.

l   So, it's time for you to wake up," she said to him.

m   "Oh, it's true," he told her.

84 a   And Wîsahkêha got up from his bed.

b   "Grandma, how long did I sleep for?" he asked her.

c   "Well, grandson, so it's now been four years, exactly," she said.

d   "Oh, so that's how long," he said to her.

e   "So, now I'm going to go walking around," he told her.

f   "I'll go around sleeping anyplace in the lodges of the other manitous," he told her.

g   "I wonder what they think about my uncle being the Spirit of Fire," he said to his grandmother.

h   "Whether or not anyone dislikes him," he told his grandmother.

i   "I wonder what *you* think about him, for instance."

j   "Oh, *I* don't dislike him in any way," the old lady said.

85 a   "Of course, I suppose some of them may perhaps dislike him," she told him.

b   "Oh come on, *who's* going to *dislike* him?" her grandson said to her.

c   "I guess it's only villainous ones that dislike him.

d   But it's not so."

e   "So tell me, who are those villainous ones," he asked her.

f   "Why, the idea of him!

g   See, the ones called the villainous ones are bad actors," she said.

h   "Oh, they're bad actors!" he said to her.

i   "Of course!" she said.

j   "Well, if I know anyone is villainous, I guess I might as well do a little something to them," he told her.

k   "It would hardly be expected that you could do anything to my brothers," she told him.

86 a   "So, you have some brothers," he said to her.

b   "Because it's as if you don't have any brothers at all," he said to her.

c   "Why, there are manitous all over that are my brothers," she told her grandson.

d   "So that's what it is!" he told her.

e   "Well, it's quite unexpected for that to be true," he told her,

f   and he left.

g   The first one whose lodge he entered was Mesôswa.

h   He found that he had him (the Spirit of Fire) set in an extremely fine bed of coals.

i   And he asked him the question.

j   "Oh, I like my grandson," he said.

k   "Excellent!" he told him,

^l   e·h=na·kwa·či.

^m   na·hkači sa·kima·wani e·yi·ki=meko e·h=menwihkeše·we·šima·niči.

ⁿ   e·h=nana·tohtawa·či.

^o   "o·´,⸤nemenwe·nama·wa no·šisema," ‖ e·h=iniči.

87 a   "o·´,⸤we·nahi·='ni," e·h=ina·či,

^b   e·h=na·kwa·či.

^c   o·ni i·niye·he owi·hka·neti·hahi, e·h=mya·šihkeše·we·šino·hiniči.| *

^d   e·h=apihapiči.

^e   e·h=nana·tohtawa·či.

^f   "o·´,⸤neša·kwe·nemopena e·h=pemenakeči," e·h=iniči.

^g   e·h=me·me·čikiha·či=meko.

^h   "o·´,⸤nepešikwa·čimopena=koh=meko e·h=ša·kwe·nemoya·ke e·h=pemenakeči," e·h=iniči.

ⁱ   "o·ho·´," e·h=ina·či.

^j   e·h=sakihta·hpe·na·či,

^k   e·h=nowa·hke·či.

^l   " 'wa·pikono·he·ha'⸤ki·h=iko·pi," e·h=ina·či.

^m   "a·kwi=meko wi·h=pešeke·nemehkini nešise·haki, neki·haki," e·h=ina·či.

ⁿ   na·hka=meko kotakani e·h=nowisaha·či.

^o   "ki·na=ča·hi 'pa·pi·hto·šketo·ha' ki·h=iko·ki nešise·haki na·hka⸤neki·haki," ‖ e·h=ina·či._†

88 a   "meše=meko·='nahi ki·h=ki·wikwe.

^b   ne·wohkini, ki·h=neškina·ko·ki.

^c   wa·wosa·h=meko ki·h=pa·pakameko·ki,"| e·h=ina·či,‡

^d   e·h=na·kwa·či.

^e   e·h=pye·notawa·či neniwani e·h=owi·kiniči.

^f   metemo·he·hani e·h=owi·winiči neniwani,

^g   e·h=aškikiniči=meko.

^h   aye=meko| e·h=išina·kwateniki aškote·wi.

ⁱ   e·h=nana·tohtawa·či,

^j   "e·ne·nema·wate·ni aškote·ne·siwa," e·h=ina·či.

^k   "ši·´,⸤pe·hki=ča·h=meko neša·kwe·nemohkatawa·wa,"| e·h=iniči.§

^l   "o·´,⸤we·nahi·='ni,"| e·h=ina·či.

^m   "neneškinawa·wa=we·=meko," e·h=iniči.

ⁿ   e·h=nowisaha·či.|

^o   mo·na·ne·hani e·h=anemipahoniči.¶

^p   "i·niya," e·h=ina·či._

^q   "i·ni=kohi⸤wi·h=išawi·hiyani," ‖ e·h=ina·či.

89 a   " 'mo·na·ne·ha'| ki·h=iko·ki nešise·haki.|

^b   a·kwi wi·h=nahi-amohkini.

---

* /i·niye·he/: syllable ⟨e⟩ over erased ⟨ne⟩.

† /pa·pi·hto·šketo·ha/ (AW): 'pocket gopher' in IP translation p. 88.

‡ /e·h=ina·či/: AK ⟨|eineči.⟩.

§ /e·h=iniči/: ⟨ni⟩ has ⟨i⟩ over erased ⟨a⟩.

¶ /anemipa/: AK ⟨anepi|pa⟩.

l   and he left.
m   And he also found that Sâkimâwa had him set in a fine bed of coals.
n   And he asked him the question.
o   "Oh, I like my grandson," he said,
87 a   "Oh, good to hear," he told him,
b   and he left.
c   And then to those two friends from before, and there he lay in a poor bed of coals.
d   He sat there
e   and asked them the question.
f   "Oh, we don't want to take care of him," one said.
g   He pressed him to make sure.
h   "Oh, we did tell the truth about not wanting to take care of him," he said.
i   "So that's it," he said to him.
j   He took him by the scruff of his neck
k   and threw him out the door.
l   "You'll be called a little mouse," he said to him.
m   "My uncles and aunts won't think you're cute," he told him.
n   And he hurled the other one out the door.
o   "So, *you* my uncles and aunts will call a pocket gopher," he told him.
88 a   "You'll burrow around just anywhere.
b   Whenever they see you, they'll despise you.
c   They'll even go so far as to club you to death," he told him,
d   and he left.
e   He came to where a man lived.
f   The man was married to an old woman,
g   but he was young.
h   It looked like there had been a fire there some time before.
i   He posed the question,
j   asking him, "I wonder what you think of the Spirit of Fire."
k   "Well, I really don't want to have anything to do with him," he said.
l   "Oh, so that's it," he said to him.
m   "I hate him, in fact," he said.
n   He hurled him out the door.
o   And a woodchuck went running off.
p   "There he goes," he said after him.
q   "That *is* how you will be," he said to him.
89 a   "My uncles will call you a woodchuck.
b   They won't make a practice of eating you.

^c mehteno·h=meko metemo·he·haki wi·ša·wi|-mya·nehka·wa·čini| ki·h=amoko·ki," e·h=ina·či.

^d o·ni ihkwe·wani e·h=ki·wi-e·niki·kwe·niči.

^e e·h=nowisaha·či.|

^f e·h=pakišino·hiniči=meko e·h=taši-nepo·hka·noniči.

^g "i·ni=kohi wi·h=išawi·hiyani.

^h e·yi·ki=meko metemo·he·haki me·či-wi·ša·wi-mya·nehka·hiwa·čini ki·h=amoko·ki," e·h=ina·či.

ⁱ " 'a·ye·ni·ha'=ke·h=mo·hči ki·h=iko·ki| neki·haki, nešise·haki·='nahi," e·h=ina·či.[*]

^j ki·ši-pa·hta·meči, e·h=pemi-we·pipahoči.

^k ke·htena=meko,

^l e·h=a·ye·ni·he·hiči=meko ke·htena i·na ‖ ihkwe·wa='yo·we.

^{90 a} na·hka=meko wi·sahke·ha e·h=na·kwa·či kotakenoki.

^b ša·watesiwani e·h=mawi-wa·pama·či.

^c e·h=pya·či i·ya·hi,

^d e·h=ki·ša·koči-=meko -menwihkeše·we·šima·soniči.

^e aka·mete·ki e·h=nana·hapiči,

^f e·h=nana·tohtawa·či,

^g "e·ne·nema·wate·ni aškote·ne·siwa," e·h=ina·či.| [†]

^h "o·´, nemenwi-pemenekwa,"| e·h=iniči.

ⁱ "ni·na=na·hka nemenwi-pemena·wa," e·h=iniči.

^j "o·´, i·ni=ča·h=we·čitawi," e·h=ina·či.

^k "i·ni=meko| aneme·hkami to·tawa·hkani," e·h=ina·či ša·watesiwani.[‡]

^l "o·´, i·ni=meko wi·h=to·tawaki ahpene·či," e·h=ina·či wi·sahke·ča·kwani.

^m "ni·n=e·yi·ki kemenwinawe·hi,‖ e·h=ki·ša·koči-=meko -menwi-to·tawači nešise·ha," e·h=išiwe·či wi·sahke·ha.[§]

^{91 a} o·ni na·hka e·h=na·kwa·či.

^b no·tatesiwani e·h=mawi-wa·pama·či.

^c i·ya·hi e·h=pya·či,

^d e·yi·ki=meko e·h=ki·ša·koči-=meko -menwi|-to·tawa·niči,[¶]

^e e·h=menwihkeše·we·šima·soniči.

^f aka·mete·ki| e·h=nana·hapiči,

^g e·h=we·pi-nana·tohtawa·či no·tatesiwani.

^h "o·´,| nete·pesi e·h=wi·či-mehtose·neni·me·hiya·ni anemi-mehtose·neniwa," e·h=iniči.|

ⁱ "ke·htena=meko netahpe·nemo.

^j ča·ki=meko neteši-awa·wa| e·h=wača·hoya·ni.

^k e·h=nepačiya·ni, netapane·hpoko·hiwa.| [*]

^l ke·htena=meko ‖ nepo·ni-nepači ki·ši-aniwešawe·ya·nini.

---

[*]/a·ye·ni·ha/ 'possum' is derived from /-a·ye·ni/ AI 'laugh', which appears in several verbs.
[†]/aškote·ne·siwa/: ⟨s⟩ in ⟨sko⟩ added later.
[‡]/aneme·hkami/ 'forever' (also found as /aneme·hkamiki/): phonemics conjectured,
[§]/ni·n=e·yi·ki/: AK ⟨.ninaye|ki.⟩.
[¶]⟨ni⟩ over erased ⟨či⟩.
[*]/netapane·hpoko·hiwa/: AK ⟨.ne|tapanopokoiwa|⟩.

^c Only old women when they greatly crave meat will eat you." he told him.

^d And then the woman was there with a smile on her face.

^e He hurled her out the door.

^f And right where she landed she played dead.

^g "That's just how you will be.

^h Old women, when they really crave meat too badly, will eat you as well," he said to her.

ⁱ "My aunts and my uncles will even call you a possum (as if, the laugher)," he told her.

^j After the curse was pronounced on her, she began running away.

^k Sure enough,

^l that woman who had been before really did become a possum.

90 a Again Wîsahkêha set out to go to someone else's.

^b He went to see South Wind.

^c He arrived over there,

^d and found that he (the Spirit of Fire) was set in an extremely fine bed of coals.

^e He sat down on the other side of the lodge,

^f and asked him the question,

^g saying, "I wonder what you think of the Spirit of Fire."

^h "Oh, he takes good care of me," the other one said.

ⁱ "And *I* take good care of *him*," the other one said.

^j "Oh, well that's excellent," he said to him.

^k "Treat him that way forever," he told South Wind.

^l "Oh, that's exactly how I'll treat him always," he told Wîsahkêha.

^m "You please *me*, also, by treating my uncle extremely well," Wîsahkêha declared.

91 a And then he set out again.

^b And he went to see Wind.

^c He arrived over there,

^d and found that he, also, treated him (the Spirit of Fire) extremely well,

^e he being set in a nice bed of coals.

^f He sat down on the other side of the lodge

^g and set to questioning Wind.

^h "Oh, I'm glad to be living with one of the People-to-Be," he said.

ⁱ "I truly rely on him.

^j I use him in every way when I cook.

^k When I'm cold, he warms me a bit with his breath.

^l I'm truly not cold anymore after I've got a good fire.

92 a ke·htena=ča·h=meko neki·ša·koči-=meko -tepa·na·wa," e·h=iniči no·tatesiwani.

b "o·´, i·ni=meko iši- ahpene·či -menwi-to·tawi ko·šisema," e·h=ina·či.*

c "kemenwinawe·hipwa| ne·h=ni·na, taswi_me·nwi-to·tawe·kwe," e·h=ina·či,

d e·h=na·kwa·či.

e meše=meko e·h=anahanemehka·či.

f aškači=meko i·ya·hi e·h=pya·či.

g e·h=pemi-pi·tike·či, e·h=nasahte·niki wi·kiya·pi.|

h aškote·wi e·h=ahte·niki e·h=apihapiči.

i meše·='nah=meko nye·wokoni i·nahi_e·h=apihapiči.

j e·h=we·pi-kakano·taki.

k "na·hina·h=meko ‖ pye·ya·kwe·ni ayo·h=we·wi·kita,

93 a ayo·h=pemi-pi·tike·te, a·ya·neši wi·h=pi·ša·kaninekwe·he·hiwa,"| e·h=iči wi·sahke·ha,

b e·h=na·kwa·či.

c kotaki e·h=na·sehkaki_wi·kiya·pi.

d i·ya·hi e·h=pya·či,

e e·h=nekoto·ke·hiniči neniwani.

f aye=meko našawaye e·h=ahpi·hčina·kwateniki aškote·wi.

g e·h=nana·tohtawa·či,|

h "e·ne·nema·wate·ni| aškote·ne·siwa," e·h=ina·či.

i "o·´, ni·na=ča·h=wi·na neneškinawa·wa," e·h=iniči.

j e·h=nowa·hke·či.

k mani| e·ši-nowa·hke·či, e·hkwa·ška·niči=meko e·h=oči-pemipenoniči masakahkwani.

l "i·ni wi·h=išawi·hiyani," e·h=ina·či.

m " ‘masakahkwa’ ‖ ki·h=iko·pi.

94 a a·kwi=wi·na| wi·h=neškino·hkini nešise·haki.

b ki·h=amohamoko·ki=meko," e·h=ina·či.

c "šewe·na a·kwi pe·hki meso·te·we.

d mehteno·h=meko ke·htesi·hičiki wi·h=amohamohkiki," e·h=ina·či.

e "a·kwi meso·te·we wi·h=wi·kamehkini," e·h=ina·či.

f o·ni_i·niya ne·sahte·nika_owi·ki e·h=na·kwa·či,

g i·ya·hi e·h=pya·či e·h=owi·ke·hiči.

h ki·ši-pi·tike·či, e·h=kohkikiči kena·či.

i kena·či=meko e·h=pi·ša·kaninekwe·hiči.

j e·h=wi·škwe·we·kesiči.

k ki·ši-=meko -ča·ki-pi·ša·kaninekwe·hiwiči, e·h=pem_anisa·či,

l pi·tike e·h=ki·ki·wisa·či.|

m saka·ki=meko e·h=kaški-nowisa·či, ‖

95 a anene·ki oči e·h=oči_nowa·ška·či.

b i·ni=meko e·h=iši-kehči-kohtaki e·h=owi·ke·hitehe.

c meše=wi·na=meko na·hina·hi e·h=ki·wita·hiči,†

d e·h=ahkawa·pataki ta·taki owi·ki, e·h=išiwe·pite·he·či.

---

*/e·h=ina·či/: ⟨na⟩ changed from ⟨ni⟩.

†/e·h=ki·wita·hiči/: AK ⟨.ekiwi|witaiči.⟩.

92 a   So, I'm truly extremely fond of him," Wind said.

b   "Ah, treat your grandchild well always, just like that," he told him.

c   "You please *me*, too, all of you who treat him well," he told him,

d   and he left.

e   He walked on and on contentedly.

f   Some time later he got where he was going.

g   He walked in and found the lodge deserted.

h   He sat there where the fire was.

i   He sat in that place for some four days.

j   And he settled for speaking to it.

k   "Whenever the one who lives here comes back,

93 a   when he walks in here, he will turn into a little bat instead," Wîsahkêha said,

b   and he left.

c   He headed for another lodge.

d   He got there

e   and found a man living there alone.

f   It looked like there had been a fire there long ago.

g   He asked him the question,

h   saying to him, "I wonder what you think of the Spirit of Fire."

i   "Oh, well *I* hate him," he answered.

j   He threw him out the door.

k   And the moment he threw him out, a badger ran away from the spot where he fell.

l   "That's how you'll be," he told him.

m   "You'll be called a badger.

94 a   But my uncles won't hate you.

b   In fact, they'll eat you," he told him.

c   "But not everyone, actually.

d   Only older people will be the ones that eat you," he told him.

e   "Not everyone will like eating you," he told him.

f   And then that other one whose house was deserted set out,

g   and he came back to where he alone lived.

h   After he came in, his bodily form slowly changed.

i   He slowly became a bat,

j   letting out a scream.

k   After he had completely turned into a bat, he flew up

l   and flew around inside.

m   He barely succeeded in flying out,

95 a   flying out through the smokehole.

b   Right away he was greatly fearful of the house where he had lived.

c   But he stayed around not so very far away.

d   In his mind he was guarding his house, in a way.

e   e·nemi-kesi·ya·hiniki,| e·h=na·hkatešitamo·hiči owi·ki,

f   we·či|-naha·winiki e·h=a·či.

g   pe·hkote·nikini e·h=penoči.

h   saka·ki=meko i·ya·hi e·h=pya·či.

i   o·ni wi·sahke·ha e·h=na·kwa·či,

j   kotakani e·h=mawi-wa·pama·či.

k   meše=meko| na·hkači e·h=anahanemehka·či.

l   aškači=meko e·h=pye·notaki wi·kiya·pi.

m   e·h=ma·ne·hto·niči=meko wa·siki·nahte·hani.

n   saka·ki=ke·h=meko=wi·na ‖ e·h=oto·škote·me·hiniči.|

96 a   ke·kya·ta=ke·h=meko e·h=pemokoči,

b   aka·mete·ki e·h=nana·hapiči.

c   e·h=pwa·wi-=ke·h=meko -kano·nekoči ke·ko·hi| e·na·čini.

d   aškači=meko e·h=kaški-keša·čiha·či.

e   "e·ne·nema·wate·ni=kohi kepye·či|-nana·tohto·ne aškote·ne·siwa," e·h=ina·či.

f   "o·´, we·nahi·='ni.

g   a·kwi=ča·h=meko paši-pešeke·nemakini i·na| keto·škote·ne·si·ma," e·h=iniči.

h   "o·´, we·nahi·='ni," e·h=ina·či.

i   "i·ni=ča·hi e·ši-nana·tohto·na·ni," e·h=ina·či.

j   i·ni=ke·h=meko='pi e·h=nana·hena·či,*

k   e·h=nowisaha·či.

l   e·hkwa·ška·hiči| e·h=taši-a·hkwe·či i·na.|

m   "i·ni=kohi wi·h=išawi·hiyani.

n   apina=meko| a·kwi wi·h=nahi-‖amohkini nešise·haki, neki·haki=ke·hi.

97 a   mehteno·h=meko me·či-kwi·natawi-mya·nehka·hiwa·čini,

b   i·ni=ye·toke| wi·h=amohki,

c   wi·h=amonokwe·ni·ma·hi," e·h=ineči.

d   " 'aka·kwa'=ča·hi ki·h=išitehka·neko·pi," e·h=ineči.

e   e·h=we·pipaho·hiči,

f   mehteko·heki e·h=ako·si·sa·či.

g   "i·ni=koh=meko wi·h=išawi·hiyani," e·h=ina·či,

h   e·h=na·kwa·či wi·sahke·ha o·hkomese·heki.

i   meše=meko e·h=anehanemehka·hiči.

j   aškači=meko e·h=pya·či o·hkomese·hani e·h=awiniči.

k   kwi·yena=meko e·h=kehči-neneka·pya·niči.

l   e·h=me·kwa·či-=meko -a·hkwamataminiči o·hkomesani.†

m   apina=meko e·h=taši-wa·wana·tetone·moniči ‖ o·hkomese·hani.‡

98 a   aka·mete·ki e·h=nana·hapiči,|

b   e·h=taši-wa·pawa·pama·či o·hkomesani.

---

*/e·h=nana·hena·či/ (AW): AK ⟨.ena|naanači.⟩.

†/e·h=me·kwa·či/: ⟨mekwa⟩ changed from ⟨mekwe⟩.

‡/wa·wana·tetone·moniči/: /na·te/ is AK ⟨nete⟩, with ⟨te⟩ over an erasure.

e When it got colder, he basically abandoned his house,
f going to where it was warm.
g Every night he went home.
h And he barely made it back.
i And then Wîsahkêha set out,
j going to see another one.
k Again he walked on and on contentedly.
l And after a while he came to a wickiup.
m The one there had a large number of sharp-pointed wooden arrows.
n And what's more, that one barely had any fire at all.
96 a And what's more that one almost shot him,
b when he sat down on the other side of the lodge.
c And what's more that one didn't speak to him when he would say anything to him.
d It took him a while to get him to be friendly.
e "I came to ask you just what you think of the Spirit of Fire," he said to him.
f "Oh, so that's it.
g Well, I just don't like that Spirit of Fire of yours one bit," he replied.
h "Oh, so that's it," he said to him.
i "Well, that's what I asked you to do," he said to him.
j And with that he grabbed hold of him
k and hurled him out the door.
l That one was in a rage there where he had landed.
m "That's exactly how you will be.
n In fact, my uncles, as well as my aunts, will even never eat you.
97 a Only when they are keenly desperate with a craving for meat,
b then maybe they'll eat you,
c I mean, if they want to eat you," he was told.
d "So, your name will be porcupine," he was told.
e He started trotting away
f and went quickly up a small tree.
g "That's just how you will do," Wîsahkêha told him,
h and he left to go to his grandmother's.
i He walked on and on quite contentedly.

j After some time he arrived at his grandmother's place.
k It was just at a time when she was having severe chills.
l His grandmother had become quite sick.
m His poor grandmother was even talking incoherently.
98 a He sat down on the other side of the lodge.
b He kept looking at his grandmother,

^c e·h=meškemeškenekoniči.

^d "wa·´, we·ta=ni·hka no·hkomese·ha," e·h=ina·či='pi,

^e e·h=taši|-mešameša·pama·či o·hkomese·hani.|

^f e·h=ki·ša·koči-=meko| -wa·peškimi·šikwe·niči.

^g e·h=kwa·kokwa·koho·mekoči.

^h kapo·twe e·h=kekye·htena·mi-=meko -se·kinotawa·či,

ⁱ e·h=so·kiha·či,

^j e·h=natoma·či mamahke·hi-metemo·he·hani,

^k e·h=mama·toma·či.

^l i·ya·h=e·h=pya·či.|

^m "nahi´, ano·hko, kepye·či-=ni·hka -mama·tomene.

ⁿ ano·hko, no·hkomese·ha wi·h=nepo·hiwa=me·kwe·he," e·h=ina·či. ‖

99 ^a "wi·h=mi·hkečihači=ča·hi| we·či-pye·či-mama·tomena·ni," e·h=ina·či wi·sahke·ha.

^b mamahke·hi-metemo·he·hani e·h=nahkomekoči.

^c i·tepi e·h=a·wa·či.

^d i·ya·h=pye·ya·wa·či,| a·hpeči=či·h=meko o·hkomese·hani sa·saka·ki=meko e·h=ne·moniči.*

^e e·h=mawinana·wa·či.

^f e·h=ana·po·sike·či mamahke·hi-mečemo·ka,

^g owi·či-metemo·hani| e·h=mi·hkečiha·či.

^h ki·š-ana·po·sike·či,

ⁱ wi·sahke·ha e·h=tahkahaki| na·tawino·na·powi.|

^j ki·ši-=meko -tahkahaki,| e·h=we·pi·hkawa·wa·či| wi·h=menaha·wa·či.

^k aškači=meko e·h=kaški-kotaminiči.|

^l masa·či=meko e·h=naha·tesihtawoči| wi·sahke·ha o·hkomese·hani.†

100 ^a kena·či=meko e·h=anemi-naha·tesiniči.

^b ki·h-=meko pe·hki -ne·se·niči,

^c e·h=na·kwa·niči mamahke·hi-metemo·he·hani.

^d e·h=a·hkwamataminiči, e·h=wačawača·ha·či wi·sahke·ha o·hkomese·hani.‡

^e ki·h-=meko -ne·se·niči,| e·h=koči-wača·ho·hiniči.

^f e·h=atosoniči aškote·wi.

^g mečemo·ka e·h=apahapane·niči.§

^h kakišaši·pye=meko metemo·he·ha e·h=apahapane·niči.

ⁱ ke·htena=´pi e·h=pwa·wi- ke·ko·hi_-iši-a·hkwamataki,

^j e·h=pwa·wi-=ke·hi -ki·hki·tesiči.

^k wa·natohka=meko e·h=ki·wi_-išawiči.|

^l wa·paniki=meko e·h=ne·se·niči,

^m e·h=po·ni-aškye·wakineče·niči ‖ o·hkomese·hani.

---

*/sa·saka·ki=meko/: AK ⟨.sasa|kaki.meko.⟩.

†⟨.okome‖seani.⟩.

‡/e·h=a·hkwamataminiči/ emends AK /e·h=ne·se·niči/, assumed to be an error; see 100*e*.

§Translation from IP.

c who kept spreading her legs open as she thrashed around.

d "Oh my, my poor grandmother!" he said to her (it is said),

e as he kept catching sight of his grandmother's snatch.

f And her pubic hair was extremely white.

g She shouted at him repeatedly.

h At some point he became seriously afraid for her,

i and he bound her

j and went to ask Old Lady Toad to come,

k to request her doctoring skills.

l And he arrived there.

m "Well, grandma, I've come to request your doctoring.

n Grandma, I think my grandmother is going to die," he told her.

99 a "So, I've come to ask for your medical aid, for you to doctor her," Wîsahkêha said to her.

b And Old Lady Toad told him yes, she would.

c And they went there.

d When they got there, they found his grandmother just barely still breathing,

e and they rushed over to her.

f Old Lady Toad boiled medicine,

g and treated the other old lady.

h After she boiled the medicine,

i Wîsahkêha stirred the medicine broth to cool it.

j When he had cooled it, they set about trying to have her drink it.

k After some time it was possible to have her swallow it.

l Only with great difficulty did Wîsahkêha see his grandmother brought back to health.

100 a It was a slow process, indeed, for her to recover.

b And after she was completely cured,

c Old Lady Toad left and went back home.

d When his grandmother was sick, Wîsahkêha would cook for her.

e And after she was well, she tried cooking for herself,

f and she burned herself in the fire.

g The old lady laughed.

h The old lady was unable to stifle a laugh.

i Truth to tell, she was not injured at all.

j And what's more, it didn't feel sore.

k She went around as if nothing had happened.

l The next day his grandmother was cured,

m and her finger was no longer raw.

101 a   o·ni kete·=’nah=meko e·h=tepa·taki aškote·wi wi·sahke·hi‿metemo·he·ha.

b   o·ni wi·sahke·ha, “ano·hko,” e·h=ina·či.|
c   “kaši=’yo ketešawi‿e·h=kehči-a·hkwamatamani,” e·h=ina·či.
d   “’šina·kwa,‿noši·hi, mani=koči e·šawiya·ni.
e   ki·h=kehke·nemi| e·hpi·hčawiya·ni e·h=a·hkwamatamo·hiya·ni,” e·h=ikoči.
f   “mani| pi·sehka·hi pi·sehkano,”| e·h=ineči.
g   e·h=se·se·tone·kwa·te·niki.
h   e·h=nana·heškaki.
i   no·make·wi|-ki·šeškaki, e·h=we·pi-mama·twe·či.
j   e·škami=meko e·h=ahpi·hči|-mama·twe·či.
k   ke·keya·h=meko e·h=we·pi-kwa·kokwa·koho·taki wi·sahke·ha,
l   e·h=wi·ša·we·či,| e·h=mama·twe·či.
m   meše=meko·=’nahi owiye·hani| e·h=anemi-‖kwa·koho·ma·či.
102 a   a·kwi=ke·h=wi·na·’pi we·te·we owiye·hani owi·ke·hiničini.
b   wi·nwa·wa=meko e·h=nešikamikesiwa·či.
c   meše=ča·h=meko e·nwe·we·kesikwe·ni e·h=inwe·we·kesiči.
d   mečemo·ka=ke·hi| wa·natohka=meko e·h=taši-ni·pito·či wi·kopye·ni, wi·kopimote·hi
         wi·h=ašihto·či.
e   aškači| mahwe·waki e·h=ka·ška·škeh-awa·wa·či wi·sahke·hani,
f   i·tepi e·h=a·wa·či.
g   ašiči=meko pye·ya·wa·či, e·h=po·nwe·we·kesiniči.
h   tepina·h=meko e·h=tanehtawa·wa·či e·h=a·wa·či nano·škwe.
i   aškači=meko e·h=pya·wa·či e·h=awiniči.|
j   wi·kiya·pi e·h=ašihto·wa·či sese·si mahwe·waki,
k   e·h=po·ni·wa·či ta·taki.
l   ki·ši-=meko -menwike·wa·či, ‖ i·ni·=’tep e·h=a·wa·či.
103 a   a·hpeči=či·h=meko e·h=ki·ši-=meko -po·ni-ne·moniči katawi pe·hki e·h=pi·tike·wa·či.
b   me·me·čiki=meko e·h=ki·ši-nepeniči.
c   metemo·he·hani e·h=wa·pamekowa·či.
d   “kaši=ča·hi išawiwa| nesese·hena·na, ano·hko,” e·h=ina·wa·či metemo·he·hani.*
e   e·h=a·čimoniči.
f   “našawaye=ča·h=meko we·pi-a·hkwamatamwa,”| e·h=ineči mahwe·waki.|
g   “a·kwi·=’nahi a·hpeči-maneto·wičini,” e·h=ina·či nekoti mahwe·wa,
h   po·si-=meko -mi·ša·te·nemota.
i   mi·na·wa·pama·či metemo·he·ha,
j   ke·htena=či·h=meko e·h=nepo·hiniči o·šiseme·hani.
k   “’šina·kwa=wi·na·=’na,” e·h=ina·či.
l   e·h=ketenamawa·či i·ni či·payi‿pi·sehka·he·hi.‖
104 a   wi·sahke·ha masa·či=meko e·h=naha·tesiči, e·h=išiwe·pite·he·či.

b   o·ni ki·ši-=meko -menwi‿pema·tesiči,

---

*/ano·hko/: in ⟨anoko.|⟩ the divider is an added dot.

101 a   And then the grandmother of Wîsahkêha, with her opinion completely changed, was proud of the fire.

b   And then Wîsahkêha said to his grandmother, "Grandma."
c   He said to her, "By the way, what was it like for you when you were very sick?"
d   "Well, Grandson, let me just show you how it was for me.
e   You shall know how sick I got when I was sick," she told him.
f   "Put on this shirt," he was told.
g   It had a ruffled collar and sleeves.
h   He put it on.
i   A little while after he had put it on, he began moaning.
j   And the intensity of his moans increased.
k   Before long Wîsahkêha began shouting.
l   He screamed in anguish and moaned.
m   He shouted to anyone and everyone.
102 a   Now, they say there wasn't one other person that had a house.
b   They lived in a single isolated house by themselves.
c   So, he was free to wail however he would wail.
d   Now, the old lady was unconcernedly setting up a warp of basswood-bark strips (on a heddle) to make a basswood-bark bag.
e   Some time later some wolves kept hearing Wîsahkêha,
f   and they went there.
g   When they got near, the wailing ceased.
h   They went towards where they thought they had heard it without being certain.
i   After quite a while they came to their place.
j   And the wolves hurriedly built a wickiup,
k   and made camp, so to speak.
l   After they had their house in good shape, they went over there.
103 a   Here he'd already almost completely stopped breathing for good when they came in.
b   They were sure he was already dead.
c   The old lady looked up at them.
d   And they said to the old lady, "So, how's our older brother, grandma?"
e   And she answered.
f   "Well, some time ago he fell sick," the wolves were told.
g   "In that case, he's not a manitou for good," one wolf said to her,
h   one who was very glad.
i   When the old lady examined him closely,
j   here, her grandson really was dead.
k   "Why, the idea of him!" she said to him.
l   And she took that ghost-shirt off of him.
104 a   Wîsahkêha felt that he had barely recovered.

b   And then after he was back in good health,

^c "ano·hko, ni·h=ota·hwi·nemi=ča·hi," e·h=ina·či.

^d "šina·kwa=ˀškwe·ˊ,| kene·ta=ma·hi·=ˀni," e·h=ina·či| o·šisemani.

^e e·h=ota·hwi·hemiči wi·sahke·ha či·payi-pi·sehka·hi,

^f e·h=a·hpeči·=meko -ki·wawiči.

^g meše| nekotenwi e·h=pya·niči| owi·hka·nani keše·maneto·wani.

^h ki·h-ki·ši-wi·seniwa·či,

ⁱ "nahi·ˊ, mani kosehkano," e·h=ineči keše·maneto·wa.

^j e·h=pemi|-nana·heškaki.

^k ki·šeškaki=meko, e·h=we·pi-a·hkwamataki.

^l "ehehye·ˊ," e·h=iniči owi·hka·nani wi·sahke·ha.*

^m e·škami=meko e·h=iši-a·hkwamataminiči owi·hka·nani.|

ⁿ ke·keya·h=meko e·h=we·pi|-a·so·noniči.

^o ke·keya·h=meko e·h=we·pi-|če·če·kamašihto·niči.

105 ^a e·h=nepa·twe·we·kesiči keše·maneto·wa.

^b wi·sahke·ha=ke·hi wa·natohka=meko e·h=we·pi-e·mehkwa·nehke·či.

^c ma·hani=wi·na owi·hka·nani e·h=taši-wi·yata·we·we·kesiniči.

^d e·nemi·=meko -kwa·koho·meta e·h=anemi-pye·čimeči.

^e ke·keya·h=meko e·h=šahkosiči keše·maneto·wa.

^f ke·keya·h=meko e·h=ma·ne·či maneto·wa.

^g apina=meko=ˀpi kapo·twe| e·h=wa·wanetone·moči.

^h ne·hi·mi·hkečihiwa·čiki=ke·hi e·h=a·nawiha·wa·či=meko.

ⁱ ke·keya·h=meko nenemehkiwaki e·h=we·pi-pya·wa·či.

^j ke·keya·h=meko we·nekwi·kaničiki ·hkwe·waki e·h=pya·wa·či.

^k ke·keya·h=meko keše·maneto·wa okwisani ‖ e·h=pya·niči,

106 ^a we·nekwi·kaniničihi, ma·ne=meko e·h=pye·či-wi·te·ma·niči.

^b e·h=asipo·hkawa·wa·či,

^c e·h=pwa·wi·=meko -we·te·wiha·wa·či.[†]

^d o·ni| nešihka=meko we·yo·sita e·h=koči·hkawa·či.

^e e·h=we·pi-kakano·na·či.

^f e·h=pwa·wi·=meko -we·te·wiha·či.

^g še·ški=meko waninawe e·h=či·kitiye·sahoniči,

^h e·h=mayo·niči.

ⁱ e·h=kehči-mayo·niči.

^j e·h=ča·ki·=meko -a·nawiha·niči,

^k "a·kwi=ye·hapa maneto·wiye·kwini," ə·h=ina·či.

^l "pa·wi·=ˀh=we·=mani!ˀ -kehke·nemiye·ke·koha!ˀ, maneto·wiye·kwe!?" e·h=ina·či.|

^m e·h=ki·ši·=ke·h=meko -nepeniči.

ⁿ e·h=we·pi-ketenamawa·či i·ni| či·payi-pi·sehka·hi.[‡]

^o ki·ši·=meko -ketenamawa·či, ‖ aškači=meko e·h=ne·moniči.[§]

---

*/ehehye·ˊ/ has been supplied as the missing complement of /e·h=iniči/.

[†]/e·h=/: ⟨.a⟩.

[‡]/či·payi/: ⟨ye.⟩ (spelling /-yi/) has the divider added.

[§]⟨kiši.meko⟩: divider added.

c he said to her, "Grandma, so, I must have it."

d "Well, you see it there, obviously," she told her grandson.

e Wîsahkêha had the ghost shirt as his own,

f and he always had it with him.

g One time his friend God arrived.

h After they had finished eating,

i "O.K., try this on," God was told.

j And he put it on.

k After he had put it on, he started to be sick.

l Wîsahkêha heard his friend say, "Uh-oh!"   (See note *.)

m His friend got sicker and sicker.

n And before long he began holding himself.

o And before long he began to cry out in pain.

105 a God screamed bloody murder.

b Now, Wîsahkêha was unconcernedly setting about to make a spoon.

c But here was his friend screaming away in terror.

d Each one shouted to in turn was in turn drawn to the cries.

e Before long God became listless.

f And before long there was many a manitou there.

g He even at some point, they say, babbled incoherently.

h What's more, skilled doctors failed with him.

i And before long the Thunderers began arriving.

j And before long angels ("winged women") came.

k And before long the son of God came,

106 a and angels, he came with many.

b The crowd of them ministered to him,

c but they got nowhere at all with him.

d And then the son tried with him by himself.

e He began speaking to him,

f but he got nowhere at all with him.

g All he did was thrust his rump all over,

h and weep.

i He wept copiously.

j Seeing them all fail with him,

k he (Wîsahkêha) said to them, "I didn't realize that you're not manitous."

l "After all, you'd hardly fail to know about him in this case, if you were manitous!" he told them.

m Now, that one was already dead.

n And he set about taking that ghost-shirt off him.

o When he had taken it off him, after a while he breathed.

107 a e·škami=meko| e·h=we·pi- čača·tepi -ne·moniči.

b ke·keya·h=meko e·h=ne·se·niči.

c e·h=a·čimoči.

d “ki·ši-=meko mana_-kehke·netake, wi·h=apahapane·niwa,” e·h=iči.

e e·h=a·nwe·še·wa·či=meko, ma·ne·he=meko.

f e·h=ma·ne·wa·či=meko a·nwe·ša·čiki.

g ki·ši-=meko -naha·tesiniči,

h kapo·twe| e·h=we·pi-apahapane·niniči owi·hka·nani.

i “’šina·kwa=ni·hka,” e·h=iniči.

j e·h=na·kwa·či.

k e·h=pye·či-=meko -mešeneči wi·sahke·ha,

l e·h=tepa·neči.|

m ki·ši-mešenekoči mači-maneto·he·hani.|

n ke·kya·ta-=mek=a·pehe e·h=na·petone·hcči si·kome·hikaneki e·šikeniki wi·sahke·ha.

o wi·na=ke·hi·=’na wi·sahke·ha i·ni e·h=ki·wawiči ‖ či·payi-pi·sehka·hi.

108 a meše=nekotenwi e·h=pye·nota·koči ke·pa·hkohokočini.|

b “nahi·´, šato, pena·´, mani| nepi·sehka·hi makeškamawino,” e·h=ina·či.

c o·ni mači-maneto·he·ha e·h=nana·heškaki.

d ki·ši-=meko no·make·we| -pi·sehkaki, e·h=we·pi-sayasaya·weška·či.

e “ši·´,” e·h=iči=’p=a·pehe.

f “me·kwe·h=meko ni·h=neneka·pya,” e·h=ina·či wi·sahke·hani.

g e·škami=meko.

h wi·na=ke·hi, “na·hina·hi·=’nahi wi·h=sa·sa·kehta·kosikwe·ni,”_e·h=išite·he·či
keše·maneto·wa.

i e·h=neškima·či=ke·hi ote·hkawa·pi·hemani.

j kapo·twe| e·h=we·pi-ka·škehtawa·či.

k “i·ni,” e·h=išite·he·či,

l e·h=mama·tomekoči.

m e·h=pwa·wi-=meko we·te·we_i·tepi -iši·ka·pa·či| keše·maneto·wa,

n e·h=kosa·či=meko ‖ owi·hka·nani,

109 a e·h=a·nomekoči wi·h=asemiha·či,|

b wi·h=asemiha·či=meko e·h=išimekoči.

c ke·keya·h=meko e·h=anohka·hkye·či.

d “ ‘a·hkwamatamwa ohtawakayani,’ ki·h=ina·wa,”_e·h=ina·či_e·nohka·na·čini.*

e i·tepi| e·h=a·či e·nohka·neta.

f kwi·yena=meko i·ya·h=pye·ya·či, e·h=šo·škinawi·niči, e·h=nepeniči.

g še·ški=meko ma·masa·či e·h=ne·moniči.

h no·make·wi-pya·či,| e·h=nepo·hiniči.

i e·h=mawi_-wa·pama·či we·mi·hkeče·wi·hemita.

j aye=či·h=meko e·h=o·če·wa·naketone·šino·hiniči.

k aškači=meko e·h=ne·moniči.

---

*/ki·h=ina·wa/: AK ⟨kiinapwa⟩, as if addressed to more than one messenger.

107 a Gradually he began breathing regularly.

b And before long he was cured.

c   And he (Wîsahkêha) had something to say.

d "When this fellow has regained his wits, he will laugh," he said.

e   They didn't believe it, quite a few of them.

f There were a lot that didn't believe.

g   After his friend was back in good health,

h at some point he started laughing.

i And he said, "Well, I'll be!"

j   And he went back.

k   Wîsahkêha was come for and arrested,

l and he was kept put away.

m After the Evil Spirit (the Devil) arrested Wîsahkêha,

n something like a three-pronged fish-spear would be nearly thrust into his mouth.

o   Now Wîsahkêha, for his part, had that ghost-shirt with him.

108 a   One time his jailer came to him.

b And he said to him, "Alright, friend, here, can you put this shirt on and make it big."

c   And then the Evil Spirit put it on.

d And after he had it on for a short time, he started getting tingling sensations.

e   "Oh my!" they say he'd say.

f   "I think I'm going to have chills," he told Wîsahkêha.

g   It was getting worse.

h   Now, *God* thought, "I wonder when his cries will be heard."

i At the same time, he admonished his guard against it.

j And at some point he began hearing him.

k "There it is," he thought,

l hearing him ask him to doctor him.

m And there was no way God would set foot there,

n as he was fearful of his friend,

109 a whose cries for his help he had ignored,

b when he asked him to help him.

c   Eventually he sent a messenger.

d And he told the one he sent, "You must tell him I have ear trouble."

e   The one sent went there.

f And just as he arrived there, he saw him straighten out and die.

g He was only breathing with difficulty.

h And shortly after he arrived, he died.

i   The one who employed him went there to see him.

j He found that he already had flies in his mouth as he lay there.

k And after a while he breathed.

l   o·ni_po·si-=meko -aškači še·ški e·h=sa·sa·kikome·sa·niči owi·wi·ne·hahi. ‖

110 a   na·hka=meko owi·pite·hani e·h=sa·sa·kisa·niki.

b   na·hka_ohkiwani e·h=po·si-=meko_-keteška·niki.

c   e·h=nešiwina·kosiči, e·h=ki·wa·kwasoči

d   "šihihwi·´," e·h=iyowa·či.

e   aškači=meko ki·ši-aye·nahkasoniči, e·h=kečipi·sehka·he·na·či.[*]

f   ki·ši-aye·nahkasoniči, e·h=we·pi-ketenamawoči i·na pi·sehka·hi._

g   ki·ši-=meko -ketenamawoči, e·h=maki-ne·moči_i·na| mači_-maneto·he·ha.

h   ki·ši-=meko me·me·čiwi_-ne·se·či, e·h=a·čimoheči.

i   "a·kwi=ma·h=na·hkači| pi·nesa·tesičiki wi·h=mešenačini," e·h=ineči.

j   "mehteno·h=ma·hi ne·ponepo·hičiki i·niki wi·h=anemi_-mešenačiki.

k   mahkwa·či=ke·hi| me·htose·neniwičiki a·kwi ‖ wi·h=mešenačini.

111 a   mehteno·h=meko wa·waneška·haki i·niki meše·='nahi wi·h=ina·hkohwa·wate·ni
        wi·h=ina·hkohwačiki," e·h=ineči.

b   "hawo·?," e·h=iči neniwa.

c   "aše=koh=meko newa·pama·wa| e·hpi·hči-maneto·wikwe·ni mana neno·te·wa.

d   ke·htena=ča·hi maneto·wiwa," e·h=ina·či i·na mači_-maneto·he·ha.

e   "a·kwi='h=we·na kehke·nemačini e·šawiwa·či anemi_-mehtose·neniwaki," e·h=ineči
        mači_-maneto·he·ha.

f   "na·hka=ke·hi i·ni| to·tawate, a·kwi=na·hkači wi·h=a·čimohakini.

g   meše=meko e·to·to·no·ke·ni ki·h=to·ta·ko·pi," e·h=ineči mači|-maneto·he·ha.

h   e·h=ki·ša·koči-=meko -pa·hta·wi-se·kiheči. ‖

112 a   ke·kya·ta=meko wa·wosa·hi e·h=kekye·htena·mi|-a·hkwamataki mači|-maneto·he·ha.[†]

b   e·h=pwa·wi-=meko -po·nite·he·či.|

c   e·h=nana·pa·hčina·kosiči.[‡]

d   meše·='nah=meko| nekotwa·hkwe_taswawahi·me e·h=pwa·wi-po·nite·he·či.

e   i·nina·h=ča·hi='pi e·h=wawi·kiha·či wi·sahke·ha aškote·ne·siwani.

f   e·h=wawi·kihiwe·či, e·h=we·we·ne·nema·či=meko wi·h=ahpi·hteše·niči|.

g   i·na mači_-maneto·ha, aškote·ne·siwa,| e·h=mya·ne·netaki owi·yawi,

h   e·h=wawi·kihiwe·niči wi·sahke·hani owi·yawi.

i   e·h=a·hkwe·či=meko.

j   kete·='nah=meko e·h=po·ni- e·šawitehe_-išawiči aškote·ne·siwa.

k   e·h=nešiwana·čihekoči wi·sahke·hani aškote·ne·siwa. ‖

---

[*]The animate obviative subject refers back to 109*l*; the translation supplies 'horns'.

[†]Page 112 is discolored on the back, showing that it was the last page of a pad and next to the
cardboard backing. The final episode was evidently summarized here to fit in the available
space.

[‡]/nana·pa·hčina·kosi-/: heard with /č/ but later with /hč/ in another stem.

l And then a lot later the tips of his horns became visible.

110 a And also his teeth started to show.

b And his nose came out more.

c He looked horrible as he lay there dead.

d "Gosh!" they said.

e Some time later, after the horns were in place, he took the shirt off him.

f After they were fully in place, the task was begun of taking the shirt off him.

g After it had been taken off him, the Devil took a deep breath.

h After he was totally cured, he was given instructions.

i "You understand, you must never again arrest people that are alive," he was told.

j "You understand, it's only dead ones that you're to be arresting in the future.

k And in particular, people who live quiet lives you must not arrest.

111 a Only bad-actors are the ones you are to imprison however you may want to imprison them," he was told.

b "Alright, I'll do that," the fellow said.

c "I'm just observing how much manitou is in this Indian.

d And truly he has manitou power," the Devil told him.

e "Well, you don't know *how* the People-to-Be *are*!" the Devil was told.

f "What's more, if you do that to them again, I won't instruct you again.

g You'll be treated however you may be treated," the Devil was told.

h He was utterly destroyed with fright.

112 a The Devil was even very nearly seriously sick.

b He just couldn't stop thinking about it.

c He had a dreadful look on his face.

d For as much as a hundred years he couldn't stop thinking about it.

e So, at that time, Wîsahkêha calmed the rage of the Spirit of Fire.

f In calming the rage, he controlled how hot he would burn.

g The bad manitou Spirit of Fire disliked himself

h when Wîsahkêha calmed the rage he had.

i He was in a rage, indeed.

j The Spirit of Fire changed completely from the way he had been.

k The Spirit of Fire (that had been) was completely destroyed by Wîsahkêha.

kyâwâchiki neniwaki êshawiwâchi nashawaye

What Some Jealous Men Did Long Ago

kyâwâchiki neniwaki êshawiwâchi nashawaye
Alfred Kiyana[*]

1 a   kya·wa·čiki neniwaki e·šawiwa·či našawaye.[†]

b   o·ni našawaye, neno·te·waki owi·wa·wahi e·ye·hi-ma·mi·hketama·ti·wa·či, mehtose·neniwaki,[‡]

c   nekoti=ye·toke‖ owi·wani pemito·pahkwe e·h=wa·woči-matamawotehe keye·hapa.

d   kapo·twe e·h=mi·na·we·nema·či.

e   e·h=wi·ke·či-='pi=mek=a·pehe -wa·keče šiniči,

f   i·tepi e·h=išitiye·šiniči či·kapahkwe.

g   wi·na·ke·hi e·h=nepe·hka·noči=meko ahpene·či,‖

h   kapo·twe='p=a·pehe e·h=neneki‖-ne·moniči.

i   o·ni=kapo·twe e·h=a·čimohekoči e·nehkawa·čini oškinawe·hani,

j   pe·hki=meko owi·hka·nani.

k   "'šina·kwa, ni·hka·ne,‖ pe·hki=meko mana ki·wa kematamatama·ko·pi.

l   tahpinawapahkwe=meko wa·woči‖-mana·pi," e·h=ina·či.‖

2 a   "našawaye·me·h=ke·h=meko‖ i·ni e·na·čimoči i·na·='na oškinawe·ha.

b   o·ni e·h=wi·te·maki.

c   i·ni=ča·h=pe·hki e·h=mehte·nemaki.

d   aye·me·h=meko oči‖-pye·či matamatamo·no·ke·ni," e·h=ina·či‖ owi·hka·nani.

e   o·ni atehči e·h=a·či, nešihka=meko,

f   oče·hte·hi·='nahi e·h=awato·či,

g   o·ni e·h=kenekahtaki·či asapye·hi.[§]

h   e·h=wi·šikya·niki=meko.

i   e·h=ki·nihto·či ma·tesi.

j   o·ni_pe·hkote·niki e·h=we·pi·hkawa·či owi·wani če·pahkwa·neki wi·h=očišiki.

k   e·h=ša·kwe·nemoči=meko ihkwe·wa.

l   "e·h=ki·škya·ki=ma·hi ki·h=pakisehko·ne, i·nahi očišinane," e·h=ina·či ona·pe·mani.

m   ke·keya·hi·='nahi e·h=kaškima·či.

n   na·hina·h=meko‖ ki·ši- či·k_atasane‖ -očišiki ihkwe·wa,

3 a   e·h=kehči_nepa·či.

b   o·ni·='na neniwa e·h=taši_pwa·wi_nepa·či.

c   ke·htena‖ aškači e·h=či·pahoči.‖

d   i·ni=meko i·tepi e·h=išinehke·či.

e   ke·htena=či·hi e·h=šahkeče·nike·či,

f   e·h=ata·hpaho·to·či.

g   i·na·ka=ke·hi neniwa e·h=ašičinawi·či.

h   na·hina·hi e·šita·hkoška·niči,

---

[*]The manuscript is NAA 2664.1:1-24; it has 24 pages.

[†]At the top as a title, below "No. 1".

[‡]/neno·te·waki/ 'people' (archaic; now 'Indians') clarified by /mehtose·neniwaki/ 'people'.

[§]/e·h=kenekahtaki·či/ (acc. by AW): AK ⟨ekэnakatakiči⟩.

What Some Jealous Men Did Long Ago
Translated by Ives Goddard

1 a　　　　　　What some jealous men did long ago.

b　　　　And long ago, when people used to chase after each other's wives,
c　　one man's wife was apparently getting fucked on him through the side of the lodge, as it
　　turned out.
d　　At some point he realized about her.
e　　She would always lie carefully with her body flexed, the story goes,
f　　and her bottom up against the lodge-wall.
g　　He would be pretending to be asleep each time,
h　　and suddenly she would be panting heavily.
i　　　　And then at some point a young man he was acquainted with told him,
j　　his close friend.
k　　　　"Well, friend, that wife of yours is getting seriously fucked on you.
l　　She's getting fucked right through the lodge-wall," he told him.
2 a　　　　"To be precise, some time back that's what *that* guy told me.
b　　And then I went with him.
c　　So, now I really know about him definitely.
d　　She must've been getting fucked on you since a good while ago," he told his friend.
e　　　　Then he went away someplace, all by himself,
f　　and he had a little sinew he took with him.
g　　And then he made some basswood-bark cordage with that braided into it.
h　　It was good and strong.
i　　And he sharpened a knife.
j　　　　And then that night he tried to get his wife to let him lie next to the lodge-wall.
k　　　　The woman was unwilling.
l　　　　"I mean, I'll crowd you over the edge if you lie on that side," she told her husband.
m　　　　Eventually, for all that, he persuaded her.
n　　And the moment the woman had lain down at the inner edge of the platform,
3 a　　she fell sound asleep.
b　　　　And the man continued to be not asleep.
c　　Sure enough, after a while, he was poked by something.
d　　And he immediately reached out his hand to it.
e　　And sure enough, here he felt something soft,
f　　and he pulled it towards him.
g　　　　And here, that other man moved nearer.
h　　　　The moment he had the other person move up against the wall,

i e·h=ki·škešaki mi·nakayi.

j i·na·ka=ke·hi neniwa nano·škwe=meko e·h=iši-pemipenoči.

k e·hkwana·moči=meko na·hina·hi e·h=mawi-ki·wa·kwasoči,|

l e·h=nešiwa·kwate·niki| meškwi.

m o·ni neniwa i·ni mi·nakayi e·h=so·kihto·či,

n owi·wani okehči·pi·heki e·h=so·kihtawa·či.

o o·ni ma·maya=meko owi·wani, ‖ "nahi´, natawi-to·hki·no=ni·hka," e·h=ina·či.

4 a naha·kanihkwe·wa e·h=to·hki·či.

b (e·h=ki·ši-='yo=ke·h=meko -ta·to·hki·niči ke·hčikiničihi.)*

c o·ni, "pena´, nawači-či·kakohike·no," e·h=ina·či| owi·wani.

d ihkwe·wa e·h=či·kakohike·či.

e wa·natohka=meko e·h=ki·wi|-tana·škahike·či.

f o·ni| e·h=mi·na·wa·pama·či| osemye·ni pašito·he·ha.

g opi·neniwiwa='yo=ke·hi='pi i·na pašito·he·ha.

h o·ni, "ši·´, metemo, pe·hki=ni·hka kesemina·na| we·weneteniwi opi·čikwa·ni," e·h=ina·či owi·wani.

i "'šina·kwa=wi·na·='na," e·h=ina·či metemo·ka ona·pe·me·hani.

j "a·kwi,=metemo, pena=ni·hka wa·pami.†

k pe·hki=ma·h=meko sa·ka·pata·ne·hiwa," e·h=iniči=meko ‖ ona·pe·me·hani.

5 a o·ni i·tepi e·h=ina·piči.

b i·na·ka=ke·hi ača·hmeko e·h=ne·taki.|

c nano·pehka e·h=inekihkwa·hkwateniki ki·wako·to·či mi·nakayi.

d na·hka i·ni='pi=meko e·h=kwa·koho·tameki e·h=ne·woči ne·peka.

e "awata·ke·no," e·h=ineči| ihkwe·wa,

f "ta·ni=ča·hi='nahi='pi," wi·h=iči.

g natawa·či=meko e·h=awato·či i·ni mi·nakayi.

h kenwe·ši·me·h=meko e·h=taši-mečime·nemoči wi·h=awatenaki i·ni mi·nakayi.

i kenwe·ši·me·h=meko e·h=ki·wi-pehkwineča·taki ihkwe·wa.

j aškači=meko e·h=šekišiniči e·h=pakitaki.|

k (pehkwapito·kwe·ni='pi.)

l sese·si=meko e·h=pemi-nowi·či.

m "we·kone·hi='yo=ča·hi," e·h=iyowa·či ‖ we·či·pa·mičiki i·nini.

6 a e·h=a·pihaki metemo·ka.

b mi·nakayi=či·hi,

c e·h=če·če·keki ihkwe·wa.|

d e·h=pye·tawomeči owi·nakayi.

e o·ni e·h=a·čimoweči e·nanohkye·niči okwiswa·wani,‡

f natawa·či=meko| e·h=pwa·wi-=ke·ko·hi -ine·nema·wa·či ne·šiwa·ničini.

g i·nini='pi=meko we·šehki·ha·wa·čini ne·šiwa·ničini.

---

*/ke·hčikiničihi/ 'the old folks (obv.)': translated 'her in-laws', as implied by /naha·kanihkwe·wa/ 'daughter-in-law living with her in-laws' (4a).

†/wa·pami/: AK ⟨wapani⟩.

‡/okwiswa·wani/: AK ⟨okwisawani⟩.

ⁱ he cut off a penis.

^j And here, that other man ran off in no particular direction.

^k He went until he ran out of breath and collapsed and died

^l in an appalling mass of blood.

^m And then the man tied (the cord to) that penis

ⁿ and tied it to his wife's belt.

^o And then quite early he said to his wife, "Alright, it's time to wake up!"

^{4 a} The daughter-in-law woke up.

^b (Now, her in-laws had both already woken up.)

^c And he said to his wife, "O.K., why don't you first sweep up."

^d The woman swept up.

^e She was going around spreading mats to sit on as if nothing were amiss.

^f And then the old man took a closer look at his daughter-in-law.

^g (Now, the old man was a jovial fellow.)

^h And then he said to his wife, " Say, Wife, our daughter-in-law's knife-case is really fine."

ⁱ "What's with *him*!" the old lady said to her husband.

^j "No, Wife, I'm *telling* you, look at her.

^k I mean, she really stands out," her husband said.

^{5 a} Then she looked over at her.

^b And here, that other woman saw it for the first time.

^c It was a penis of huge girth that she had hanging from her belt.

^d And also, just then (the story goes) there was a shout when the dead one was seen.

^e "Take it back," the woman was told,

^f leaving it for her to ask, "Where did they say?"

^g And making the best of it, she took that penis back.

^h For quite a while the woman hesitated to deliver that penis.

ⁱ For quite a while she kept it clutched in her hand.

^j After some time she threw it down where he lay.

^k (To hear it told, she must have tied it in a bundle.)

^l And she hurried on out.

^m "Well, so what's this?" said the family of the decedent.

^{6 a} The old lady untied it.

^b And here it was a penis,

^c and the woman let out a scream.

^d His penis had been brought back to him.

^e And then the things their son did were told about.

^f They accordingly decided not to hold anything against him who had done the killing.

^g The very one that had done the killing was who they adopted (for their son), the story goes.

^h o·ni·=ʼna kotakani e·h=owi·wiči še·škesi·he·hani.

ⁱ mahkwa·či=meko e·h=awiči ihkwe·wa.

^j e·h=pwa·wi-=meko -mi·hketi·či.

^k o·ni=kapo·twe=meko e·h=we·pi-kya·we·či,

^l e·h=nano·či-=meko -kya·we·či neniwa.

^m e·h=wi·tamawa·či| we·to·hkwe·yo·miničihi,

ⁿ e·h=te·pwe·htawoči.

^o e·h=nana·tohtawoči ‖ ihkwe·wa.

^{7 a} "a·kwi=ča·h=ni·na owiye·ha me·h-mi·hkemičini," e·h=iči.

^b o·ni e·h=na·katawe·nemeči, taswi=meko či·nawe·ma·či.

^c e·h=na·katawe·nema·wa·či.*

^d o·ni e·h=pwa·wi-=meko -kehke·nema·wa·či ke·htena wi·h=mi·hketi·niči.†

^e o·ni·=ʼna| neniwa e·h=ašiha·či pehkwitepe·hani.

^f ki·ši-ašiha·či pehkwitepe·hani, e·h=ki·škikwe·šwa·či.

^g o·ni| e·h=aša·šiko·hiwitepe·na·či.

^h o·ni peteki e·h=iši·kwe·seto·či keno·še·wi-owi·pitani.

ⁱ meše·=ʼnah=meko nano·pehka e·h=sa·kikome·seto·či.

^j o·ni i·nini| na·meki e·h=išisahtawa·či.

^k kana·kwa wi·h=ketenamawoči i·na ihkwe·wa.

^l ki·hka=meko=ʼpi anene·ki e·h=a·čimoči e·to·ta·koči ‖ i·nini ona·pe·mani,‡

^{8 a} e·h=nepo·hiči ki·ši-a·čimoči.

^b ke·htena=ke·h=meko e·h=pwa·wi-mi·hketi·či.

^c o·ni·=ʼna neniwa we·wi·tepi=meko| e·h=ayi·hkwiči.

^d i·ni=ʼpi=meko e·h=očiwe·pi-a·hkwamataki.

^e kapo·twe=meko e·h=kekye·htena·mi|-a·hkwamataki.

^f kapo·twe=meko ašikani e·h=po·hkeška·niki oški·šekwi,|

^g e·ye·ši-pwa·wi-=meko -a·hkwamataki.

^h o·ni·=ʼpi owi·naniwi e·h=we·pi-aneteniki.

ⁱ e·h=e·škami-=meko| -aneteniki.

^j ki·ši-=meko| -ča·kaneteniki owi·naniwi,

^k a·šowi=na·hka| e·h=oči-po·hkeška·niki oški·šekwi.

^l če·wi·šwi| e·h=po·hkeška·niki.

^m aškači·meki·hi e·h=nepo·hiči.

ⁿ i·ni=ʼpi_i·na e·šawiči kya·wa·ta. ‖ §

*   *   *

^{9 a} o·ni=kotaka na·hka kya·wa·ta.

^b i·na=wi·na ke·htena=meko e·h=mi·hketi·niči owi·wani.

---

*⟨wači⟩ over erased ⟨či⟩.

†⟨wači⟩ over erased ⟨či⟩.

‡/ki·hka/: ⟨kaʼ⟩ or ⟨ke⟩.

§One line left blank after this at the bottom of the page.

h   And then that man married another young girl.
i   The woman stayed around quietly.
j   She didn't have men friends.
k   And then at some point he began to be jealous.
l   The man couldn't stop being jealous.
m   He told her male relatives,
n   and he was believed.
o   When the woman was asked,
7 a she said, "Well, no one has yet sought *my* company."
b   And then her every move was followed, by all her relatives.
c   They followed her every move.
d   And they were unable to learn that she was really having an affair.
e   And then that man made a snowsnake.
f   After he made the snowsnake, he cut the head off it.
g   Then he put a head of slippery elm on it.
h   And he set pike teeth in place to point backwards.
i   He put on a good many with their tips sticking out.
j   And then he shoved that inside her.
k   It was impossible to pull it out of that woman.
l   Around all sides of the smokehole, she told what her husband had done to her.
8 a And she died after telling what had happened to her.
b   Now, it was really true that she was not having an affair.
c   And then that man for a while was tired.
d   And from that exact time on, he was sick, the story goes.
e   And at some point he was seriously sick.
f   And at some point his eye on one side burst open,
g   even before he was sick.
h   And then his tongue began to rot.
i   It got more and more rotten.
j   And after his tongue had rotted away,
k   his eye on the other side also burst open.
l   Both of them burst open.
m   And a little after that he died.
n   That's what happened to the one who was jealous, the story goes.

*   *   *

9 a And there was another one who was jealous.
b   But *his* wife really *was* fooling around.

c e·h=pwa·wi-=ke·hi -wi·kwa·na·či aškiča·hi.

d kenwe·ši=we·=meko e·h=pwa·wi-ame·notawa·či.

e meše=meko e·h=taši-ša·ši·ša·či.

f   o·ni we·to·hkwe·yo·mičiki e·h=pwa·wi-=meko -kehke·nema·wa·či.

g o·ni| we·ta·nesita ihkwe·wa| nešihka e·h=kehke·nema·či.|

h e·h=pwa·wi-=meko -neškima·či.

i   i·na·ka=ke·hi neniwa, "wi·h=pwa·wi-'hi·'yo -kehke·nema·pi!?" e·h=išite·he·či.|

j   kapo·twe e·h=a·nawapwi·htesiči neniwa.

k o·ni| owi·hta·wani e·h=a·čimoha·či.

l "me·ša," e·h=ina·či owi·hta·wani,[*]

m "kekehke·nema·pwa? mana ketehkwe·mwa·wa? e·h=mi·hketi·či?"| e·h=ina·či.[†]

n   "a·kwi," e·h=iniči.

o   pye·ya·či=meko, ‖ e·h=a·čimoči.

10 a "me·kwe·h=ma·hi ma·hiya_mi·hketi·wa," e·h=ina·či.[‡]

b o·ni e·h=mya·ne·netaminiči osese·hahi.[§]

c (še·ški·'yo=ke·hi_e·h=okiwa·či.)

d   "o·´, kehke·nemake,| ni·na=meko ni·h=kehči-nesa·wa," e·h=iči kehkiwesa.

e   o·ni okiwa·wani.

f "ni·na=ke·hi aše=meko a·kwi-ke·ko·hi inakini," e·h=iči_mečemo·ka.

g mehto·či=meko e·h=wi·to·hkawa·či e·h=išiwe·powe·či.

h   "kete·='nahi·'yo=ča·h=ye·toke a·mi|-mya·ne·netamani pakinete," e·h=ina·či okiwa·wani.

i   "ni·na=wi·na a·kwi=meko ke·ko·hi wi·h=ine·netama·nini=ye·hapa," e·h=iči.

j   "na·hina·hi e·hkwi-neškinawe·hka·nokwe·ni," e·h=iči.

k   "menwawiniwani=ke·hi i·nini ona·pe·mani,

l na·hka_kehtwe·wesiniwani.

m a·kwi=ke·ko·hi·='nahi inekočini ‖ e·h=mi·hketi·či.

11 a meše=meko še·ški taši-ma·mi·hketi·toke.

b o·ni·='nini=na·hka meše=meko_taši-ša·ši·še·niwani," e·h=ina·či okiwa·wani.[¶]

c   a·kwi-kana·kwa=meko.

d metemo·ka e·h=a·hkwe·či=meko.

e "nešiwihto·wa=meko neta·nesa," e·h=išite·he·či.

f   o·ni·='na neniwa me·no·hkami·niki e·h=mehči-=meko -ne·ne·wa·či owi·wani
e·h=taši·hka·ti·niči.

g   (i·niki=ke·hi| e·h=a·noma·wa·či=meko we·tehkwe·mičiki e·h=neškima·wa·či.)

h   o·ni=ye·toke na·hina·hi e·h=ni·peniki| e·h=anenwi·či,

---

[*] /me·ša/ 'brother-in-law!' (a colloquial form of address) is here translated 'pal'.

[†] ⟨mwa⟩ changed from ⟨ma⟩.

[‡] /ma·hiya/ 'the recently departed one'; here translated 'the one that's no longer here'.

[§] ⟨ta⟩ like ⟨to⟩.

[¶] /o·ni·='nini/: AK ⟨onini⟩; /taši-ša·ši·še·niwani/: AK ⟨šašiyeniwa|ni⟩.

c   Now, he paid no attention to her at first.

d   In fact, for a long time he didn't react to what she was doing.

e   He contentedly kept on going out to hunt.

f   And her male relatives didn't know what she was doing at all.

g   The woman whose daughter she was alone knew about her.

h   And she did *not* admonish her.

i   Meanwhile, that other man thought she would hardly fail to be known about.

j   There came a time when the man lost his patience.

k   And then he spoke to his brother-in-law.

l   "Say, pal," he said to his brother-in-law.

m   "Do you guys know that your sister is having an affair?" he said to him.

n   "No," the other one said.

o   As soon as he got back, he reported it.

10 a "I think the one that's no longer here is having an affair," he told them.

b   And his older brothers were angered by it.

c   (Now, they had only their mother living.)

d   "Well, if I know who, *I'll* beat him up *myself*," said the eldest.

e   And then their mother weighed in.

f   "*I* didn't say anything to her on purpose," the old lady said.

g   She made it sound like she was letting her do it.

h   "Well, what you probably *wouldn't* like is if she gets thrown out," he said to their mother.

i   "But *I* won't actually think anything of it, come to that," he said.

j   "Whenever she eventually makes everyone mad by what she's doing," he said.

k   "Remember, now, her husband is a nice guy,

l   and also a good hunter.

m   And here he doesn't say anything to her about her having an affair.

11 a She just happily keeps on with it.

b   And he, also, happily keeps on hunting," he said to their mother.

c   It was no use.

d   The old lady was quite angry.

e   "My daughter is getting the best of it," she thought.

f   And then that spring that man kept seeing his wife carrying on openly.

g   (Now, her brothers had failed to persuade her when they admonished her.)

h   And then, it seems, at the time the garden crops were ripe, he went swimming.

i   e·h=mešena·či mahkohtawaka·hani me·nwi-ʼnekino·hiničini.*
j   o·ni meše=nekotenwi pe·hkote·niki wi·h=mana·či e·h=iši·hkawa·či.|
k   ki·ši-meškišima·či, ki·ši-šoweška·niči,
12 a   "i·ni=koh=meko wi·h=na·kwa·ya·ni," e·h=ina·či.
b   e·h=šo·škwisahtawa·či i·nini| mahkohtawaka·hani. ‖
c   e·h=nana·hi·hta·či,
d   e·h=pemi-nowi·či,
e   omehte·hani še·ški e·h=awana·či.†
f   (kotakeki=ʼyo=ke·hi o·te·weneki e·h=taši-neniwiči, e·ye·h=ma·ne·wa·či meškwahki·haki.)
g   o·ni·=ʼna ihkwe·wa,
h   ki·ši-na·kwa·niči, e·h=kehke·nema·či ača·hmeko na·meki e·h=apiniči neme·sani.
i   kete·=ʼnahi e·h=se·kesiči.
j   kotaki wa·paniki i·ni=meko e·h=ki·ši-makwi·taki.‡
k   o·ni ki·h-meči-=meko -wi·ša·wamataki,
l   e·h=a·čimoči,
m   "neta·hkwamata we·či-ihkwe·wiya·ni," e·h=iči.
n   metemo·ka e·h=mi·hkečihiwe·či| ota·nesani,
o   e·h=e·škamesiniči=meko.
p   aškači=meko e·h=a·čimoči.
q   i·ni=ke·h=wi·na,| "natomehko," e·h=ina·či okwisahi,
r   onekwanani=ča·hi ‖ wi·h=natomemeči.
13 a   "nahi=ni·hka´," e·h=iniči=meko.§
b   "pakina·petoke=ma·hi·=ʼna keta·nesa," e·h=inekoči okwisahi.
c   o·ni·=ʼna ihkwe·wa e·h=nepo·hiči.
d   metemo·ka e·h=kehči|-mayo·či,
e   e·h=neške·nema·či=meko i·nini onekwanani=ʼyo·we.
f   o·ni=kapo·twe e·h=a·čimohekoči| maneto·wani.
g   "po·ne·nemi| kenekwana=ʼyo·we," e·h=ineči.
h   "pwa·wi-po·nima·te=ke·hi, ki·na=meko ki·h=nepe,| e·h=ineči.
i   "ka·ta=na·hka ke·ko·hi ki·wi-išihišiye·kani| ayo·h=ma·wa·ka·neki,"ʼe·h=ineči.
j   "ki·na=ma·hi keta·nesa wa·waneška·hiwa," e·h=ineči.
k   i·ni=ča·hi·=ʼpi=meko e·h=iši-po·ni-=ke·ko·hi -inahina·či.|
l   aniwe·we=meko mi·ša·tesiweni kehči-nekoti-wi·hkwe·wana·ne e·h=awato·tamawa·či,
m   wi·h=okwisiči e·h=išima·či. ‖
14 a   ahpene·či=meko e·h=awatawa·či ke·ko·he·hi.
b   na·hka| i·na neniwa ahpene·či=meko e·h=pi·tipi·tikawa·či=ye·toke.¶

───────────────────

*/mahkohtawaka·ha/ (HWB in 1998), 'sunfish' (TM from AK in NAA 2647).
†⟨wanači⟩ over erasure of ⟨šiači⟩.
‡Divider added later after ⟨kotaki⟩.
§/nahi=ni·hká/ 'what do I care!' (refusing a request): 'Oh I don't care' (HP, K-W160; acc. AW).
¶/=ye·toke/: AK ⟨.yetoke.⟩.

ⁱ And he caught a sunfish of pretty good size.

^j   And then at a certain moment that night he got her arranged for fucking.

^k After he spread her open, and after she opened wide,

12 a he said to her, "Right now, I am leaving."

^b And he quickly slipped that sunfish into her.

^c And he got dressed

^d and walked out,

^e taking only his bow.

^f (Now, he was a man of another village, back when there were many Meskwakis.)

^g   And then that woman,

^h after he had gone, realized for the first time that there was a fish inside her.

ⁱ *Now* she was scared.

^j And the day after that she already had a swelling.

^k And then after she was already feeling a troubling pain,

^l she spoke up

^m and said, "I have an illness in my womanly part."

ⁿ   The old lady was a doctor to her daughter.

^o She saw her get steadily worse.

^p And some time later she spoke up.

^q And after all, "Ask him to come," she told her sons,

^r for her son-in-law to be asked to come.

13 a   And he said bluntly, "What do I care!"

^b   And her sons told her, "See, your daughter must have been thrown out."

^c   And then the woman died.

^d   And the old lady wept loudly,

^e bearing great ill will towards her former son-in-law.

^f   And then at some point a manitou spoke to her.

^g "Stop thinking about your former son-in-law," she was told.

^h "And if you don't stop thinking about him, you yourself will die," she was told.

ⁱ "Also, don't go around saying bad things about him in this village," she was told.

^j "As you know, it was your own daughter that was bad," she was told.

^k   So, she immediately stopped saying things about him.

^l On the contrary, she took over to him a large bundle of fancy clothing,

^m telling him he would be her son.

14 a She always took him things.

^b   And also that man was always going in to visit her, it seems.

* * *

c   o·ni=na·hka kotaka e·yi·ki=meko kya·wa·ta.
d   ša·ka e·h=tašiniči i·na ihkwe·wa| otawe·ma·wahi,
e   e·h=nekotihekoči.
f   wi·na=ke·h=meko e·h=ma·wači-aškikiči i·na ihkwe·wa,
g   e·h=ahkoweči·hiči.
h   o·ni| kapo·twe_e·h=a·šimekoči osese·hahi neniwani nekoti.
i   wi·na| i·na ihkwe·wa i·nini e·h=neškinawa·či neniwani.
j   koči·hi=ʼpi e·h=kehtwe·wesiniči.|
k   ča·ki=meko e·h=iši-awe·weniwiniči.
l   wi·na=ke·hi i·na ihkwe·he·ha| e·h=ma·wači-=meko -we·wenesiči.
m   če·w_ahpi·hčiki hičihi e·h=ma·wači-=meko -we·wenesiči. ‖
15 a   o·ni=ʼna oškinawe·ha e·h=mya·nesiči=meko| ma·wači če·w_ahpi·hčikičihi.
b   šewe·na e·h=ani·hwa·či=meko ma·wači ča·kenwi ke·ko·hi.
c   e·h=ma·wači-=ke·h=meko -kehtwe·wesiči.
d   e·h=nahi·hkawa·či mahkwahi,
e   na·hka meše·we·wahi e·h=nahi-kwa·koho·ma·či.
f   o·ni=ye·toke i·na| e·h=a·šimemeči owi·yawi.
g   kotaka=ke·hi e·h=mešoška·či i·nini_še·škesi·he·hani.
h   e·h=nawe·ni-neni·he·hiči,|
i   e·h=menwe·nemekoči.
j   e·h=ki·ši-=meko -a·we·nemoči wi·h=owi·wiči.
k   e·ye·ši-_pwa·wi-=meko -tane·nema·či wi·h=ona·pe·miniči,
l   e·h=ona·pe·miniči.
m   e·h=wa·wana·tesiči=meko,|
n   e·h=wa·wana·čite·he·či.
o   ke·kya·ta=meko ‖ e·h=asa·mehka·či-we·pesi·hiwiči i·na neniwa,|
16 a   oškinawe·ha=ʼh=we·na.
b   wi·na=ke·hi·=ʼna ihkwe·wa e·h=mya·ne·nema·či=meko i·nini ona·pe·mani.
c   kotakani=meko e·h=pwa·wi_wani·hka·na·či nana·ši.
d   ahpene·či=meko e·h=nenehke·nema·či.
e   kapo·twe=ʼpi nanawi=meko e·h=mena·ni-=meko -iši_ne·woti·wa·či,
f   e·h=pwa·wi-=ke·hi -ki·šiti·wa·či.
g   pi·neši=meko e·h=ne·woti·wa·či.
h   ihkwe·wa=ʼpi wa·wosa·h=meko e·h=mawinahkye·či.
i   o·ni=meko očiwe·pi e·h=we·pi-mi·hketi·wa·či.
j   kapo·twe e·h=we·pi-natawe·netaki wi·h=iši-neškinawe·ha·kwe·ni i·nini ona·pe·mani.
k   aškači e·h=mehkaki wi·h=iši-ka·hka·winawe·ha·či.
l   atehči e·h=mawi-taši-anahanahtaki·či pi·minihkwa·ni,
m   asapi_pi·minihkwa·ni=ma·hi.*
17 a   o·ni mehtekwi e·h=papaka·škikahaki,|
b   kehči-tehkina·kani e·h=ašihto·či ihkwe·wa.

---

*⟨pimi‖nikwani⟩.

*   *   *

^c   And then there was another man who was jealous as well.

^d   The woman had nine brothers,

^e and she was their only sister.

^f What's more, that woman was herself the youngest of all,

^g the baby of the family.

^h   And then at some point her older brothers urged a certain man on her.

ⁱ And the woman for her part didn't like the man.

^j Although, to be sure, he was a good hunter, to hear the tale.

^k And people gave him all kinds of tasks to do.

^l   Now, the young woman herself was the prettiest of all.

^m She was the prettiest of all those of her age.

15 a   And that young man was the ugliest of all his peers.

^b But he was the best of any at beating them at everything.

^c What's more, he was the best hunter.

^d He knew how to get bears,

^e and he also knew how to call elk.

^f And it seems *he* was the one urged on her.

^g   Now, there was another one, who was smitten with that young girl.

^h He was handsome,

ⁱ and she liked him.

^j He already thought he would marry her.

^k And before he was even thinking that she would get married,

^l she got married.

^m He didn't know *what* to do,

ⁿ and he didn't know what to think.

^o That man was almost too crazy,

16 a or rather that young man.

^b   Meanwhile that woman for her part disliked her husband.

^c And she could never forget the other one.

^d She was always thinking about him.

^e   At some point, off in some isolated place, they saw each other unexpectedly.

^f Now, they had not made an arrangement.

^g Their meeting happened unplanned.

^h The woman even ran over.

ⁱ And from right then, the story goes, they began an affair.

^j   At some point she began searching for a way to make her husband mad.

^k And after a while she found a way to make him exceedingly angry.

^l She went away someplace to braid some string,

^m Indian-hemp string, of course.

17 a And then the woman chipped away at a piece of wood to get it flat

^b and made a large cradle-board.

c   atehči=meko taši.

d   na·wi·kwe·ho·ni=ke·hi e·h=mi·ša·čihto·či,

e   e·si·hahi e·h=po·hpo·hkahwa·či.

f   ki·h‿ki·šihto·či=meko me·me·čiwi, e·h=nawasehkawa·či ona·pe·mani| atehči.[*]

g   o·ni·=’ya·hi e·h=ahte·niki·=’ni kehči‿tehkina·kani.

h   e·h=anemi‿ana·swiha·či i·ya·h=po·s=ašiči.[†]

i   pe·hki=meko e·h=ana·swiha·či.

j   "kokwe·či-tehkineti·yakwe," e·h=ina·či.

k   "ni·na menehta| ki·h=tehkiši," e·h=ineči neniwa.

l   "hawo·?," e·h=iči.

m   i·ni| i·tepi e·h=ahte·niki e·h=a·wa·či,|

n   e·h=we·pi-tehkina·či owi·wani.

o   "meškapišino=wi·no·!" e·h=išiwe·či ihkwe·wa.

p   "me·mye·hči!?" e·h=ineči.

q   "meškapiso·hiwaki=koč=a·pehe iškwe·se·he·haki," e·h=iči ihkwe·wa. ‖

18 a   o·ni taka·wi=meko e·h=meškapineči.

b   e·h=ki·ši-tehkineči ihkwe·wa,

c   "o·ni=ni·na," e·h=iči.

d   o·ni neniwa e·h=we·pi-tehkineči.

e   "ši·=’ni·ya·pi wi·h=mehto·nwe·pinena·ni," e·h=ineči.

f   "o·´‿meše=meko," e·h=iči=neniwa,

g   e·h=mehto·nwe·pineči,

h   e·h=ma·čikanwe·neči.|

i   "ya·´, kwi·yese·he·ha ma·čikanwe·wa," e·h=iči ihkwe·wa.|

j   ki·ši-=meko -a·yači·či-wi·šikapina·či,

k   e·h=nasawape·piči,[‡]

l   e·h=nawači-manekoči.

m   wi·na·=ke·hi·=’na| neniwa e·h=katawi-=meko -wa·wanana·moči,

n   e·h=asa·mi‿wi·šikapisoči.

o   ki·ši‿ma·hkwiči te·hkina·so·ha,

p   e·h=wi·wahoki,

q   e·h=anemi-nepiwinakaye·či.

r   e·h=pano·meči e·h=išiwe·pi·hka·noki,[§]

s   e·h=te·witepe·šiki‿neniwa.|

t   (a·hpeči·=’yo=ke·h=meko a·kwi‿kana·kwa ‖ wi·h=keteški·či.)

19 a   nepina·to·hkana·ki e·h=mawi‿a·hči·ya·hkwahkaneči.

b   ma·ne=meko e·h=ne·wokoči ihkwe·wahi.

c   še·ški=’p=a·pehe paya·hkiči e·h=ina·piniči a·neta.[¶]

---

[*]/me·me·čiwi/ (JAG, changed from earlier /me·mečiwi/): AK ⟨memyečiwi⟩.

[†]⟨po⟩ over erased ⟨a⟩.

[‡]⟨wa⟩ changed from ⟨we⟩.

[§]⟨ki⟩ over erased ⟨či⟩.

[¶]/e·h=ina·piniči/: ⟨ni⟩ over erasure of start of ⟨č⟩.

^c It was well away from everyone.
^d And she decorated the bow of the cradle-board,
^e poking holes in shells (to hang them).
^f After she had it completely finished, she asked her husband to come away.
^g And over there was that large cradle-board.
^h And she began to horse around with him very near there.
ⁱ She really horsed around with him.
^j "What if we try tying each other on the cradle-board," she said to him.
^k "You must tie *me* on first," the man was told.
^l "O.K." he said.
^m Then they went to where it was,
ⁿ and he set to tying his wife on it.
^o "Oh, tie me with my legs apart!" the woman ordered.
^p "That's hardly necessary!" he said.
^q "Little girls are always tied on with the legs apart, of course," the woman said.
18 a And then she was tied with her legs slightly apart.
^b The woman finished being tied on the cradle-board
^c and said, "Now me!"
^d And then the man began to be tied on the cradle-board.
^e "Well, alright now, I'm going to tie you with your penis exposed," he was told.
^f "Oh, go ahead," the man said.
^g He was tied with his penis exposed,
^h and it made him have an erection.
ⁱ "Mercy! The little boy has a hard on!" said the woman.
^j After she had tied him double and tied him tight,
^k she sat with her thighs astraddle,
^l and he had a quick moment to fuck her.
^m Now, come to the man, though, he was almost out of breath,
ⁿ as he was tied too tightly.
^o And after the cradle-baby had his fuck,
^p he was put on someone's back and carried,
^q going off with wet prick.
^r A pretense was made of having the man fall off,
^s and he bumped his head when he landed.
^t (Now, all this time it was impossible for him to get loose.)
19 a He was taken and leaned up against a tree on the water path.
^b And he was seen by many women.
^c Except that some would look away.

^d   wi·na=ke·hi| mehto·či=meko a·mo·wahi e·h=ina·pata·niniči o·če·wahi owi·nakayi
e·taši·hkaminičihi.

^e   kapo·twe owi·nemo·ni=ta·taki e·h=pya·niči,

^f   oto·te·mani owi·wani we·to·te·ma·ko·ma·ničini.

^g   e·h=pye·či-šo·ška·pihokoči.

^h   e·h=ki·ša·koči·=meko -te·pihekoči.

ⁱ   "apeno·heki='škwe iši|-ka·čimeno·ke·ni," e·h=ikoči.

^j   "ke·htena=kohi," e·h=ina·či.

^k   "nahi´, natawi·=meko -a·šitawa·ha·hkani," e·h=inekoči.

^l   "koči·h,| 'ni·h=nesa·wa,' ikwa otawe·ma·wani,

^m   'pwa·wi|-pya·nite ona·pe·mani,' ‖ ikwa.

20 a   i·tepi_pwa·wi-iha·yane, šo·ški=meko wi·h=nesa·pi," e·h=iniči.

^b   o·ni=ye·toke i·tepi=meko e·h=a·či.

^c   e·h=me·nešite·he·niči kete·='nahi owi·wani.

^d   wa·natohka=meko e·h=ki·wi·'šawiči.

^e   o·ni_te·kwa·kiniki, ke·tawi·=meko -nenye·škote·wa·či na·hina·hi,

^f   e·h=wanima·či,

^g   "na·čikoyakwe," e·h=ina·či_owi·wani.

^h   e·h=anwa·či·či ihkwe·wa,

ⁱ   e·h=anemi-ana·sowa·či.

^j   kapo·twe, "mečemo·ke, pena´, pešekesiwi·hka·nono.

^k   ki·h=nesene='pi," e·h=ineči ihkwe·wa.

^l   "hawo·?," e·h=iči,

^m   e·h=pemipenoči.| *

ⁿ   o·ni_neniwa e·h=anemi|-ši·še·hka·noči.

^o   kapo·twe| e·h=ašihkawoči,

^p   e·h=pemoči=ta·taki,

^q   e·h=nepo·hka·noči ihkwe·wa.

^r   e·h=we·pi-peši·neči.

^s   menehta opi·sehka·hi ‖ e·h=ketenamawoči,

21 a   ahkowi_oko·te·hani.

^b   akoše·we=ke·h=meko e·h=so·kiheči| e·h=išiwe·pite·he·či,

^c   na·hka| e·h=ni·šo·ka·pineči.

^d   akoše·we_kapo·twe_če·wina·hi e·h=ši·pata·pye·sahto·či.

^e   e·h=ki·ša·kotapisoči_ihkwe·wa.

^f   e·h=pepye·tekwapineči,

^g   e·h=mo·škapiso·hiniči ohketenani.

^h   "šihihwi·´, mešihketene·wa| mana pešekesiwa,"_e·h=iči=neniwa.

ⁱ   e·h=nawači|-mana·či,

^j   e·h=wi·wahoči,

^k   e·h=na·kwa·či, e·h=we·po·ma·či.

---

*/mi/: AK ⟨ni⟩.

d   What's more, he had flies looking like bees swarming on his penis.

e   At some point a woman who was by extension his sister-in-law came,

f   one who was like a sister to his brother's wife.

g   She came and readily untied him.

h   And he was extremely grateful to her.

i   "You must've been talked into it like a child," she said to him.

j   "That's certainly true," he told her.

k   "Alright, find a way to get back at her," she said to him.

l   "Although her brother did say about her, 'I'll kill her

m   if her husband doesn't come back.'

20 a   If you don't go back there, she'll be killed directly," she said.

b   And then, it seems, he went right there.

c   Now his wife was ashamed.

d   He acted as if nothing were amiss.

e   And then that fall, right when all were about to disperse to the hunting camps,

f   he said something deceptive to his wife,

g   saying to her, "Let's go retrieve our cached meat."

h   The woman agreed,

i   and they were horsing around as they went off.

j   At some point the woman was told, "O.K. now, wife, pretend to be a deer.

k   And I'll kill you, say."

l   "Alright," she said

m   and went running off.

n   And then the man went on pretending to hunt.

o   At some point the woman was started out of concealment,

p   and shot, as it were,

q   and pretended to die.

r   And her skinning began.

s   First her top was taken off,

21 a   and afterwards her skirts.

b   What's more, she could tell, with some misgivings, that she was being tied up,

c   and also that her two legs were being tied together.

d   And with misgivings she abruptly yanked the ropes taut at the same time.

e   The woman was tied as tight as could be.

f   She was tied bent over double,

g   and tied in a way that her snatch poked out a little.

h   "Boy, this deer has a big twat," the man said.

i   And pausing to fuck her,

j   he loaded her on his back

k   and, carrying her off on his back, set out.

l e·h=tanwe·we·kahki_ma·mahkese·haki,

m atehči na·me·ya·hkwe e·taši|-ma·mahkese·hičiki.

n o·ni·='niye e·h=anemi_-'no·meči i·na ihkwe·wa,

o e·h=ča·ki-mehčiheči.

p "neki·wa·ni=kohi´," e·h=iči=neniwa.[*]

q "newani-nehta·we,

r mana me·šihketena·ta pešekesiwa‖ e·h=nesaki.

22 a apina=meko a·kwi_kehke·netamo·hiya·nini we·či·ya·ni," e·h=iči.|

b (i·niye·ne=ke·hi mi·hkemekočini i·nahi e·h=awiniči.)

c e·h=awato·meči e·h=owi·ke·hiwa·či,

d či·ki|-wi·kiya·pihkiwe e·h=anemi_-'no·meči.

e i·ya·h=sa·kiči e·h=po·no·meči e·h=owi·kiwa·či.

f "e·h=pya·wa·či na·čikočiki," e·h=iniči pi·tike e·winičihi.

g metemo·ka| e·h=nowi·či,

h e·h=aka·wi_-kesa·piči.

i onekwanani=meko e·h=išite·he·či.

j "nahi´,_mawi-a·pihwi," e·h=ina·či ona·pe·mani.

k mani_e·ši_-nowi·či pašito·ha,

l onekwanani=či·hi.

m "ma·haki=ma·hi a·m_-a·pihwa·čiki we·wi·hta·wičiki," e·h=iči_pašito·ha.

n e·h=nowi·wa·či_kekimesi neniwaki,

o e·h=mi·na·wa·piwa·či. ‖

23 a otehkwe·mwa·wani=či·hi.

b kekimesi=meko e·h=po·ni_-wa·pama·wa·či,

c e·h=me·nešite·he·wa·či.

d "ki·na=ma·hi·='na ki·h=mawi|-a·pihwa·wa," e·h=ina·wa·či| okiwa·wani.

e mečemo·ka e·h=nowi·či.

f e·h=mama·kinowe·tiye·šiniči ota·nesani.|

g e·h=taši-_-meko_mayo·či| e·h=taši-a·pihwa·či.

h "a·kwi=koh-wi·na, neta·ha, owiye·ha ke·ko·hi to·to·hkini.

i ki·na=meko keto·ta=ki·yawi," e·h=ina·či.

j e·h=ki·ša·koči-ahtehahtehte·wineče·pisoniči,

k na·hka ohka·teki| e·h=ahtahahtehte·wika·pisoniči ota·neswa·wani.[†]

l ki·ši-pi·tikana·wa·či,

m e·h=we·pi-a·ya·čimoha·či neniwa_we·ta·nesita.

n "i·ni we·či|-, 'mahkwa·či,' -inena·ni, neta·ha," ‖ e·h=ina·či.[‡]

24 a "i·noki=ča·h=wa·wosa·h=meko i·ni| wi·h=kohtamani e·hkwi|-ona·pe·miwane·ni,

b e·hkwi-nahe·nemenokwe·ni_owiye·ha.

c i·niya='yo=wi·na kena·pe·ma,| i·ni=meko e·h=nakanehki=ye·toke," e·h=ina·či.

---

[*] /=kohi´/: AK ⟨ko.i.⟩.

[†] /e·h=ahtahahtehte·wika·pisoniči/: AK ⟨|eataatatewikapiso|niči.⟩.

[‡] /we·či|- ... -inena·ni/: AK ⟨weči| ... .einenani.⟩.

l And there was a noise from moccasin-game players,

m ones playing the moccasin game off in the woods.

n And then that woman was carried off to go there,

o with everything exposed to view.

p "I really got lost!" said the man.

q "I made a kill just as a diversion,

r killing this deer with a big twat.

22 a I don't even really know where I've been," he said.

b (Now, the one who had had the affair with her was there.)

c And she was carried over to where she and her family lived,

d being carried off to the edge of where the houses were.

e And she was set down over there outside her family's lodge.

f "The ones who went after the cached meat are back," those inside said.

g The old lady went out,

h and she barely glanced out the door,

i thinking it was her son-in-law.

j "Alright, go and untie it," she said to her husband.

k And as soon as the old man came out,

l here he saw his son-in-law.

m "Well, the brothers-in-law should be the ones to untie it," said the old man.

n Every one of the men came out,

o and they looked closely.

23 a And here it was their sister.

b Every one of them stopped looking at her,

c being ashamed.

d "Well, *you* must be the one to go and untie it," they told their mother.

e The old lady went out.

f And here were the large buttocks of her daughter.

g She kept weeping as she untied her.

h "No one *else* did *anything* to you.

i *You* did it to *yourself*," she told her.

j Their daughter's hands were terribly black and blue from being tied,

k and on her feet she was also black and blue from her feet being tied.

l After they had brought her inside,

m her father had words to say to her.

n "That's why I told you to behave nice-and-quietly, daughter," he told her.

24 a "So, now, not surprisingly, you face the scary prospect of no longer being married,

b of no longer having anyone think you're fit (to marry).

c For your husband, it seems, has right now left you," he told her.

d   "ki·nwa·wa=na·hka, a·kwi| ke·ko·hi wi·h=iši-mya·ne·neme·kwini
keme·ša·hemwa·wa='yo·we," e·h=ineči.
e   "mana=ča·h=a·mi|-mya·ne·neme·kwa, wi·h=mya·ne·neme·kwe išite·he·ye·kwe:|
f   mi·hkema·ta ma·hani ketehkwe·me·hwa·wani.
g   i·na| me·nešiha·ta," e·h=ineči| neniwaki.
h   i·ni=meko='pi aškači·meki·hi e·h=nepo·hiči i·na ihkwe·wa,
i   e·h=pi·ke·wi-me·nešite·he·či, ma·ne| e·h=ne·wokoči_neniwahi.
j   i·ni e·na·čimeči. ‖

d   "And *you*, you're not to dislike your former brother-in-law in any way," (the brothers)
were told.
e   "So, this is who you should dislike, if you wish to dislike him:
f   the one who had an affair with your poor sister here.
g   He's the one who shamed her," the men were told.
h   Then, not long after that, the story goes, that woman died,
i   dying of shame because many men had seen her.
j   That's what is told about her.